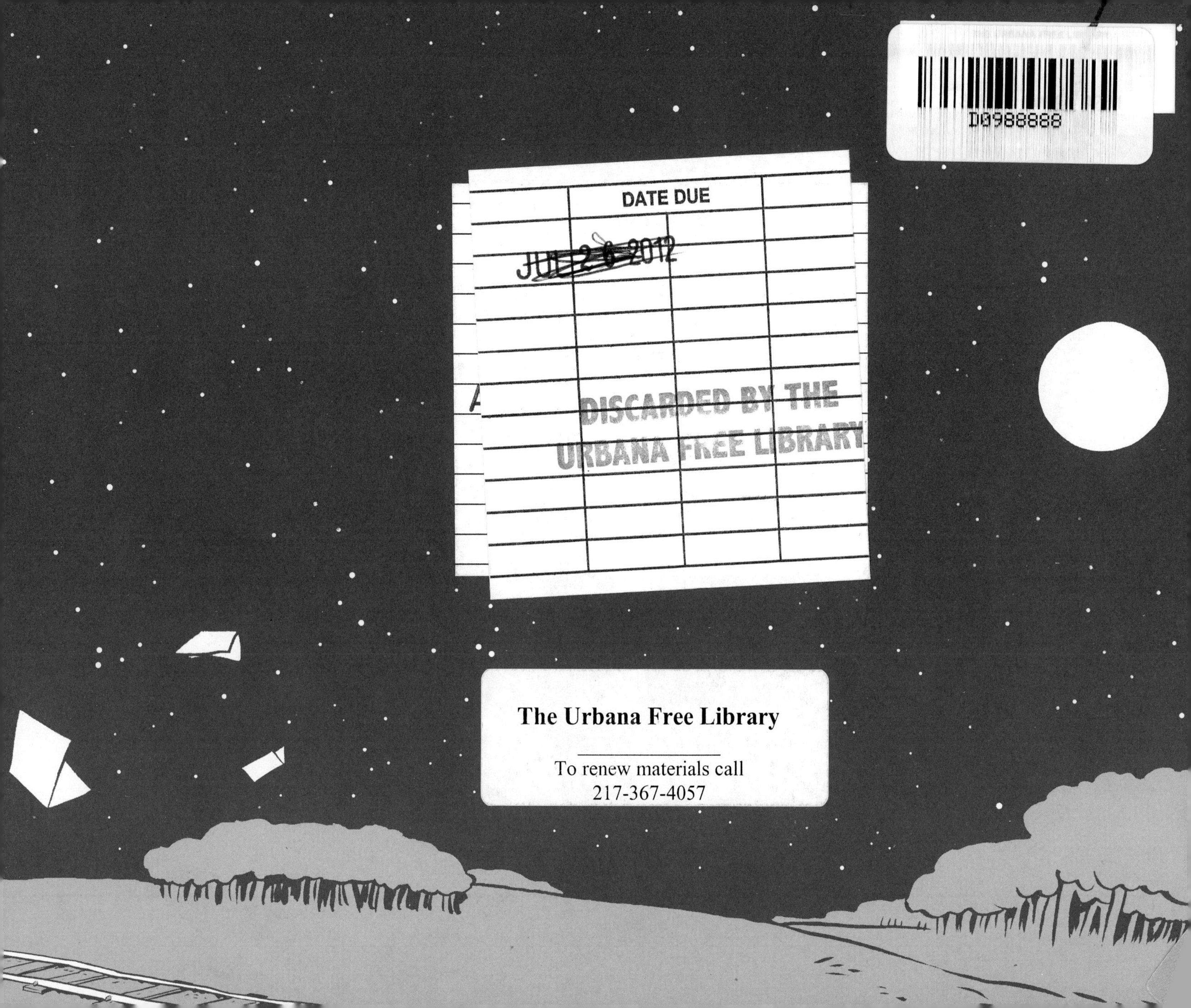

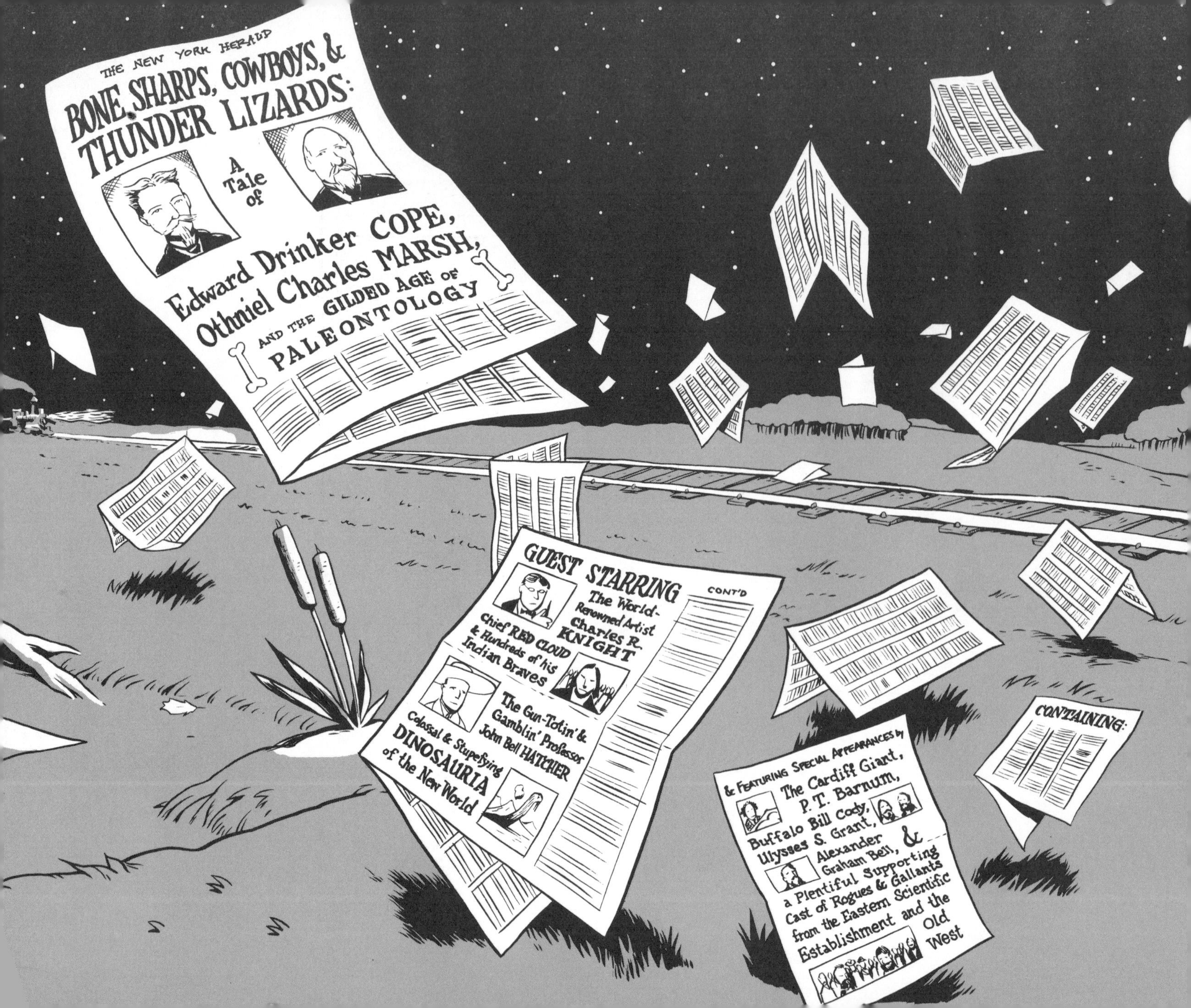
THE NEW YORK HERALD
BONE SHARPS, COWBOYS, & THUNDER LIZARDS:
A Tale of
Edward Drinker COPE, Othniel Charles MARSH, & THE GILDED AGE OF PALEONTOLOGY
GUEST STARRING
The World-Renowned Artist Charles R. KNIGHT
Chief RED CLOUD & Hundreds of his Indian Braves
The Gun-Totin' & Gamblin' Professor John Bell HATCHER
Colossal & Stupefying DINOSAURIA of the New World
CONT'D
CONTAINING:
& FEATURING SPECIAL APPEARANCES by
The Cardiff Giant, P.T. Barnum, Buffalo Bill Cody, Ulysses S. Grant, Alexander Graham Bell, & a Plentiful Supporting Cast of Rogues & Gallants from the Eastern Scientific Establishment and the Old West

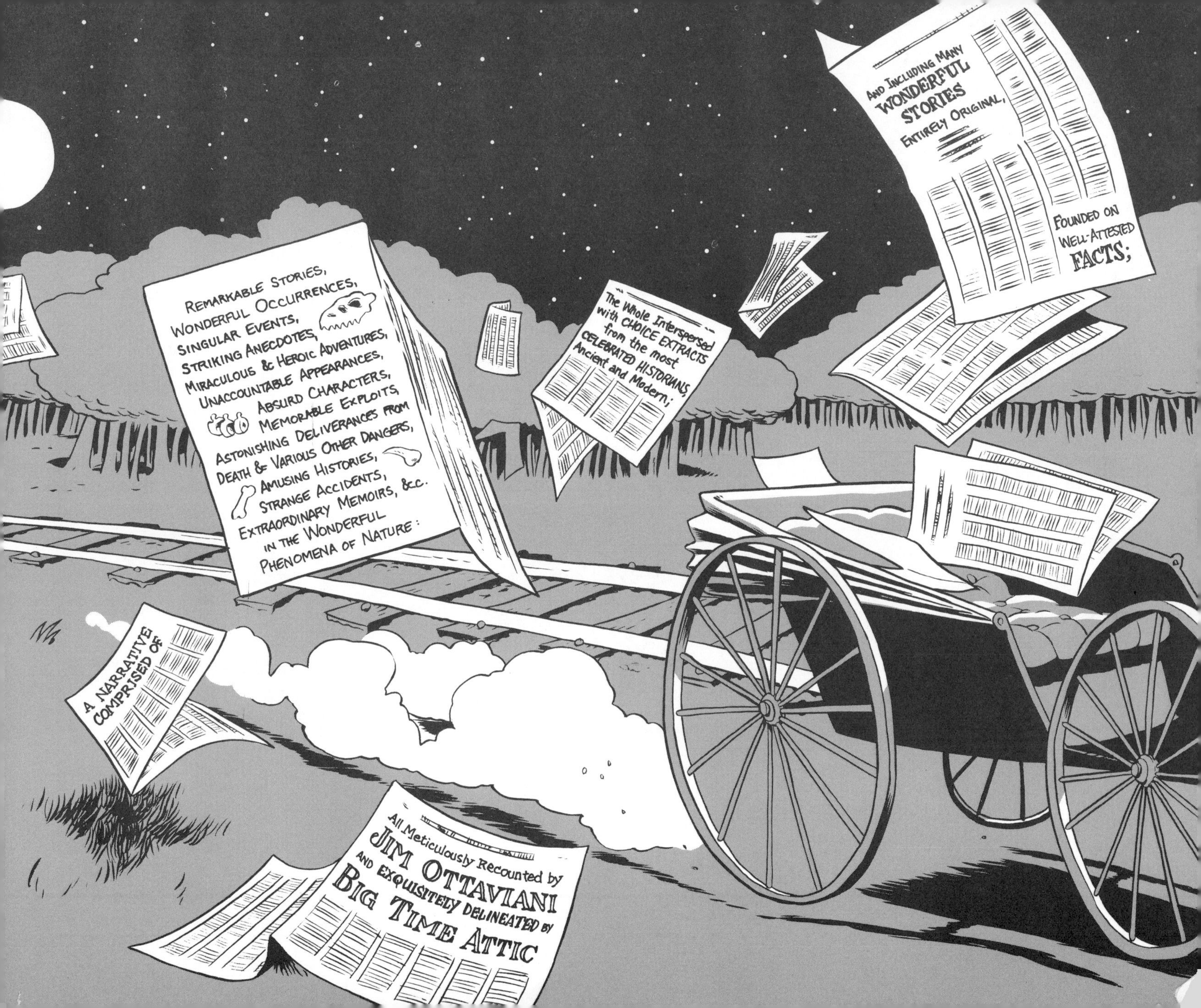
A Narrative Comprised of
Remarkable Stories, Wonderful Occurrences, Singular Events, Striking Anecdotes, Miraculous & Heroic Adventures, Unaccountable Appearances, Absurd Characters, Memorable Exploits, Astonishing Deliverances from Death & Various Other Dangers, Amusing Histories, Strange Accidents, Extraordinary Memoirs, &c. in the Wonderful Phenomena of Nature:
The Whole Interspersed with CHOICE EXTRACTS from the most CELEBRATED HISTORIANS, Ancient and Modern;
And Including Many WONDERFUL STORIES Entirely Original,
Founded on Well-Attested FACTS;
All Meticulously Recounted by JIM OTTAVIANI
and Exquisitely Delineated by BIG TIME ATTIC

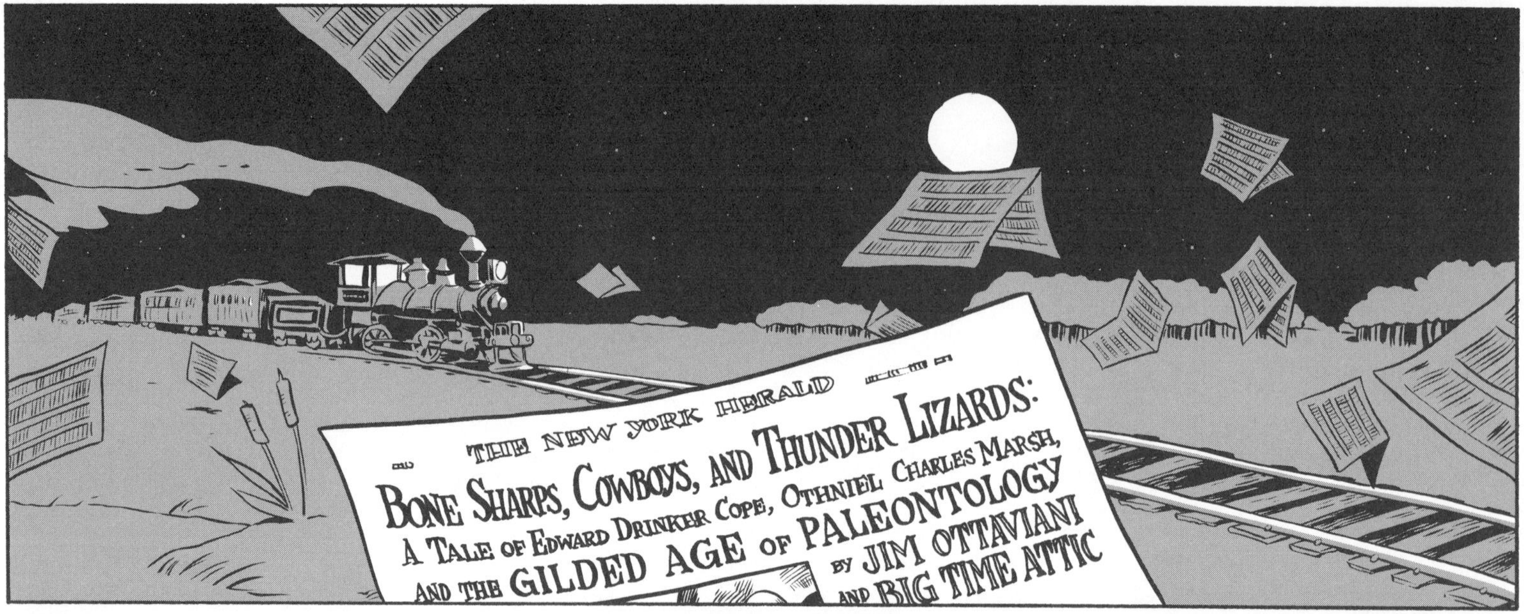
THE NEW YORK HERALD
BONE SHARPS, COWBOYS, AND THUNDER LIZARDS:
A TALE OF EDWARD DRINKER COPE, OTHNIEL CHARLES MARSH, AND THE GILDED AGE OF PALEONTOLOGY
BY JIM OTTAVIANI AND BIG TIME ATTIC

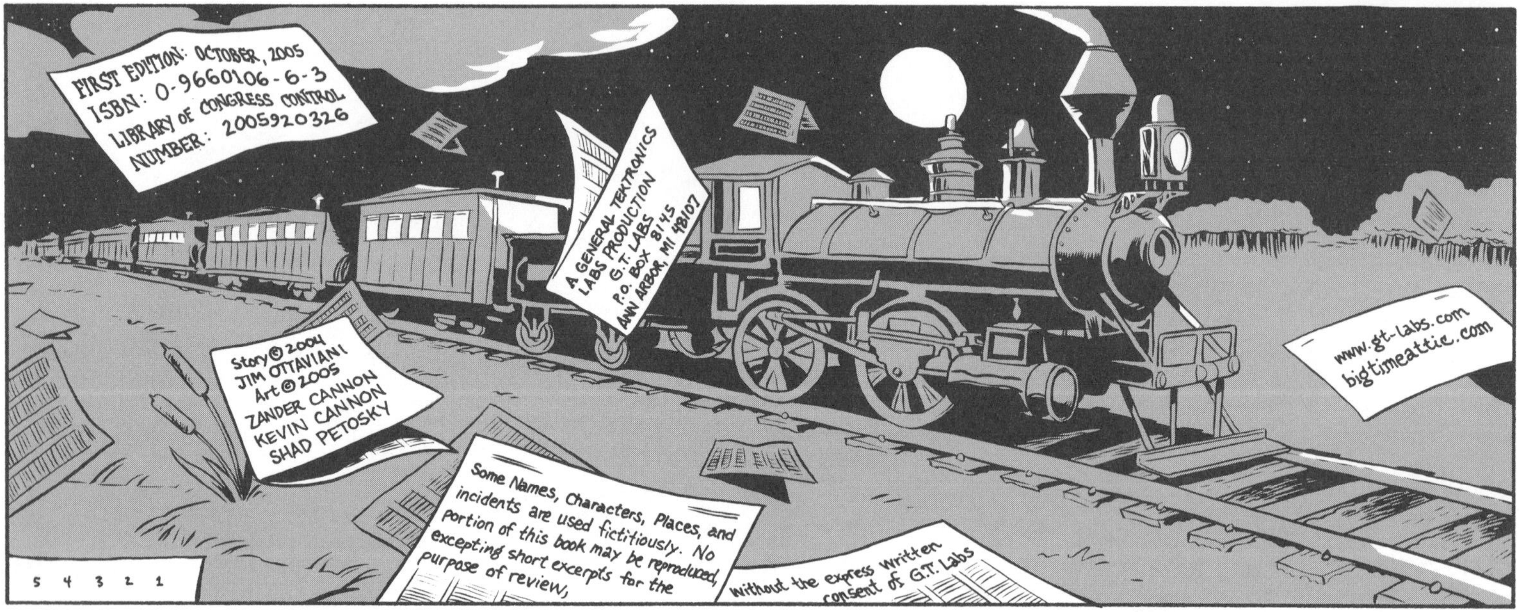
FIRST EDITION: OCTOBER, 2005
ISBN: 0-9660106-6-3
LIBRARY OF CONGRESS CONTROL NUMBER: 2005920326
A GENERAL TEKTRONICS LABS PRODUCTION
G.T. LABS
P.O. BOX 8145
ANN ARBOR, MI 48107
Story © 2004 JIM OTTAVIANI
Art © 2005 ZANDER CANNON KEVIN CANNON SHAD PETOSKY
www.gt-labs.com
bigtimeattic.com
Some Names, Characters, Places, and incidents are used fictitiously. No portion of this book may be reproduced, excepting short excerpts for the purpose of review,
without the express written consent of G.T. Labs
5 4 3 2 1

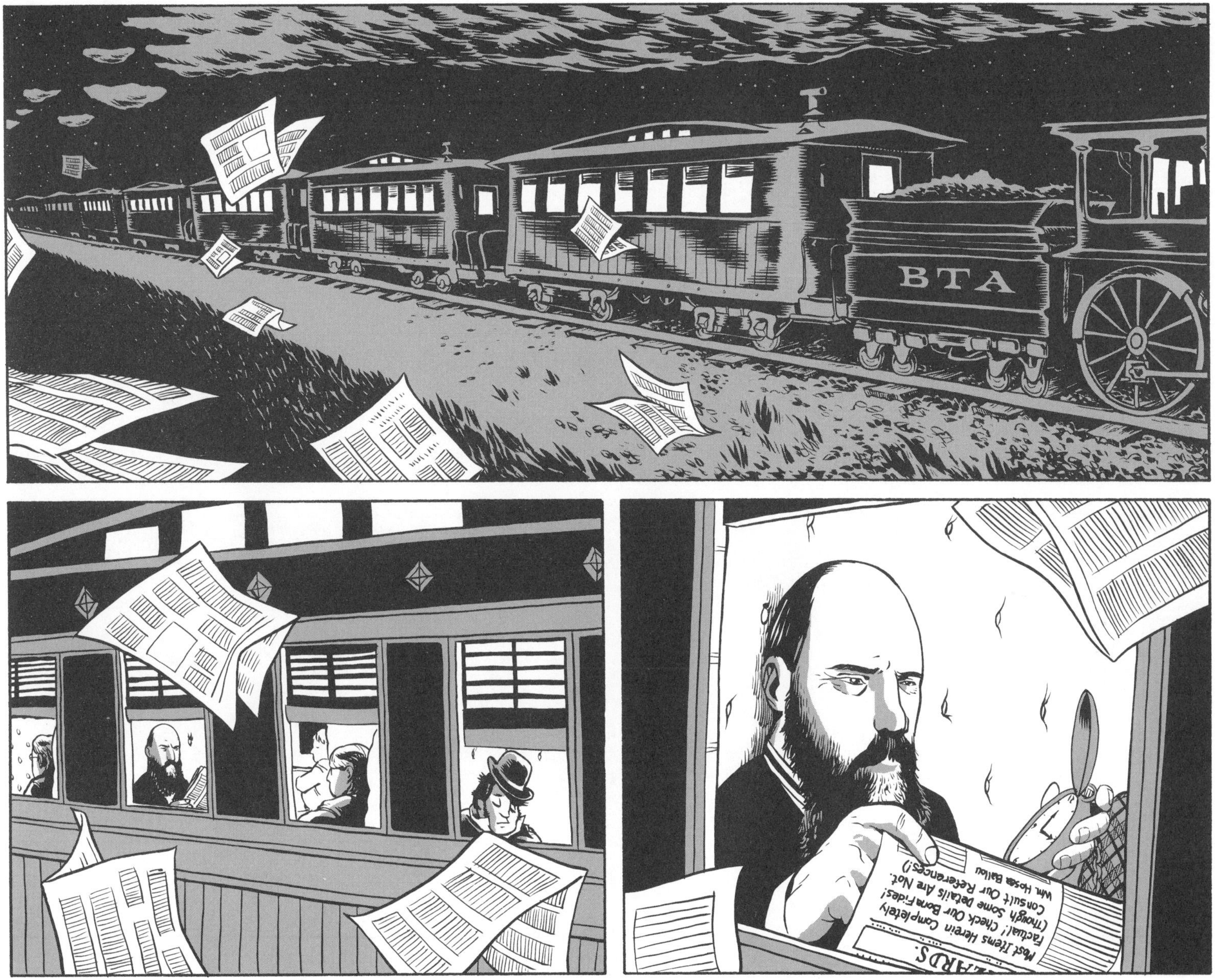
BTA
Most Items Herein Completely
Factual! Check Our Bona Fides!
(Though Some Details Are Not.
Consult Our References!)
Wm. Hosea Ballou

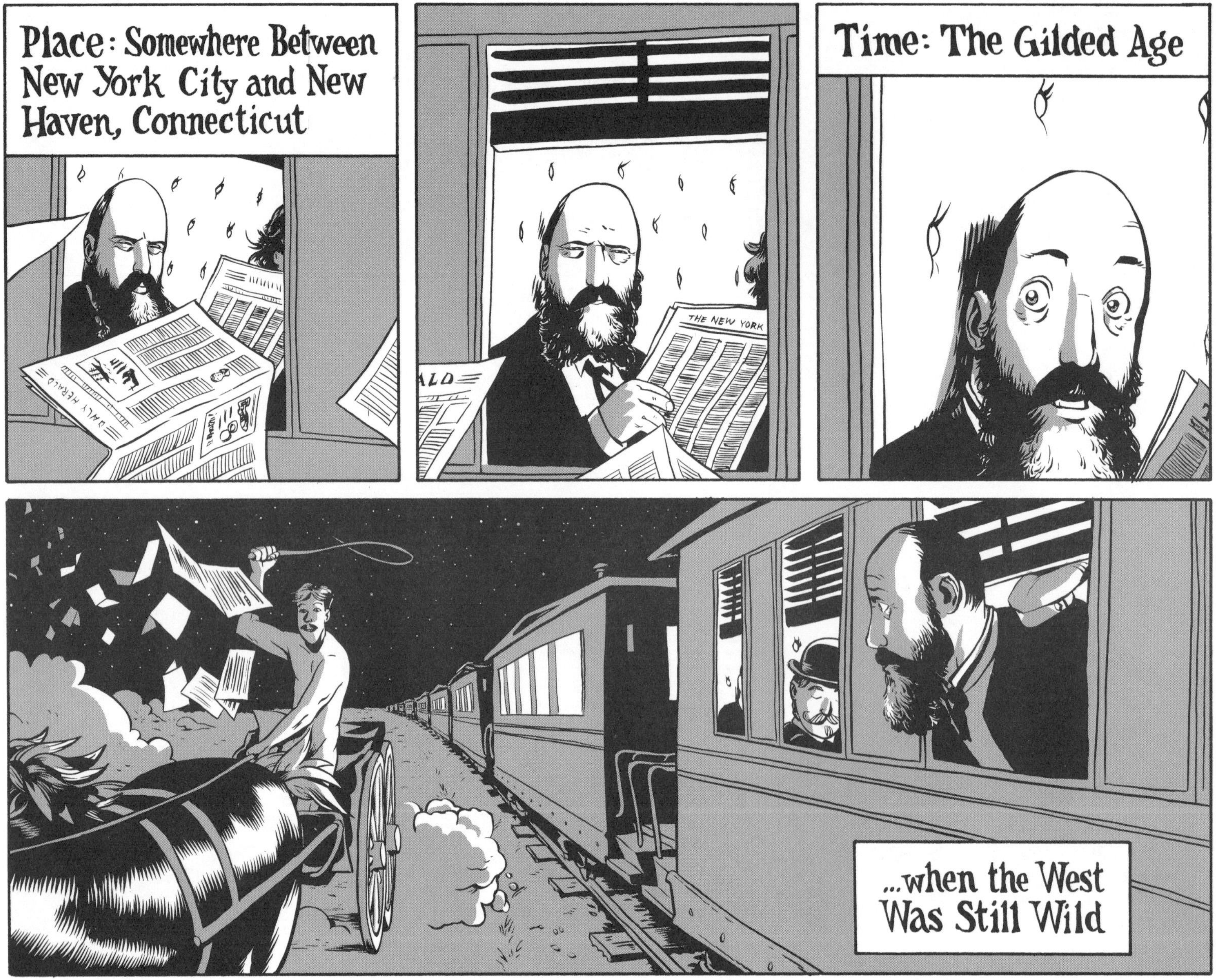
Place: Somewhere Between New York City and New Haven, Connecticut
THE NEW YORK
Time: The Gilded Age
...when the West Was Still Wild

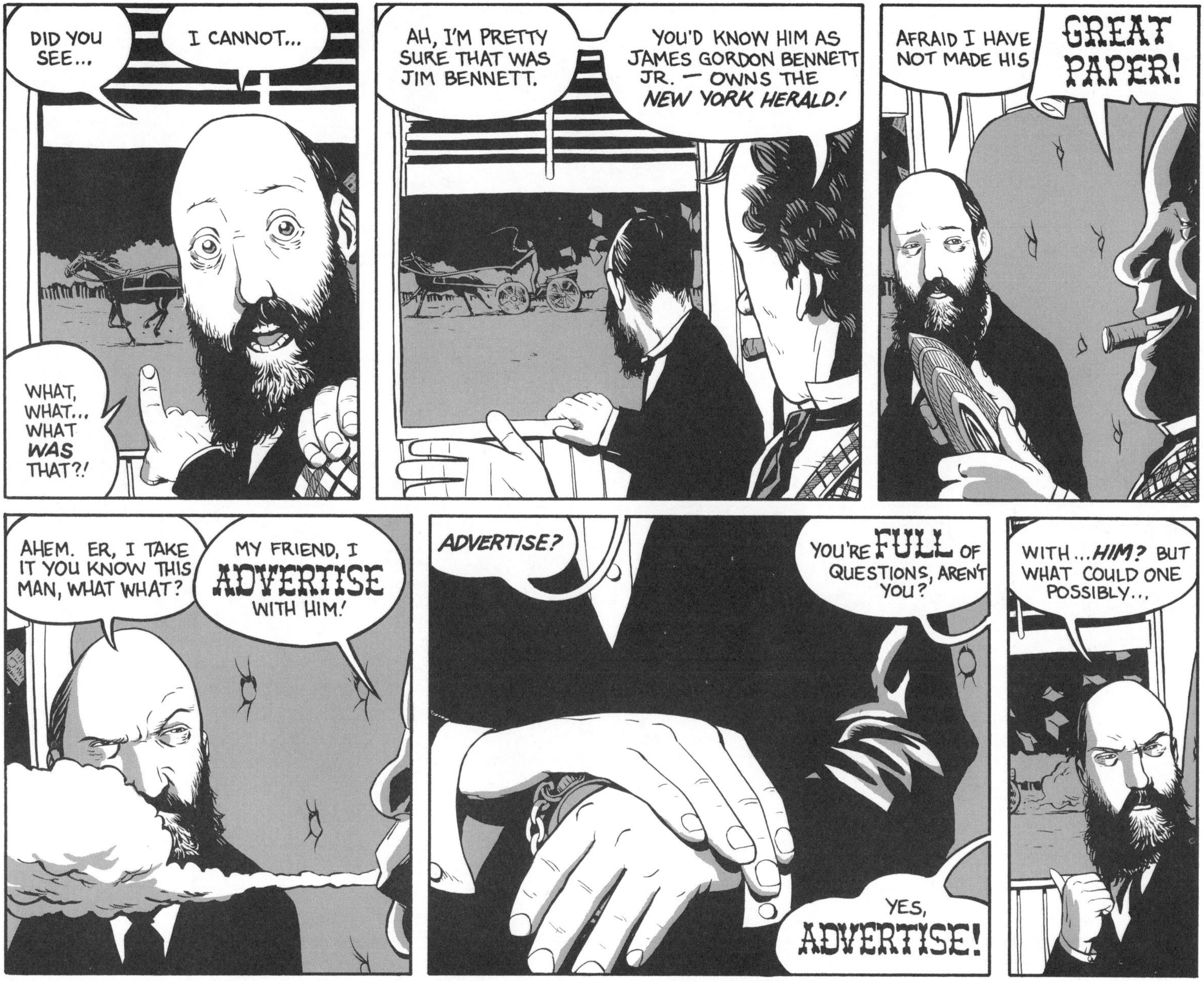
DID YOU SEE...
I CANNOT...
WHAT, WHAT... WHAT *WAS* THAT?!
AH, I'M PRETTY SURE THAT WAS JIM BENNETT.
YOU'D KNOW HIM AS JAMES GORDON BENNETT JR. — OWNS THE *NEW YORK HERALD!*
AFRAID I HAVE NOT MADE HIS
GREAT PAPER!
AHEM. ER, I TAKE IT YOU KNOW THIS MAN, WHAT WHAT?
MY FRIEND, I ADVERTISE WITH HIM!
ADVERTISE?
YOU'RE FULL OF QUESTIONS, AREN'T YOU?
YES, ADVERTISE!
WITH ...*HIM?* BUT WHAT COULD ONE POSSIBLY...

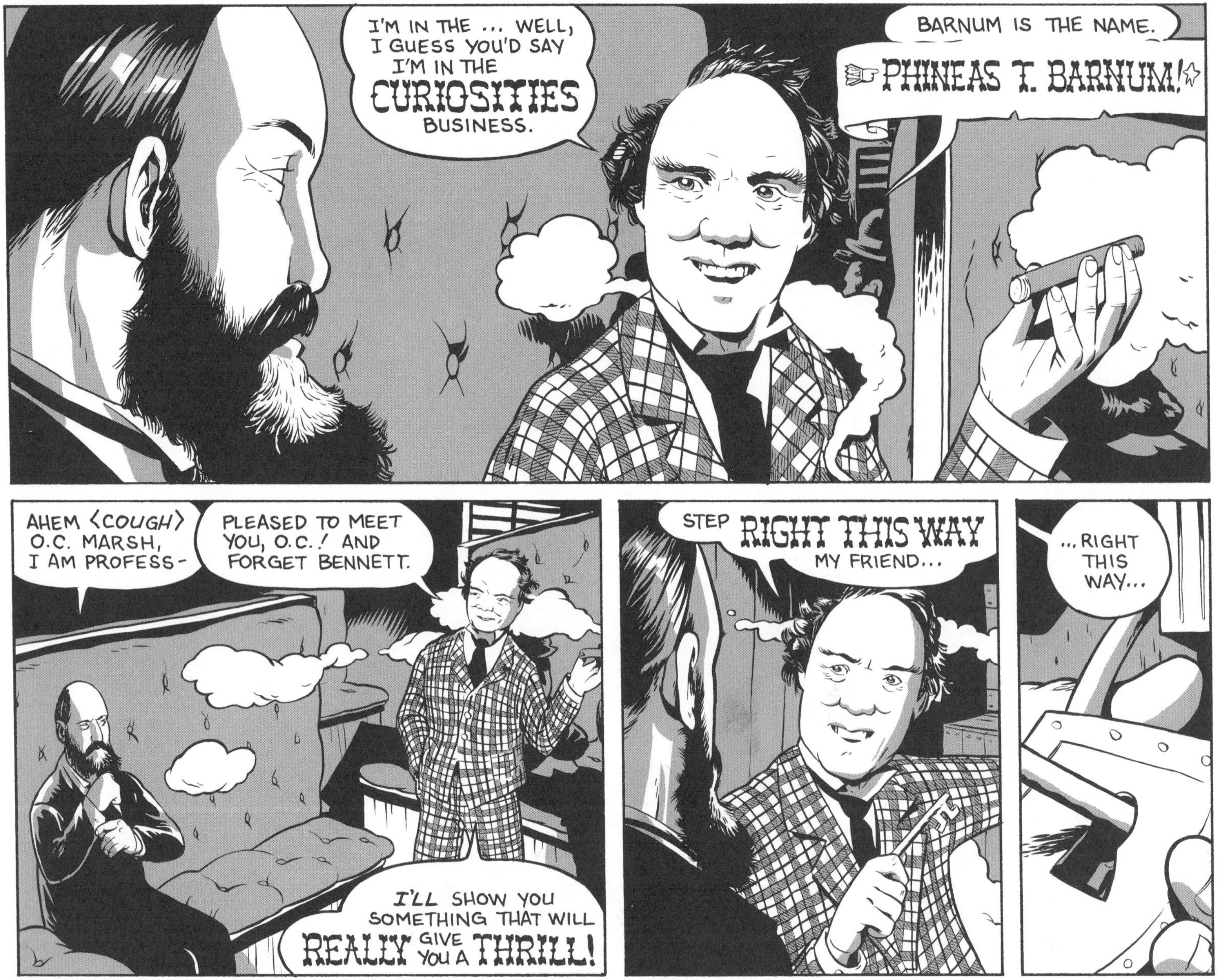
I'M IN THE ... WELL, I GUESS YOU'D SAY I'M IN THE CURIOSITIES BUSINESS.
BARNUM IS THE NAME.
PHINEAS T. BARNUM!
AHEM <COUGH> O.C. MARSH, I AM PROFESS-
PLEASED TO MEET YOU, O.C.! AND FORGET BENNETT.
I'LL SHOW YOU SOMETHING THAT WILL REALLY GIVE YOU A THRILL!
STEP RIGHT THIS WAY MY FRIEND...
...RIGHT THIS WAY...

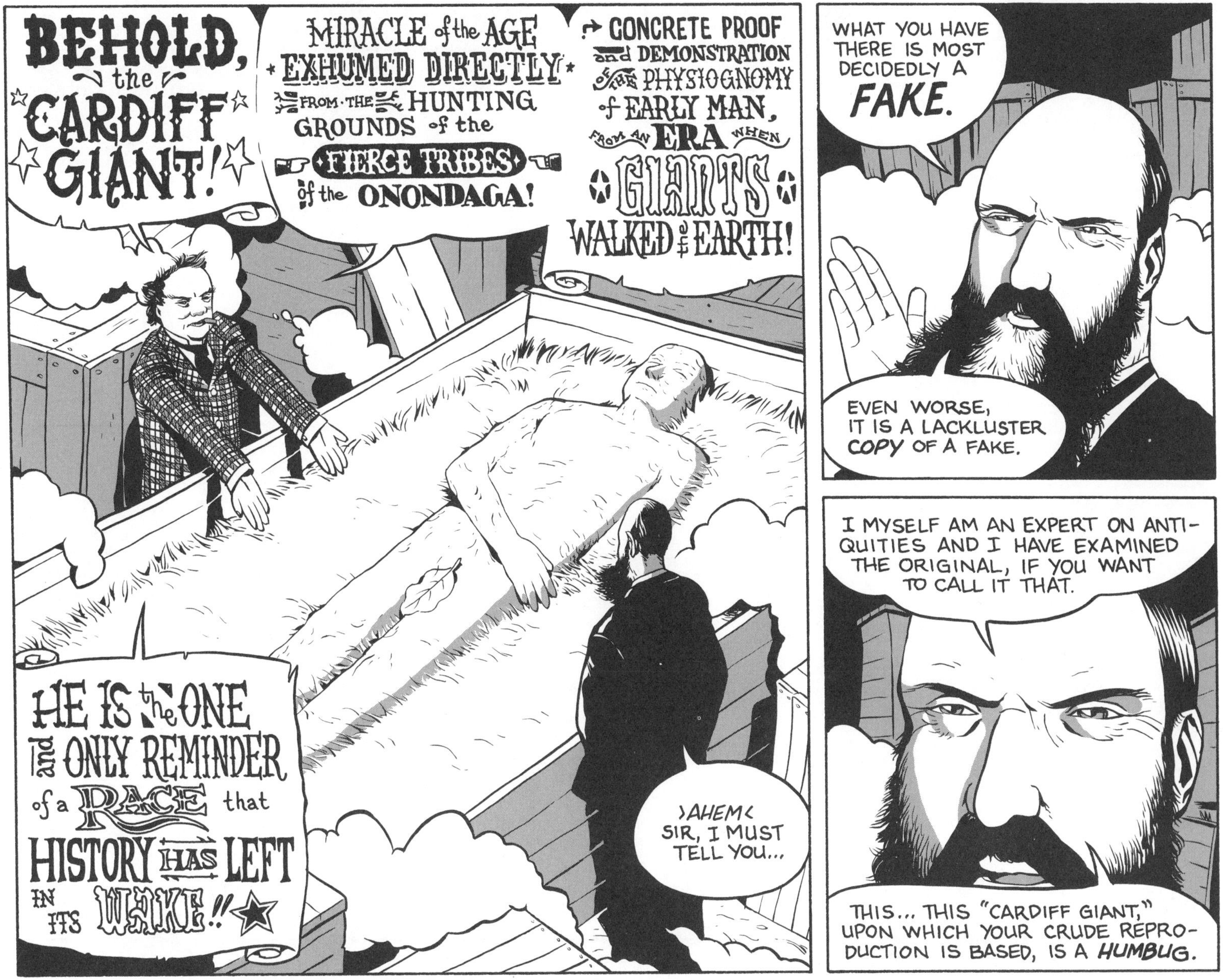
BEHOLD, the CARDIFF GIANT!
MIRACLE of the AGE EXHUMED DIRECTLY FROM THE HUNTING GROUNDS of the FIERCE TRIBES of the ONONDAGA!
CONCRETE PROOF and DEMONSTRATION OF THE PHYSIOGNOMY of EARLY MAN, FROM AN ERA WHEN GIANTS WALKED the EARTH!
HE IS the ONE and ONLY REMINDER of a RACE that HISTORY HAS LEFT IN ITS WAKE!!
›AHEM‹ SIR, I MUST TELL YOU...
WHAT YOU HAVE THERE IS MOST DECIDEDLY A FAKE.
EVEN WORSE, IT IS A LACKLUSTER COPY OF A FAKE.
I MYSELF AM AN EXPERT ON ANTI-QUITIES AND I HAVE EXAMINED THE ORIGINAL, IF YOU WANT TO CALL IT THAT.
THIS... THIS "CARDIFF GIANT," UPON WHICH YOUR CRUDE REPRO-DUCTION IS BASED, IS A HUMBUG.

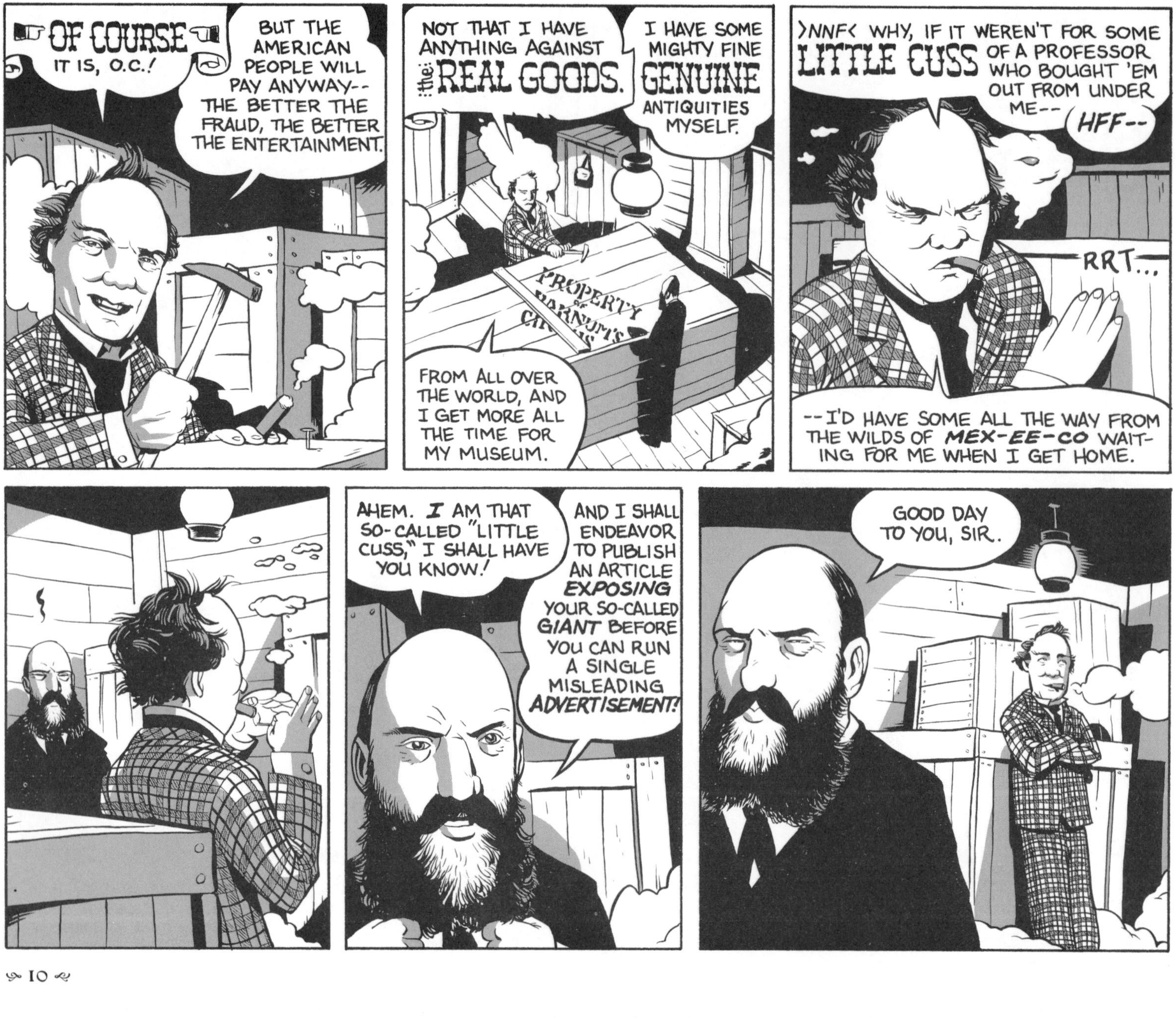
OF COURSE IT IS, O.C.!
BUT THE AMERICAN PEOPLE WILL PAY ANYWAY-- THE BETTER THE FRAUD, THE BETTER THE ENTERTAINMENT.
NOT THAT I HAVE ANYTHING AGAINST the REAL GOODS.
I HAVE SOME MIGHTY FINE GENUINE ANTIQUITIES MYSELF.
PROPERTY of BARNUM'S CIRCUS
FROM ALL OVER THE WORLD, AND I GET MORE ALL THE TIME FOR MY MUSEUM.
>NNF< WHY, IF IT WEREN'T FOR SOME LITTLE CUSS OF A PROFESSOR WHO BOUGHT 'EM OUT FROM UNDER ME--
HFF--
RRT...
--I'D HAVE SOME ALL THE WAY FROM THE WILDS OF MEX-EE-CO WAITING FOR ME WHEN I GET HOME.
AHEM. I AM THAT SO-CALLED "LITTLE CUSS," I SHALL HAVE YOU KNOW!
AND I SHALL ENDEAVOR TO PUBLISH AN ARTICLE EXPOSING YOUR SO-CALLED GIANT BEFORE YOU CAN RUN A SINGLE MISLEADING ADVERTISEMENT!
GOOD DAY TO YOU, SIR.

BONE SHARPS

In which we encounter the rest of our
protagonists, witness a stunning betrayal, &c.

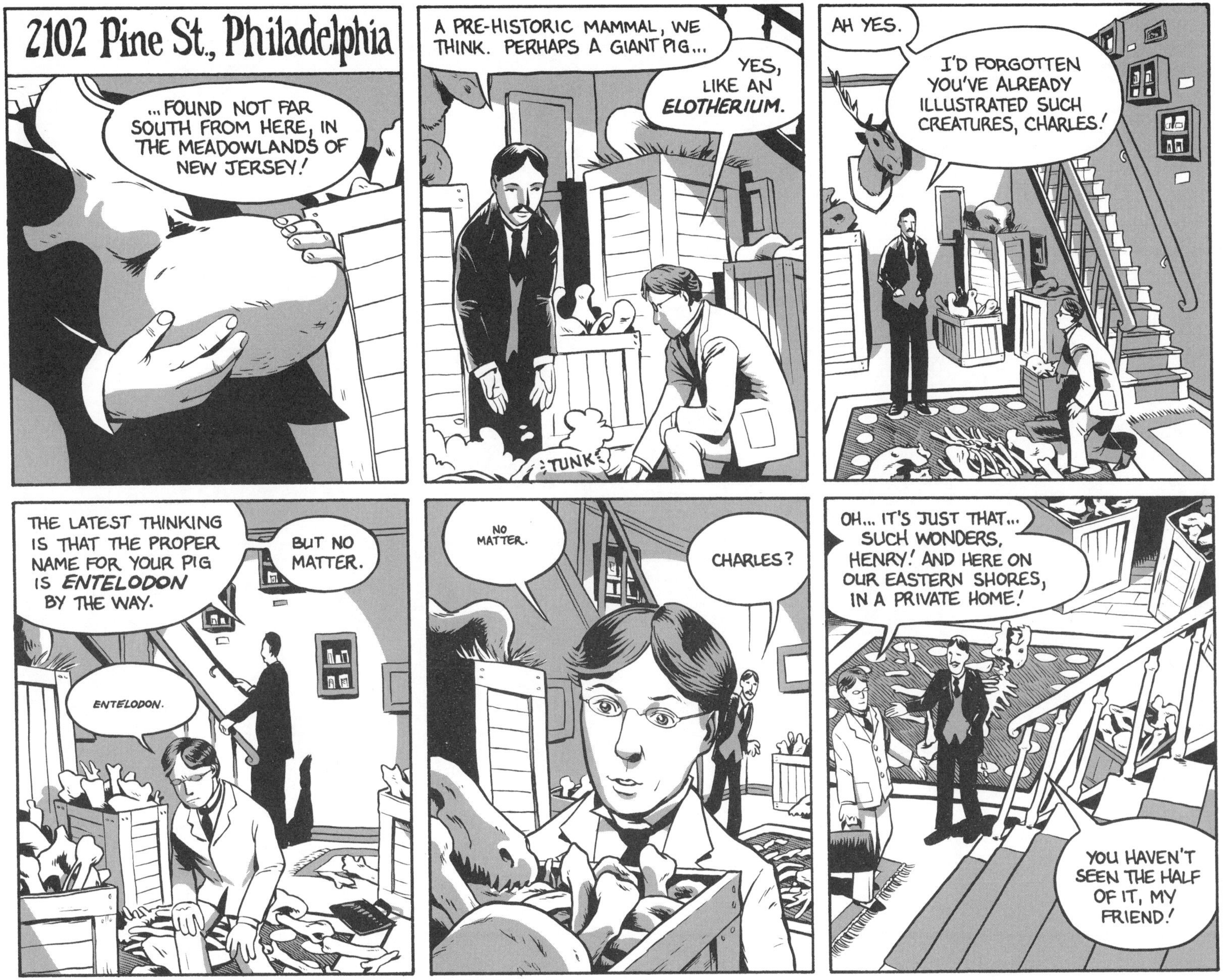
2102 Pine St., Philadelphia
...FOUND NOT FAR SOUTH FROM HERE, IN THE MEADOWLANDS OF NEW JERSEY!
A PRE-HISTORIC MAMMAL, WE THINK. PERHAPS A GIANT PIG...
YES, LIKE AN ELOTHERIUM.
TUNK
AH YES.
I'D FORGOTTEN YOU'VE ALREADY ILLUSTRATED SUCH CREATURES, CHARLES!
THE LATEST THINKING IS THAT THE PROPER NAME FOR YOUR PIG IS ENTELODON BY THE WAY.
BUT NO MATTER.
ENTELODON.
NO MATTER.
CHARLES?
OH... IT'S JUST THAT... SUCH WONDERS, HENRY! AND HERE ON OUR EASTERN SHORES, IN A PRIVATE HOME!
YOU HAVEN'T SEEN THE HALF OF IT, MY FRIEND!

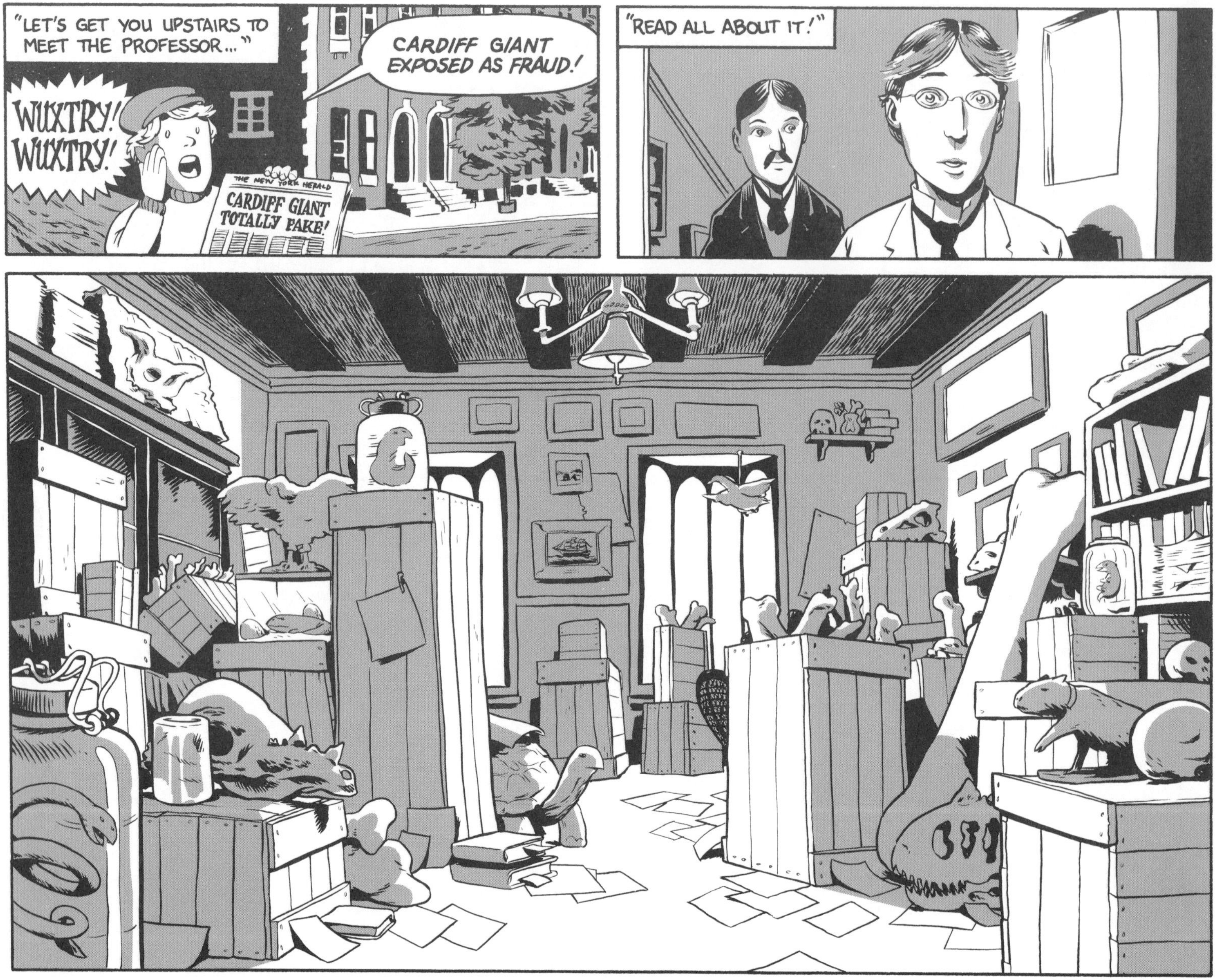

"LET'S GET YOU UPSTAIRS TO MEET THE PROFESSOR..."
WUXTRY! WUXTRY!
CARDIFF GIANT EXPOSED AS FRAUD!
THE NEW YORK HERALD
CARDIFF GIANT TOTALLY FAKE!
"READ ALL ABOUT IT!"

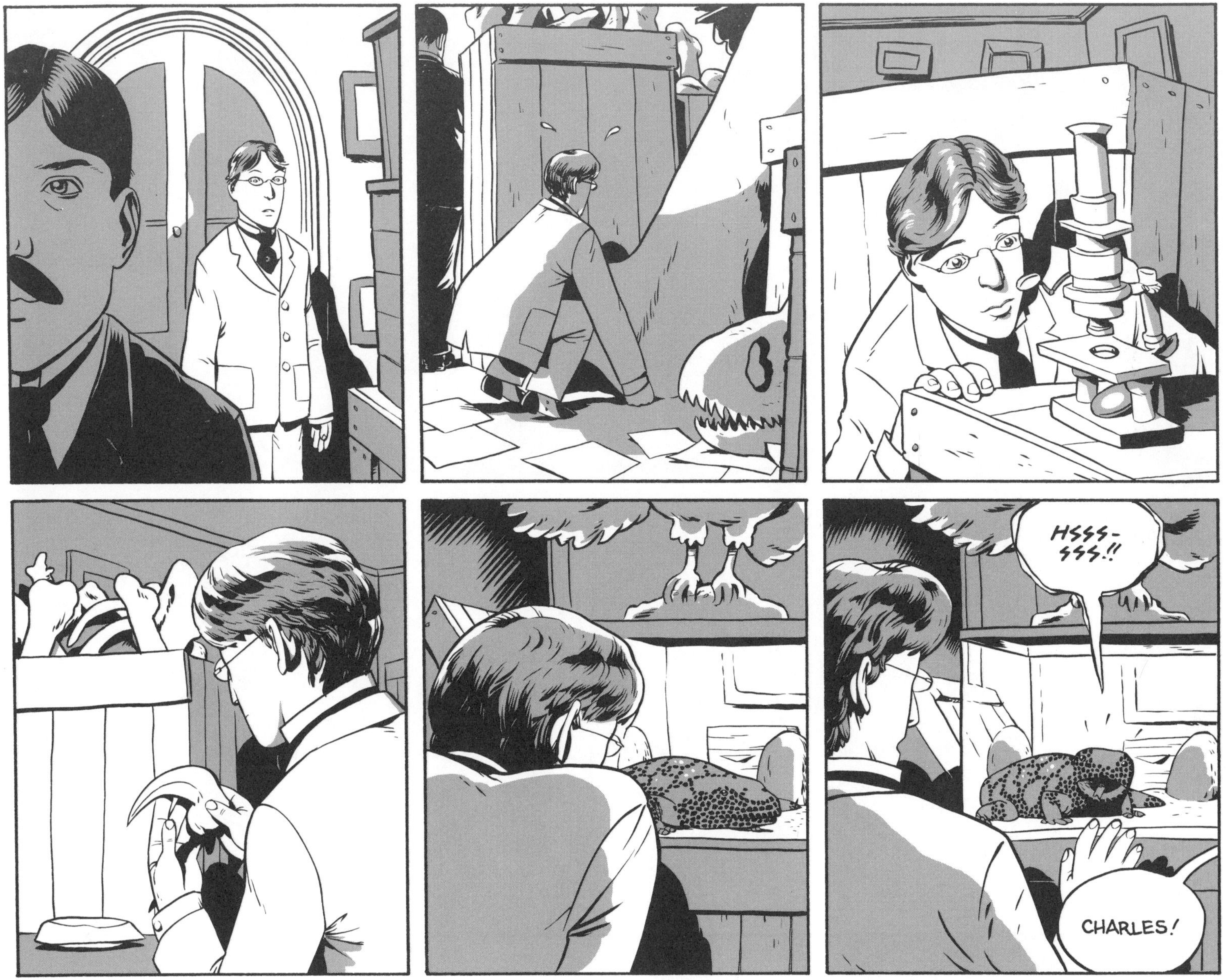
HSSS-
SSS!!
CHARLES!

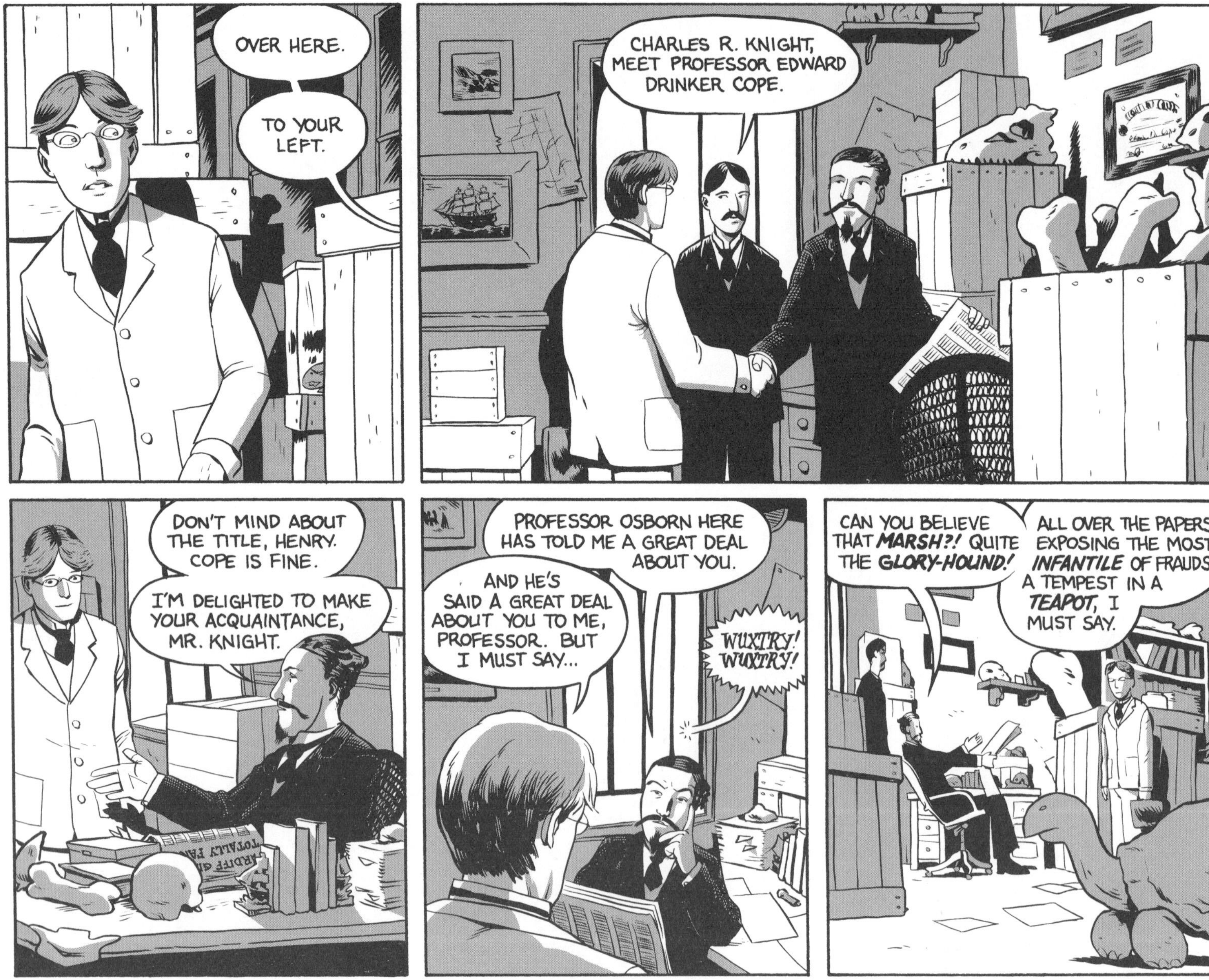
OVER HERE.
TO YOUR LEFT.
CHARLES R. KNIGHT, MEET PROFESSOR EDWARD DRINKER COPE.
DON'T MIND ABOUT THE TITLE, HENRY. COPE IS FINE.
I'M DELIGHTED TO MAKE YOUR ACQUAINTANCE, MR. KNIGHT.
PROFESSOR OSBORN HERE HAS TOLD ME A GREAT DEAL ABOUT YOU.
AND HE'S SAID A GREAT DEAL ABOUT YOU TO ME, PROFESSOR. BUT I MUST SAY...
WUXTRY! WUXTRY!
CAN YOU BELIEVE THAT **MARSH?!** QUITE THE **GLORY-HOUND!**
ALL OVER THE PAPERS, EXPOSING THE MOST **INFANTILE** OF FRAUDS. A TEMPEST IN A **TEAPOT**, I MUST SAY.

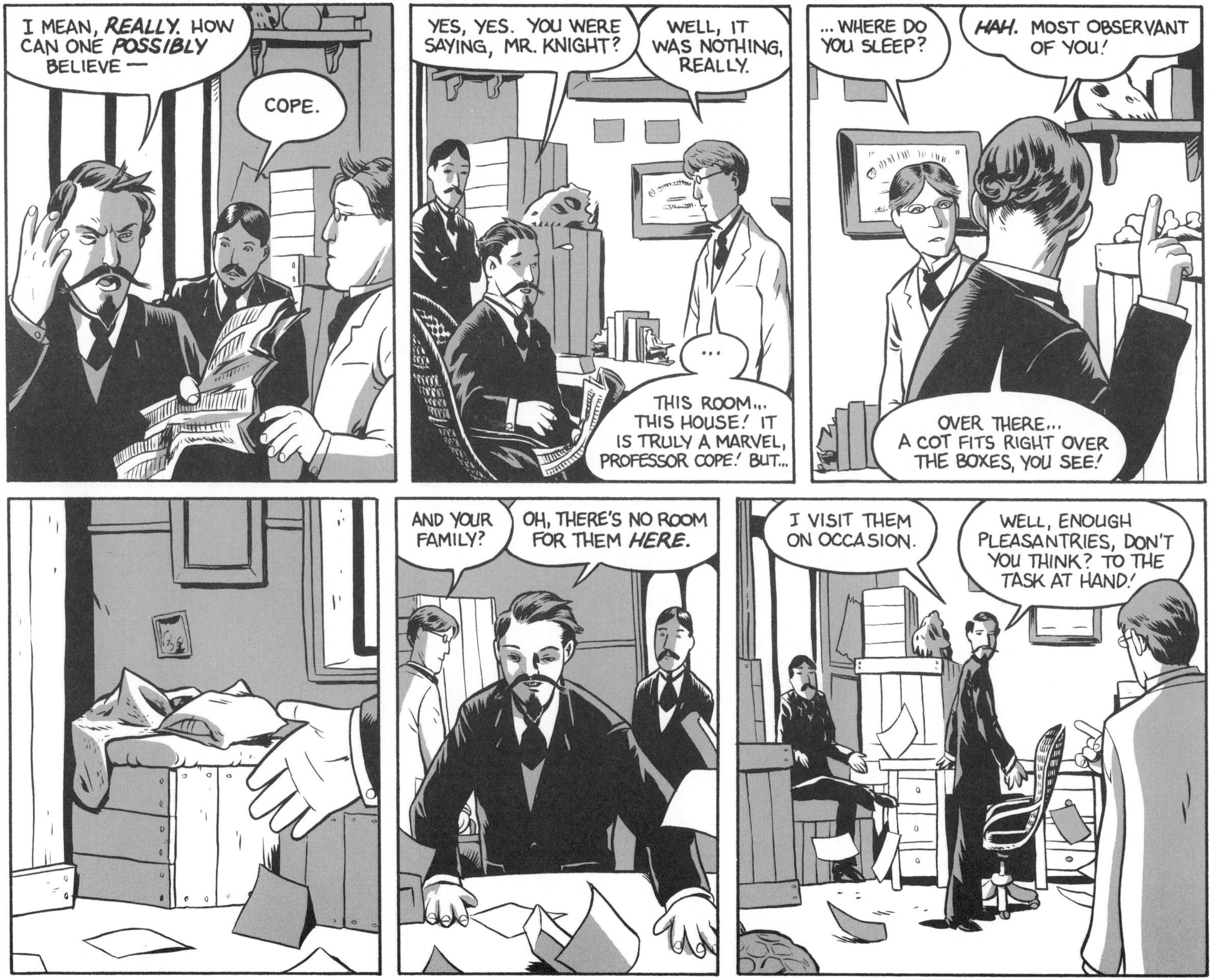

I MEAN, *REALLY*. HOW CAN ONE *POSSIBLY* BELIEVE —
COPE.
YES, YES. YOU WERE SAYING, MR. KNIGHT?
WELL, IT WAS NOTHING, REALLY.
...
THIS ROOM... THIS HOUSE! IT IS TRULY A MARVEL, PROFESSOR COPE! BUT...
... WHERE DO YOU SLEEP?
HAH. MOST OBSERVANT OF YOU!
OVER THERE... A COT FITS RIGHT OVER THE BOXES, YOU SEE!
AND YOUR FAMILY?
OH, THERE'S NO ROOM FOR THEM *HERE*.
I VISIT THEM ON OCCASION.
WELL, ENOUGH PLEASANTRIES, DON'T YOU THINK? TO THE *TASK* AT HAND!

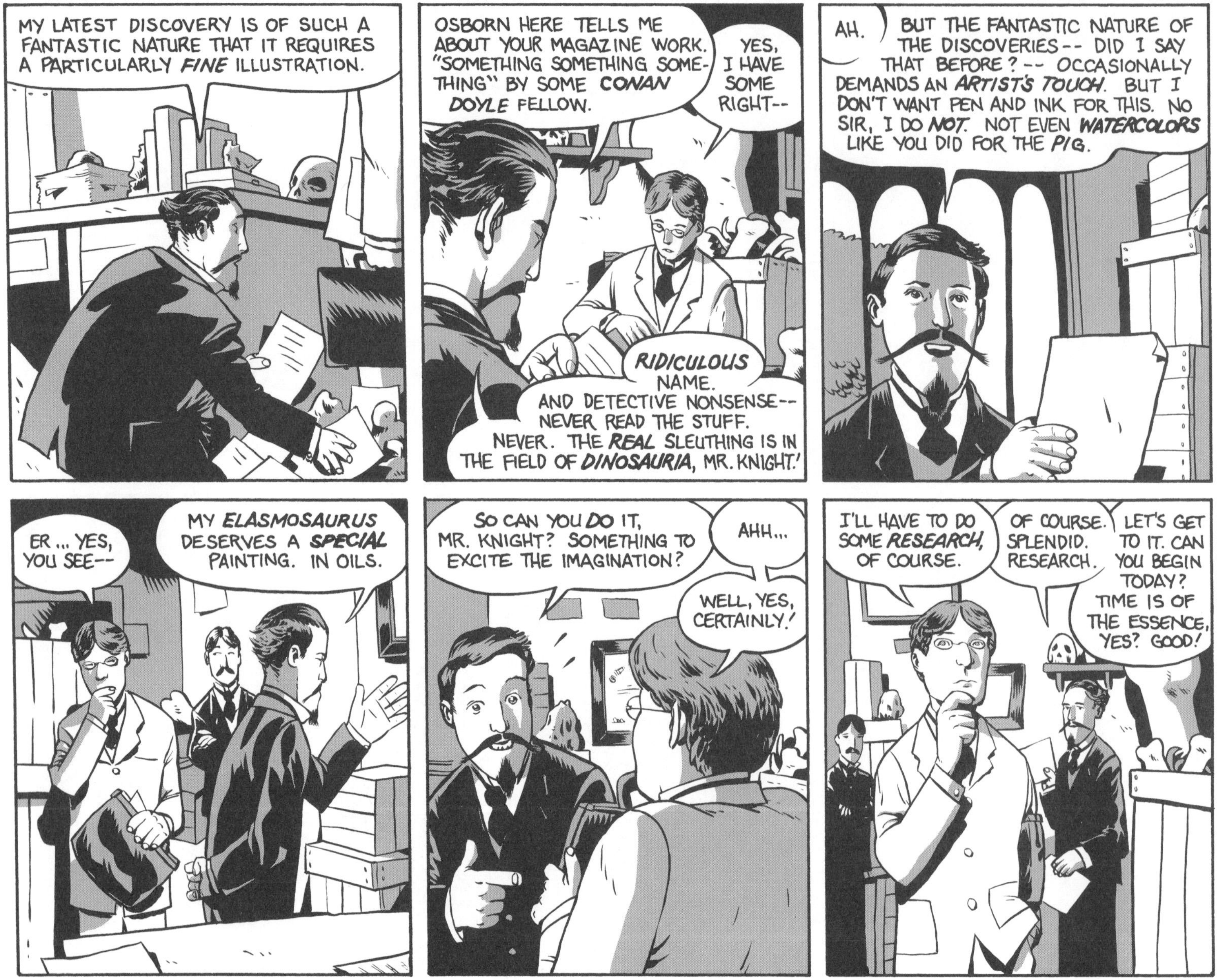
MY LATEST DISCOVERY IS OF SUCH A FANTASTIC NATURE THAT IT REQUIRES A PARTICULARLY *FINE* ILLUSTRATION.
OSBORN HERE TELLS ME ABOUT YOUR MAGAZINE WORK. "SOMETHING SOMETHING SOMETHING" BY SOME *CONAN DOYLE* FELLOW.
YES, I HAVE SOME RIGHT--
RIDICULOUS NAME.
AND DETECTIVE NONSENSE-- NEVER READ THE STUFF.
NEVER. THE *REAL* SLEUTHING IS IN THE FIELD OF *DINOSAURIA*, MR. KNIGHT!
AH.
BUT THE FANTASTIC NATURE OF THE DISCOVERIES -- DID I SAY THAT BEFORE? -- OCCASIONALLY DEMANDS AN *ARTIST'S TOUCH*. BUT I DON'T WANT PEN AND INK FOR THIS. NO SIR, I DO *NOT*. NOT EVEN *WATERCOLORS* LIKE YOU DID FOR THE *PIG*.
ER ... YES, YOU SEE--
MY *ELASMOSAURUS* DESERVES A *SPECIAL* PAINTING. IN OILS.
SO CAN YOU *DO* IT, MR. KNIGHT? SOMETHING TO EXCITE THE IMAGINATION?
AHH...
WELL, YES, CERTAINLY!
I'LL HAVE TO DO SOME *RESEARCH*, OF COURSE.
OF COURSE. SPLENDID. RESEARCH.
LET'S GET TO IT. CAN YOU BEGIN TODAY? TIME IS OF THE ESSENCE, YES? GOOD!

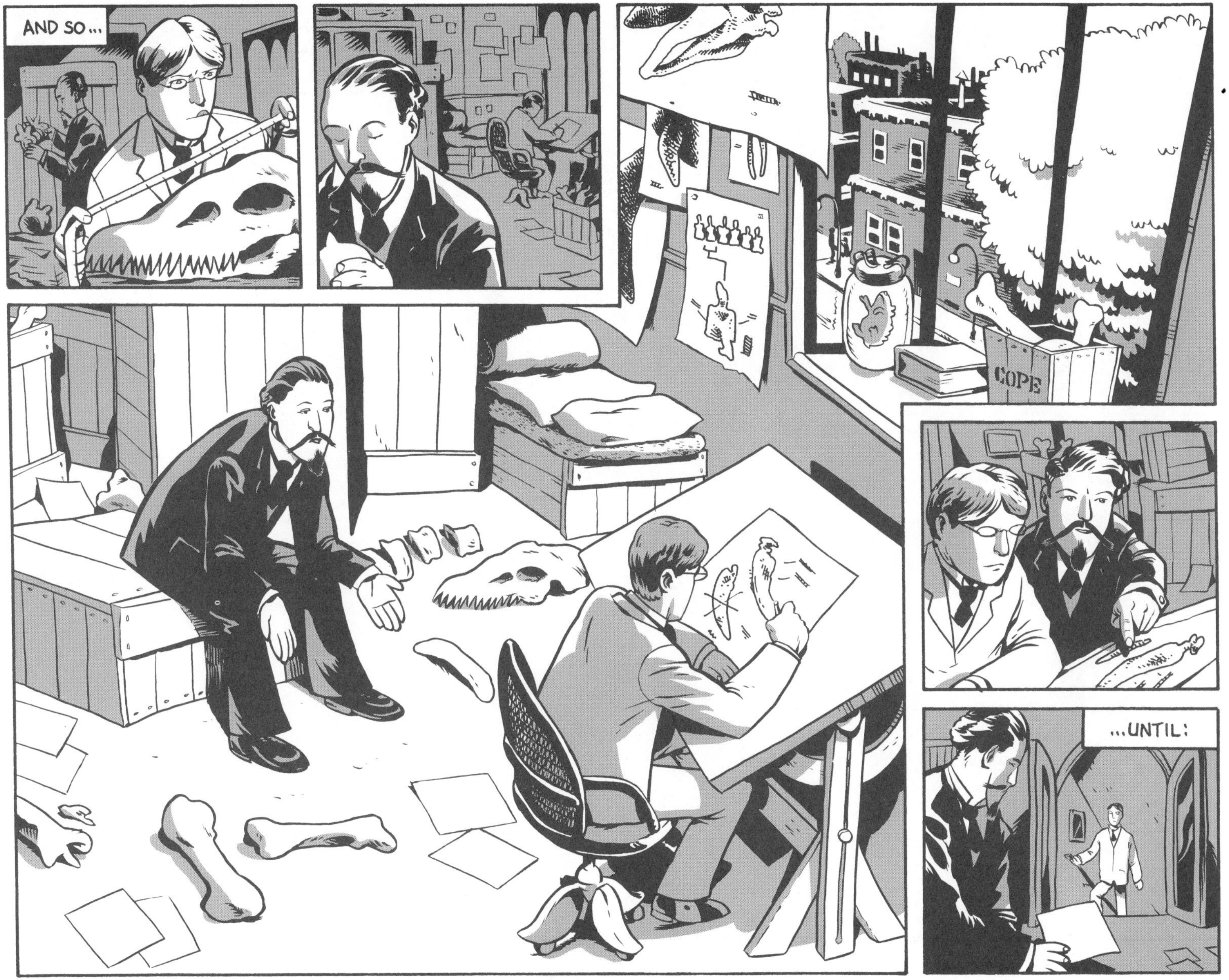
AND SO...
COPE
...UNTIL:

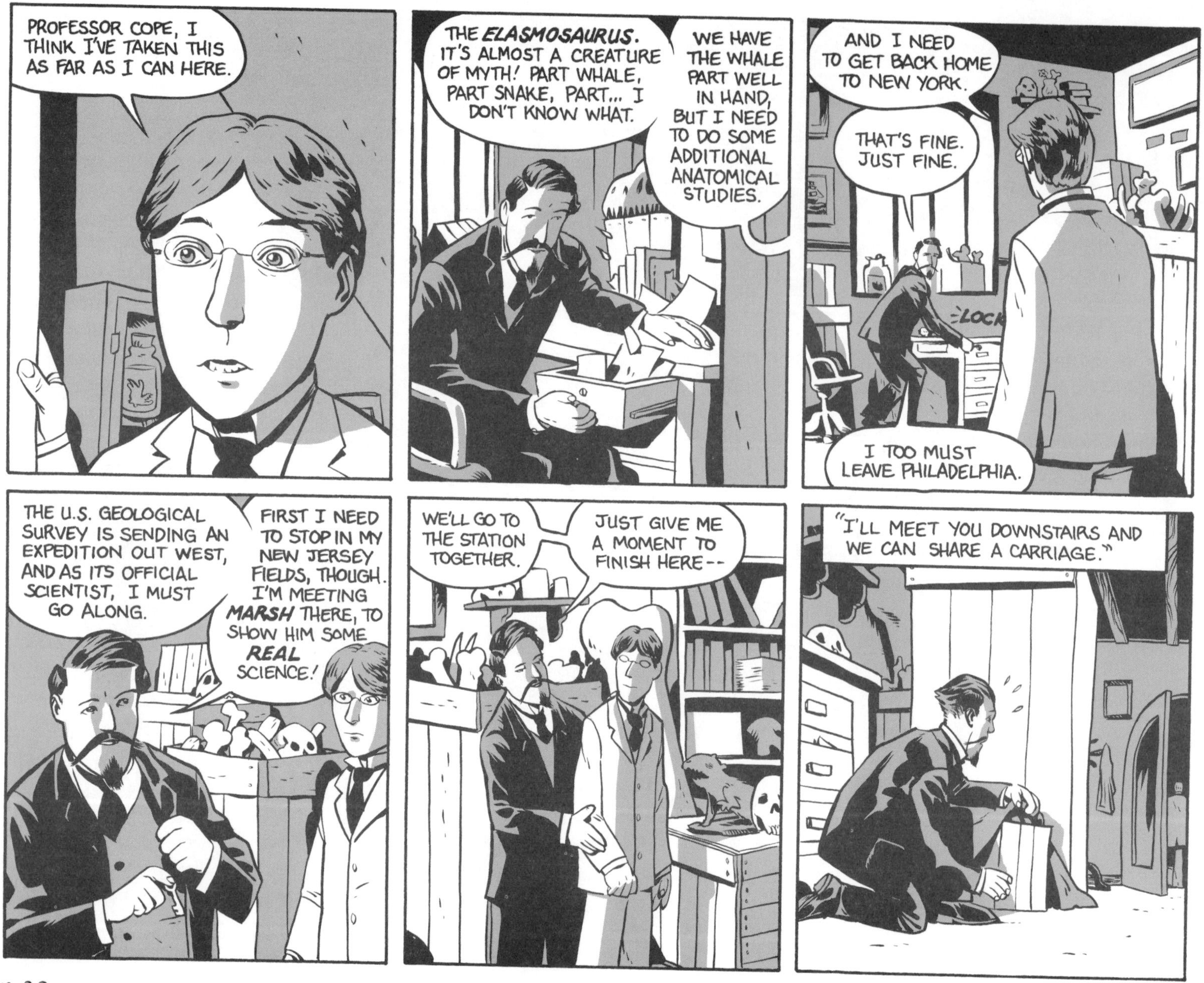
PROFESSOR COPE, I THINK I'VE TAKEN THIS AS FAR AS I CAN HERE.
THE ELASMOSAURUS. IT'S ALMOST A CREATURE OF MYTH! PART WHALE, PART SNAKE, PART... I DON'T KNOW WHAT.
WE HAVE THE WHALE PART WELL IN HAND, BUT I NEED TO DO SOME ADDITIONAL ANATOMICAL STUDIES.
AND I NEED TO GET BACK HOME TO NEW YORK.
THAT'S FINE. JUST FINE.
LOCK
I TOO MUST LEAVE PHILADELPHIA.
THE U.S. GEOLOGICAL SURVEY IS SENDING AN EXPEDITION OUT WEST, AND AS ITS OFFICIAL SCIENTIST, I MUST GO ALONG.
FIRST I NEED TO STOP IN MY NEW JERSEY FIELDS, THOUGH. I'M MEETING MARSH THERE, TO SHOW HIM SOME REAL SCIENCE!
WE'LL GO TO THE STATION TOGETHER.
JUST GIVE ME A MOMENT TO FINISH HERE--
"I'LL MEET YOU DOWNSTAIRS AND WE CAN SHARE A CARRIAGE."

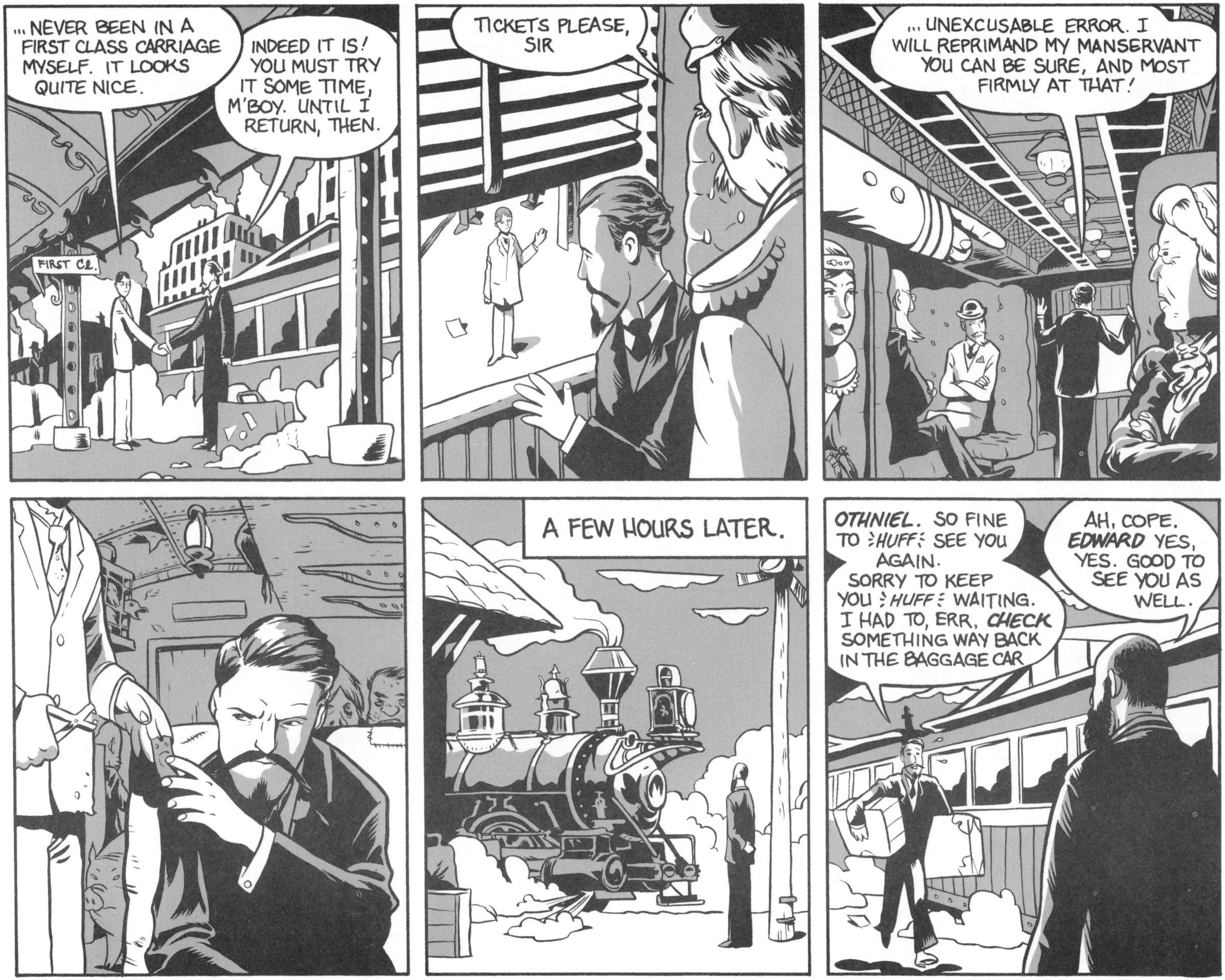
...NEVER BEEN IN A FIRST CLASS CARRIAGE MYSELF. IT LOOKS QUITE NICE.
INDEED IT IS! YOU MUST TRY IT SOME TIME, M'BOY. UNTIL I RETURN, THEN.
FIRST CL.
TICKETS PLEASE, SIR
...UNEXCUSABLE ERROR. I WILL REPRIMAND MY MANSERVANT YOU CAN BE SURE, AND MOST FIRMLY AT THAT!
A FEW HOURS LATER.
OTHNIEL. SO FINE TO HUFF SEE YOU AGAIN. SORRY TO KEEP YOU HUFF WAITING. I HAD TO, ERR, CHECK SOMETHING WAY BACK IN THE BAGGAGE CAR
AH, COPE. EDWARD YES, YES. GOOD TO SEE YOU AS WELL.

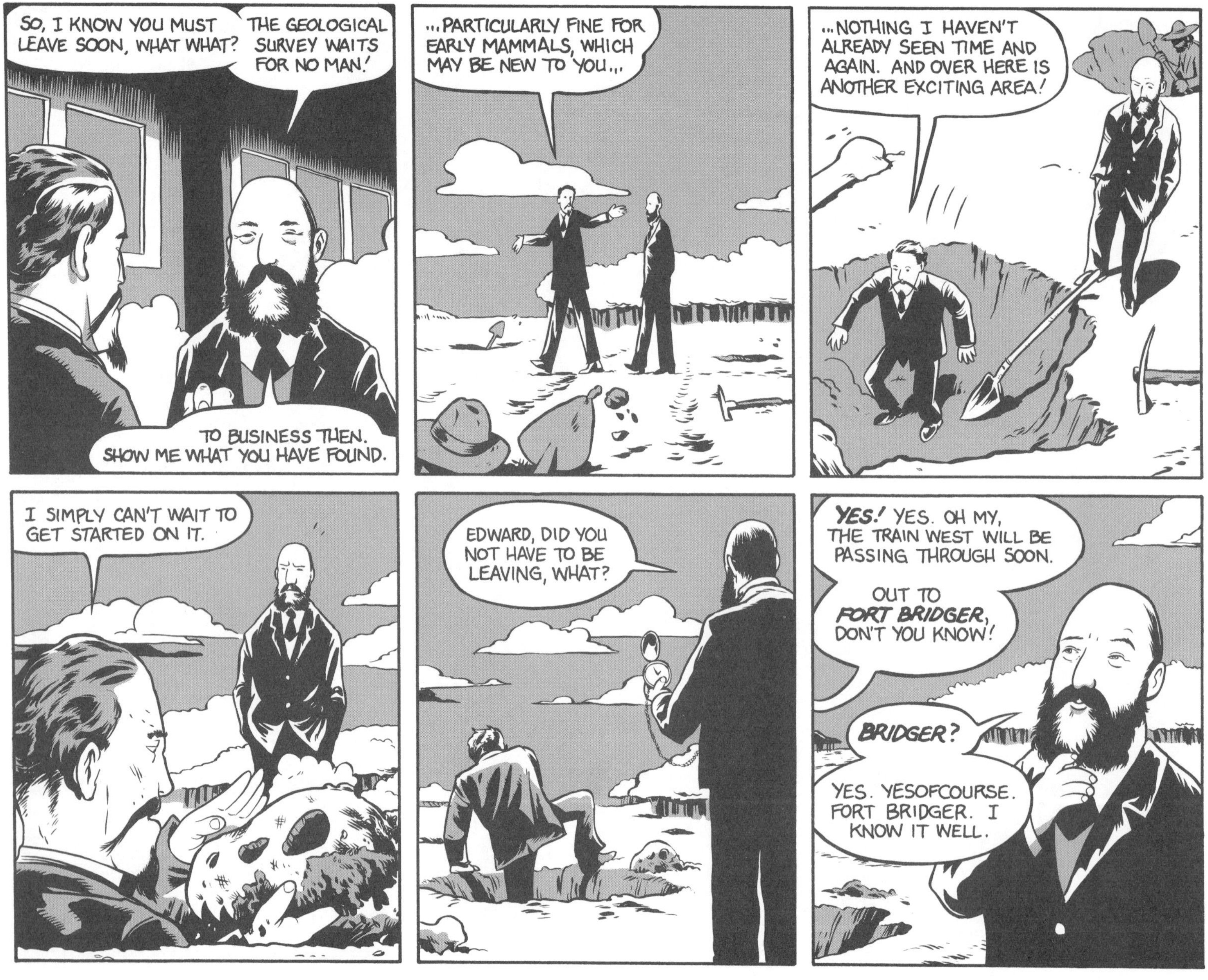
SO, I KNOW YOU MUST LEAVE SOON, WHAT WHAT?
THE GEOLOGICAL SURVEY WAITS FOR NO MAN!
TO BUSINESS THEN. SHOW ME WHAT YOU HAVE FOUND.
...PARTICULARLY FINE FOR EARLY MAMMALS, WHICH MAY BE NEW TO YOU...
...NOTHING I HAVEN'T ALREADY SEEN TIME AND AGAIN. AND OVER HERE IS ANOTHER EXCITING AREA!
I SIMPLY CAN'T WAIT TO GET STARTED ON IT.
EDWARD, DID YOU NOT HAVE TO BE LEAVING, WHAT?
YES! YES. OH MY, THE TRAIN WEST WILL BE PASSING THROUGH SOON.
OUT TO FORT BRIDGER, DON'T YOU KNOW!
BRIDGER?
YES. YESOFCOURSE. FORT BRIDGER. I KNOW IT WELL.

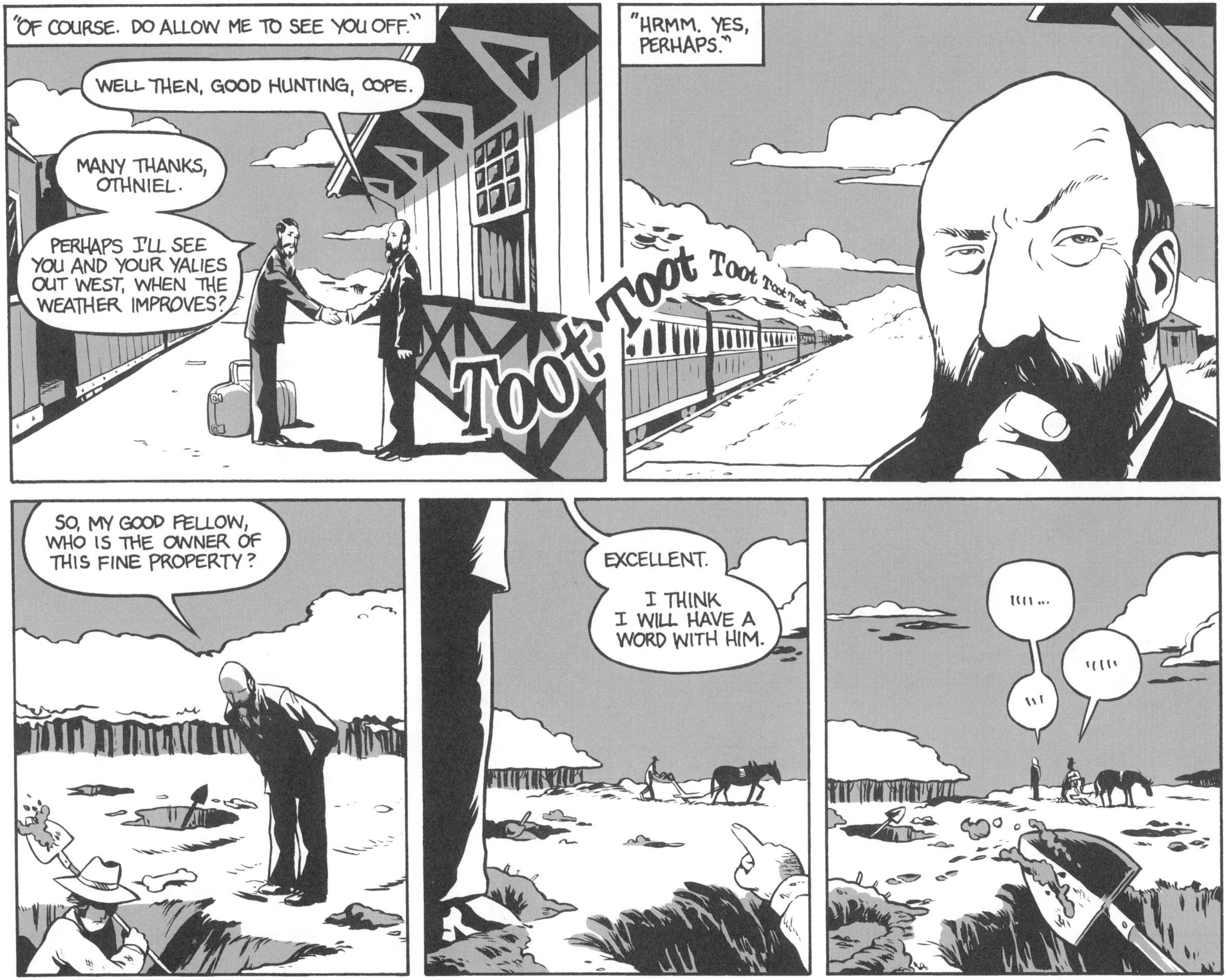
"OF COURSE. DO ALLOW ME TO SEE YOU OFF."
WELL THEN, GOOD HUNTING, COPE.
MANY THANKS, OTHNIEL.
PERHAPS I'LL SEE YOU AND YOUR YALIES OUT WEST, WHEN THE WEATHER IMPROVES?
Toot Toot Toot Toot Toot
"HRMM. YES, PERHAPS."
SO, MY GOOD FELLOW, WHO IS THE OWNER OF THIS FINE PROPERTY?
EXCELLENT.
I THINK I WILL HAVE A WORD WITH HIM.

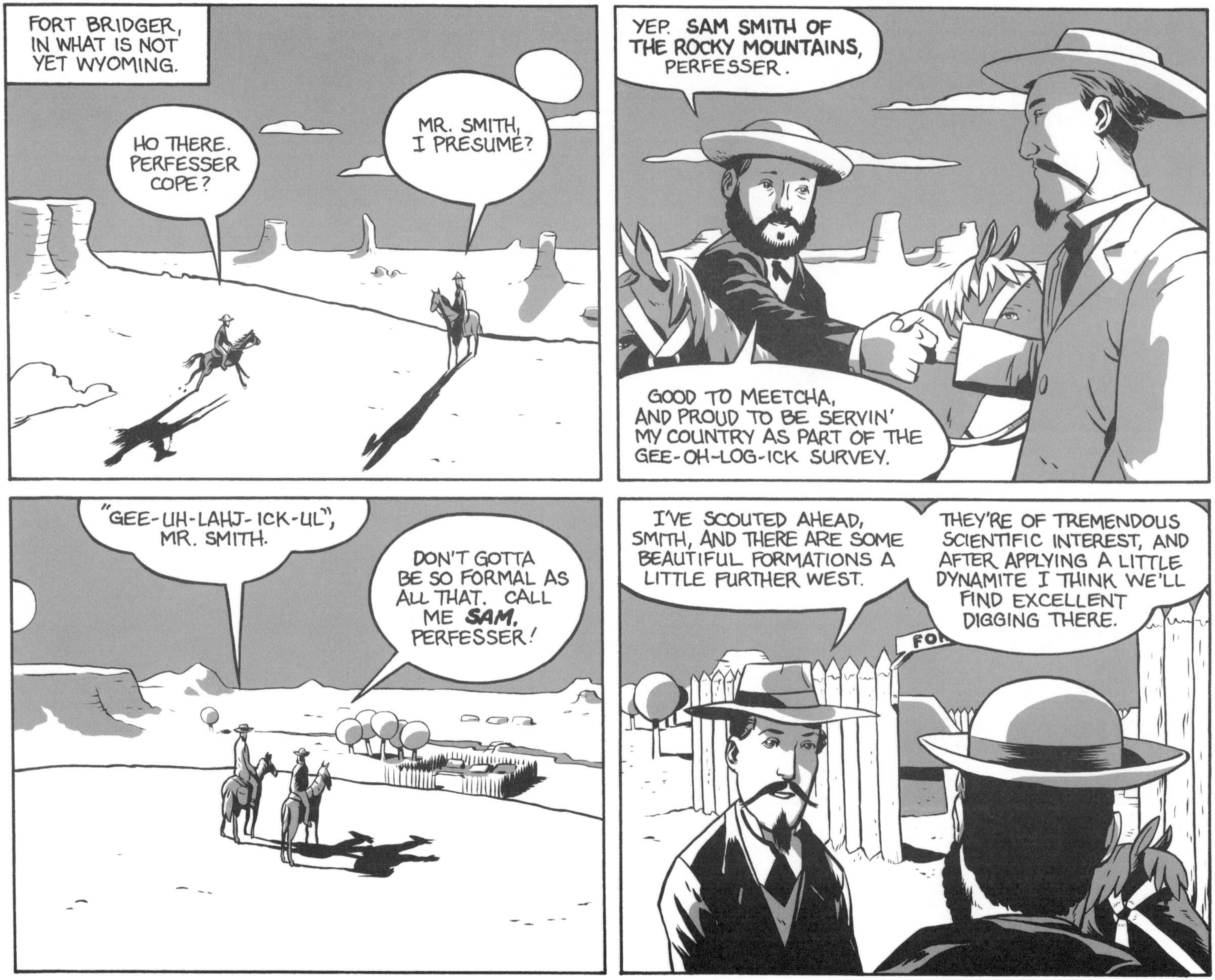
FORT BRIDGER, IN WHAT IS NOT YET WYOMING.
HO THERE. PERFESSER COPE?
MR. SMITH, I PRESUME?
YEP. SAM SMITH OF THE ROCKY MOUNTAINS, PERFESSER.
GOOD TO MEETCHA, AND PROUD TO BE SERVIN' MY COUNTRY AS PART OF THE GEE-OH-LOG-ICK SURVEY.
"GEE-UH-LAHJ-ICK-UL", MR. SMITH.
DON'T GOTTA BE SO FORMAL AS ALL THAT. CALL ME SAM, PERFESSER!
I'VE SCOUTED AHEAD, SMITH, AND THERE ARE SOME BEAUTIFUL FORMATIONS A LITTLE FURTHER WEST.
THEY'RE OF TREMENDOUS SCIENTIFIC INTEREST, AND AFTER APPLYING A LITTLE DYNAMITE I THINK WE'LL FIND EXCELLENT DIGGING THERE.

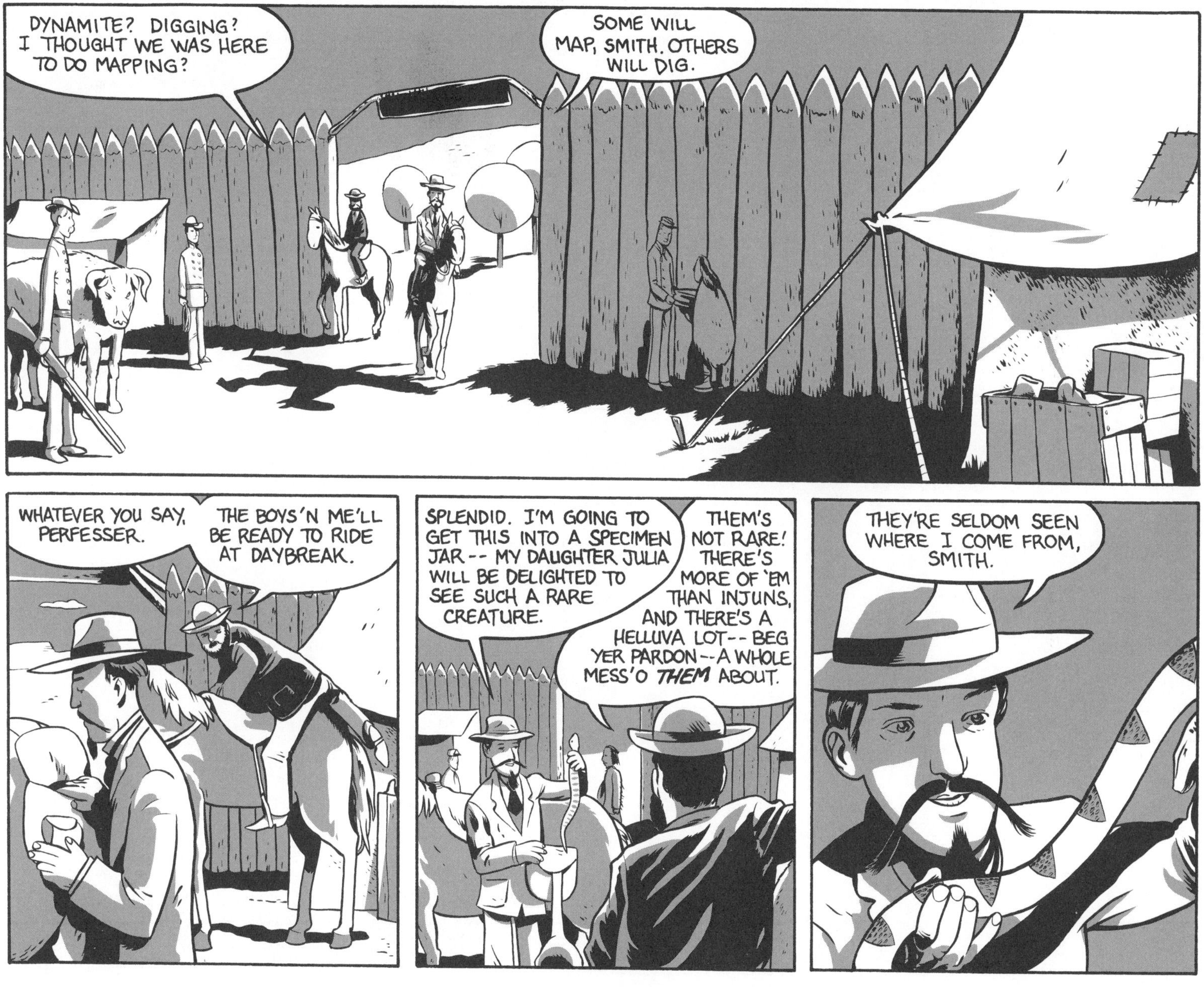
DYNAMITE? DIGGING? I THOUGHT WE WAS HERE TO DO MAPPING?
SOME WILL MAP, SMITH. OTHERS WILL DIG.
WHATEVER YOU SAY, PERFESSER.
THE BOYS'N ME'LL BE READY TO RIDE AT DAYBREAK.
SPLENDID. I'M GOING TO GET THIS INTO A SPECIMEN JAR-- MY DAUGHTER JULIA WILL BE DELIGHTED TO SEE SUCH A RARE CREATURE.
THEM'S NOT RARE! THERE'S MORE OF 'EM THAN INJUNS, AND THERE'S A HELLUVA LOT-- BEG YER PARDON--A WHOLE MESS'O THEM ABOUT.
THEY'RE SELDOM SEEN WHERE I COME FROM, SMITH.

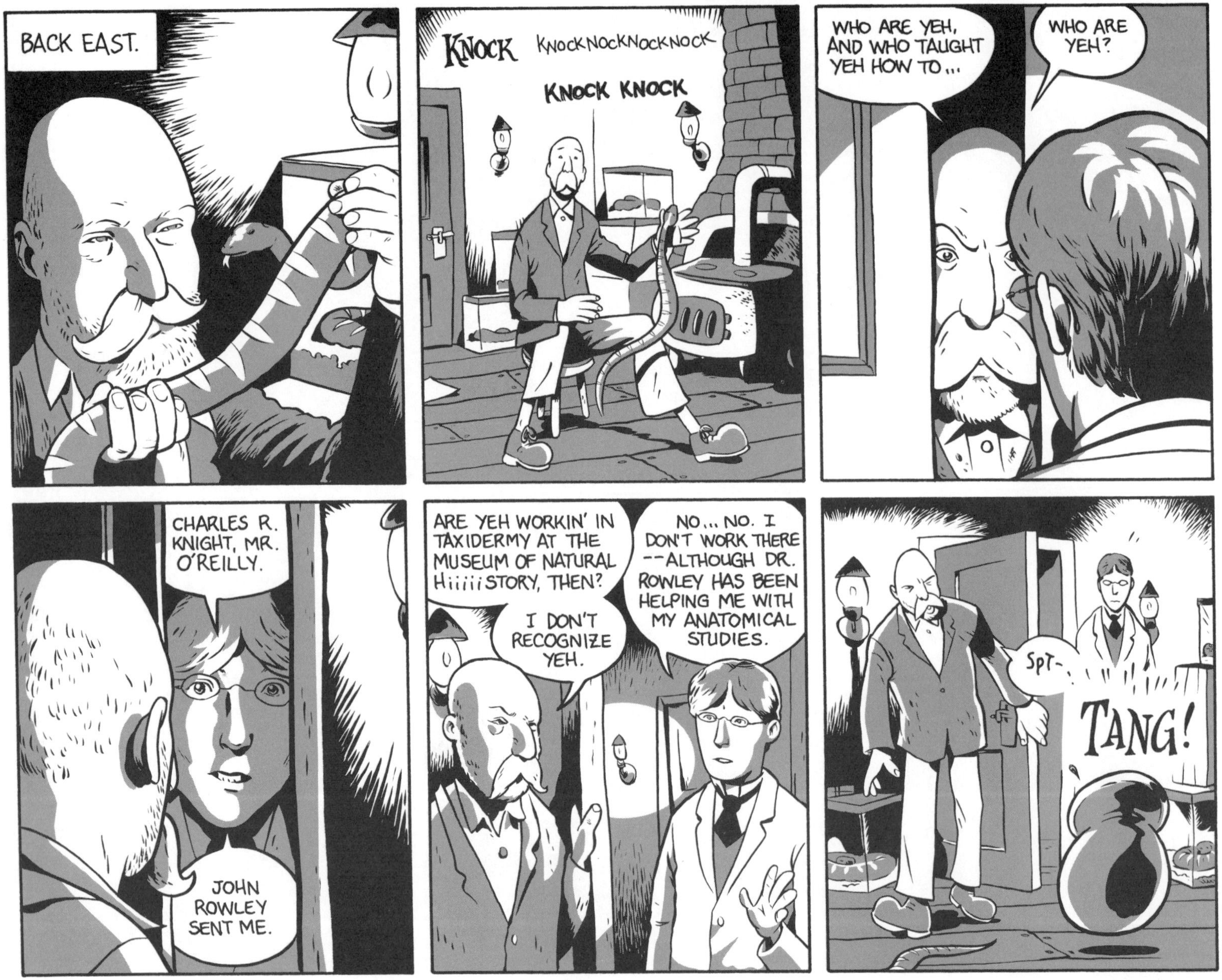
BACK EAST.
KNOCK KNOCKNOCKNOCKNOCK
KNOCK KNOCK
WHO ARE YEH, AND WHO TAUGHT YEH HOW TO...
WHO ARE YEH?
CHARLES R. KNIGHT, MR. O'REILLY.
JOHN ROWLEY SENT ME.
ARE YEH WORKIN' IN TAXIDERMY AT THE MUSEUM OF NATURAL HiiiiiSTORY, THEN?
I DON'T RECOGNIZE YEH.
NO... NO. I DON'T WORK THERE --ALTHOUGH DR. ROWLEY HAS BEEN HELPING ME WITH MY ANATOMICAL STUDIES.
SpT-
TANG!

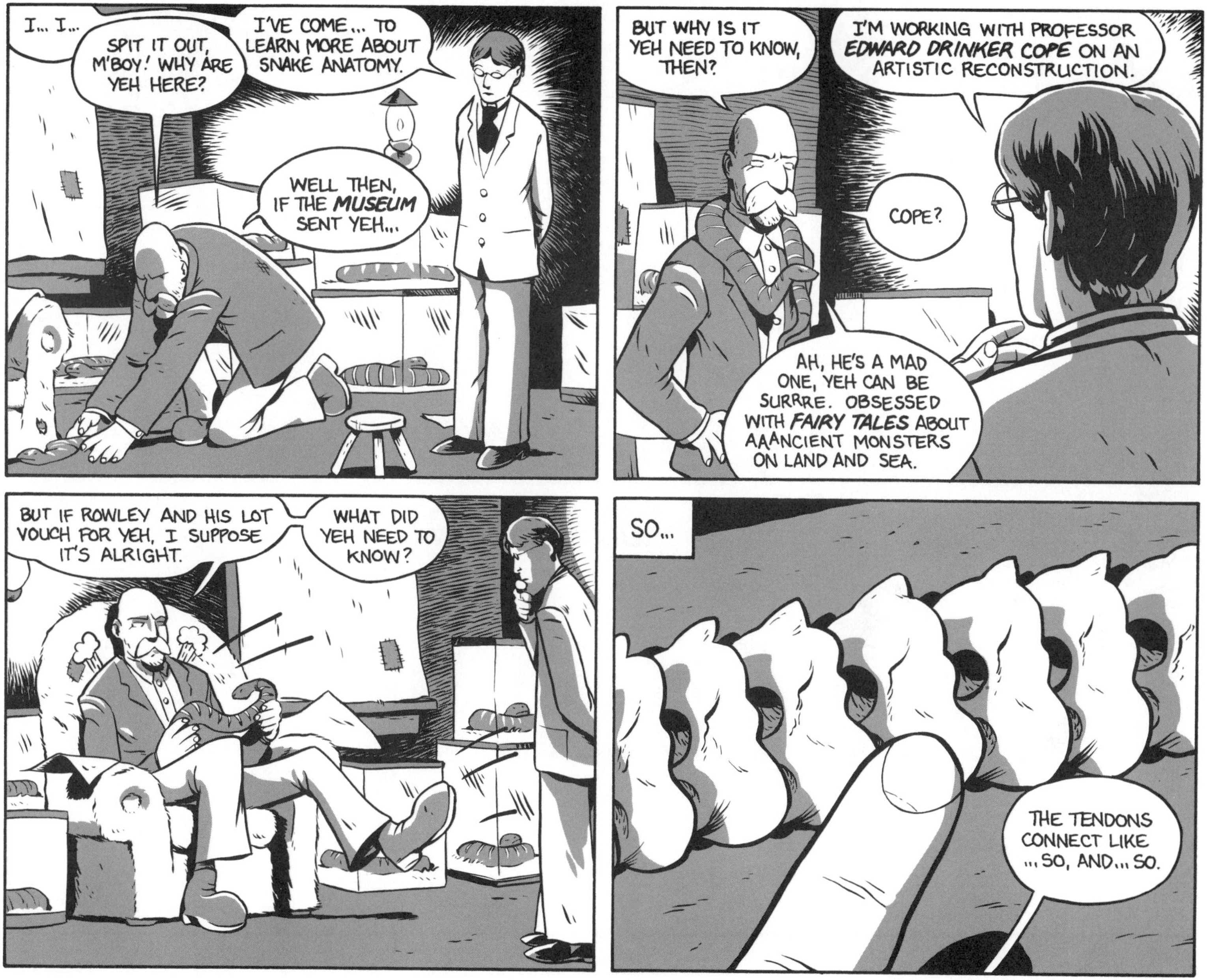
I... I...
SPIT IT OUT, M'BOY! WHY ARE YEH HERE?
I'VE COME... TO LEARN MORE ABOUT SNAKE ANATOMY.
WELL THEN, IF THE MUSEUM SENT YEH...
BUT WHY IS IT YEH NEED TO KNOW, THEN?
I'M WORKING WITH PROFESSOR EDWARD DRINKER COPE ON AN ARTISTIC RECONSTRUCTION.
COPE?
AH, HE'S A MAD ONE, YEH CAN BE SURRRE. OBSESSED WITH FAIRY TALES ABOUT AAANCIENT MONSTERS ON LAND AND SEA.
BUT IF ROWLEY AND HIS LOT VOUCH FOR YEH, I SUPPOSE IT'S ALRIGHT.
WHAT DID YEH NEED TO KNOW?
SO...
THE TENDONS CONNECT LIKE ...SO, AND... SO.

AND...

NAH, NAH, M'BOY. NEEEEVER THAT WAY.

OBSERVE THIS FINE FELLA HERE, THEN. YOU'LL SEE THAT...

AND...

SURE, AND THEY COULD COIL UP LIKE THAT, YES. VERY GOOD.

FINALLY...

YER A TALENTED FELLA, I'LL SAY THAT. BUT IT'S TIME FOR ME *FEE*.

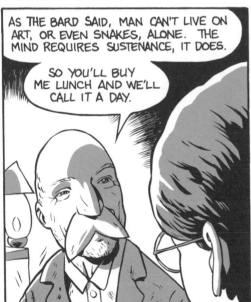

AS THE BARD SAID, MAN CAN'T LIVE ON ART, OR EVEN SNAKES, ALONE. THE MIND REQUIRES SUSTENANCE, IT DOES.

SO YOU'LL BUY ME LUNCH AND WE'LL CALL IT A DAY.

SP-

TANG!

HMM...

I THINK I KNOW OF A PLACE THAT WILL ... SUIT.

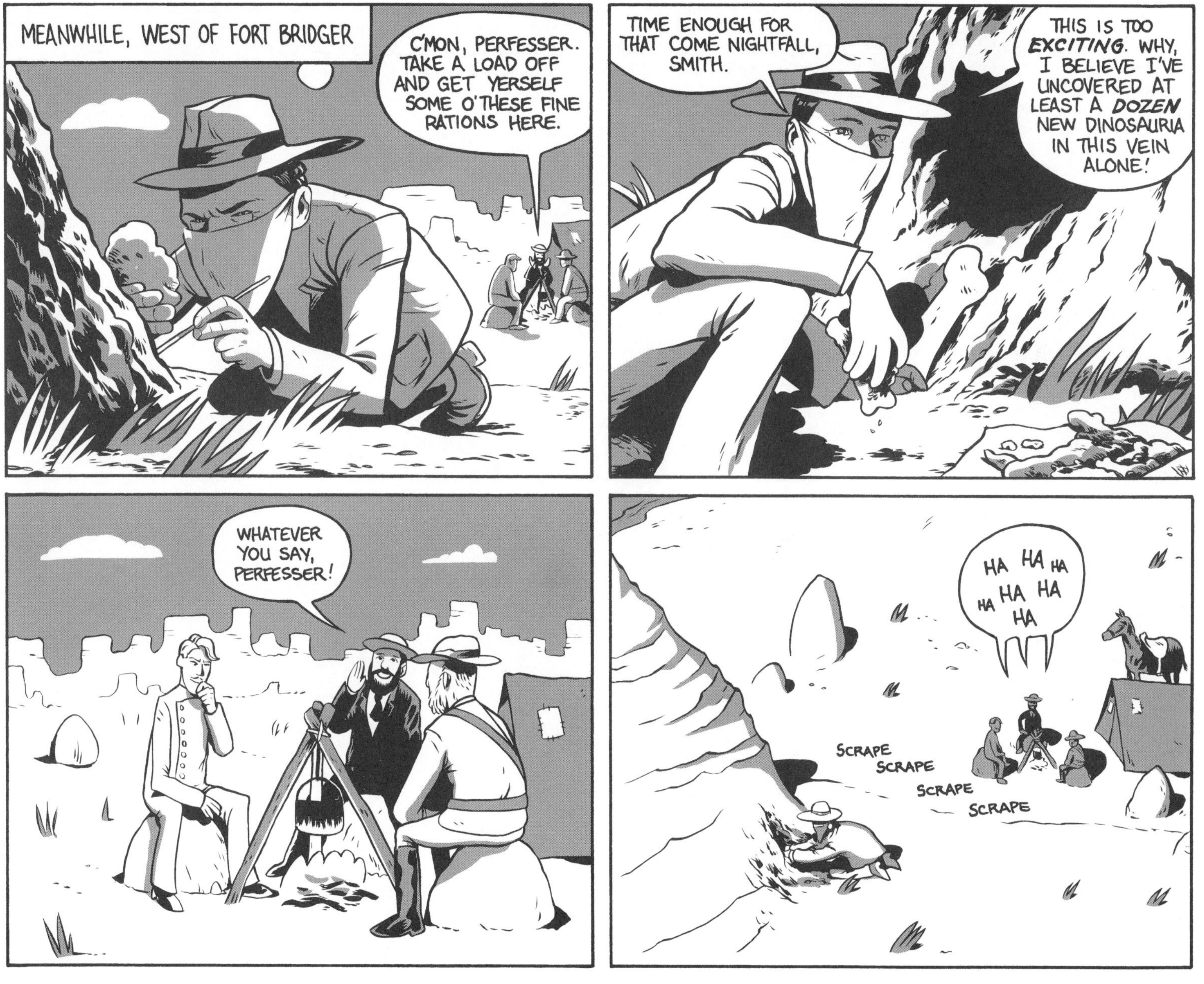
MEANWHILE, WEST OF FORT BRIDGER
C'MON, PERFESSER. TAKE A LOAD OFF AND GET YERSELF SOME O'THESE FINE RATIONS HERE.
TIME ENOUGH FOR THAT COME NIGHTFALL, SMITH.
THIS IS TOO EXCITING. WHY, I BELIEVE I'VE UNCOVERED AT LEAST A DOZEN NEW DINOSAURIA IN THIS VEIN ALONE!
WHATEVER YOU SAY, PERFESSER!
HA HA HA HA HA HA HA
SCRAPE SCRAPE SCRAPE SCRAPE

THAT NIGHT...

THESE BONES -- YOU SAY THEY'RE FROM... FROM *DAH-NO-SEWER-UH*? AND THIS IS WHERE THEY WUZ WALKIN' AROUND, THEN?

HA! HA! *DINOSAURIA*, MR. SMITH. ANCIENT CREATURES FROM A TIME LONG PAST. AND NOT *WALKED*, SIR.

SWAM!

YES, THIS WAS ONCE A *SEA*, A GREAT SALT OCEAN OF A PERIOD CALLED THE *CRETACEOUS*, AT THE TIME WHEN THE CHALK OF ENGLAND WAS BEING DEPOSITED.

ENGLAND? I THOUGHT WE WAS TALKING ABOUT HERE IN WYOMING TERRITORY? AIN'T NO CHALK, AND DAMN LITTLE WATER NEITHER.

MILLIONS OF YEARS AGO, SMITH.

MANY MILLIONS.

THE OCEAN WAS VAST, SHALLOW, AND MOST FULL OF LIFE... OVER THIRTY-SEVEN SPECIES OF REPTILE -- ONLY ONE TERRESTRIAL, AND FOUR AIRBORNE.

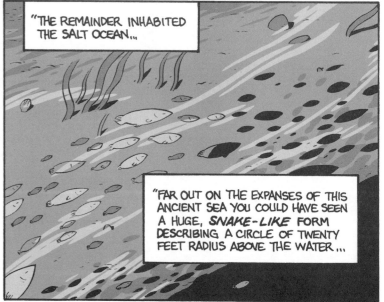

"THE REMAINDER INHABITED THE SALT OCEAN...

"FAR OUT ON THE EXPANSES OF THIS ANCIENT SEA YOU COULD HAVE SEEN A HUGE, *SNAKE-LIKE* FORM DESCRIBING A CIRCLE OF TWENTY FEET RADIUS ABOVE THE WATER ....

"THIS IS THE *ELASMOSAURUS PLATYURUS*. A MAGNIFICENT, CARNIVOROUS SEA REPTILE.

"IT PROBABLY SWAM MANY FEET BELOW THE SURFACE, RAISING ITS HEAD TO THE DISTANT AIR FOR BREATH, THEN WITHDRAWING IT AND EXPLORING THE DEPTHS BELOW WITHOUT ONCE ALTERING THE POSITION OF ITS BODY...

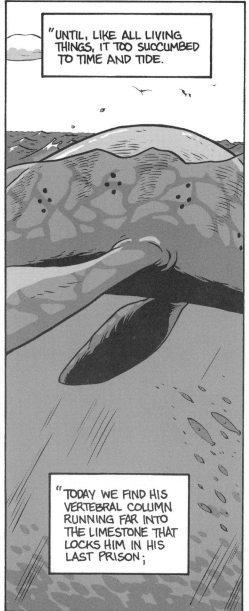

"UNTIL, LIKE ALL LIVING THINGS, IT TOO SUCCUMBED TO TIME AND TIDE.

"TODAY WE FIND HIS VERTEBRAL COLUMN RUNNING FAR INTO THE LIMESTONE THAT LOCKS HIM IN HIS LAST PRISON;

"OR A PADDLE EXTENDED ON THE SLOPE, AS THOUGH ENTREATING AID;

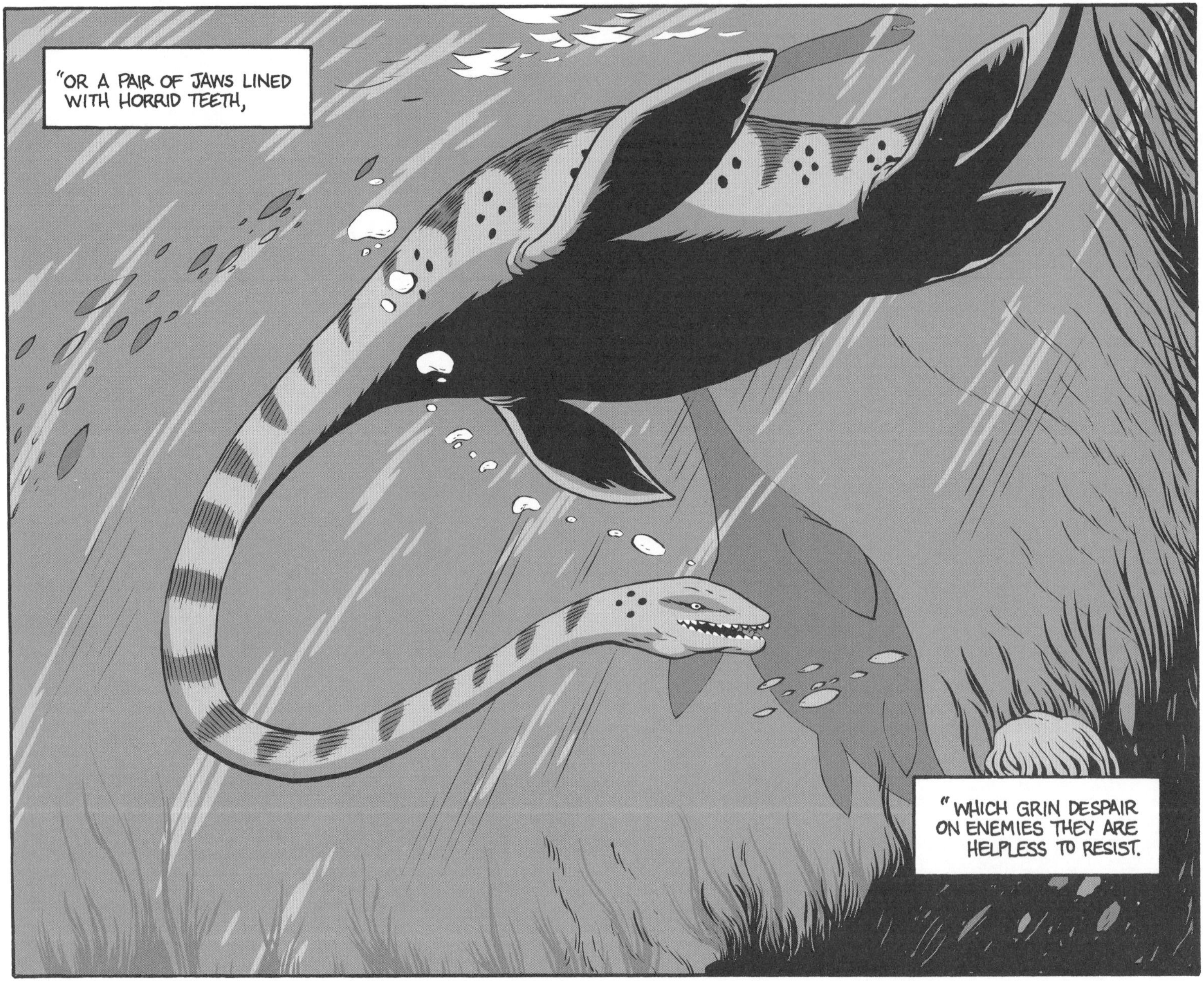
"OR A PAIR OF JAWS LINED WITH HORRID TEETH,
"WHICH GRIN DESPAIR ON ENEMIES THEY ARE HELPLESS TO RESIST.

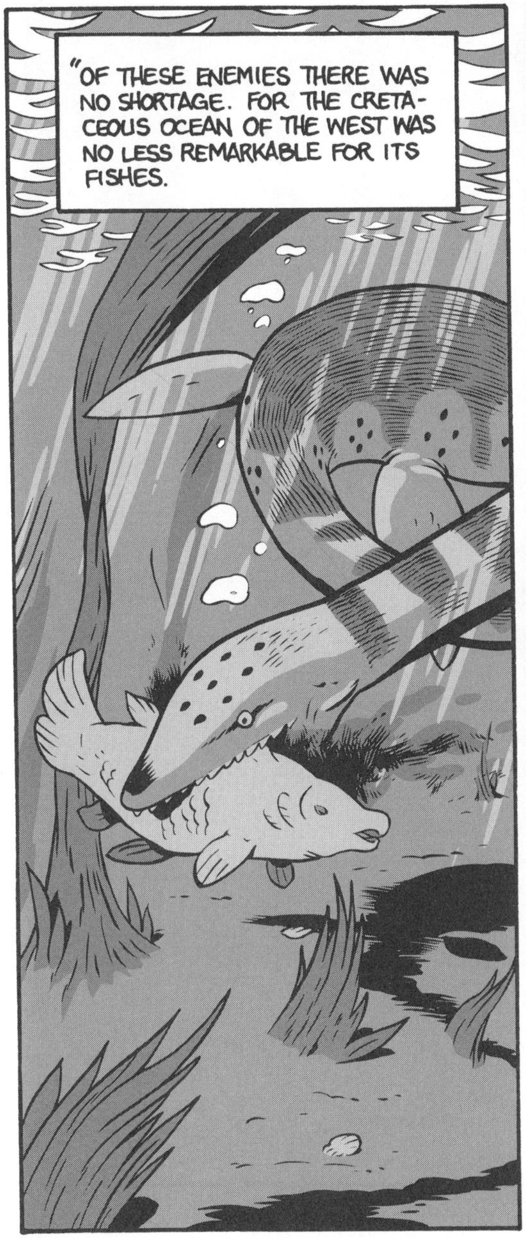
"OF THESE ENEMIES THERE WAS NO SHORTAGE. FOR THE CRETACEOUS OCEAN OF THE WEST WAS NO LESS REMARKABLE FOR ITS FISHES.

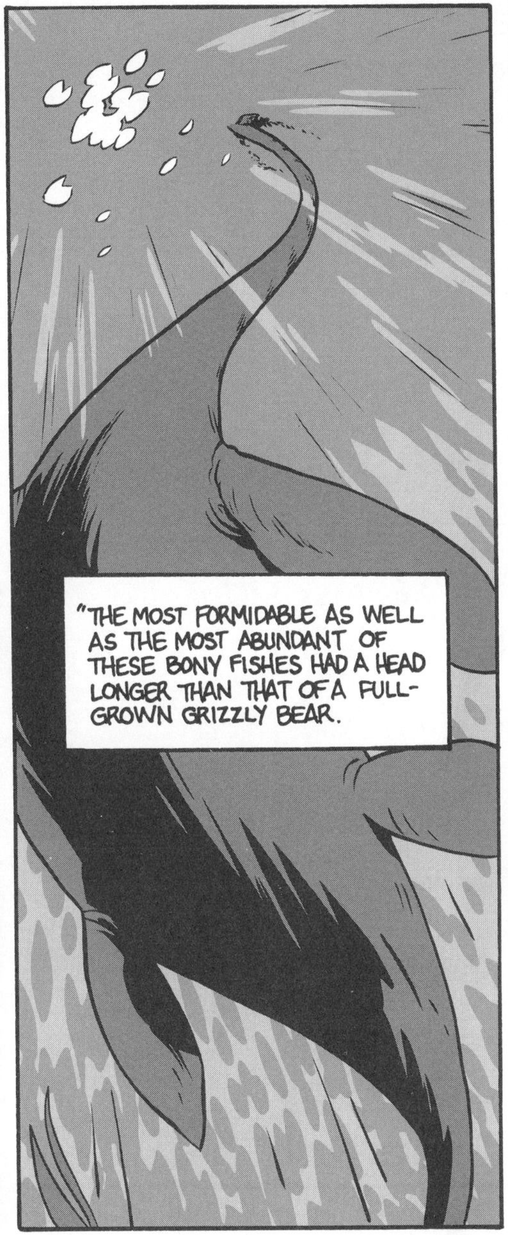
"THE MOST FORMIDABLE AS WELL AS THE MOST ABUNDANT OF THESE BONY FISHES HAD A HEAD LONGER THAN THAT OF A FULL-GROWN GRIZZLY BEAR.

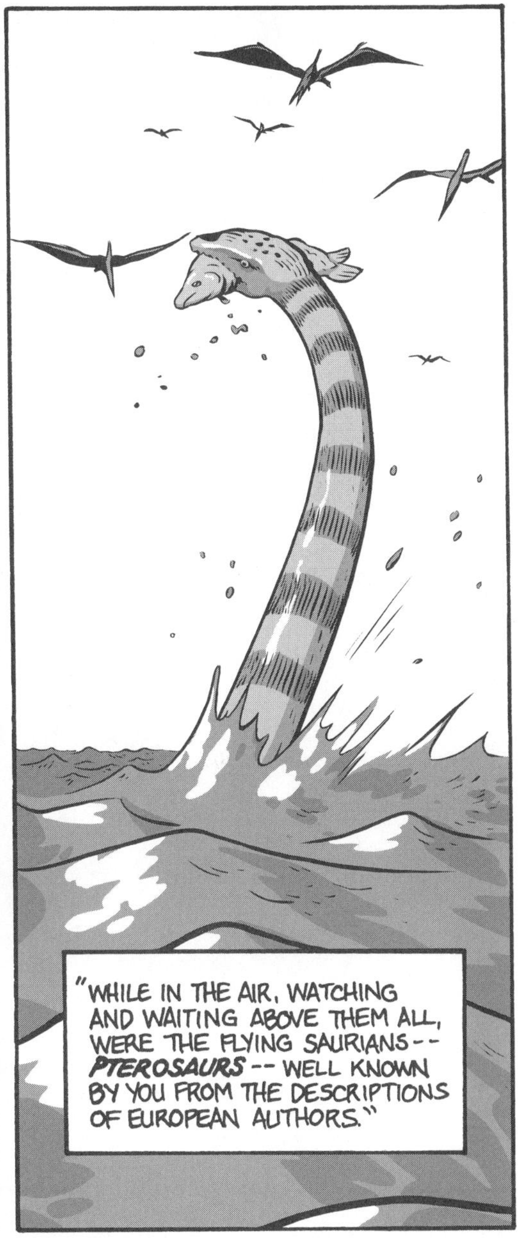
"WHILE IN THE AIR, WATCHING AND WAITING ABOVE THEM ALL, WERE THE FLYING SAURIANS-- PTEROSAURS -- WELL KNOWN BY YOU FROM THE DESCRIPTIONS OF EUROPEAN AUTHORS."

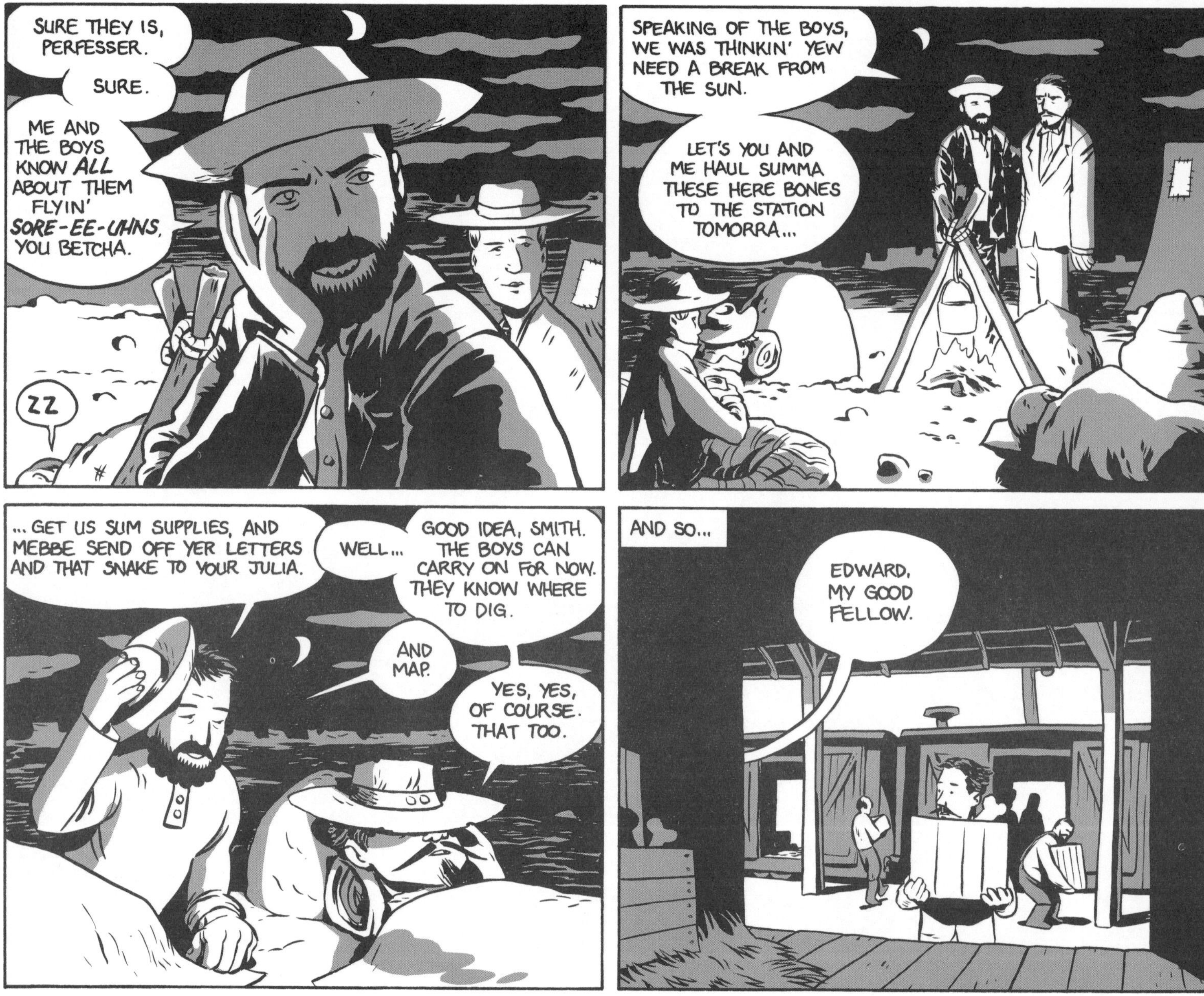
SURE THEY IS, PERFESSER.
SURE.
ME AND THE BOYS KNOW ALL ABOUT THEM FLYIN' SORE-EE-UHNS, YOU BETCHA.
ZZ
SPEAKING OF THE BOYS, WE WAS THINKIN' YEW NEED A BREAK FROM THE SUN.
LET'S YOU AND ME HAUL SUMMA THESE HERE BONES TO THE STATION TOMORRA...
... GET US SUM SUPPLIES, AND MEBBE SEND OFF YER LETTERS AND THAT SNAKE TO YOUR JULIA.
WELL...
GOOD IDEA, SMITH. THE BOYS CAN CARRY ON FOR NOW. THEY KNOW WHERE TO DIG.
AND MAP.
YES, YES, OF COURSE. THAT TOO.
AND SO...
EDWARD, MY GOOD FELLOW.

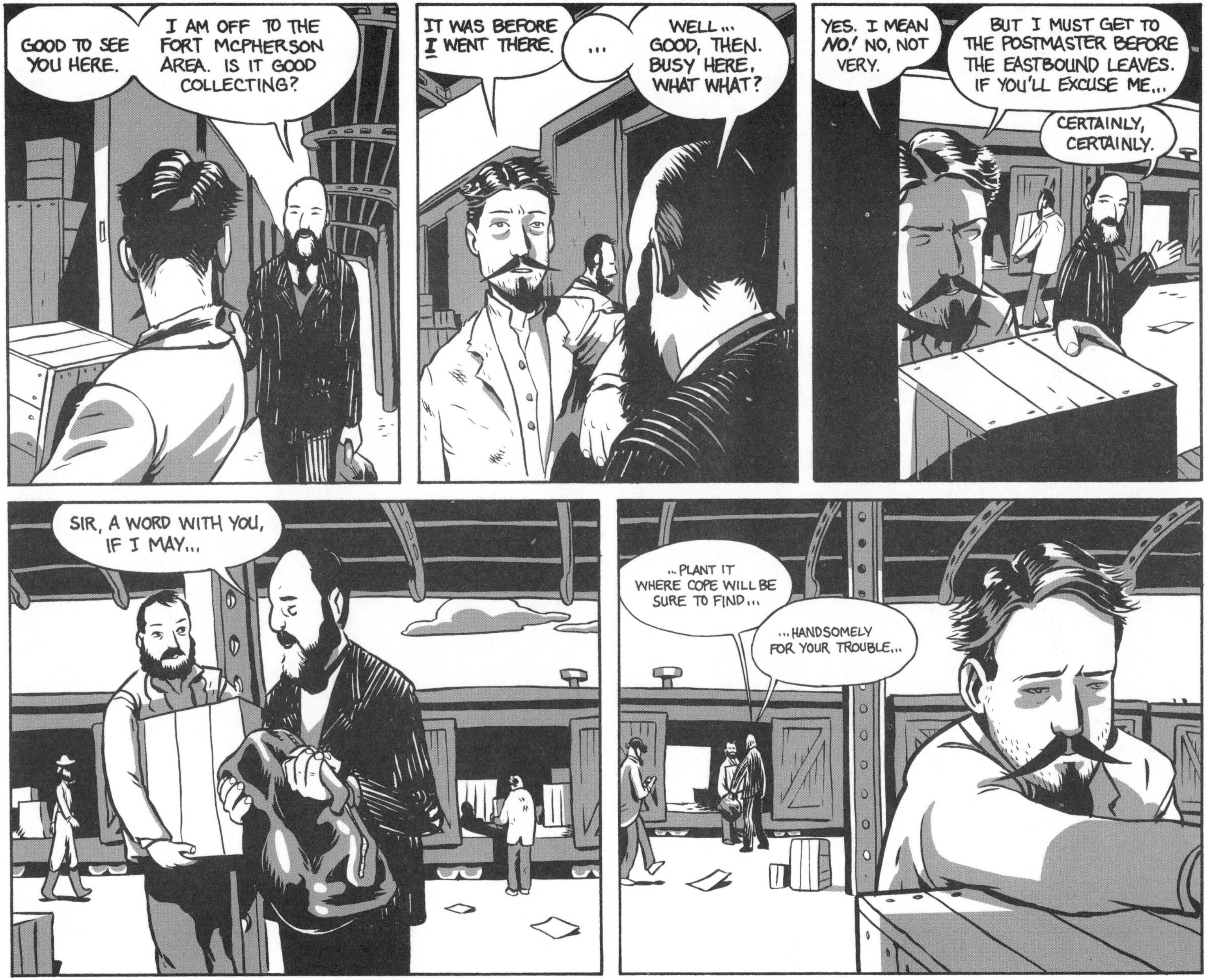
GOOD TO SEE YOU HERE.
I AM OFF TO THE FORT McPHERSON AREA. IS IT GOOD COLLECTING?
IT WAS BEFORE I WENT THERE.
...
WELL... GOOD, THEN. BUSY HERE, WHAT WHAT?
YES. I MEAN NO! NO, NOT VERY.
BUT I MUST GET TO THE POSTMASTER BEFORE THE EASTBOUND LEAVES. IF YOU'LL EXCUSE ME...
CERTAINLY, CERTAINLY.
SIR, A WORD WITH YOU, IF I MAY...
...PLANT IT WHERE COPE WILL BE SURE TO FIND...
...HANDSOMELY FOR YOUR TROUBLE...

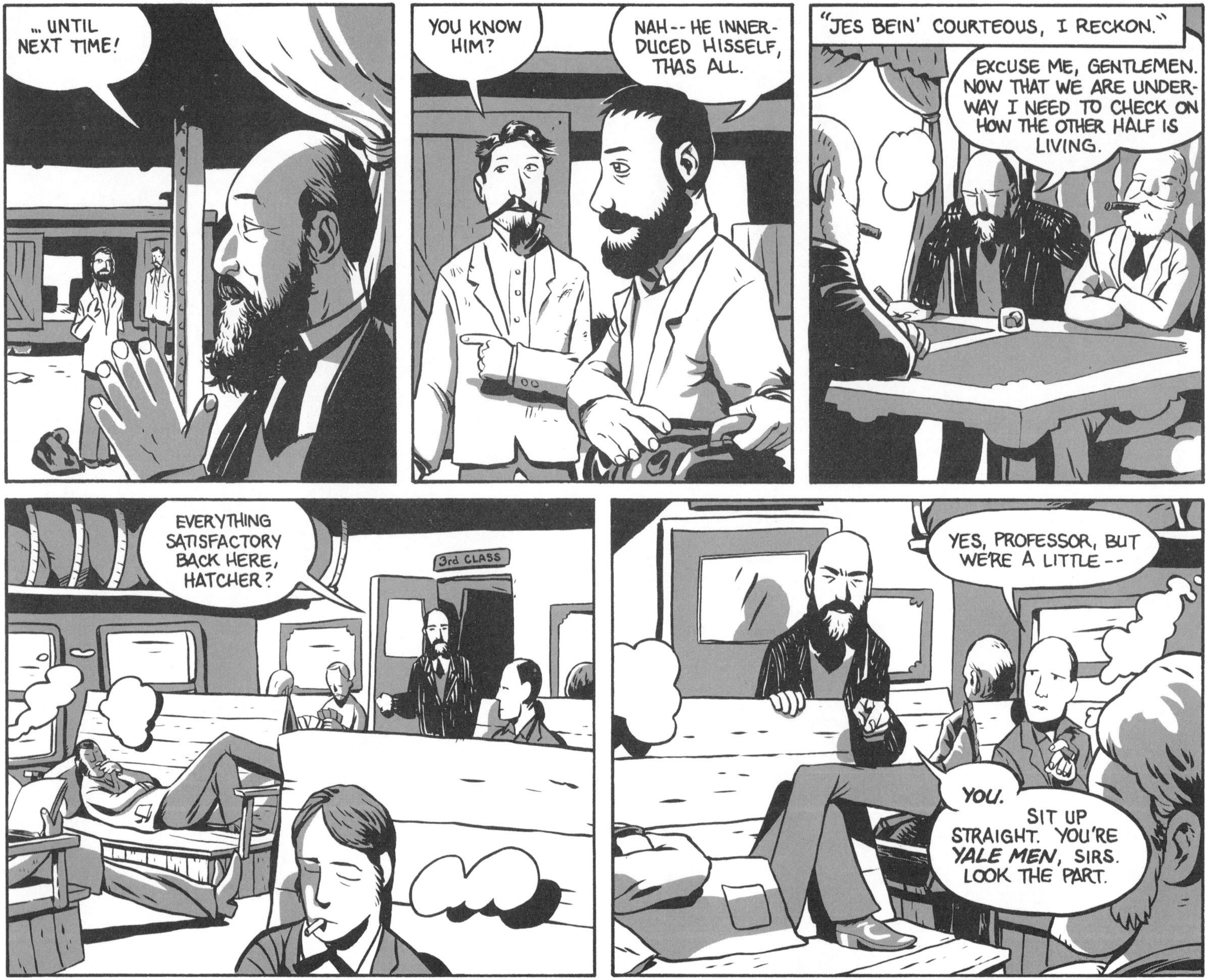

... UNTIL NEXT TIME!
YOU KNOW HIM?
NAH -- HE INNER-DUCED HISSELF, THAS ALL.
"JES BEIN' COURTEOUS, I RECKON."
EXCUSE ME, GENTLEMEN. NOW THAT WE ARE UNDERWAY I NEED TO CHECK ON HOW THE OTHER HALF IS LIVING.
EVERYTHING SATISFACTORY BACK HERE, HATCHER?
3rd CLASS
YES, PROFESSOR, BUT WE'RE A LITTLE --
YOU.
SIT UP STRAIGHT. YOU'RE YALE MEN, SIRS. LOOK THE PART.

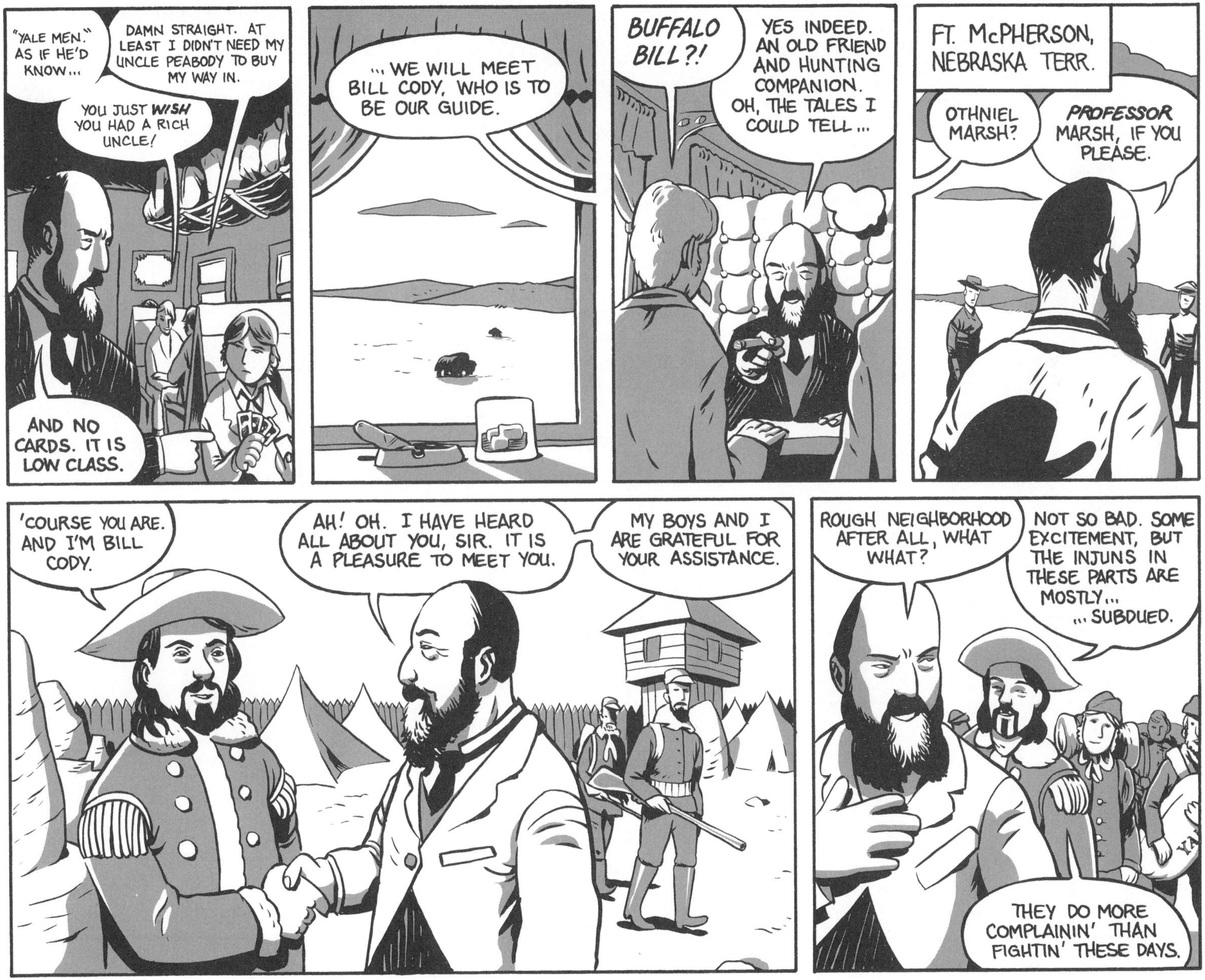
"YALE MEN." AS IF HE'D KNOW...
DAMN STRAIGHT. AT LEAST I DIDN'T NEED MY UNCLE PEABODY TO BUY MY WAY IN.
YOU JUST WISH YOU HAD A RICH UNCLE!
AND NO CARDS. IT IS LOW CLASS.
...WE WILL MEET BILL CODY, WHO IS TO BE OUR GUIDE.
BUFFALO BILL?!
YES INDEED. AN OLD FRIEND AND HUNTING COMPANION. OH, THE TALES I COULD TELL...
FT. McPHERSON, NEBRASKA TERR.
OTHNIEL MARSH?
PROFESSOR MARSH, IF YOU PLEASE.
'COURSE YOU ARE. AND I'M BILL CODY.
AH! OH. I HAVE HEARD ALL ABOUT YOU, SIR. IT IS A PLEASURE TO MEET YOU.
MY BOYS AND I ARE GRATEFUL FOR YOUR ASSISTANCE.
ROUGH NEIGHBORHOOD AFTER ALL, WHAT WHAT?
NOT SO BAD. SOME EXCITEMENT, BUT THE INJUNS IN THESE PARTS ARE MOSTLY...
...SUBDUED.
THEY DO MORE COMPLAININ' THAN FIGHTIN' THESE DAYS.

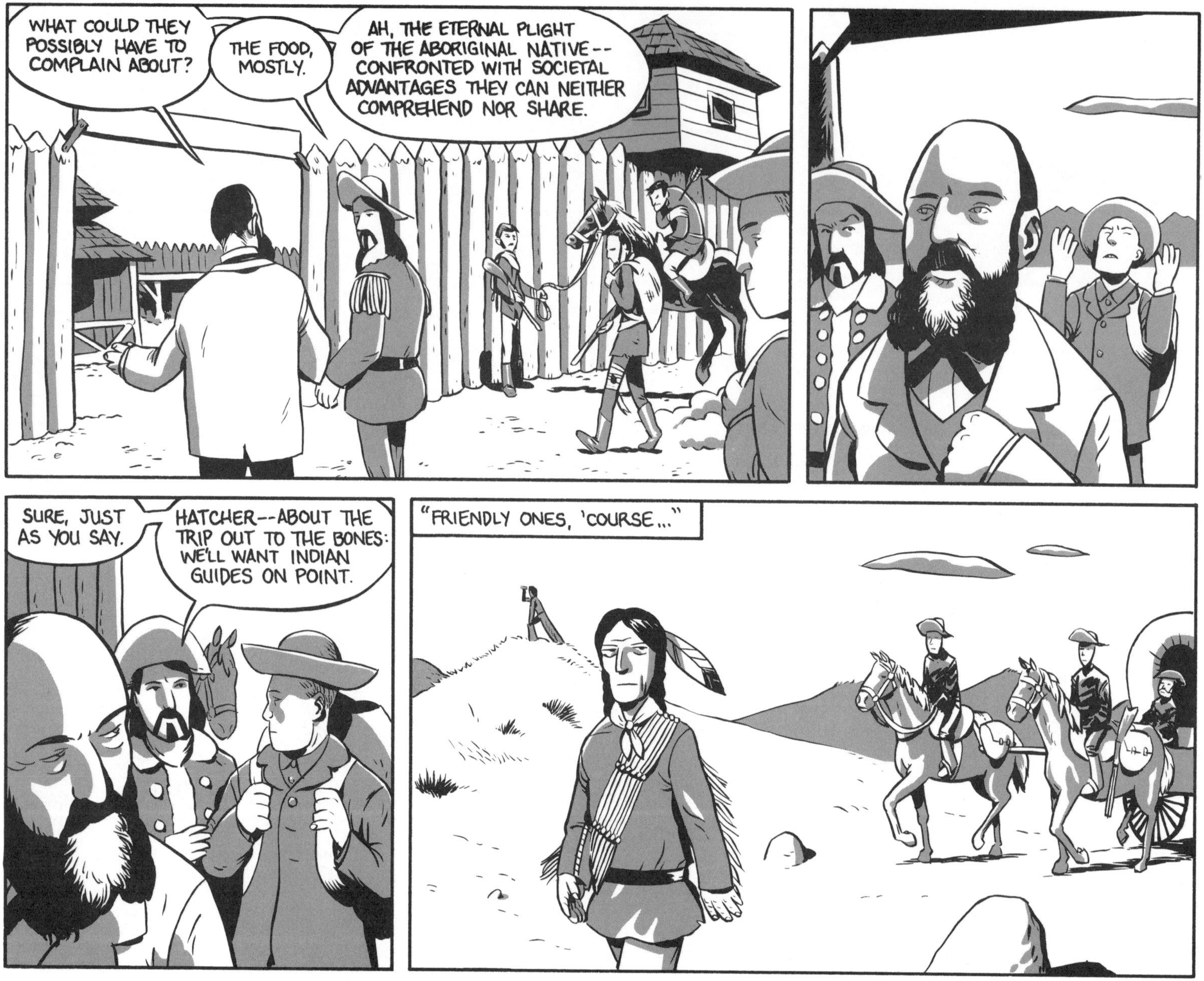

WHAT COULD THEY POSSIBLY HAVE TO COMPLAIN ABOUT?
THE FOOD, MOSTLY.
AH, THE ETERNAL PLIGHT OF THE ABORIGINAL NATIVE-- CONFRONTED WITH SOCIETAL ADVANTAGES THEY CAN NEITHER COMPREHEND NOR SHARE.
SURE, JUST AS YOU SAY.
HATCHER--ABOUT THE TRIP OUT TO THE BONES: WE'LL WANT INDIAN GUIDES ON POINT.
"FRIENDLY ONES, 'COURSE..."

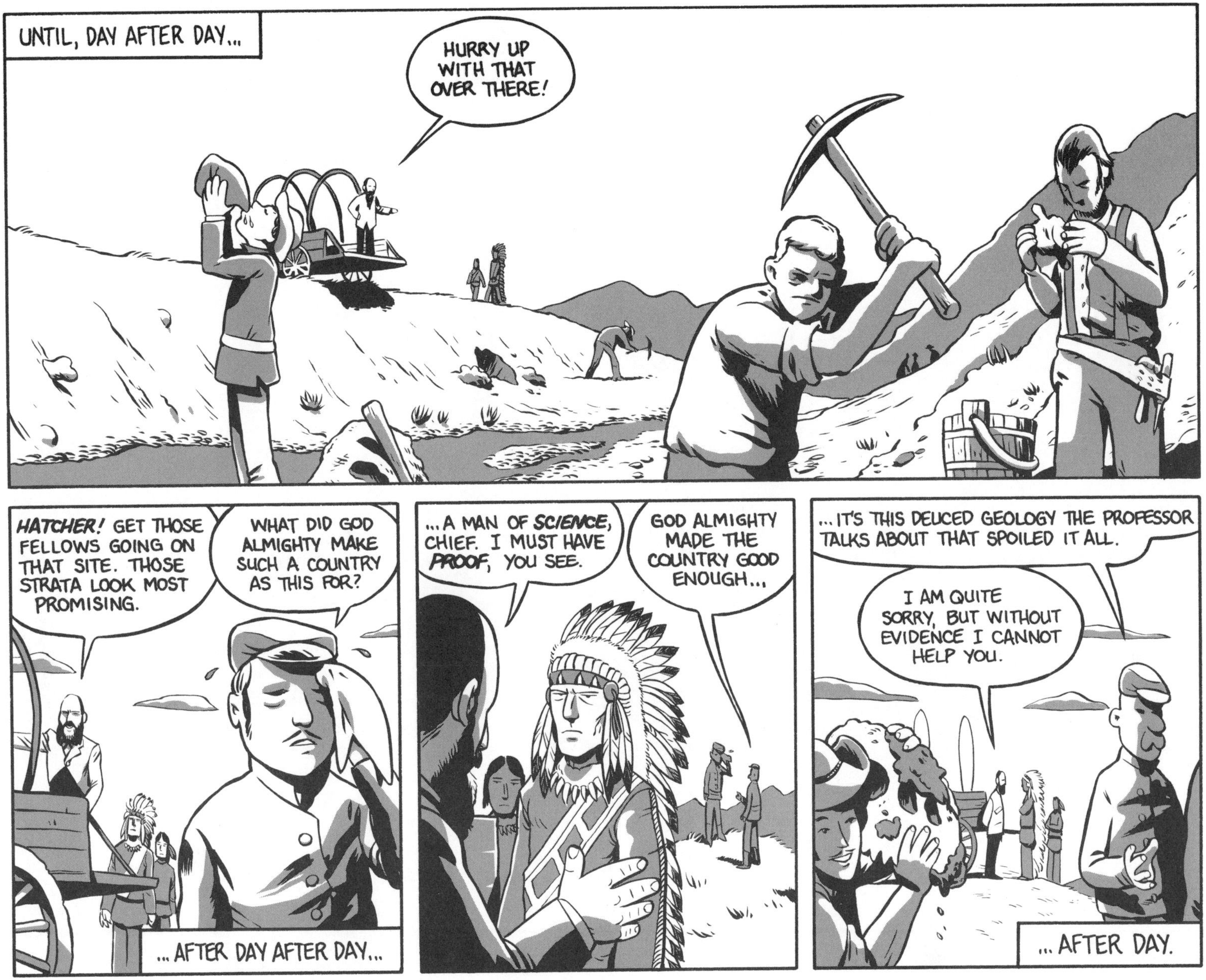

UNTIL, DAY AFTER DAY...
HURRY UP WITH THAT OVER THERE!
HATCHER! GET THOSE FELLOWS GOING ON THAT SITE. THOSE STRATA LOOK MOST PROMISING.
WHAT DID GOD ALMIGHTY MAKE SUCH A COUNTRY AS THIS FOR?
...AFTER DAY AFTER DAY...
...A MAN OF SCIENCE, CHIEF. I MUST HAVE PROOF, YOU SEE.
GOD ALMIGHTY MADE THE COUNTRY GOOD ENOUGH...
...IT'S THIS DEUCED GEOLOGY THE PROFESSOR TALKS ABOUT THAT SPOILED IT ALL.
I AM QUITE SORRY, BUT WITHOUT EVIDENCE I CANNOT HELP YOU.
...AFTER DAY.

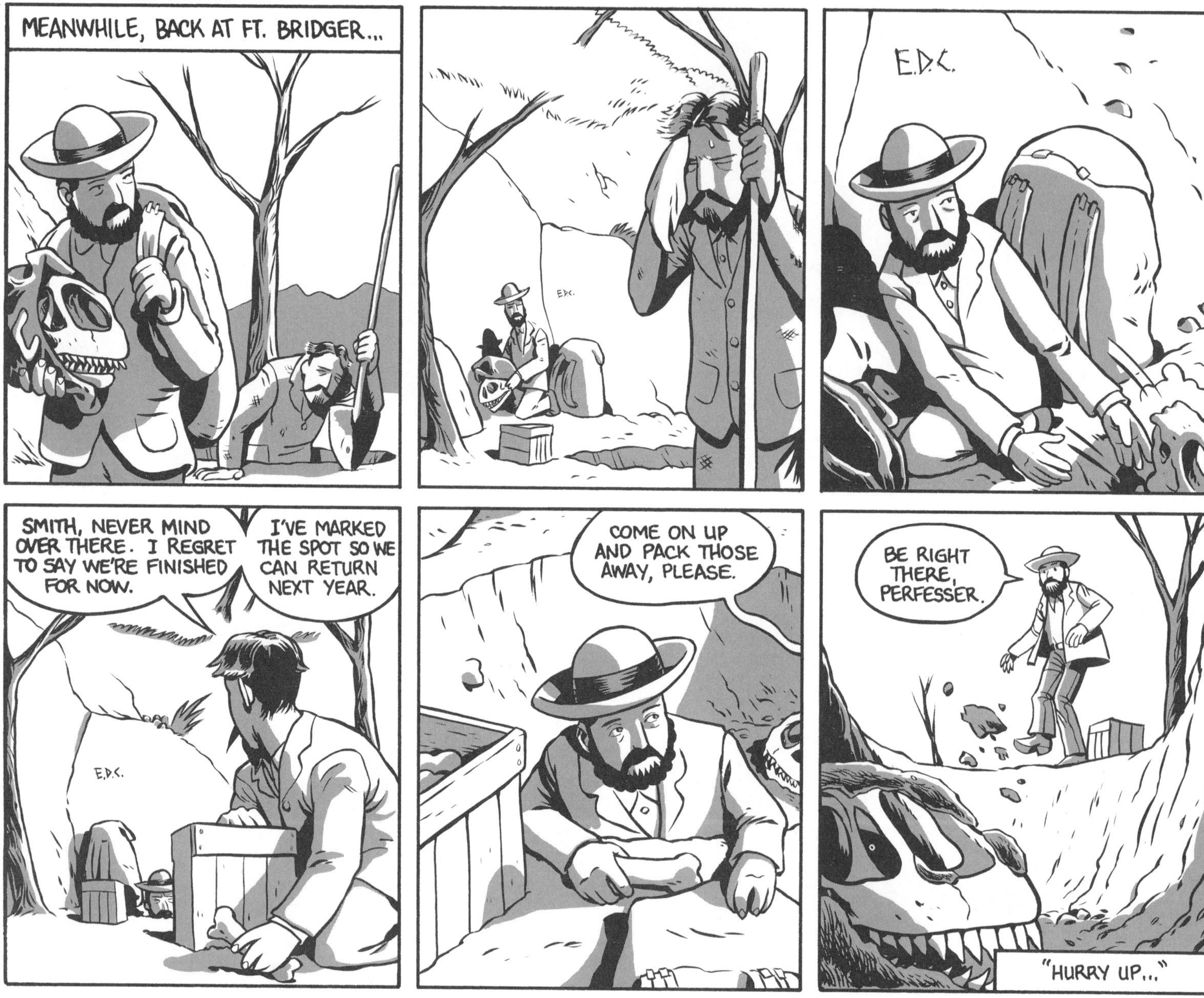
MEANWHILE, BACK AT FT. BRIDGER...
E.D.C.
SMITH, NEVER MIND OVER THERE. I REGRET TO SAY WE'RE FINISHED FOR NOW.
I'VE MARKED THE SPOT SO WE CAN RETURN NEXT YEAR.
E.D.C.
COME ON UP AND PACK THOSE AWAY, PLEASE.
BE RIGHT THERE, PERFESSER.
"HURRY UP..."

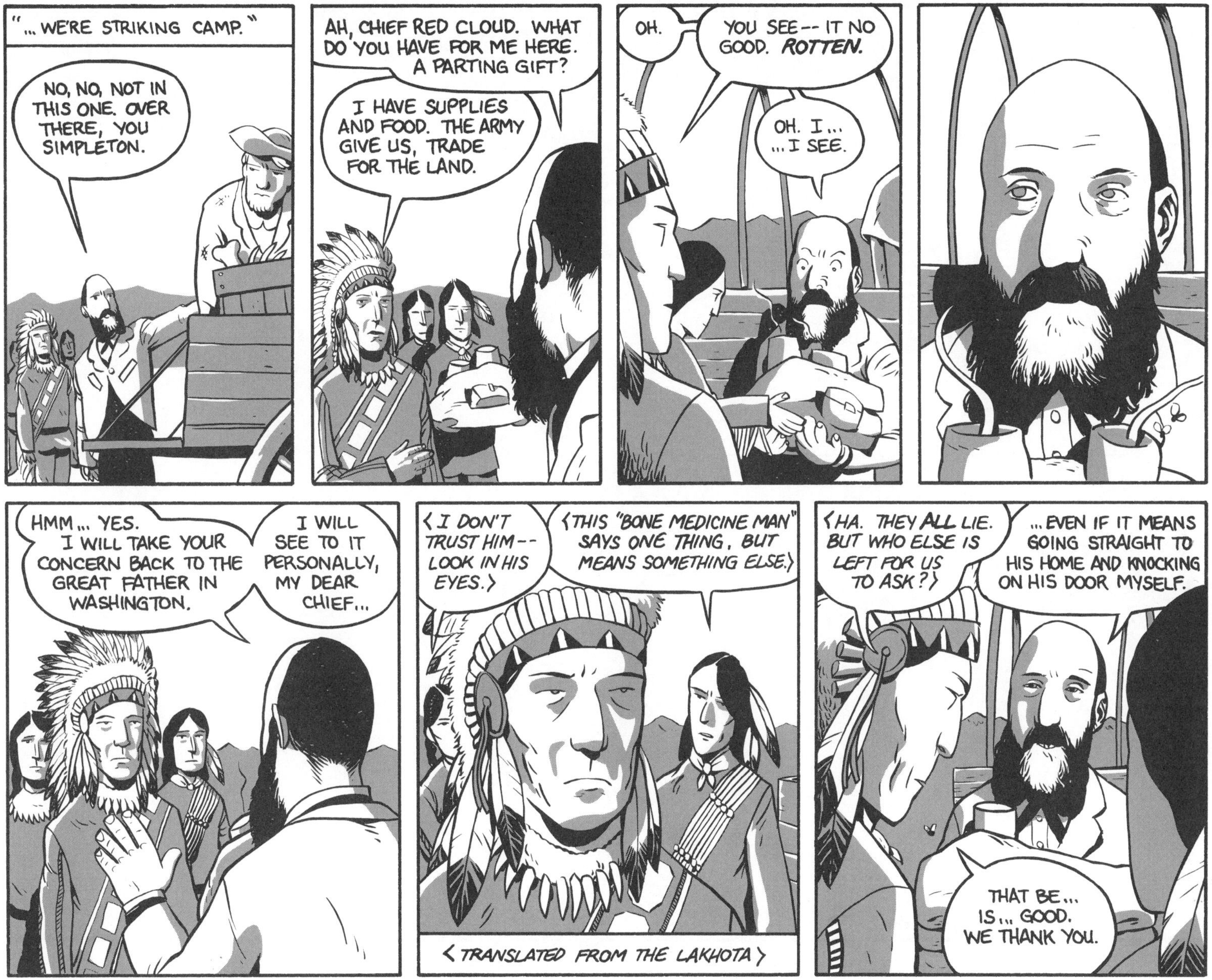
"... WE'RE STRIKING CAMP."
NO, NO, NOT IN THIS ONE. OVER THERE, YOU SIMPLETON.
AH, CHIEF RED CLOUD. WHAT DO YOU HAVE FOR ME HERE. A PARTING GIFT?
I HAVE SUPPLIES AND FOOD. THE ARMY GIVE US, TRADE FOR THE LAND.
OH.
YOU SEE-- IT NO GOOD. *ROTTEN.*
OH. I... ...I SEE.
HMM... YES. I WILL TAKE YOUR CONCERN BACK TO THE GREAT FATHER IN WASHINGTON.
I WILL SEE TO IT PERSONALLY, MY DEAR CHIEF...
<I DON'T TRUST HIM-- LOOK IN HIS EYES.>
<THIS "BONE MEDICINE MAN" SAYS ONE THING, BUT MEANS SOMETHING ELSE.>
<TRANSLATED FROM THE LAKHOTA>
*<HA. THEY **ALL** LIE. BUT WHO ELSE IS LEFT FOR US TO ASK?>*
...EVEN IF IT MEANS GOING STRAIGHT TO HIS HOME AND KNOCKING ON HIS DOOR MYSELF.
THAT BE... IS... GOOD. WE THANK YOU.

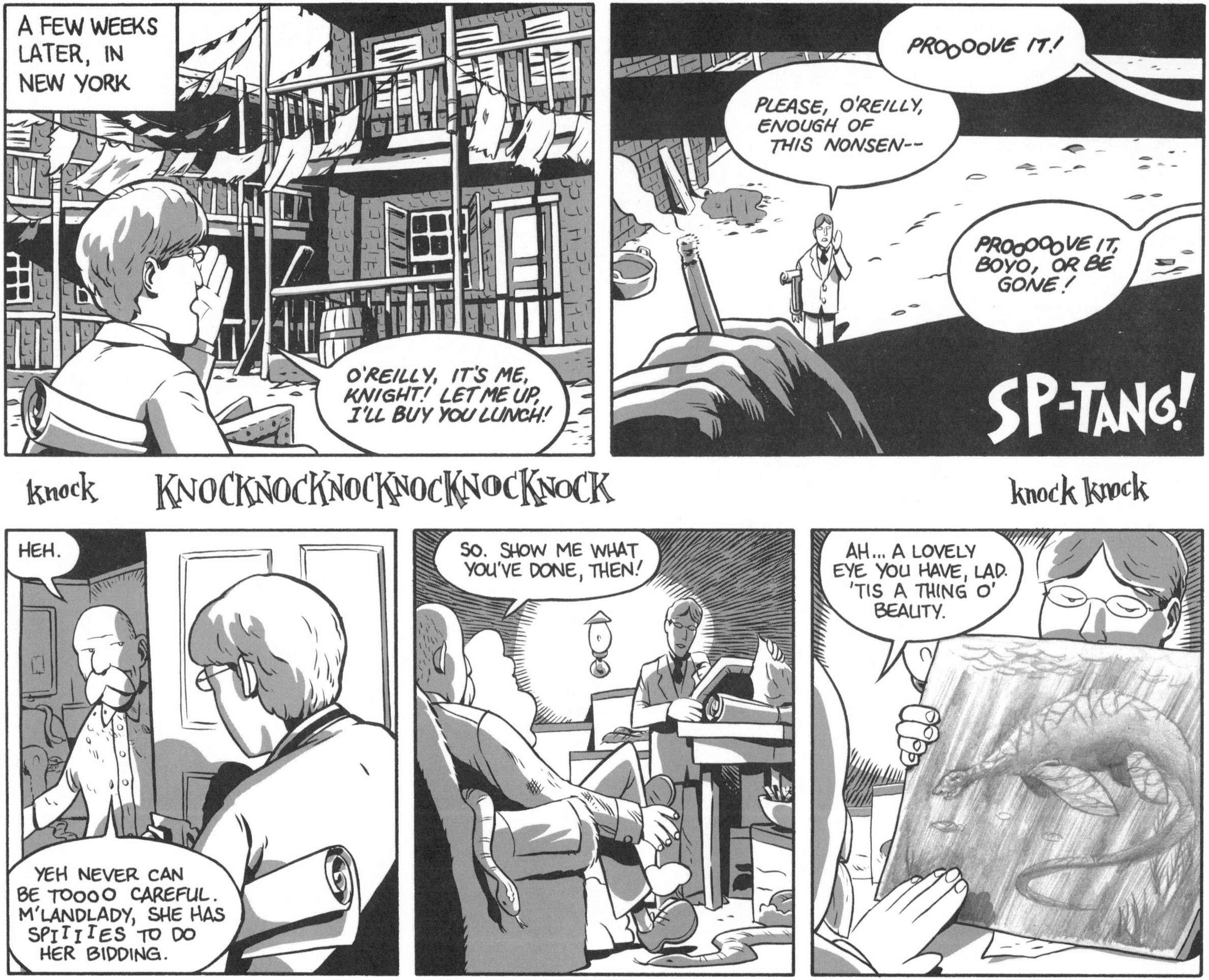
A FEW WEEKS LATER, IN NEW YORK
O'REILLY, IT'S ME, KNIGHT! LET ME UP, I'LL BUY YOU LUNCH!
PROOOOVE IT!
PLEASE, O'REILLY, ENOUGH OF THIS NONSEN--
PROOOOOVE IT, BOYO, OR BE GONE!
SP-TANG!
knock
KNOCKNOCKNOCKNOCKNOCKNOCK
knock knock
HEH.
YEH NEVER CAN BE TOOOO CAREFUL. M'LANDLADY, SHE HAS SPIIIIES TO DO HER BIDDING.
SO. SHOW ME WHAT YOU'VE DONE, THEN!
AH... A LOVELY EYE YOU HAVE, LAD. 'TIS A THING O' BEAUTY.

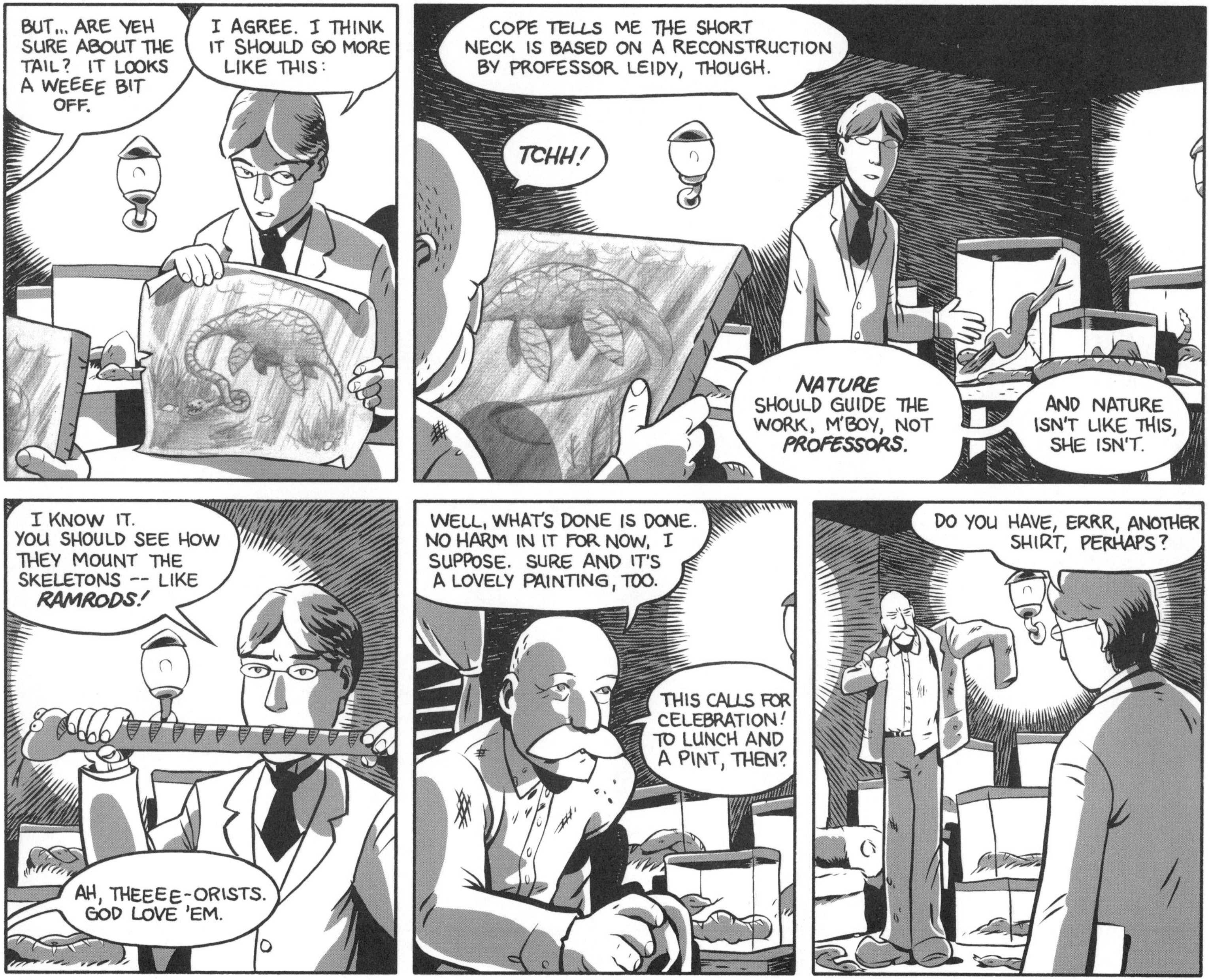
BUT... ARE YEH SURE ABOUT THE TAIL? IT LOOKS A WEEEE BIT OFF.
I AGREE. I THINK IT SHOULD GO MORE LIKE THIS:
COPE TELLS ME THE SHORT NECK IS BASED ON A RECONSTRUCTION BY PROFESSOR LEIDY, THOUGH.
TCHH!
NATURE SHOULD GUIDE THE WORK, M'BOY, NOT PROFESSORS.
AND NATURE ISN'T LIKE THIS, SHE ISN'T.
I KNOW IT. YOU SHOULD SEE HOW THEY MOUNT THE SKELETONS -- LIKE RAMRODS!
AH, THEEEE-ORISTS. GOD LOVE 'EM.
WELL, WHAT'S DONE IS DONE. NO HARM IN IT FOR NOW, I SUPPOSE. SURE AND IT'S A LOVELY PAINTING, TOO.
THIS CALLS FOR CELEBRATION! TO LUNCH AND A PINT, THEN?
DO YOU HAVE, ERRR, ANOTHER SHIRT, PERHAPS?

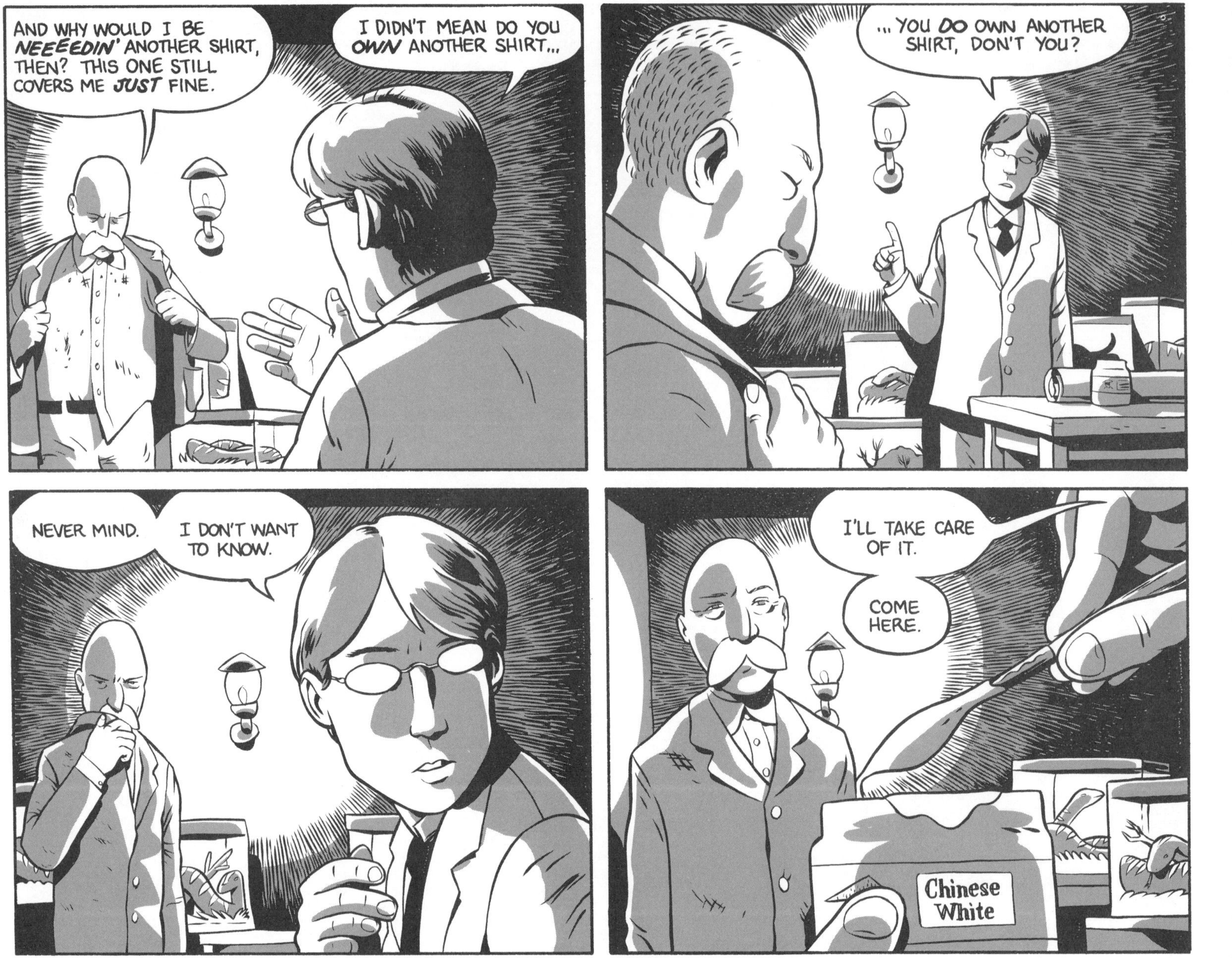
AND WHY WOULD I BE NEEEEDIN' ANOTHER SHIRT, THEN? THIS ONE STILL COVERS ME JUST FINE.
I DIDN'T MEAN DO YOU OWN ANOTHER SHIRT...
... YOU DO OWN ANOTHER SHIRT, DON'T YOU?
NEVER MIND.
I DON'T WANT TO KNOW.
I'LL TAKE CARE OF IT.
COME HERE.
Chinese White

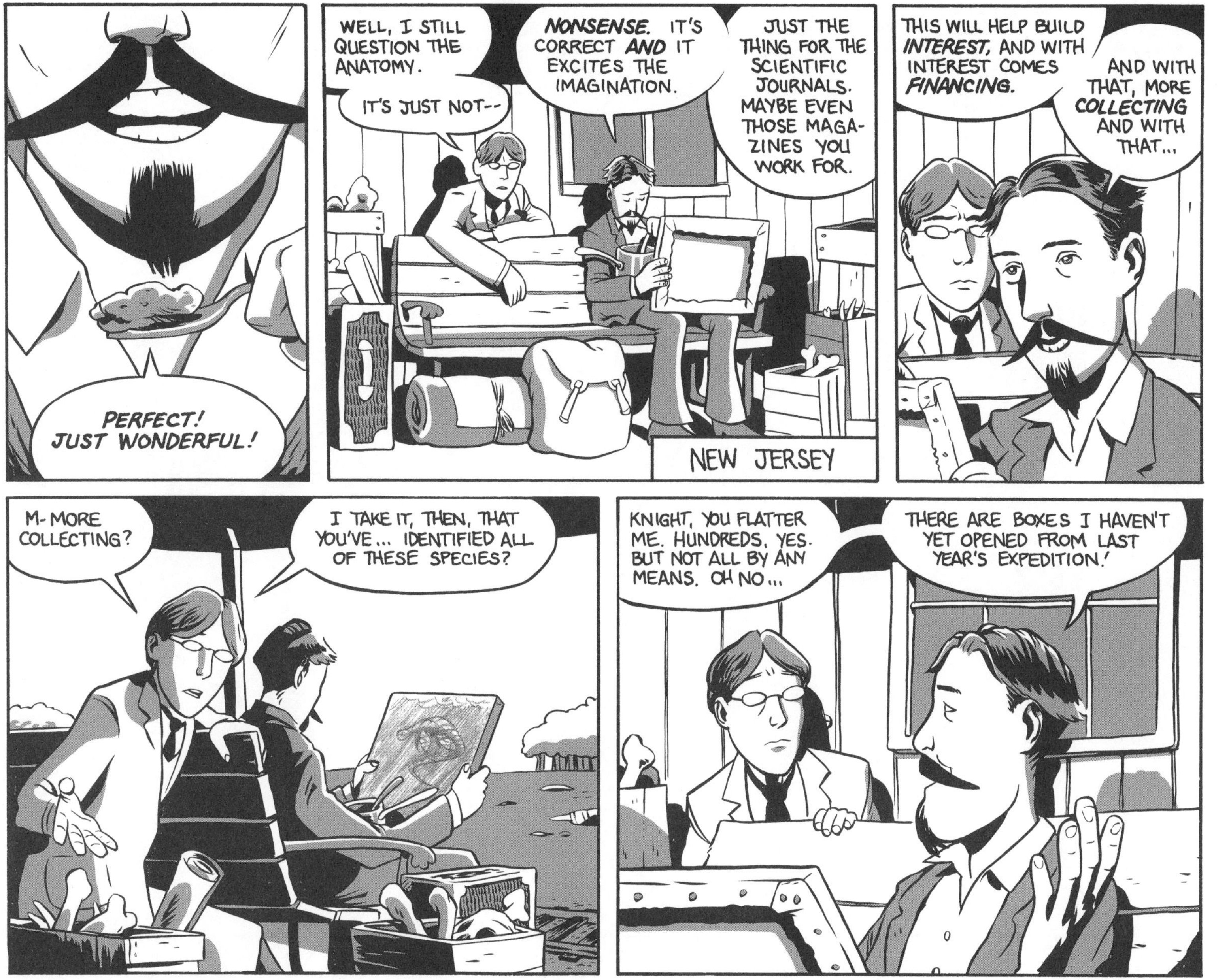
PERFECT! JUST WONDERFUL!
WELL, I STILL QUESTION THE ANATOMY.
IT'S JUST NOT--
NONSENSE. IT'S CORRECT AND IT EXCITES THE IMAGINATION.
JUST THE THING FOR THE SCIENTIFIC JOURNALS. MAYBE EVEN THOSE MAGA-ZINES YOU WORK FOR.
NEW JERSEY
THIS WILL HELP BUILD INTEREST, AND WITH INTEREST COMES FINANCING.
AND WITH THAT, MORE COLLECTING AND WITH THAT...
M-MORE COLLECTING?
I TAKE IT, THEN, THAT YOU'VE... IDENTIFIED ALL OF THESE SPECIES?
KNIGHT, YOU FLATTER ME. HUNDREDS, YES. BUT NOT ALL BY ANY MEANS. OH NO...
THERE ARE BOXES I HAVEN'T YET OPENED FROM LAST YEAR'S EXPEDITION!

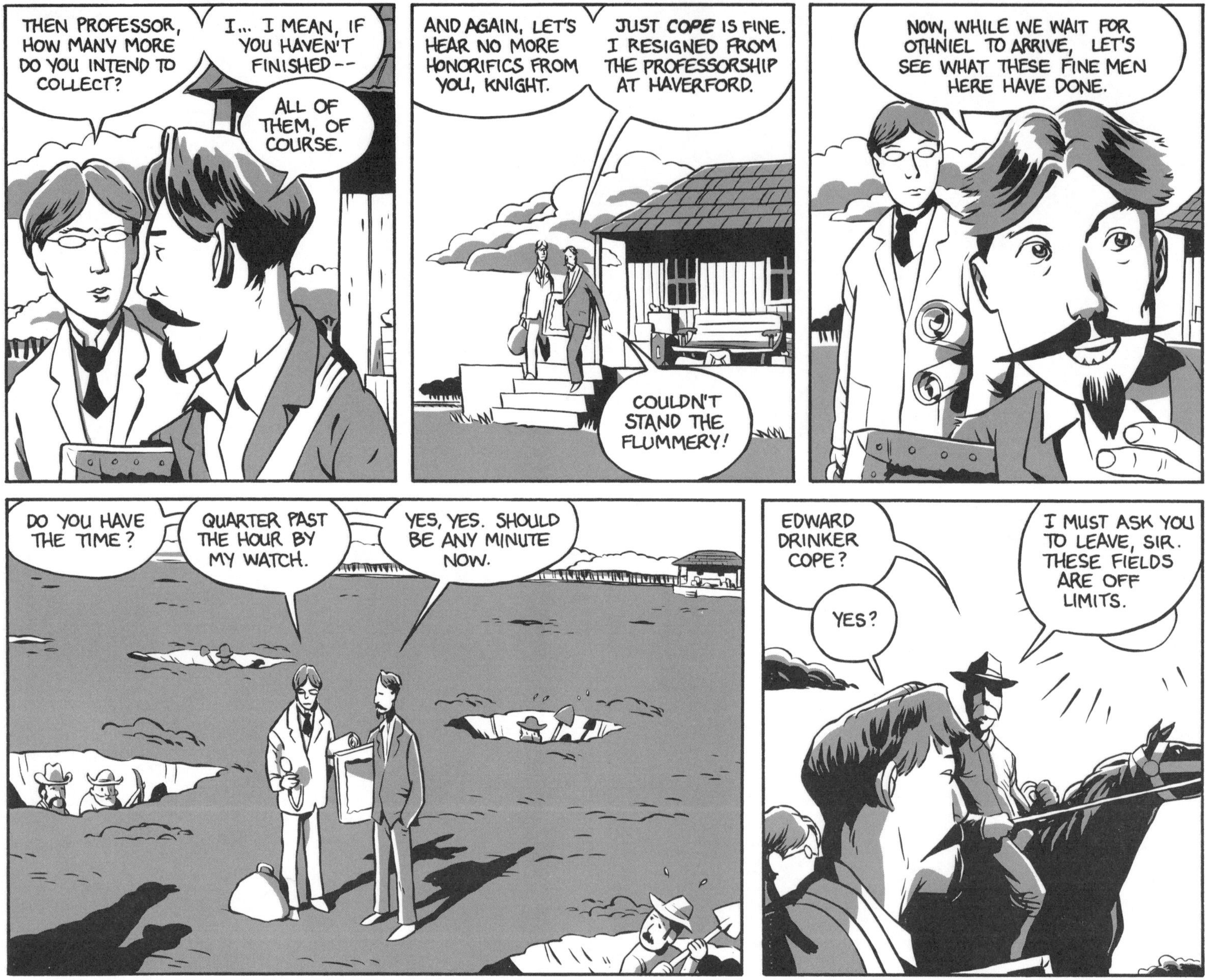
THEN PROFESSOR, HOW MANY MORE DO YOU INTEND TO COLLECT?
I... I MEAN, IF YOU HAVEN'T FINISHED--
ALL OF THEM, OF COURSE.
AND AGAIN, LET'S HEAR NO MORE HONORIFICS FROM YOU, KNIGHT.
JUST COPE IS FINE. I RESIGNED FROM THE PROFESSORSHIP AT HAVERFORD.
COULDN'T STAND THE FLUMMERY!
NOW, WHILE WE WAIT FOR OTHNIEL TO ARRIVE, LET'S SEE WHAT THESE FINE MEN HERE HAVE DONE.
DO YOU HAVE THE TIME?
QUARTER PAST THE HOUR BY MY WATCH.
YES, YES. SHOULD BE ANY MINUTE NOW.
EDWARD DRINKER COPE?
YES?
I MUST ASK YOU TO LEAVE, SIR. THESE FIELDS ARE OFF LIMITS.

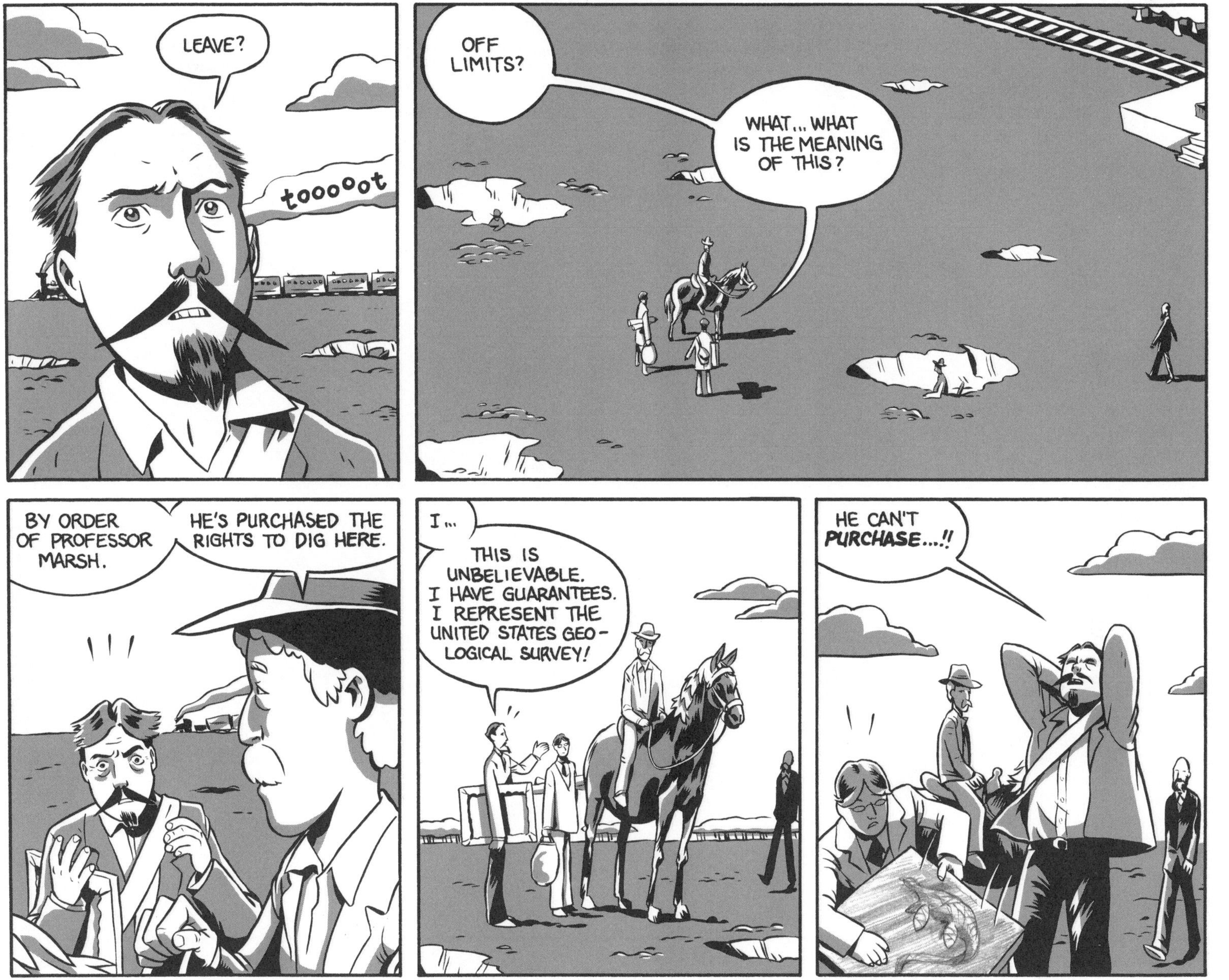
LEAVE?
tooooot
OFF LIMITS?
WHAT... WHAT IS THE MEANING OF THIS?
BY ORDER OF PROFESSOR MARSH.
HE'S PURCHASED THE RIGHTS TO DIG HERE.
I...
THIS IS UNBELIEVABLE. I HAVE GUARANTEES. I REPRESENT THE UNITED STATES GEO-LOGICAL SURVEY!
HE CAN'T *PURCHASE*...!!

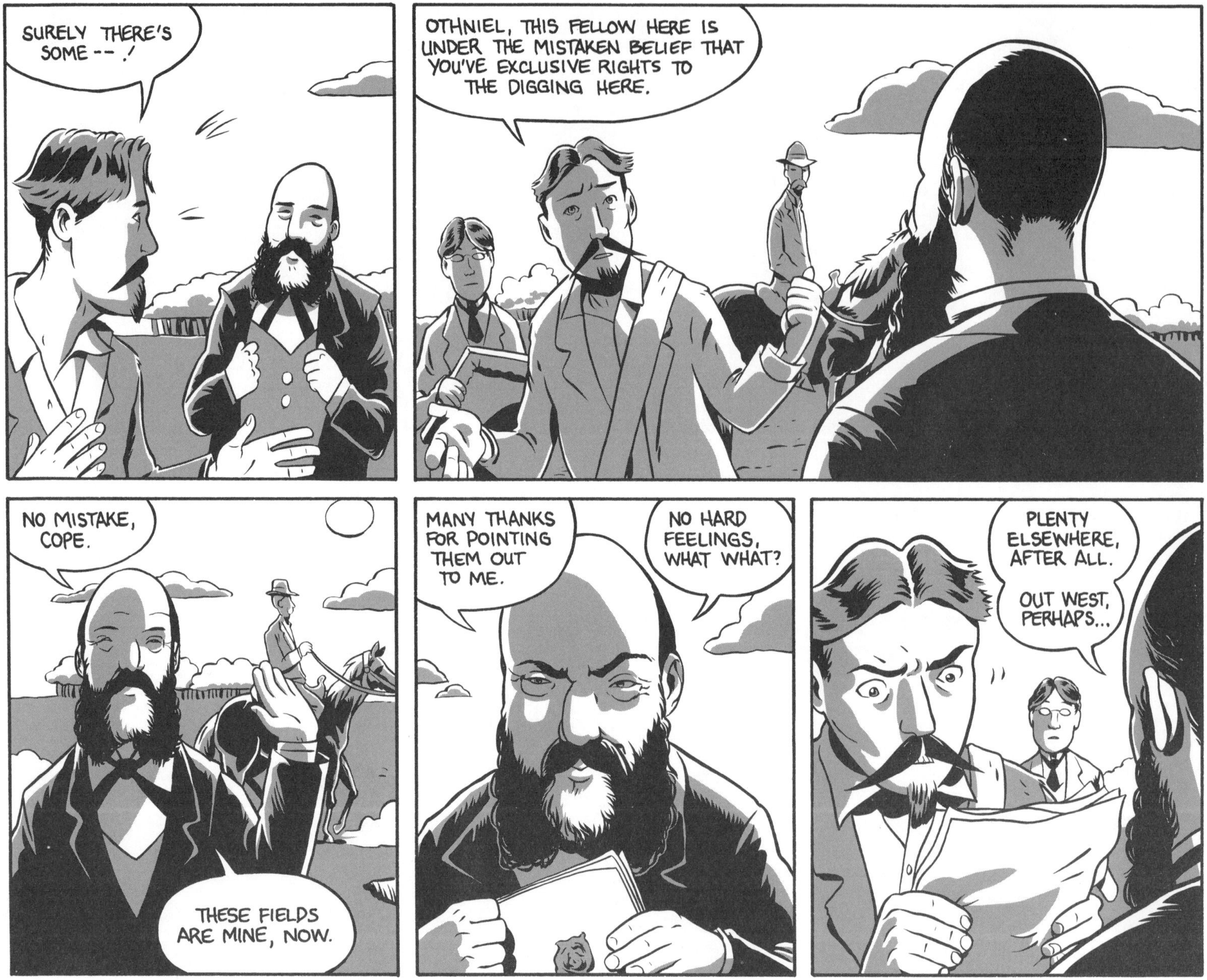

SURELY THERE'S SOME --!
OTHNIEL, THIS FELLOW HERE IS UNDER THE MISTAKEN BELIEF THAT YOU'VE EXCLUSIVE RIGHTS TO THE DIGGING HERE.
NO MISTAKE, COPE.
THESE FIELDS ARE MINE, NOW.
MANY THANKS FOR POINTING THEM OUT TO ME.
NO HARD FEELINGS, WHAT WHAT?
PLENTY ELSEWHERE, AFTER ALL.
OUT WEST, PERHAPS...

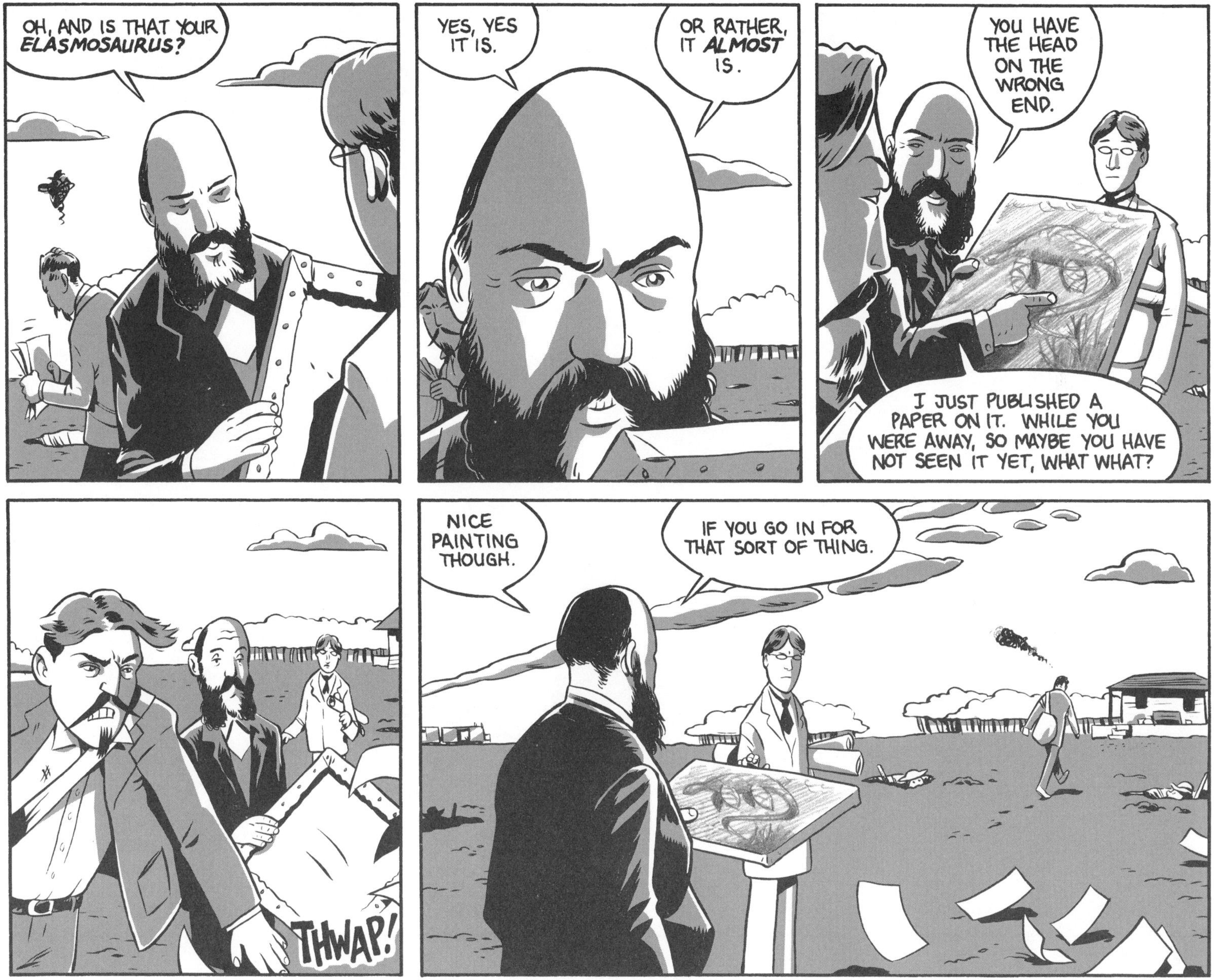
OH, AND IS THAT YOUR *ELASMOSAURUS?*
YES, YES IT IS.
OR RATHER, IT *ALMOST* IS.
YOU HAVE THE HEAD ON THE WRONG END.
I JUST PUBLISHED A PAPER ON IT. WHILE YOU WERE AWAY, SO MAYBE YOU HAVE NOT SEEN IT YET, WHAT WHAT?
THWAP!
NICE PAINTING THOUGH.
IF YOU GO IN FOR THAT SORT OF THING.

COWBOYS

In which we learn of numerous means of acquiring and disposing of fortunes, said means being known to scientists and scoundrels alike

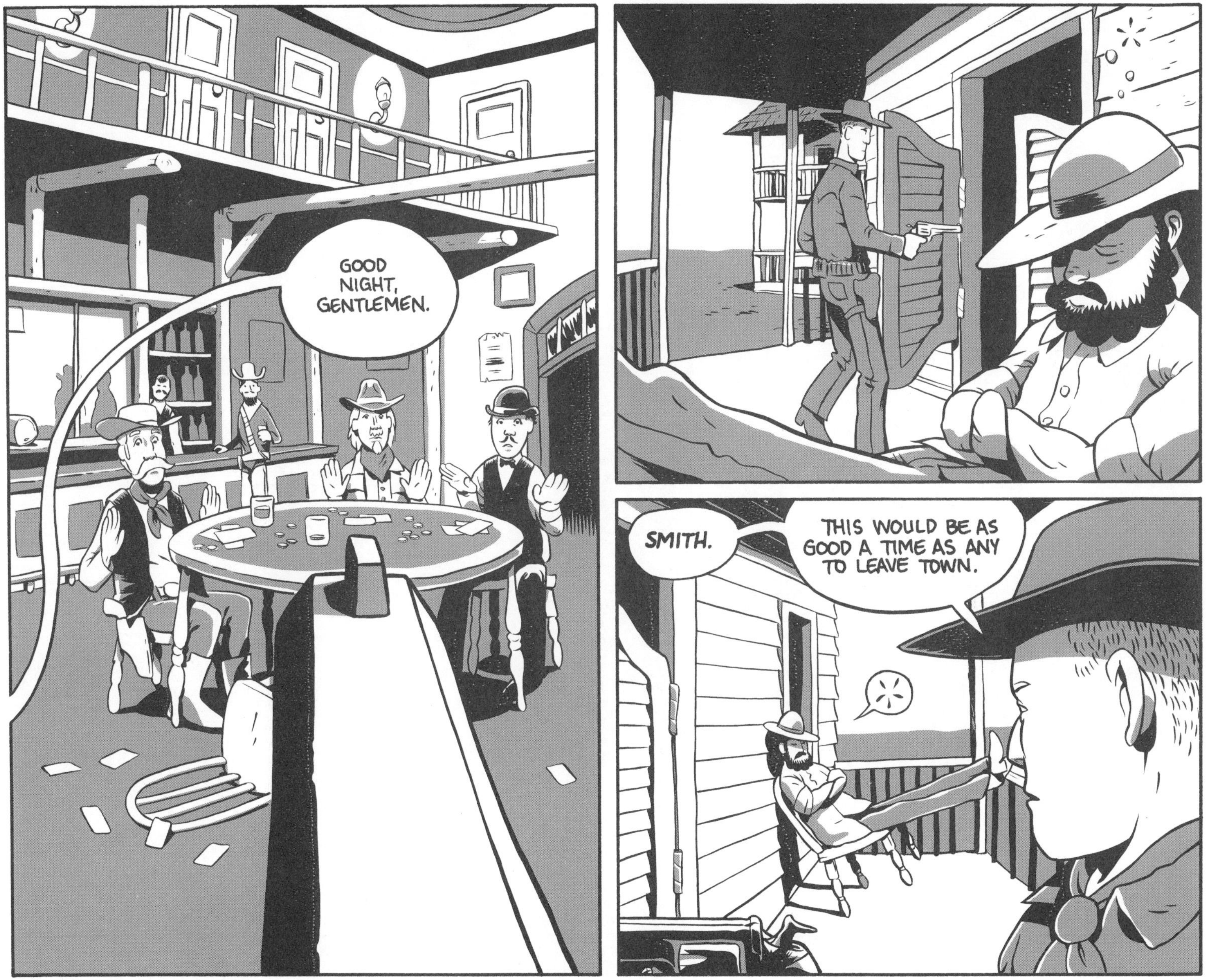
GOOD NIGHT, GENTLEMEN.
SMITH.
THIS WOULD BE AS GOOD A TIME AS ANY TO LEAVE TOWN.

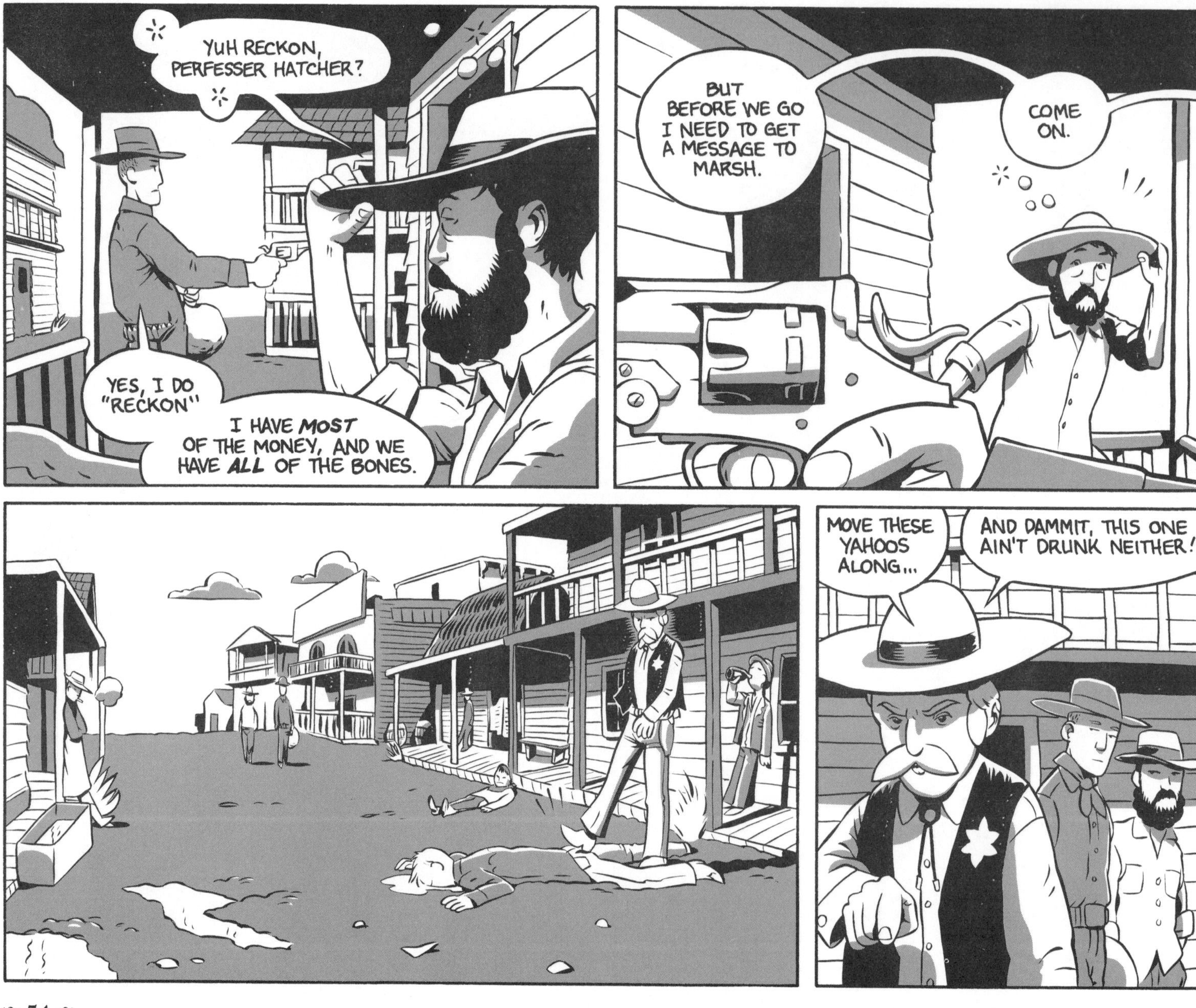
YUH RECKON, PERFESSER HATCHER?
YES, I DO "RECKON"
I HAVE MOST OF THE MONEY, AND WE HAVE ALL OF THE BONES.
BUT BEFORE WE GO I NEED TO GET A MESSAGE TO MARSH.
COME ON.
MOVE THESE YAHOOS ALONG...
AND DAMMIT, THIS ONE AIN'T DRUNK NEITHER!

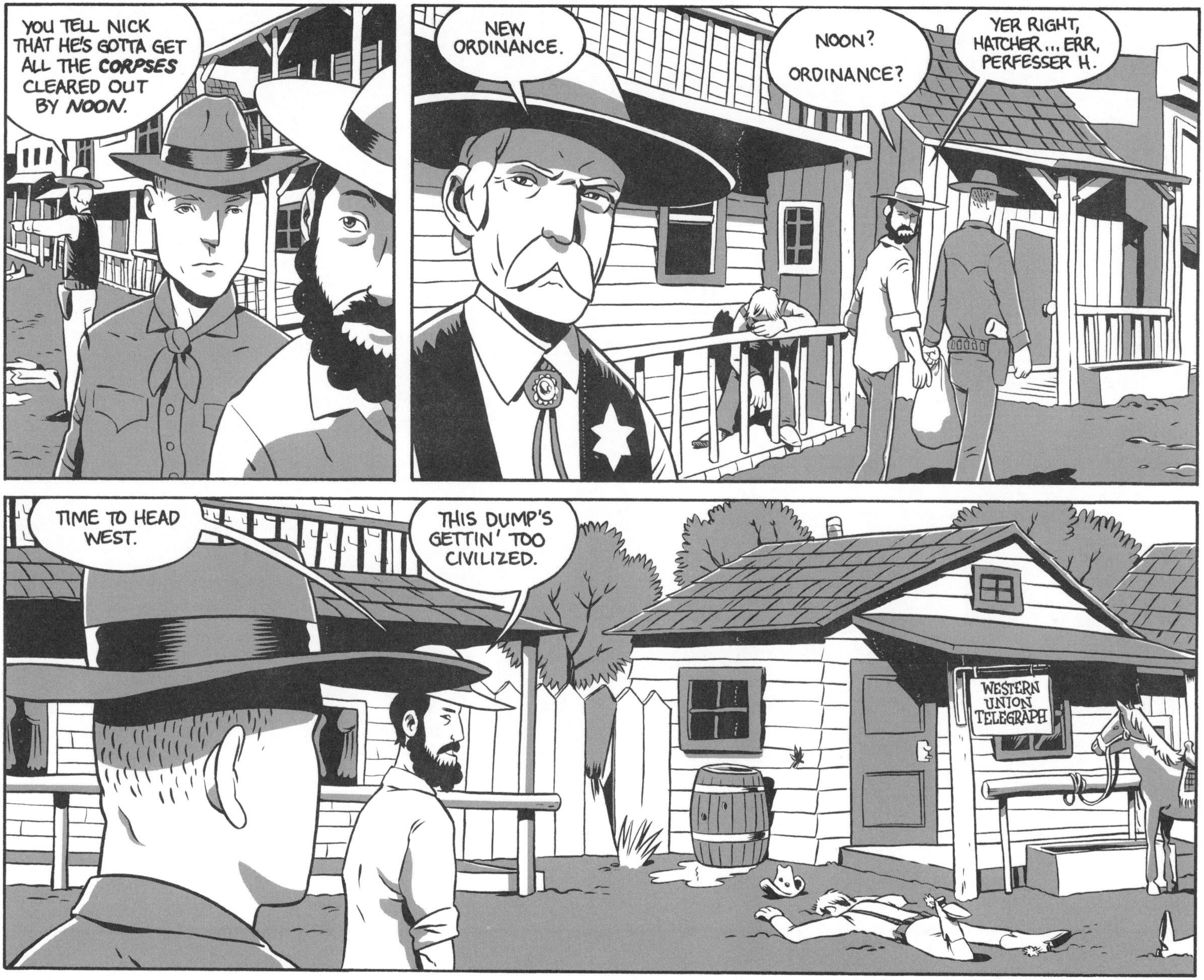
YOU TELL NICK THAT HE'S GOTTA GET ALL THE CORPSES CLEARED OUT BY NOON.
NEW ORDINANCE.
NOON? ORDINANCE?
YER RIGHT, HATCHER... ERR, PERFESSER H.
TIME TO HEAD WEST.
THIS DUMP'S GETTIN' TOO CIVILIZED.
WESTERN UNION TELEGRAPH

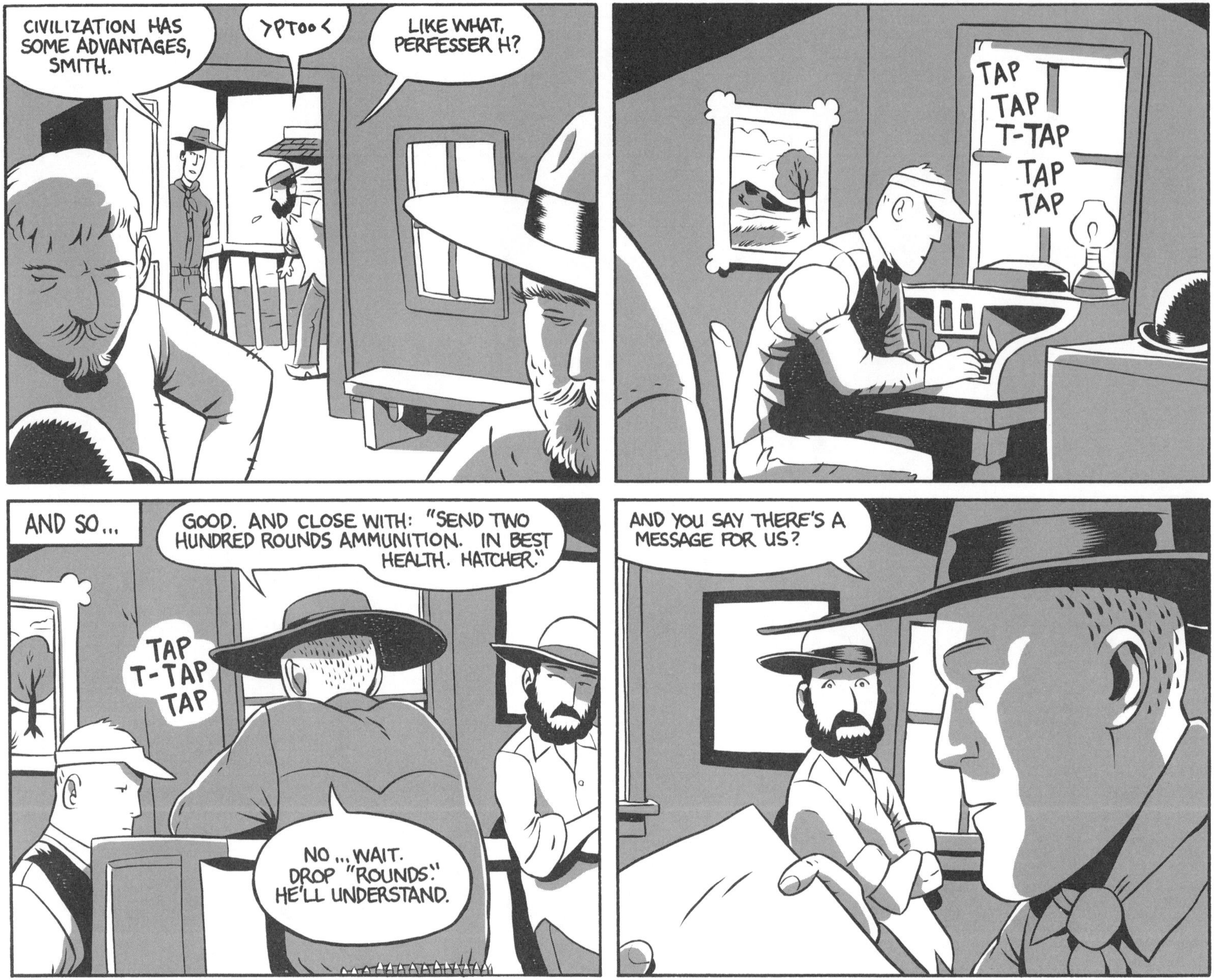
CIVILIZATION HAS SOME ADVANTAGES, SMITH.
>PTOO<
LIKE WHAT, PERFESSER H?
TAP TAP T-TAP TAP TAP
AND SO...
GOOD. AND CLOSE WITH: "SEND TWO HUNDRED ROUNDS AMMUNITION. IN BEST HEALTH. HATCHER."
TAP T-TAP TAP
NO ... WAIT. DROP "ROUNDS." HE'LL UNDERSTAND.
AND YOU SAY THERE'S A MESSAGE FOR US?

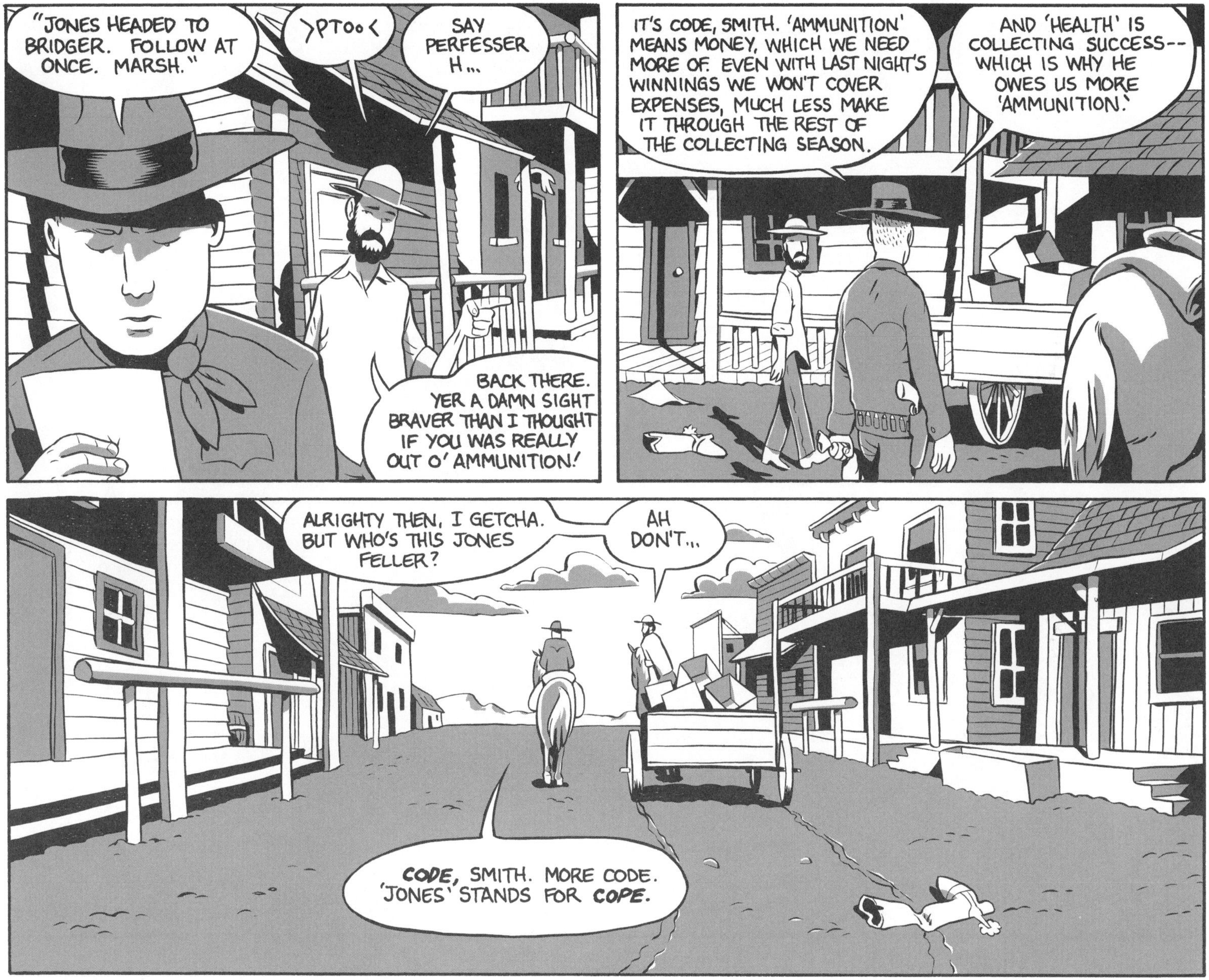
"JONES HEADED TO BRIDGER. FOLLOW AT ONCE. MARSH."
>PTOO<
SAY PERFESSER H...
BACK THERE. YER A DAMN SIGHT BRAVER THAN I THOUGHT IF YOU WAS REALLY OUT O' AMMUNITION!
IT'S CODE, SMITH. 'AMMUNITION' MEANS MONEY, WHICH WE NEED MORE OF. EVEN WITH LAST NIGHT'S WINNINGS WE WON'T COVER EXPENSES, MUCH LESS MAKE IT THROUGH THE REST OF THE COLLECTING SEASON.
AND 'HEALTH' IS COLLECTING SUCCESS-- WHICH IS WHY HE OWES US MORE 'AMMUNITION.'
ALRIGHTY THEN, I GETCHA. BUT WHO'S THIS JONES FELLER?
AH DON'T...
CODE, SMITH. MORE CODE. 'JONES' STANDS FOR **COPE.**

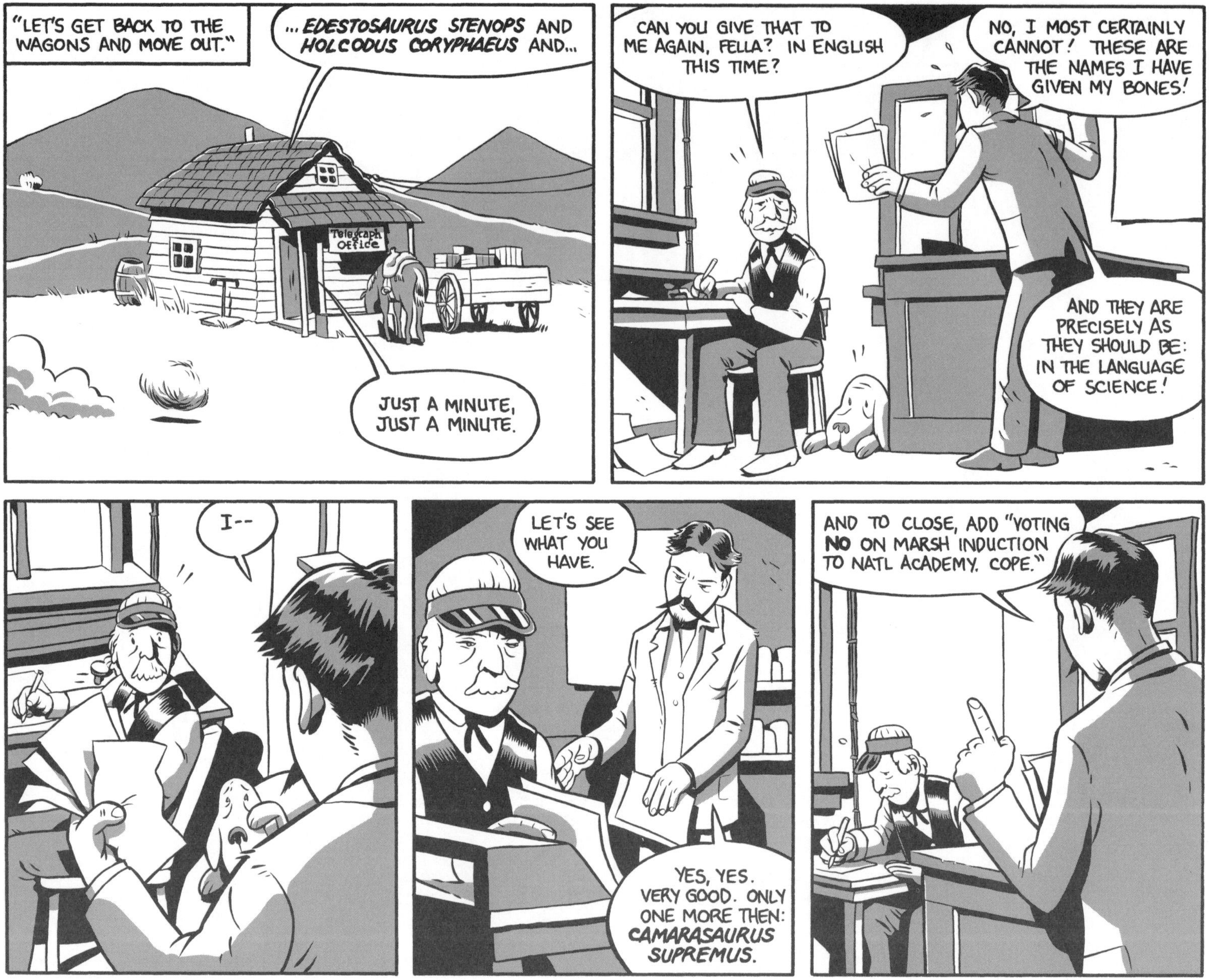
"LET'S GET BACK TO THE WAGONS AND MOVE OUT."
...EDESTOSAURUS STENOPS AND HOLCODUS CORYPHAEUS AND...
Telegraph Office
JUST A MINUTE, JUST A MINUTE.
CAN YOU GIVE THAT TO ME AGAIN, FELLA? IN ENGLISH THIS TIME?
NO, I MOST CERTAINLY CANNOT! THESE ARE THE NAMES I HAVE GIVEN MY BONES!
AND THEY ARE PRECISELY AS THEY SHOULD BE: IN THE LANGUAGE OF SCIENCE!
I--
LET'S SEE WHAT YOU HAVE.
YES, YES. VERY GOOD. ONLY ONE MORE THEN: CAMARASAURUS SUPREMUS.
AND TO CLOSE, ADD "VOTING NO ON MARSH INDUCTION TO NATL ACADEMY. COPE."

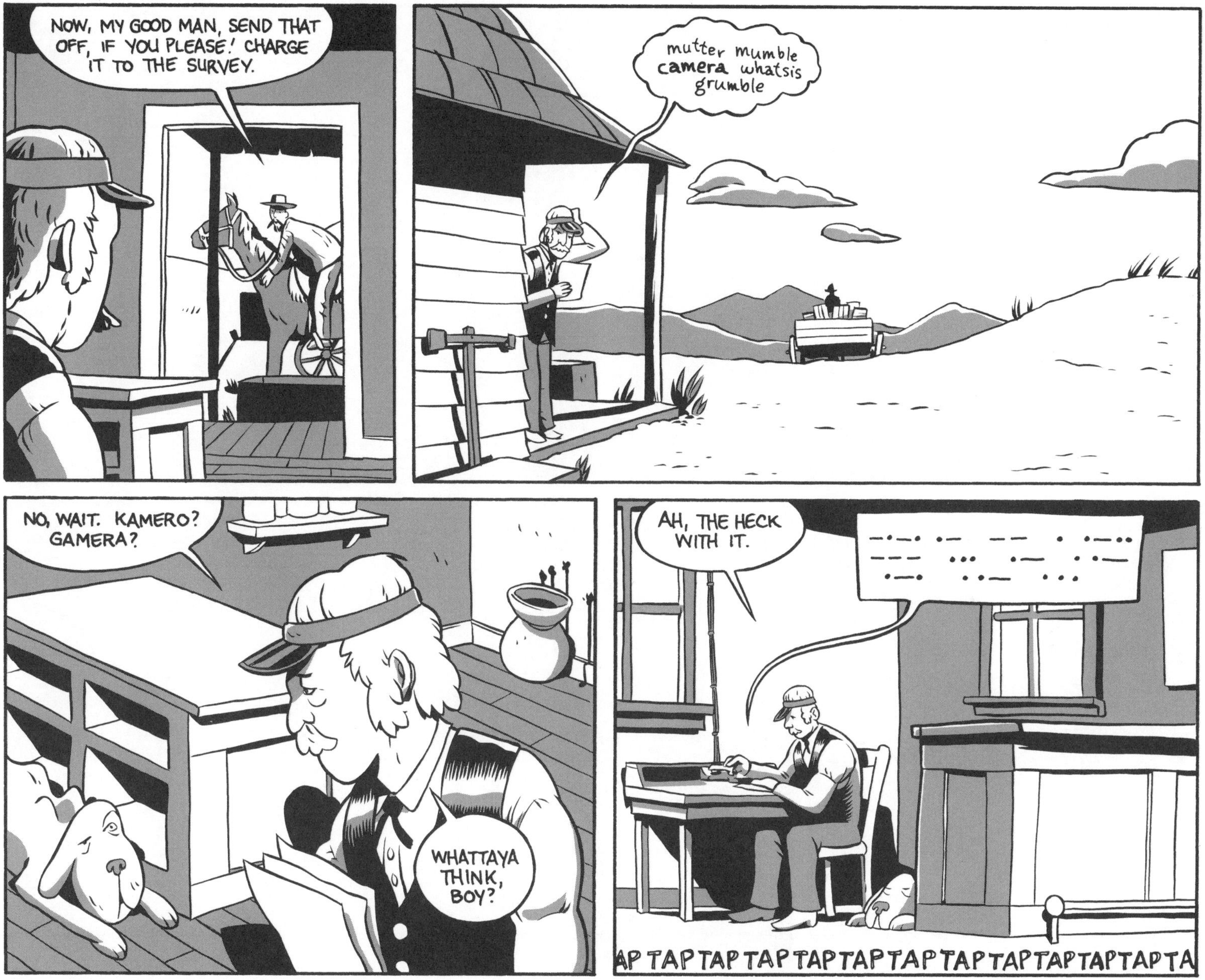
NOW, MY GOOD MAN, SEND THAT OFF, IF YOU PLEASE! CHARGE IT TO THE SURVEY.
mutter mumble camera whatsis grumble
NO, WAIT. KAMERO? GAMERA?
WHATTAYA THINK, BOY?
AH, THE HECK WITH IT.
AP TAP TAP TAP TAP TAP TAP TAP TAP TAP TAP TAP TA

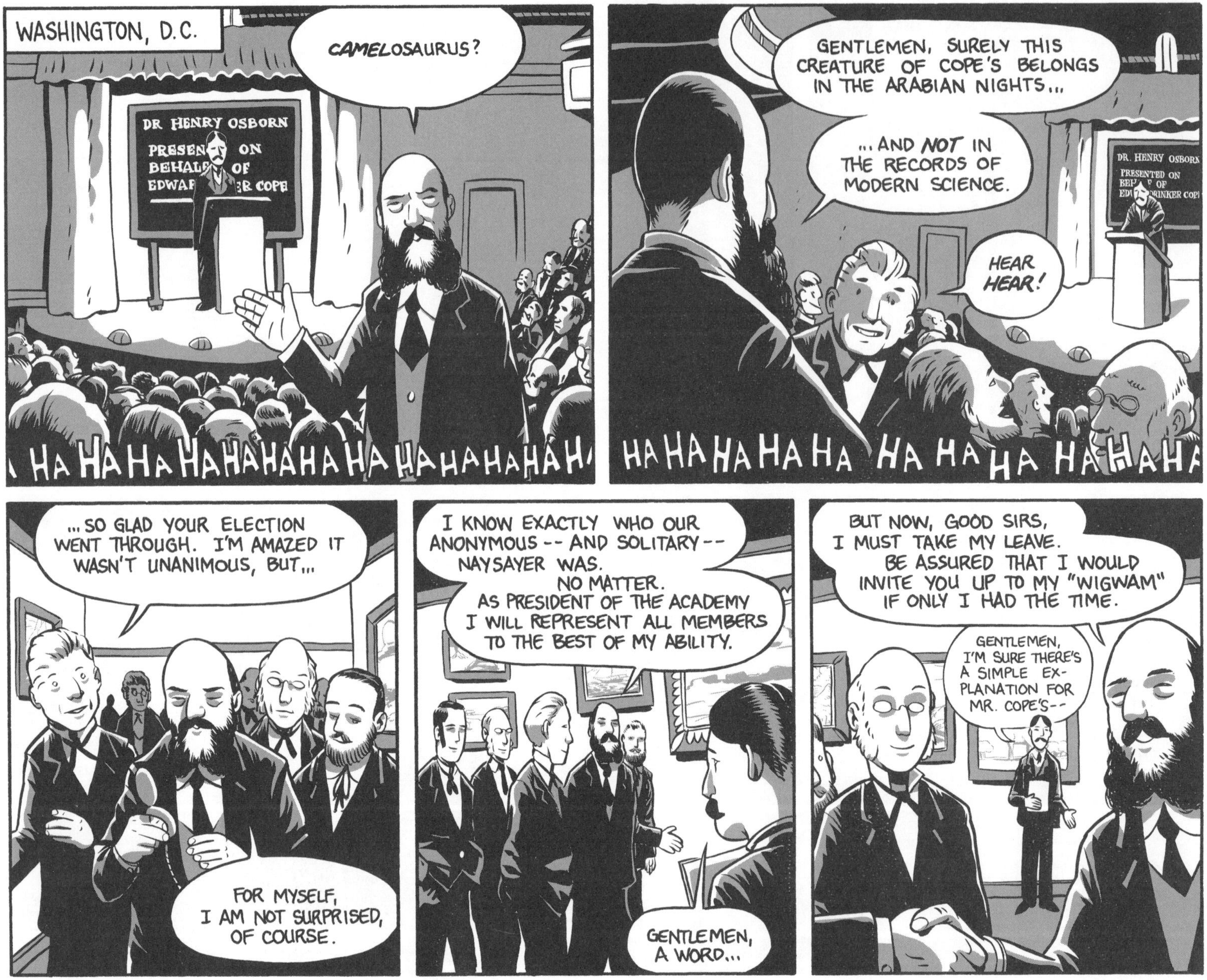
WASHINGTON, D.C.
DR HENRY OSBORN PRESEN ON BEHALF OF EDWAR ER COPE
CAMELOSAURUS?
GENTLEMEN, SURELY THIS CREATURE OF COPE'S BELONGS IN THE ARABIAN NIGHTS...
...AND NOT IN THE RECORDS OF MODERN SCIENCE.
HEAR HEAR!
HA HA HA HA HA HA HA HA HA HA HA HA HA HA HA HA
HA HA HA HA HA HA HA HA HA HA HA HA HA
...SO GLAD YOUR ELECTION WENT THROUGH. I'M AMAZED IT WASN'T UNANIMOUS, BUT...
FOR MYSELF, I AM NOT SURPRISED, OF COURSE.
I KNOW EXACTLY WHO OUR ANONYMOUS -- AND SOLITARY -- NAYSAYER WAS.
NO MATTER. AS PRESIDENT OF THE ACADEMY I WILL REPRESENT ALL MEMBERS TO THE BEST OF MY ABILITY.
GENTLEMEN, A WORD...
BUT NOW, GOOD SIRS, I MUST TAKE MY LEAVE.
BE ASSURED THAT I WOULD INVITE YOU UP TO MY "WIGWAM" IF ONLY I HAD THE TIME.
GENTLEMEN, I'M SURE THERE'S A SIMPLE EXPLANATION FOR MR. COPE'S--

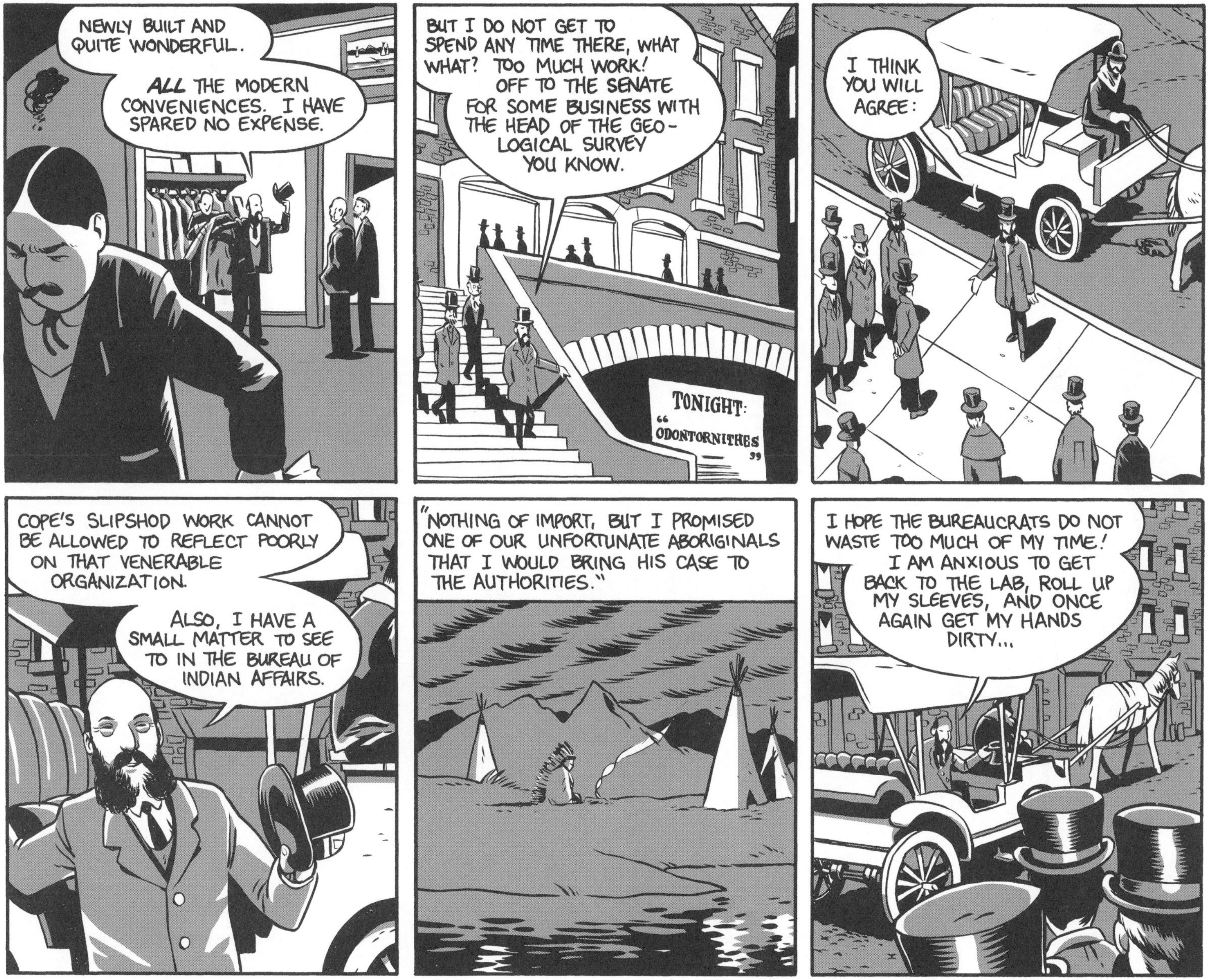
NEWLY BUILT AND QUITE WONDERFUL.
ALL THE MODERN CONVENIENCES. I HAVE SPARED NO EXPENSE.
BUT I DO NOT GET TO SPEND ANY TIME THERE, WHAT WHAT? TOO MUCH WORK!
OFF TO THE SENATE FOR SOME BUSINESS WITH THE HEAD OF THE GEO-LOGICAL SURVEY YOU KNOW.
TONIGHT: "ODONTORNITHES"
I THINK YOU WILL AGREE:
COPE'S SLIPSHOD WORK CANNOT BE ALLOWED TO REFLECT POORLY ON THAT VENERABLE ORGANIZATION.
ALSO, I HAVE A SMALL MATTER TO SEE TO IN THE BUREAU OF INDIAN AFFAIRS.
"NOTHING OF IMPORT, BUT I PROMISED ONE OF OUR UNFORTUNATE ABORIGINALS THAT I WOULD BRING HIS CASE TO THE AUTHORITIES."
I HOPE THE BUREAUCRATS DO NOT WASTE TOO MUCH OF MY TIME!
I AM ANXIOUS TO GET BACK TO THE LAB, ROLL UP MY SLEEVES, AND ONCE AGAIN GET MY HANDS DIRTY...

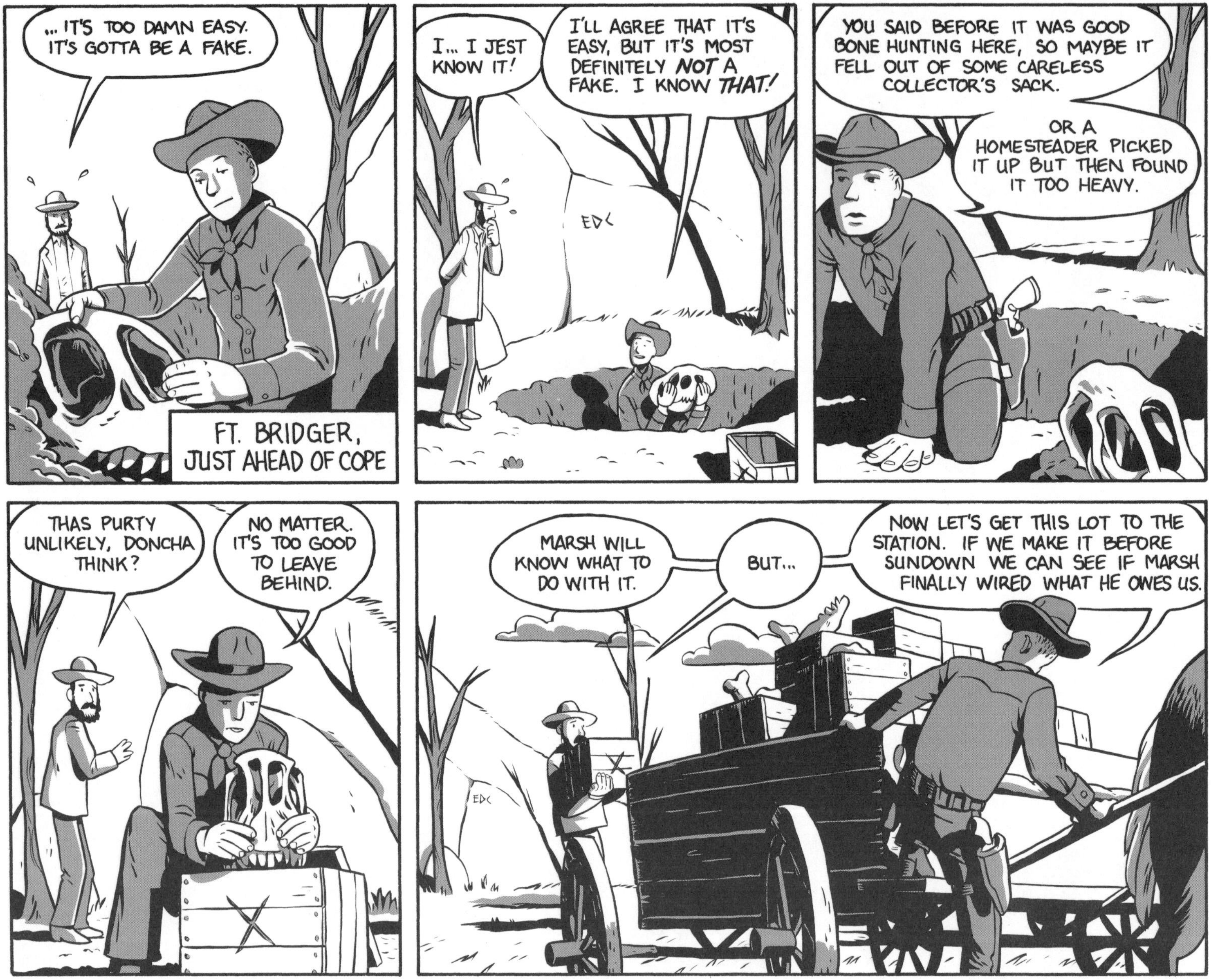
... IT'S TOO DAMN EASY. IT'S GOTTA BE A FAKE.
FT. BRIDGER, JUST AHEAD OF COPE
I... I JEST KNOW IT!
I'LL AGREE THAT IT'S EASY, BUT IT'S MOST DEFINITELY *NOT* A FAKE. I KNOW *THAT!*
EDC
YOU SAID BEFORE IT WAS GOOD BONE HUNTING HERE, SO MAYBE IT FELL OUT OF SOME CARELESS COLLECTOR'S SACK.
OR A HOMESTEADER PICKED IT UP BUT THEN FOUND IT TOO HEAVY.
THAS PURTY UNLIKELY, DONCHA THINK?
NO MATTER. IT'S TOO GOOD TO LEAVE BEHIND.
MARSH WILL KNOW WHAT TO DO WITH IT.
BUT...
NOW LET'S GET THIS LOT TO THE STATION. IF WE MAKE IT BEFORE SUNDOWN WE CAN SEE IF MARSH FINALLY WIRED WHAT HE OWES US.
EDC

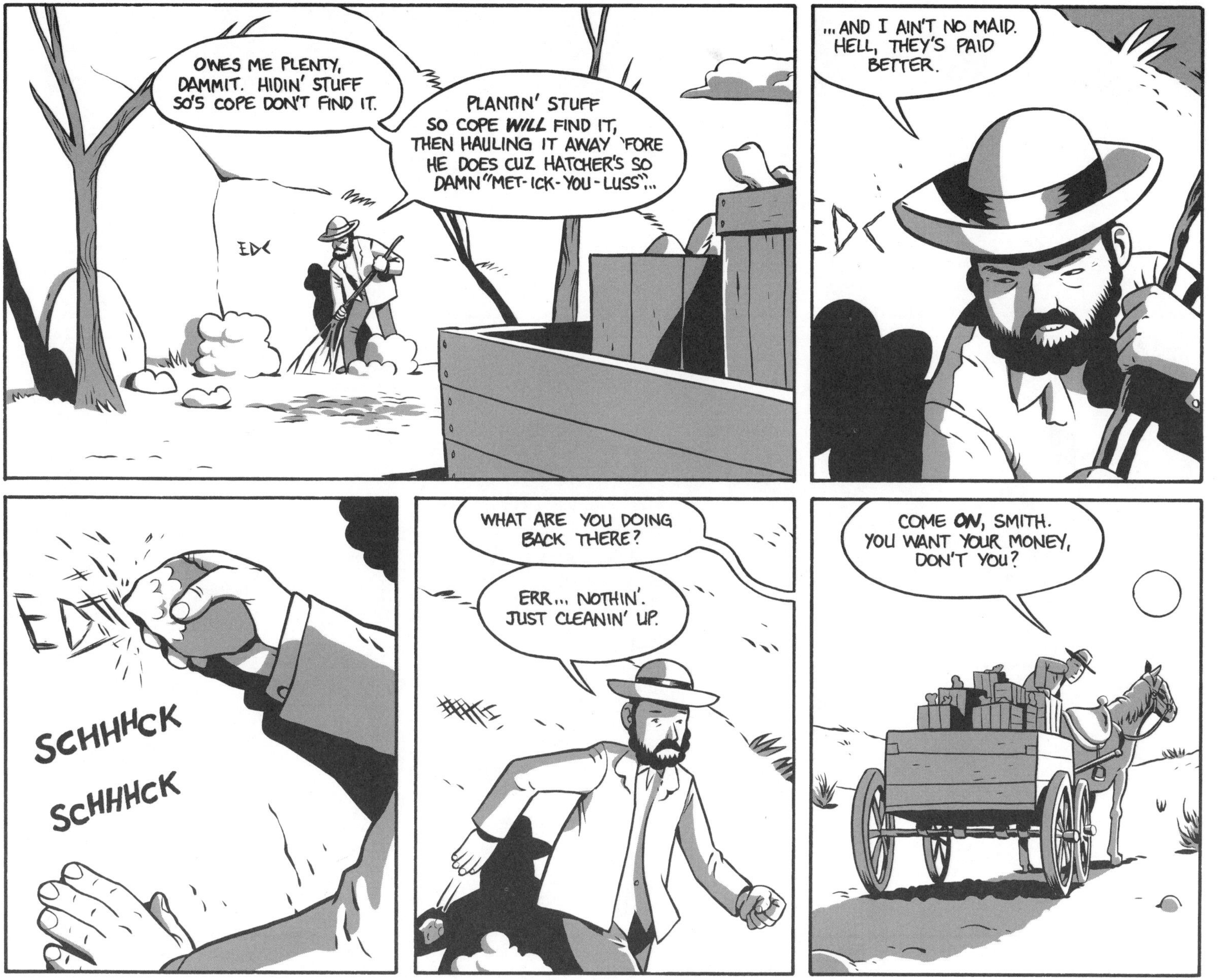
OWES ME PLENTY, DAMMIT. HIDIN' STUFF SO'S COPE DON'T FIND IT.
PLANTIN' STUFF SO COPE WILL FIND IT, THEN HAULING IT AWAY 'FORE HE DOES CUZ HATCHER'S SO DAMN "MET-ICK-YOU-LUSS"...
EDC
...AND I AIN'T NO MAID. HELL, THEY'S PAID BETTER.
SCHHHCK
SCHHHCK
WHAT ARE YOU DOING BACK THERE?
ERR... NOTHIN'. JUST CLEANIN' UP.
COME ON, SMITH. YOU WANT YOUR MONEY, DON'T YOU?

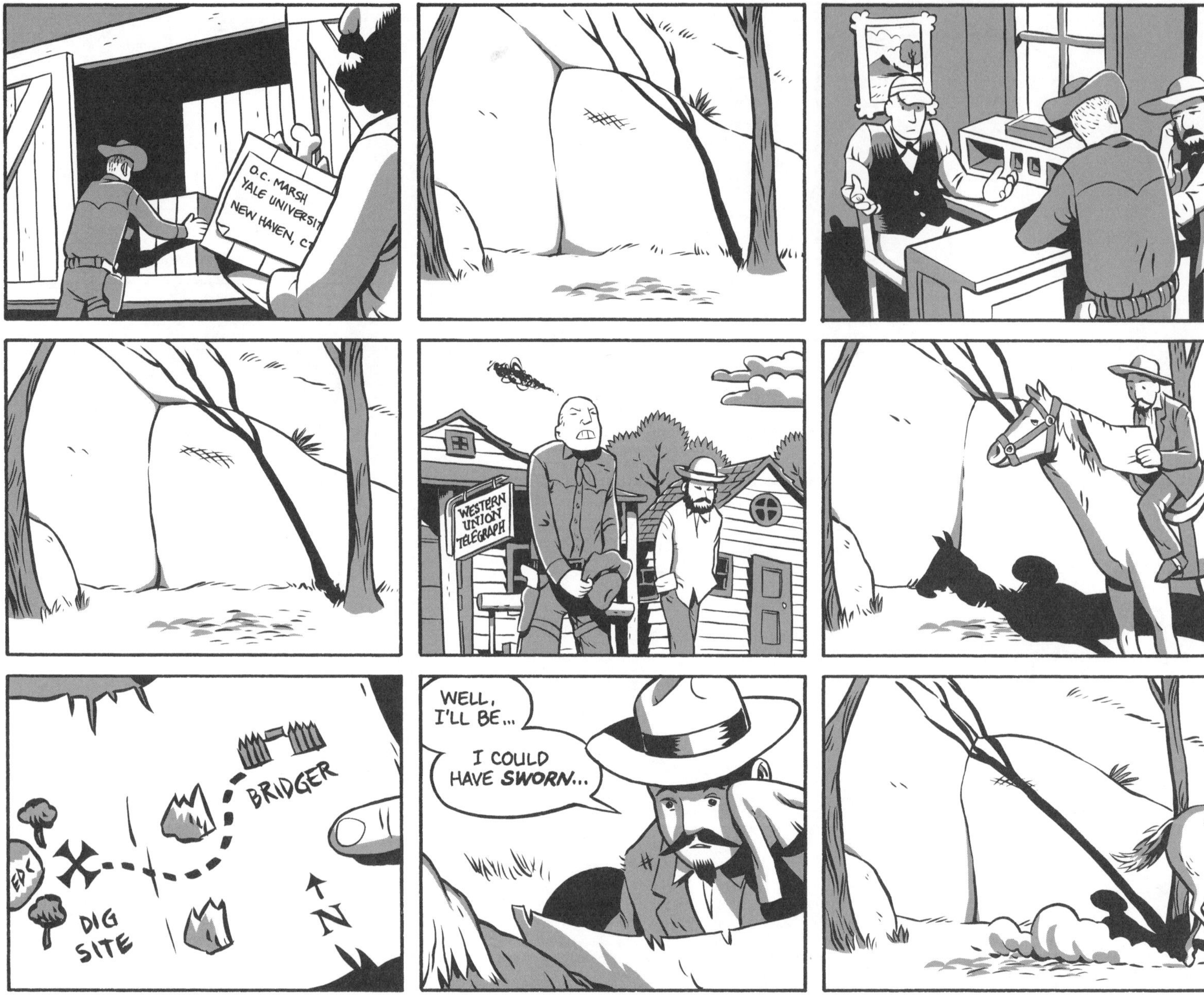
O.C. MARSH
YALE UNIVERSIT
NEW HAVEN, CT
WESTERN UNION TELEGRAPH
BRIDGER
EDC
DIG SITE
N
WELL, I'LL BE...
I COULD HAVE **SWORN**...

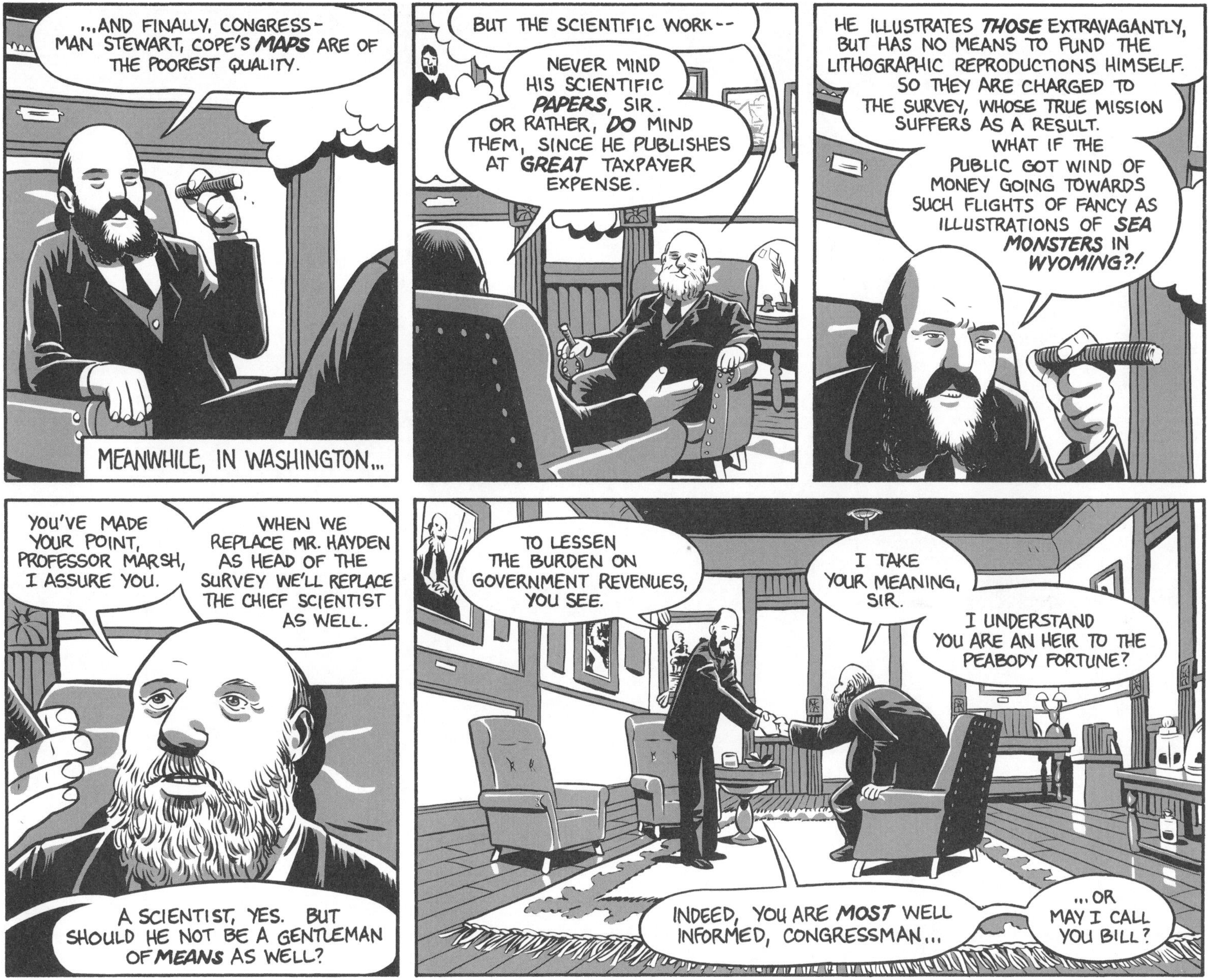

...AND FINALLY, CONGRESSMAN STEWART, COPE'S MAPS ARE OF THE POOREST QUALITY.
MEANWHILE, IN WASHINGTON...
BUT THE SCIENTIFIC WORK--
NEVER MIND HIS SCIENTIFIC PAPERS, SIR. OR RATHER, DO MIND THEM, SINCE HE PUBLISHES AT GREAT TAXPAYER EXPENSE.
HE ILLUSTRATES THOSE EXTRAVAGANTLY, BUT HAS NO MEANS TO FUND THE LITHOGRAPHIC REPRODUCTIONS HIMSELF. SO THEY ARE CHARGED TO THE SURVEY, WHOSE TRUE MISSION SUFFERS AS A RESULT.
WHAT IF THE PUBLIC GOT WIND OF MONEY GOING TOWARDS SUCH FLIGHTS OF FANCY AS ILLUSTRATIONS OF SEA MONSTERS IN WYOMING?!
YOU'VE MADE YOUR POINT, PROFESSOR MARSH, I ASSURE YOU.
WHEN WE REPLACE MR. HAYDEN AS HEAD OF THE SURVEY WE'LL REPLACE THE CHIEF SCIENTIST AS WELL.
A SCIENTIST, YES. BUT SHOULD HE NOT BE A GENTLEMAN OF MEANS AS WELL?
TO LESSEN THE BURDEN ON GOVERNMENT REVENUES, YOU SEE.
I TAKE YOUR MEANING, SIR.
I UNDERSTAND YOU ARE AN HEIR TO THE PEABODY FORTUNE?
INDEED, YOU ARE MOST WELL INFORMED, CONGRESSMAN...
...OR MAY I CALL YOU BILL?

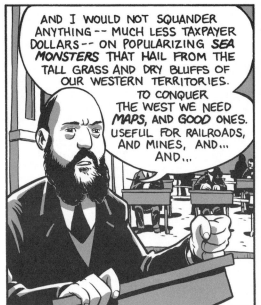

AND I WOULD NOT SQUANDER ANYTHING -- MUCH LESS TAXPAYER DOLLARS -- ON POPULARIZING *SEA MONSTERS* THAT HAIL FROM THE TALL GRASS AND DRY BLUFFS OF OUR WESTERN TERRITORIES.

TO CONQUER THE WEST WE NEED *MAPS*, AND *GOOD* ONES. USEFUL FOR RAILROADS, AND MINES, AND... AND...

PROGRESS. *PROGRESS!*

I THANK YOU FOR YOUR TIME, AND HOPE FOR YOUR ENDORSEMENT AS LEAD SCIENTIST OF THE U.S. GEOLOGICAL SURVEY UNDER THE DIRECTION OF JOHN WESLEY POWELL.

"NOW, IF CONGRESS WILL EXCUSE ME I HAVE AN APPOINTMENT WITH THE PRESIDENT."

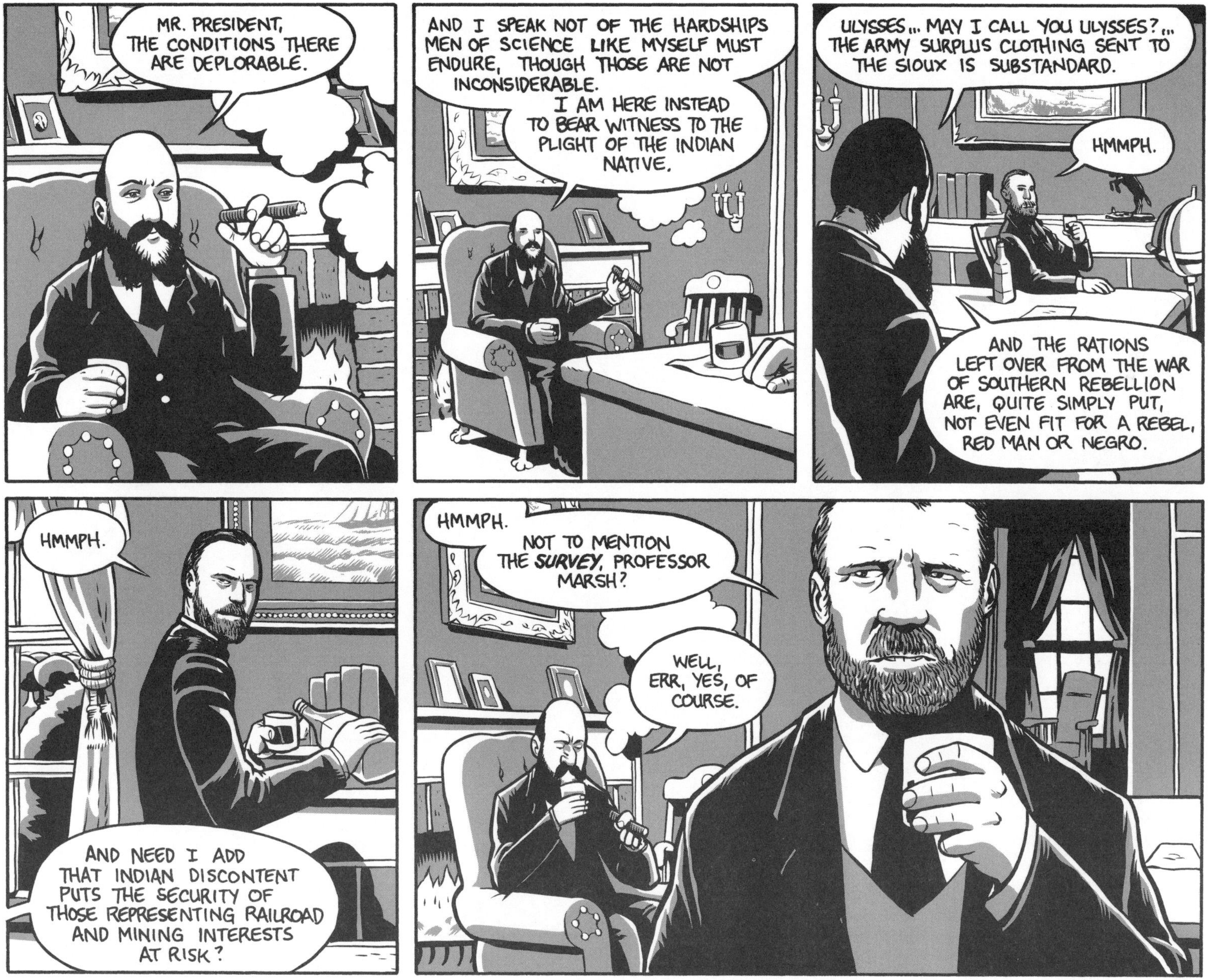
MR. PRESIDENT, THE CONDITIONS THERE ARE DEPLORABLE.
AND I SPEAK NOT OF THE HARDSHIPS MEN OF SCIENCE LIKE MYSELF MUST ENDURE, THOUGH THOSE ARE NOT INCONSIDERABLE.
I AM HERE INSTEAD TO BEAR WITNESS TO THE PLIGHT OF THE INDIAN NATIVE.
ULYSSES... MAY I CALL YOU ULYSSES?... THE ARMY SURPLUS CLOTHING SENT TO THE SIOUX IS SUBSTANDARD.
HMMPH.
AND THE RATIONS LEFT OVER FROM THE WAR OF SOUTHERN REBELLION ARE, QUITE SIMPLY PUT, NOT EVEN FIT FOR A REBEL, RED MAN OR NEGRO.
HMMPH.
AND NEED I ADD THAT INDIAN DISCONTENT PUTS THE SECURITY OF THOSE REPRESENTING RAILROAD AND MINING INTERESTS AT RISK?
HMMPH.
NOT TO MENTION THE *SURVEY*, PROFESSOR MARSH?
WELL, ERR, YES, OF COURSE.

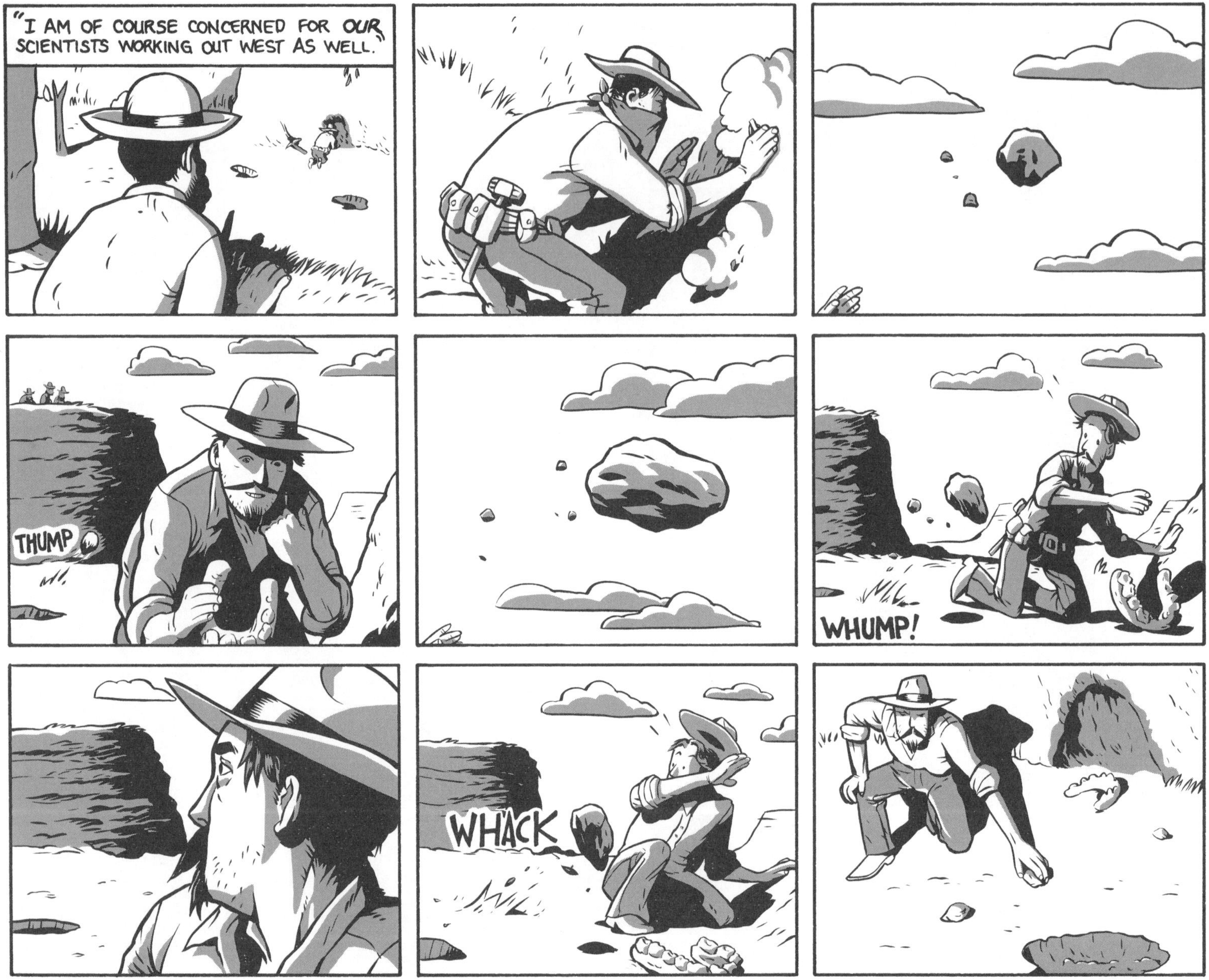
"I AM OF COURSE CONCERNED FOR OUR SCIENTISTS WORKING OUT WEST AS WELL."
THUMP
WHUMP!
WHACK

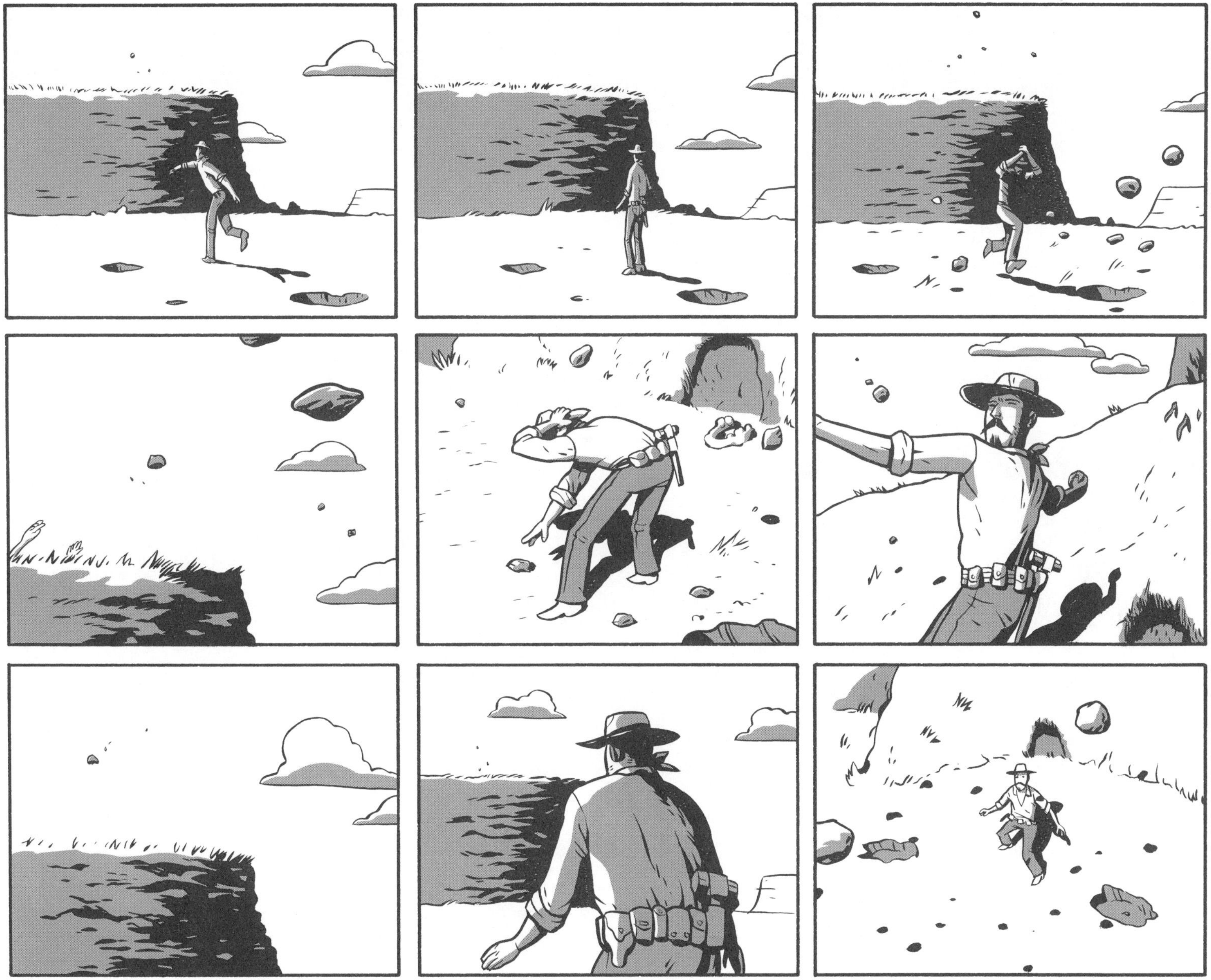

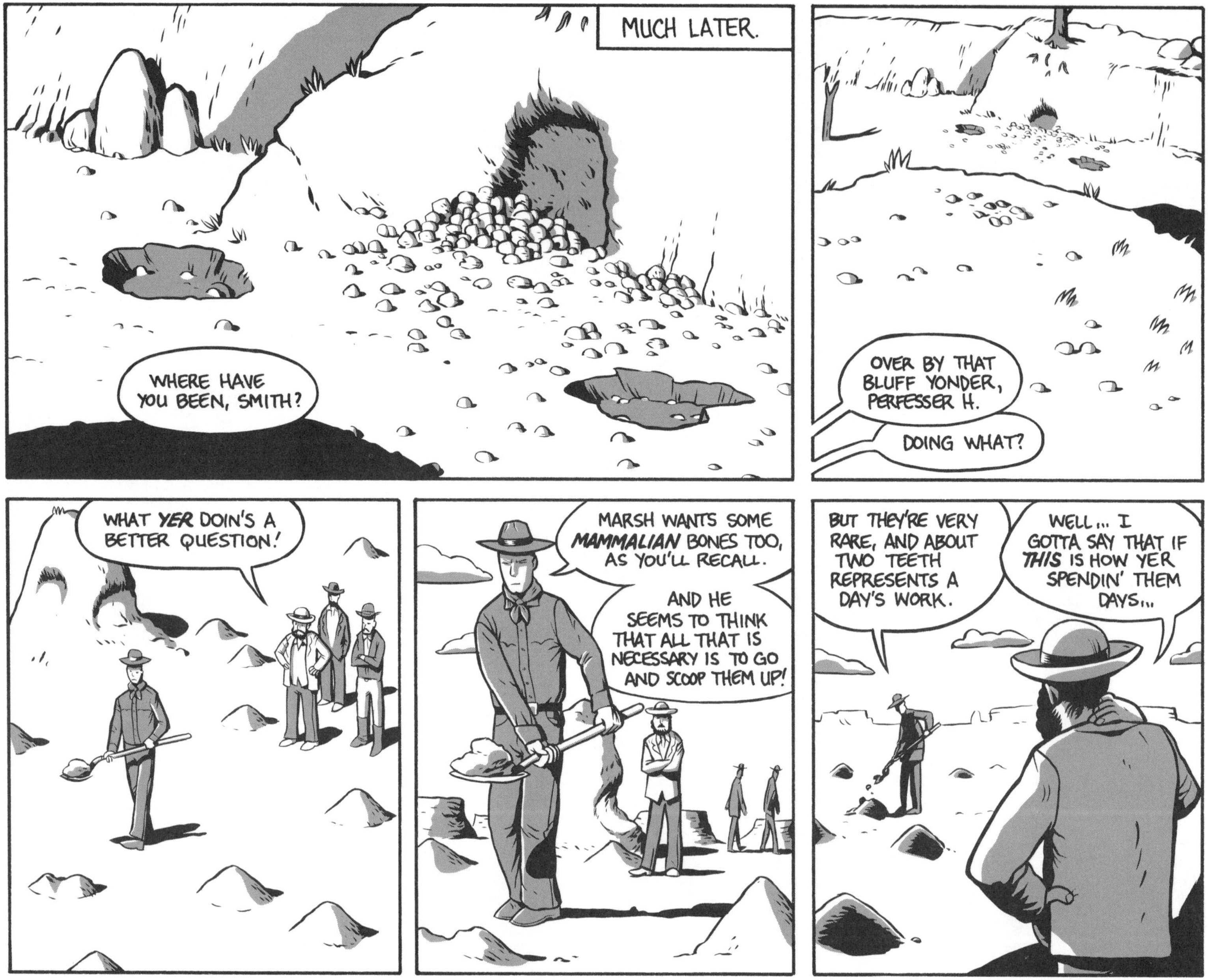
MUCH LATER.
WHERE HAVE YOU BEEN, SMITH?
OVER BY THAT BLUFF YONDER, PERFESSER H.
DOING WHAT?
WHAT YER DOIN'S A BETTER QUESTION!
MARSH WANTS SOME MAMMALIAN BONES TOO, AS YOU'LL RECALL.
AND HE SEEMS TO THINK THAT ALL THAT IS NECESSARY IS TO GO AND SCOOP THEM UP!
BUT THEY'RE VERY RARE, AND ABOUT TWO TEETH REPRESENTS A DAY'S WORK.
WELL... I GOTTA SAY THAT IF THIS IS HOW YER SPENDIN' THEM DAYS...

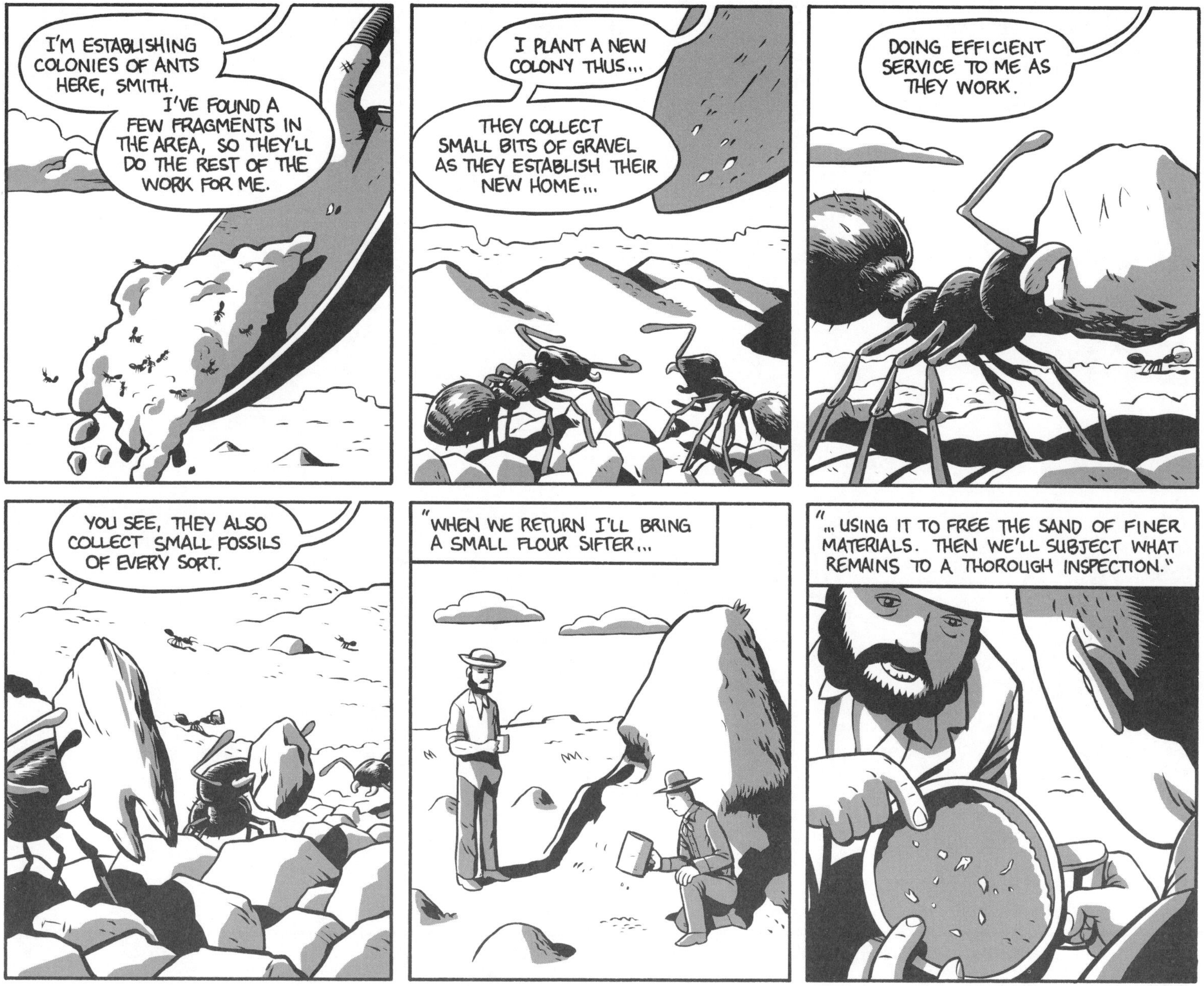
I'M ESTABLISHING COLONIES OF ANTS HERE, SMITH.
I'VE FOUND A FEW FRAGMENTS IN THE AREA, SO THEY'LL DO THE REST OF THE WORK FOR ME.
I PLANT A NEW COLONY THUS...
THEY COLLECT SMALL BITS OF GRAVEL AS THEY ESTABLISH THEIR NEW HOME...
DOING EFFICIENT SERVICE TO ME AS THEY WORK.
YOU SEE, THEY ALSO COLLECT SMALL FOSSILS OF EVERY SORT.
"WHEN WE RETURN I'LL BRING A SMALL FLOUR SIFTER...
"...USING IT TO FREE THE SAND OF FINER MATERIALS. THEN WE'LL SUBJECT WHAT REMAINS TO A THOROUGH INSPECTION."

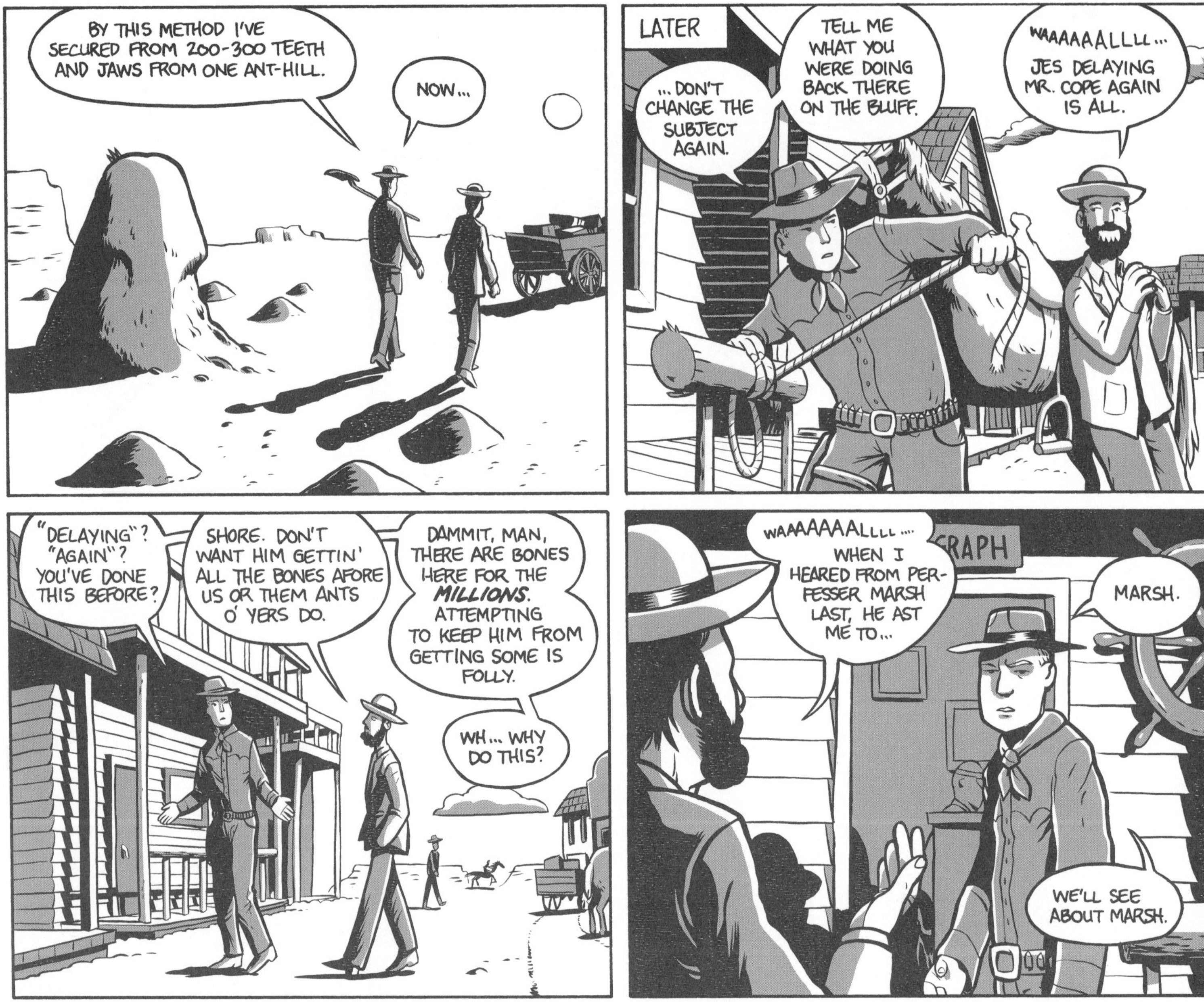
BY THIS METHOD I'VE SECURED FROM 200-300 TEETH AND JAWS FROM ONE ANT-HILL.
NOW...
LATER
...DON'T CHANGE THE SUBJECT AGAIN.
TELL ME WHAT YOU WERE DOING BACK THERE ON THE BLUFF.
WAAAAAALLLL... JES DELAYING MR. COPE AGAIN IS ALL.
"DELAYING"? "AGAIN"? YOU'VE DONE THIS BEFORE?
SHORE. DON'T WANT HIM GETTIN' ALL THE BONES AFORE US OR THEM ANTS O' YERS DO.
DAMMIT, MAN, THERE ARE BONES HERE FOR THE ***MILLIONS***. ATTEMPTING TO KEEP HIM FROM GETTING SOME IS FOLLY.
WH... WHY DO THIS?
WAAAAAAALLLL.... WHEN I HEARED FROM PER-FESSER MARSH LAST, HE AST ME TO...
RAPH
MARSH.
WE'LL SEE ABOUT MARSH.

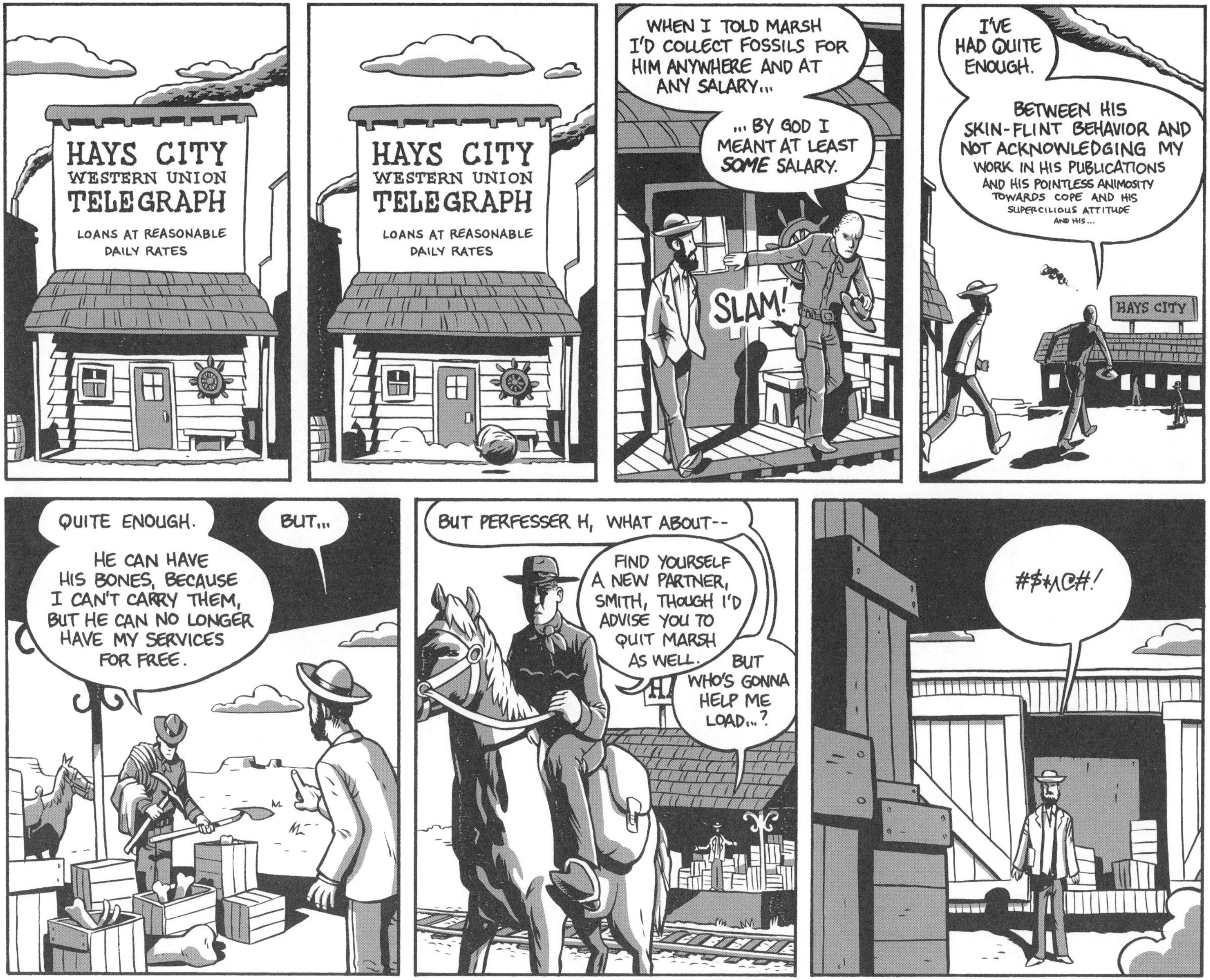
HAYS CITY
WESTERN UNION
TELEGRAPH
LOANS AT REASONABLE DAILY RATES
HAYS CITY
WESTERN UNION
TELEGRAPH
LOANS AT REASONABLE DAILY RATES
WHEN I TOLD MARSH I'D COLLECT FOSSILS FOR HIM ANYWHERE AND AT ANY SALARY...
...BY GOD I MEANT AT LEAST SOME SALARY.
SLAM!
I'VE HAD QUITE ENOUGH.
BETWEEN HIS SKIN-FLINT BEHAVIOR AND NOT ACKNOWLEDGING MY WORK IN HIS PUBLICATIONS AND HIS POINTLESS ANIMOSITY TOWARDS COPE AND HIS SUPERCILIOUS ATTITUDE AND HIS...
HAYS CITY
QUITE ENOUGH.
HE CAN HAVE HIS BONES, BECAUSE I CAN'T CARRY THEM, BUT HE CAN NO LONGER HAVE MY SERVICES FOR FREE.
BUT...
BUT PERFESSER H, WHAT ABOUT--
FIND YOURSELF A NEW PARTNER, SMITH, THOUGH I'D ADVISE YOU TO QUIT MARSH AS WELL.
BUT WHO'S GONNA HELP ME LOAD...?
#$*ʌ@#!

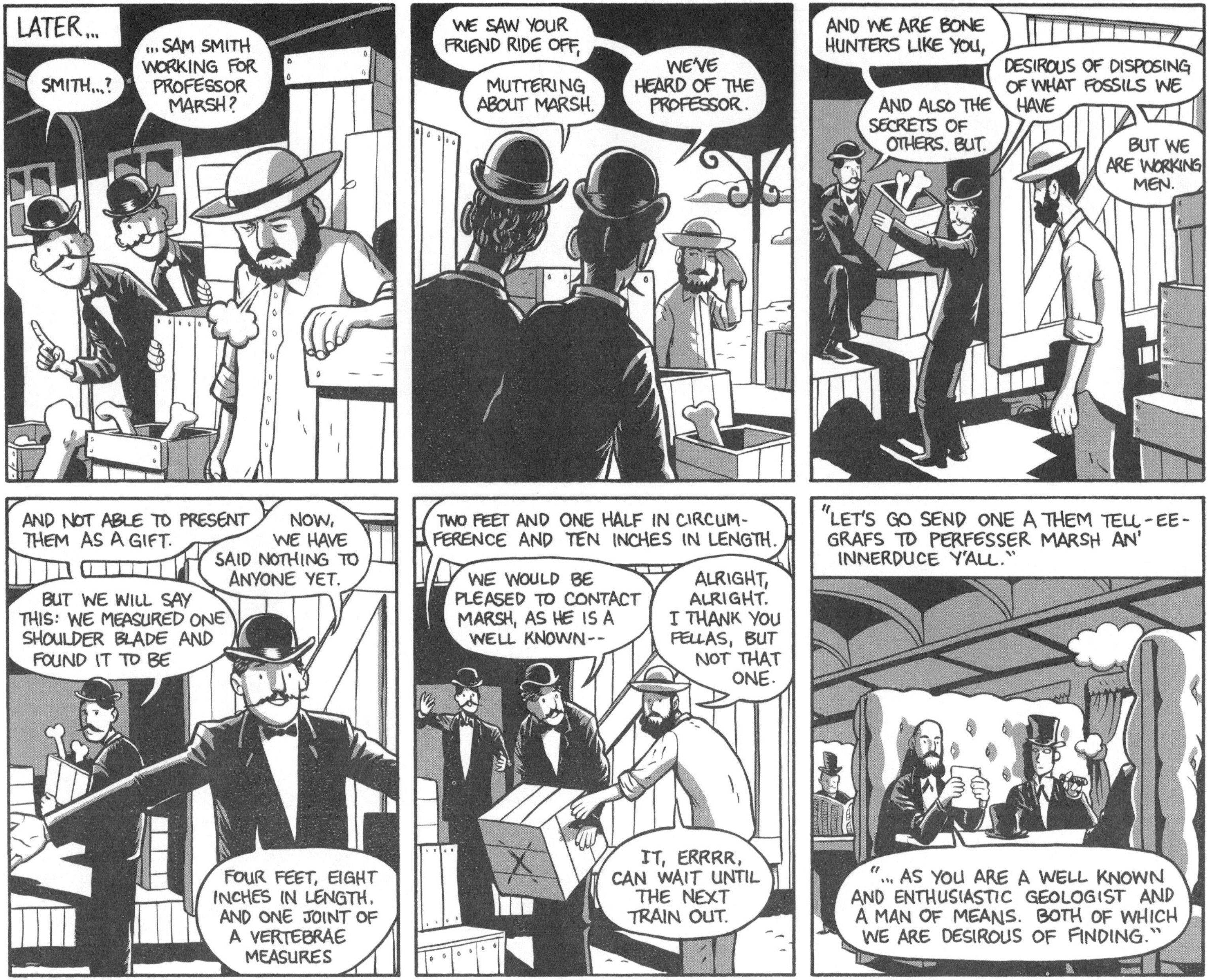
LATER...
SMITH...?
...SAM SMITH WORKING FOR PROFESSOR MARSH?
WE SAW YOUR FRIEND RIDE OFF,
MUTTERING ABOUT MARSH.
WE'VE HEARD OF THE PROFESSOR.
AND WE ARE BONE HUNTERS LIKE YOU,
AND ALSO THE SECRETS OF OTHERS. BUT.
DESIROUS OF DISPOSING OF WHAT FOSSILS WE HAVE
BUT WE ARE WORKING MEN.
AND NOT ABLE TO PRESENT THEM AS A GIFT.
NOW, WE HAVE SAID NOTHING TO ANYONE YET.
BUT WE WILL SAY THIS: WE MEASURED ONE SHOULDER BLADE AND FOUND IT TO BE
FOUR FEET, EIGHT INCHES IN LENGTH. AND ONE JOINT OF A VERTEBRAE MEASURES
TWO FEET AND ONE HALF IN CIRCUMFERENCE AND TEN INCHES IN LENGTH.
WE WOULD BE PLEASED TO CONTACT MARSH, AS HE IS A WELL KNOWN--
ALRIGHT, ALRIGHT. I THANK YOU FELLAS, BUT NOT THAT ONE.
IT, ERRRR, CAN WAIT UNTIL THE NEXT TRAIN OUT.
"LET'S GO SEND ONE A THEM TELL-EE-GRAFS TO PERFESSER MARSH AN' INNERDUCE Y'ALL."
"... AS YOU ARE A WELL KNOWN AND ENTHUSIASTIC GEOLOGIST AND A MAN OF MEANS. BOTH OF WHICH WE ARE DESIROUS OF FINDING."

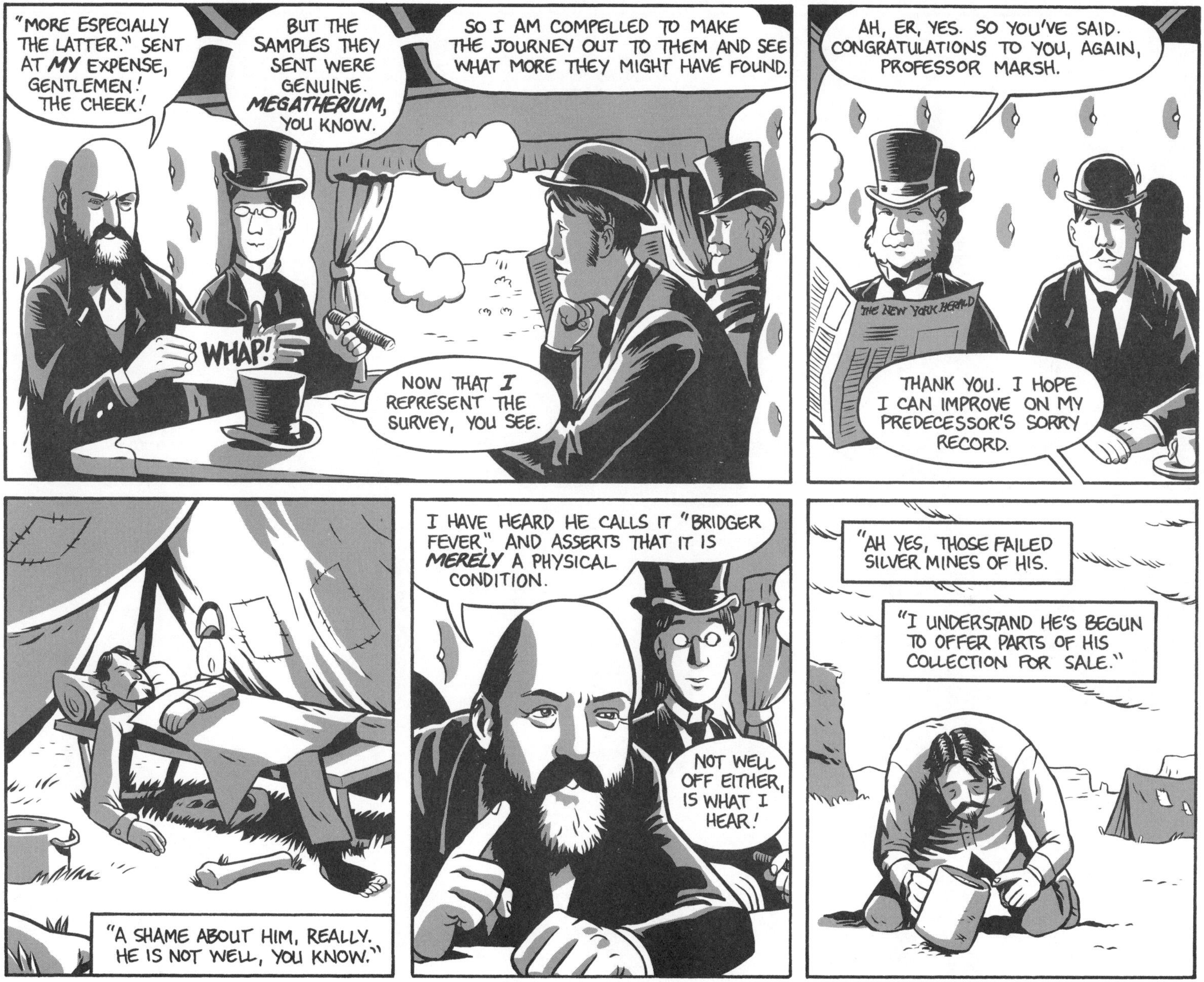
"MORE ESPECIALLY THE LATTER." SENT AT MY EXPENSE, GENTLEMEN! THE CHEEK!
BUT THE SAMPLES THEY SENT WERE GENUINE. MEGATHERIUM, YOU KNOW.
SO I AM COMPELLED TO MAKE THE JOURNEY OUT TO THEM AND SEE WHAT MORE THEY MIGHT HAVE FOUND.
WHAP!
NOW THAT I REPRESENT THE SURVEY, YOU SEE.
AH, ER, YES. SO YOU'VE SAID. CONGRATULATIONS TO YOU, AGAIN, PROFESSOR MARSH.
THE NEW YORK HERALD
THANK YOU. I HOPE I CAN IMPROVE ON MY PREDECESSOR'S SORRY RECORD.
"A SHAME ABOUT HIM, REALLY. HE IS NOT WELL, YOU KNOW."
I HAVE HEARD HE CALLS IT "BRIDGER FEVER," AND ASSERTS THAT IT IS MERELY A PHYSICAL CONDITION.
NOT WELL OFF EITHER, IS WHAT I HEAR!
"AH YES, THOSE FAILED SILVER MINES OF HIS.
"I UNDERSTAND HE'S BEGUN TO OFFER PARTS OF HIS COLLECTION FOR SALE."

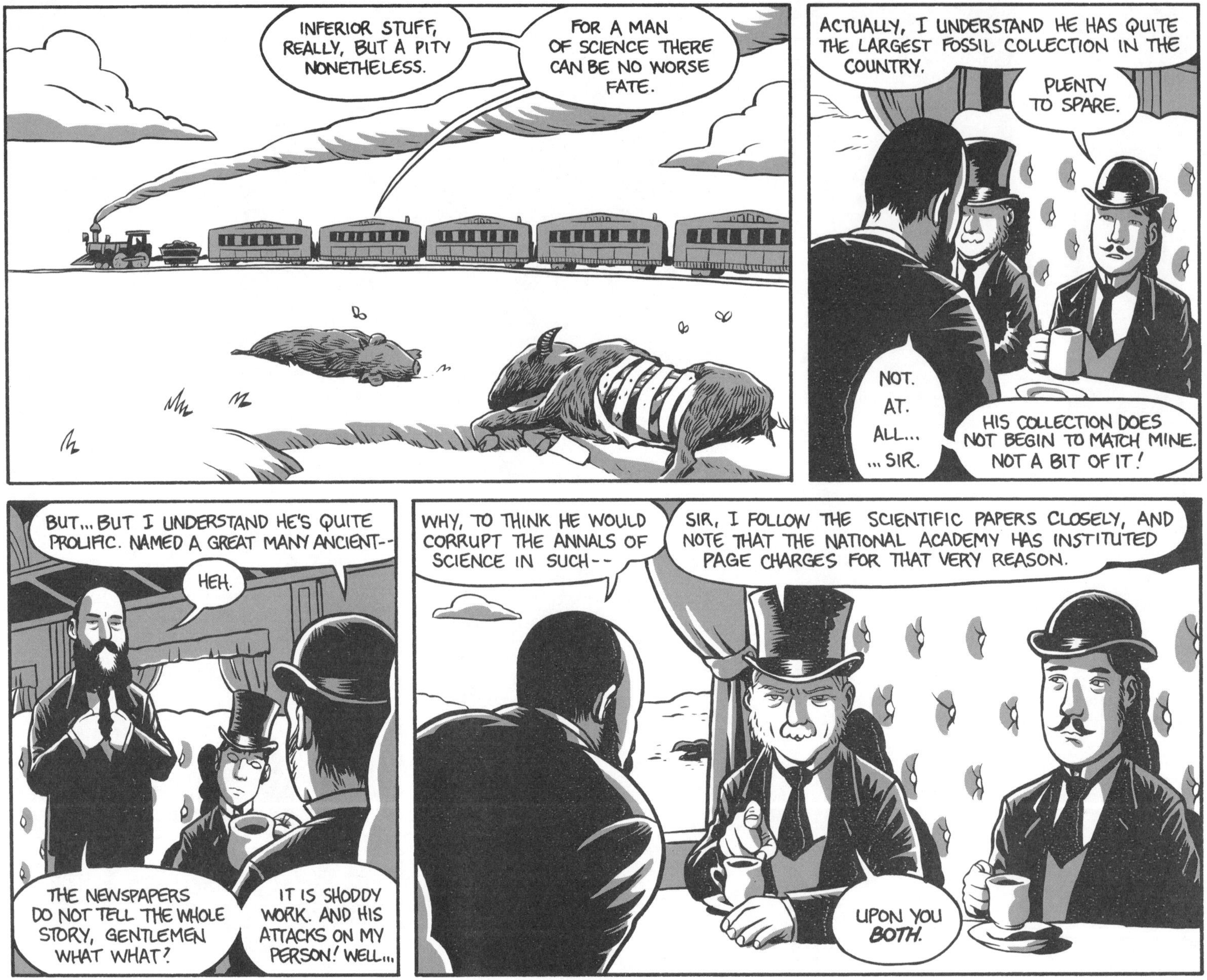
INFERIOR STUFF, REALLY, BUT A PITY NONETHELESS.
FOR A MAN OF SCIENCE THERE CAN BE NO WORSE FATE.
ACTUALLY, I UNDERSTAND HE HAS QUITE THE LARGEST FOSSIL COLLECTION IN THE COUNTRY.
PLENTY TO SPARE.
NOT. AT. ALL... ...SIR.
HIS COLLECTION DOES NOT BEGIN TO MATCH MINE. NOT A BIT OF IT!
BUT... BUT I UNDERSTAND HE'S QUITE PROLIFIC. NAMED A GREAT MANY ANCIENT--
HEH.
THE NEWSPAPERS DO NOT TELL THE WHOLE STORY, GENTLEMEN WHAT WHAT?
IT IS SHODDY WORK. AND HIS ATTACKS ON MY PERSON! WELL...
WHY, TO THINK HE WOULD CORRUPT THE ANNALS OF SCIENCE IN SUCH--
SIR, I FOLLOW THE SCIENTIFIC PAPERS CLOSELY, AND NOTE THAT THE NATIONAL ACADEMY HAS INSTITUTED PAGE CHARGES FOR THAT VERY REASON.
UPON YOU *BOTH*.

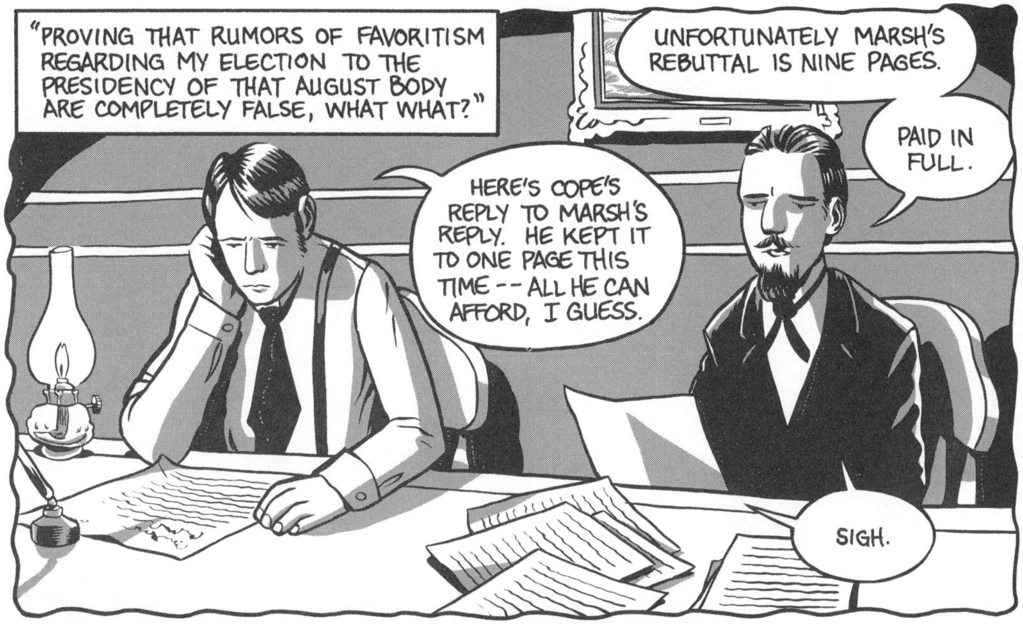
"PROVING THAT RUMORS OF FAVORITISM REGARDING MY ELECTION TO THE PRESIDENCY OF THAT AUGUST BODY ARE COMPLETELY FALSE, WHAT WHAT?"
HERE'S COPE'S REPLY TO MARSH'S REPLY. HE KEPT IT TO ONE PAGE THIS TIME -- ALL HE CAN AFFORD, I GUESS.
UNFORTUNATELY MARSH'S REBUTTAL IS NINE PAGES.
PAID IN FULL.
SIGH.

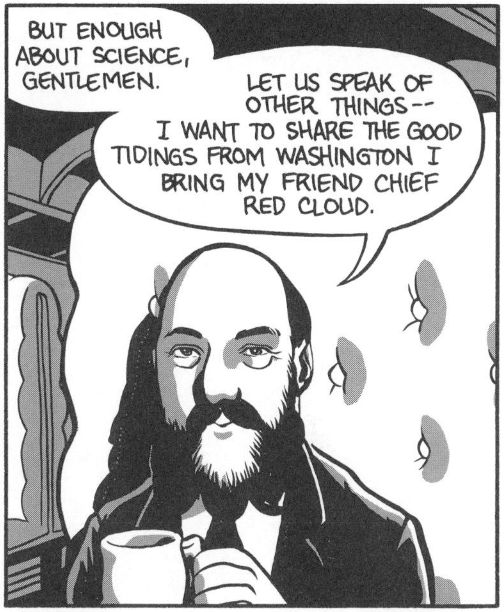
BUT ENOUGH ABOUT SCIENCE, GENTLEMEN.
LET US SPEAK OF OTHER THINGS -- I WANT TO SHARE THE GOOD TIDINGS FROM WASHINGTON I BRING MY FRIEND CHIEF RED CLOUD.

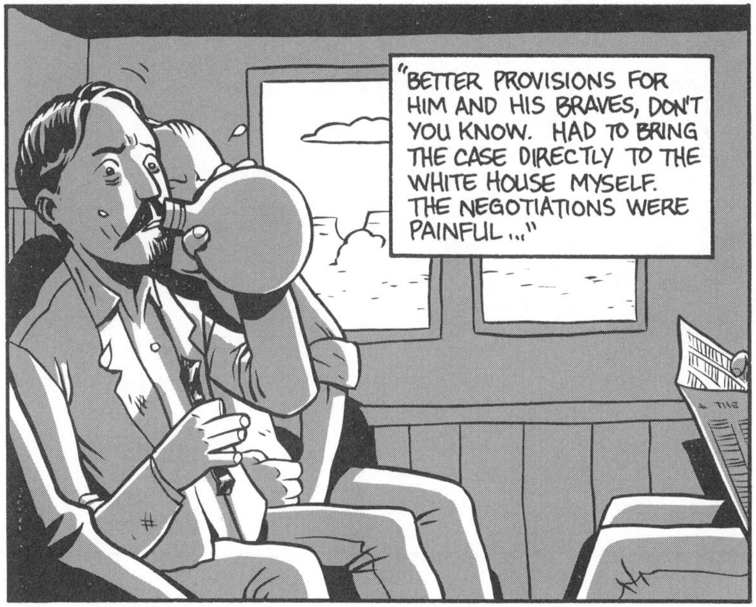
"BETTER PROVISIONS FOR HIM AND HIS BRAVES, DON'T YOU KNOW. HAD TO BRING THE CASE DIRECTLY TO THE WHITE HOUSE MYSELF. THE NEGOTIATIONS WERE PAINFUL..."

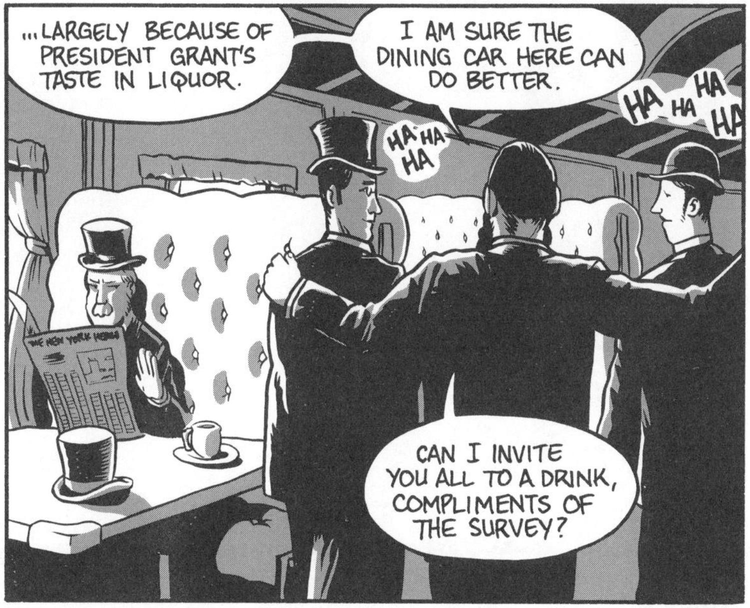
...LARGELY BECAUSE OF PRESIDENT GRANT'S TASTE IN LIQUOR.
I AM SURE THE DINING CAR HERE CAN DO BETTER.
HA HA HA HA
HA HA HA
THE NEW YORK HERALD
CAN I INVITE YOU ALL TO A DRINK, COMPLIMENTS OF THE SURVEY?

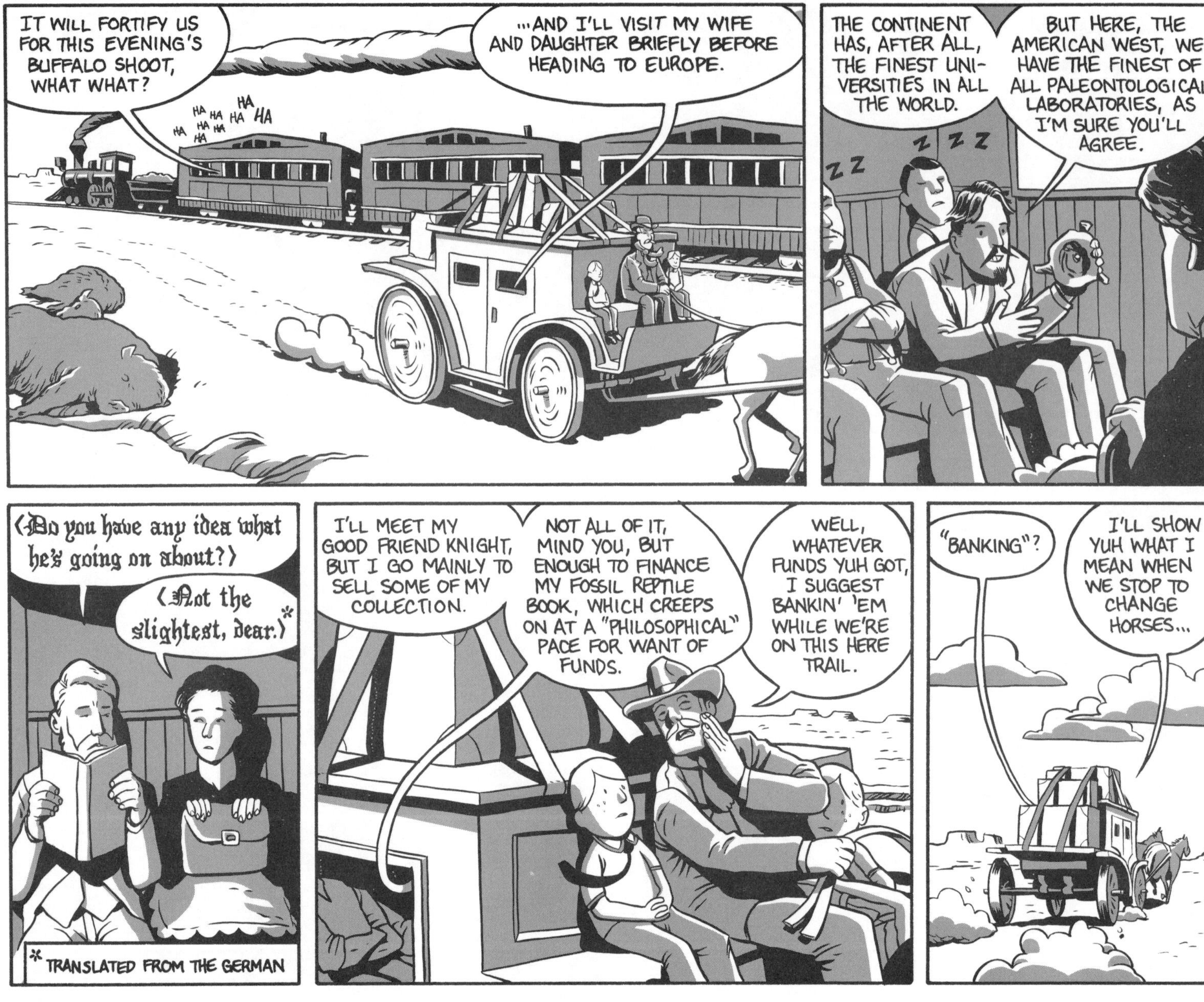
IT WILL FORTIFY US FOR THIS EVENING'S BUFFALO SHOOT, WHAT WHAT?
HA HA HA HA HA HA HA HA HA
...AND I'LL VISIT MY WIFE AND DAUGHTER BRIEFLY BEFORE HEADING TO EUROPE.
THE CONTINENT HAS, AFTER ALL, THE FINEST UNIVERSITIES IN ALL THE WORLD.
BUT HERE, THE AMERICAN WEST, WE HAVE THE FINEST OF ALL PALEONTOLOGICAL LABORATORIES, AS I'M SURE YOU'LL AGREE.
Z Z
Z Z Z
‹Do you have any idea what he's going on about?›
‹Not the slightest, dear.›*
*TRANSLATED FROM THE GERMAN
I'LL MEET MY GOOD FRIEND KNIGHT, BUT I GO MAINLY TO SELL SOME OF MY COLLECTION.
NOT ALL OF IT, MIND YOU, BUT ENOUGH TO FINANCE MY FOSSIL REPTILE BOOK, WHICH CREEPS ON AT A "PHILOSOPHICAL" PACE FOR WANT OF FUNDS.
WELL, WHATEVER FUNDS YUH GOT, I SUGGEST BANKIN' 'EM WHILE WE'RE ON THIS HERE TRAIL.
"BANKING"?
I'LL SHOW YUH WHAT I MEAN WHEN WE STOP TO CHANGE HORSES...

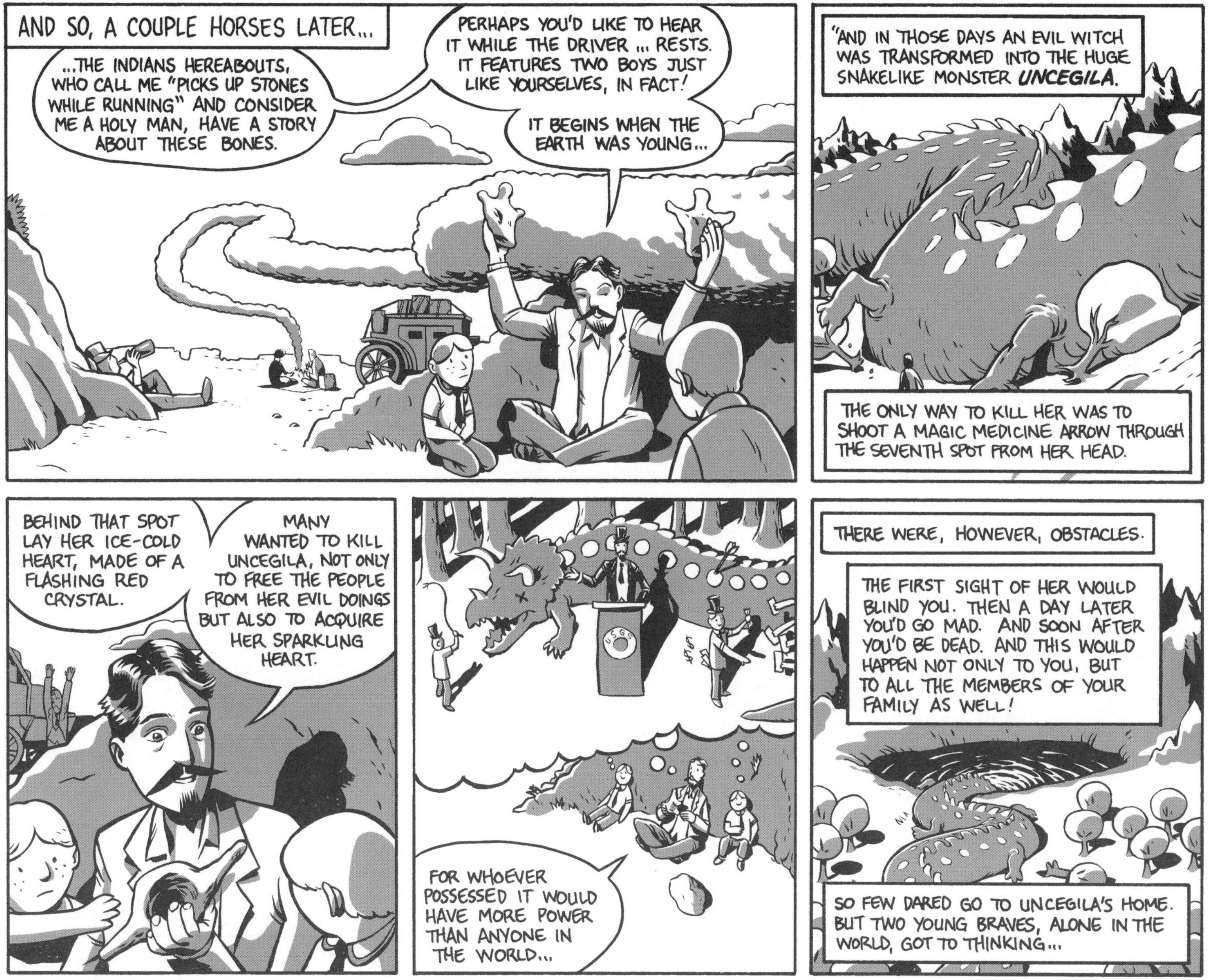
AND SO, A COUPLE HORSES LATER...
...THE INDIANS HEREABOUTS, WHO CALL ME "PICKS UP STONES WHILE RUNNING" AND CONSIDER ME A HOLY MAN, HAVE A STORY ABOUT THESE BONES.
PERHAPS YOU'D LIKE TO HEAR IT WHILE THE DRIVER ... RESTS. IT FEATURES TWO BOYS JUST LIKE YOURSELVES, IN FACT!
IT BEGINS WHEN THE EARTH WAS YOUNG...
"AND IN THOSE DAYS AN EVIL WITCH WAS TRANSFORMED INTO THE HUGE SNAKELIKE MONSTER ***UNCEGILA***.
THE ONLY WAY TO KILL HER WAS TO SHOOT A MAGIC MEDICINE ARROW THROUGH THE SEVENTH SPOT FROM HER HEAD.
BEHIND THAT SPOT LAY HER ICE-COLD HEART, MADE OF A FLASHING RED CRYSTAL.
MANY WANTED TO KILL UNCEGILA, NOT ONLY TO FREE THE PEOPLE FROM HER EVIL DOINGS BUT ALSO TO ACQUIRE HER SPARKLING HEART.
USGS
FOR WHOEVER POSSESSED IT WOULD HAVE MORE POWER THAN ANYONE IN THE WORLD...
THERE WERE, HOWEVER, OBSTACLES.
THE FIRST SIGHT OF HER WOULD BLIND YOU. THEN A DAY LATER YOU'D GO MAD. AND SOON AFTER YOU'D BE DEAD. AND THIS WOULD HAPPEN NOT ONLY TO YOU, BUT TO ALL THE MEMBERS OF YOUR FAMILY AS WELL!
SO FEW DARED GO TO UNCEGILA'S HOME. BUT TWO YOUNG BRAVES, ALONE IN THE WORLD, GOT TO THINKING...

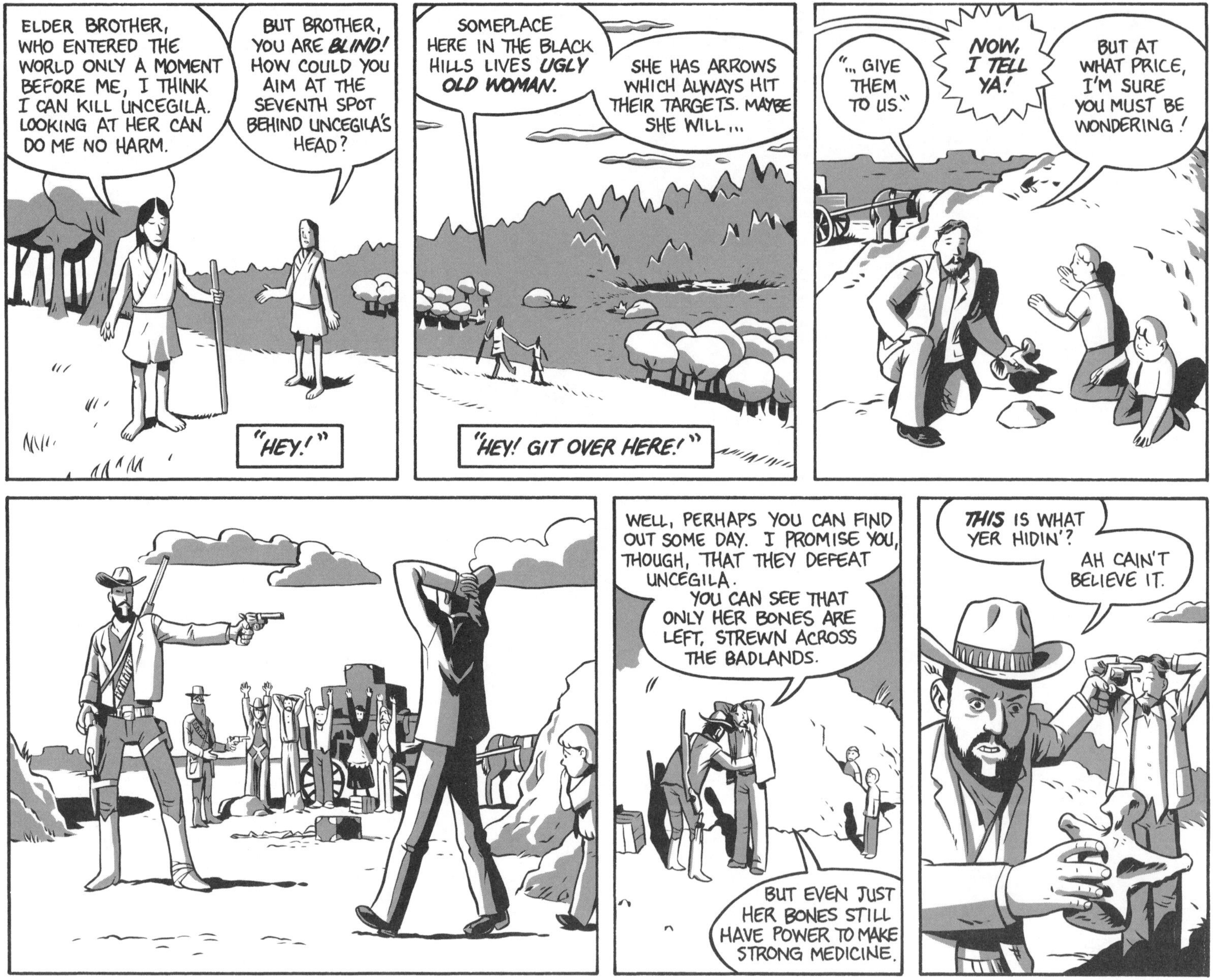

ELDER BROTHER, WHO ENTERED THE WORLD ONLY A MOMENT BEFORE ME, I THINK I CAN KILL UNCEGILA. LOOKING AT HER CAN DO ME NO HARM.
BUT BROTHER, YOU ARE BLIND! HOW COULD YOU AIM AT THE SEVENTH SPOT BEHIND UNCEGILA'S HEAD?
"HEY!"
SOMEPLACE HERE IN THE BLACK HILLS LIVES UGLY OLD WOMAN.
SHE HAS ARROWS WHICH ALWAYS HIT THEIR TARGETS. MAYBE SHE WILL...
"HEY! GIT OVER HERE!"
"... GIVE THEM TO US."
NOW, I TELL YA!
BUT AT WHAT PRICE, I'M SURE YOU MUST BE WONDERING!
WELL, PERHAPS YOU CAN FIND OUT SOME DAY. I PROMISE YOU, THOUGH, THAT THEY DEFEAT UNCEGILA.
YOU CAN SEE THAT ONLY HER BONES ARE LEFT, STREWN ACROSS THE BADLANDS.
BUT EVEN JUST HER BONES STILL HAVE POWER TO MAKE STRONG MEDICINE.
THIS IS WHAT YER HIDIN'?
AH CAIN'T BELIEVE IT.

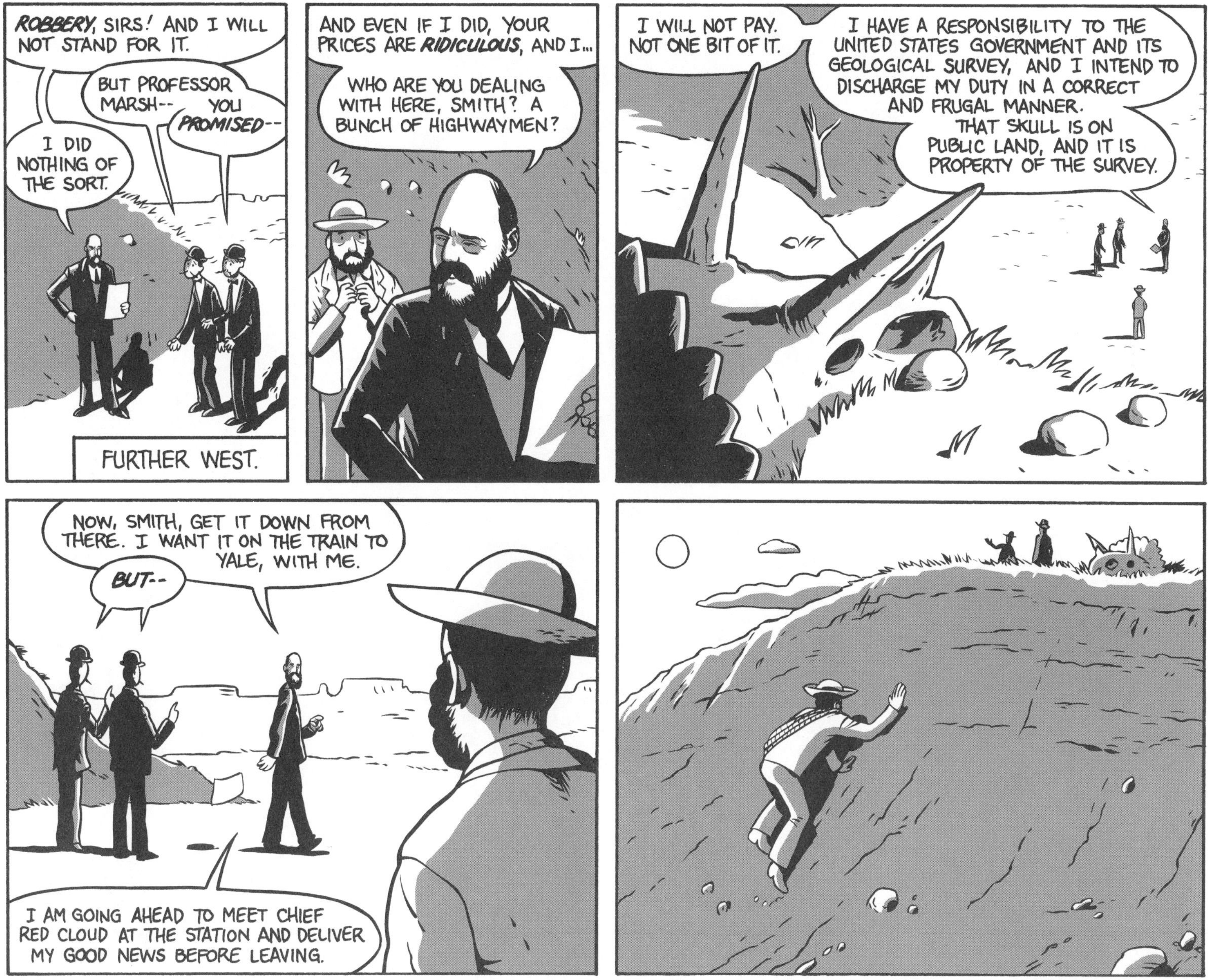
ROBBERY, SIRS! AND I WILL NOT STAND FOR IT.
BUT PROFESSOR MARSH--
YOU PROMISED--
I DID NOTHING OF THE SORT.
FURTHER WEST.
AND EVEN IF I DID, YOUR PRICES ARE RIDICULOUS, AND I...
WHO ARE YOU DEALING WITH HERE, SMITH? A BUNCH OF HIGHWAYMEN?
I WILL NOT PAY. NOT ONE BIT OF IT.
I HAVE A RESPONSIBILITY TO THE UNITED STATES GOVERNMENT AND ITS GEOLOGICAL SURVEY, AND I INTEND TO DISCHARGE MY DUTY IN A CORRECT AND FRUGAL MANNER.
THAT SKULL IS ON PUBLIC LAND, AND IT IS PROPERTY OF THE SURVEY.
NOW, SMITH, GET IT DOWN FROM THERE. I WANT IT ON THE TRAIN TO YALE, WITH ME.
BUT--
I AM GOING AHEAD TO MEET CHIEF RED CLOUD AT THE STATION AND DELIVER MY GOOD NEWS BEFORE LEAVING.

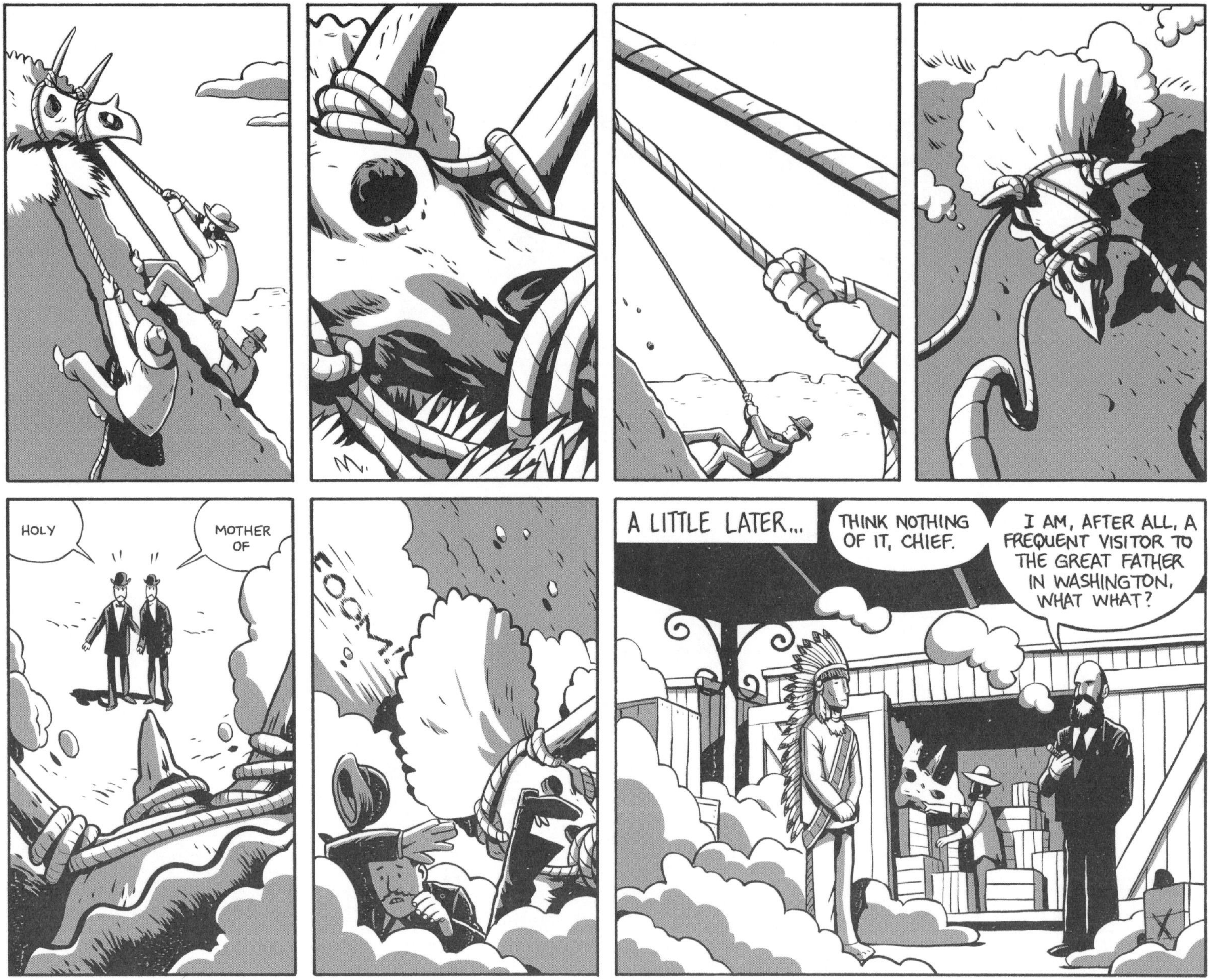
HOLY
MOTHER OF
FOOM!
A LITTLE LATER...
THINK NOTHING OF IT, CHIEF.
I AM, AFTER ALL, A FREQUENT VISITOR TO THE GREAT FATHER IN WASHINGTON, WHAT WHAT?

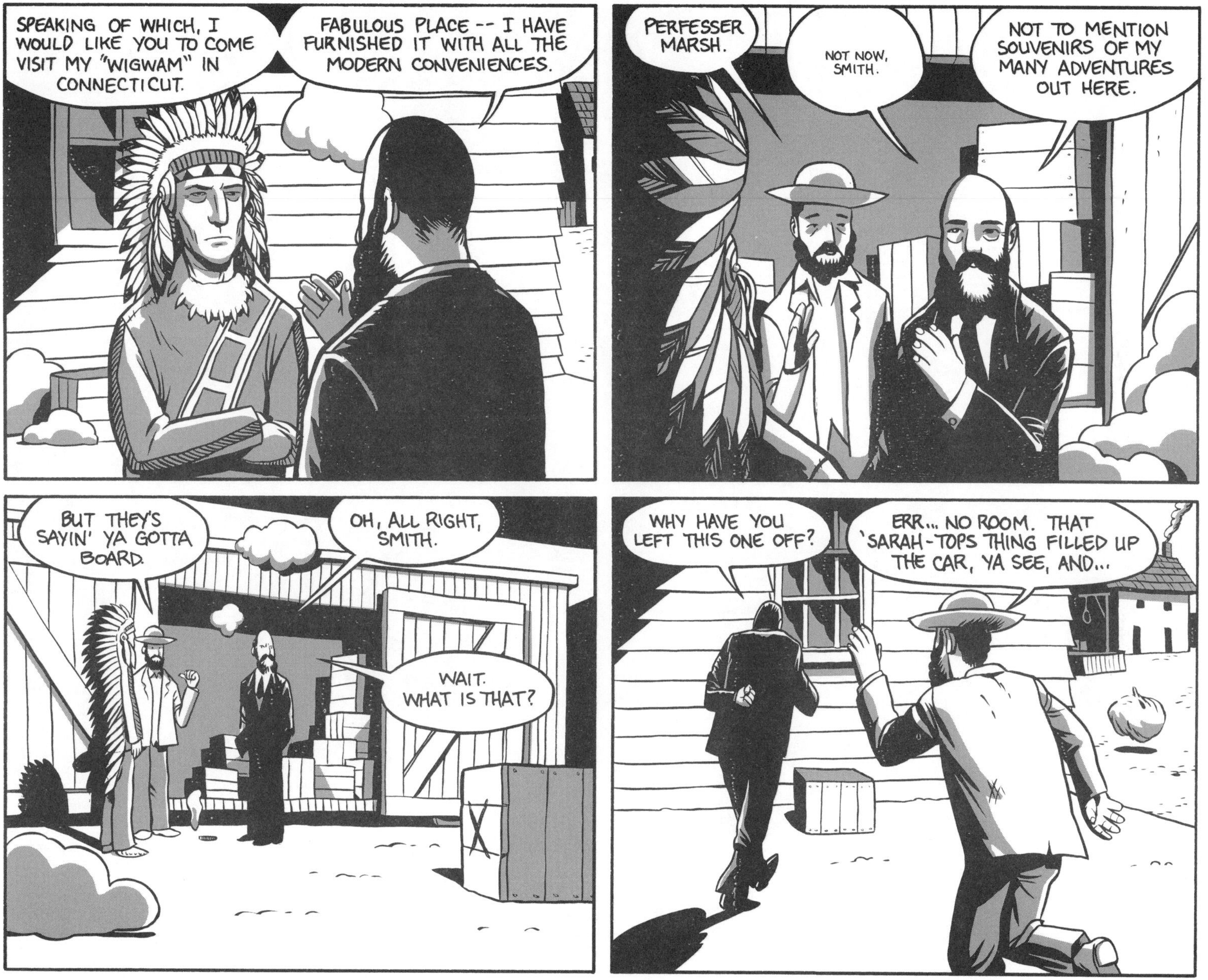
SPEAKING OF WHICH, I WOULD LIKE YOU TO COME VISIT MY "WIGWAM" IN CONNECTICUT.
FABULOUS PLACE -- I HAVE FURNISHED IT WITH ALL THE MODERN CONVENIENCES.
PERFESSER MARSH.
NOT NOW, SMITH.
NOT TO MENTION SOUVENIRS OF MY MANY ADVENTURES OUT HERE.
BUT THEY'S SAYIN' YA GOTTA BOARD.
OH, ALL RIGHT, SMITH.
WAIT. WHAT IS THAT?
WHY HAVE YOU LEFT THIS ONE OFF?
ERR... NO ROOM. THAT 'SARAH-TOPS THING FILLED UP THE CAR, YA SEE, AND...

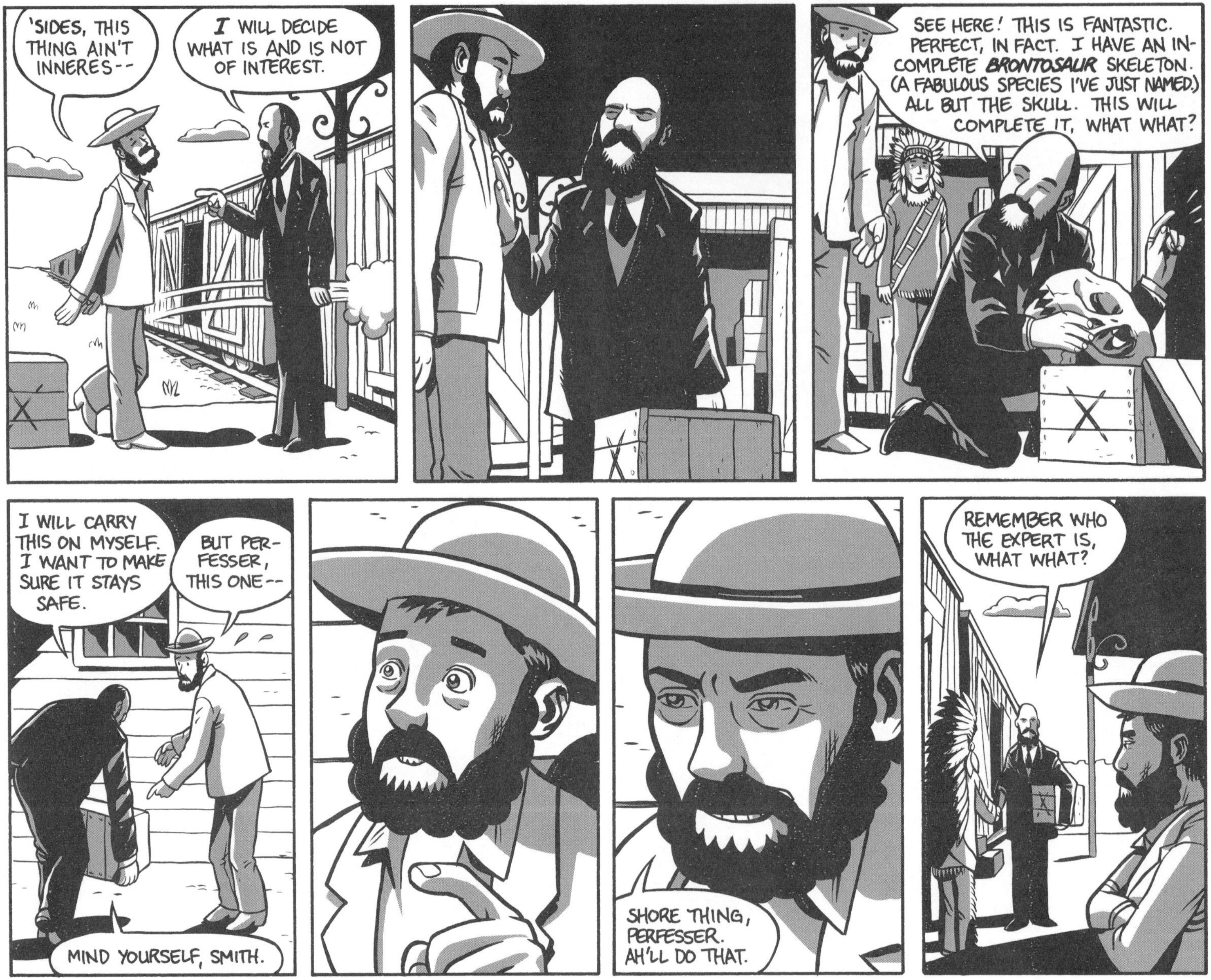
'SIDES, THIS THING AIN'T INNERES--
I WILL DECIDE WHAT IS AND IS NOT OF INTEREST.
SEE HERE! THIS IS FANTASTIC. PERFECT, IN FACT. I HAVE AN INCOMPLETE BRONTOSAUR SKELETON. (A FABULOUS SPECIES I'VE JUST NAMED.) ALL BUT THE SKULL. THIS WILL COMPLETE IT, WHAT WHAT?
I WILL CARRY THIS ON MYSELF. I WANT TO MAKE SURE IT STAYS SAFE.
BUT PERFESSER, THIS ONE--
MIND YOURSELF, SMITH.
SHORE THING, PERFESSER. AH'LL DO THAT.
REMEMBER WHO THE EXPERT IS, WHAT WHAT?

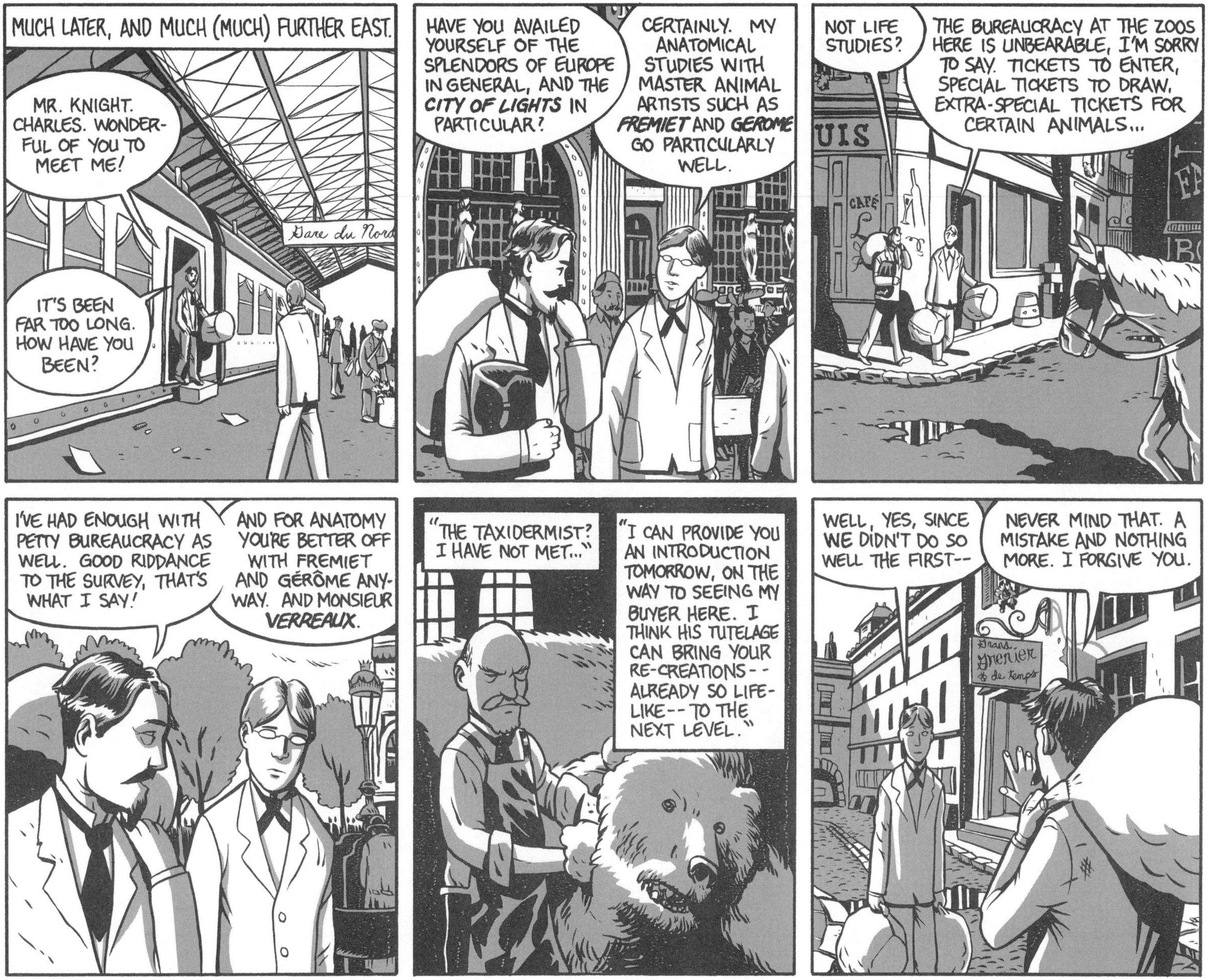
MUCH LATER, AND MUCH (MUCH) FURTHER EAST.
MR. KNIGHT. CHARLES. WONDERFUL OF YOU TO MEET ME!
IT'S BEEN FAR TOO LONG. HOW HAVE YOU BEEN?
Gare du Nord
HAVE YOU AVAILED YOURSELF OF THE SPLENDORS OF EUROPE IN GENERAL, AND THE CITY OF LIGHTS IN PARTICULAR?
CERTAINLY. MY ANATOMICAL STUDIES WITH MASTER ANIMAL ARTISTS SUCH AS FREMIET AND GEROME GO PARTICULARLY WELL.
NOT LIFE STUDIES?
THE BUREAUCRACY AT THE ZOOS HERE IS UNBEARABLE, I'M SORRY TO SAY. TICKETS TO ENTER, SPECIAL TICKETS TO DRAW, EXTRA-SPECIAL TICKETS FOR CERTAIN ANIMALS...
UIS
CAFÉ
I'VE HAD ENOUGH WITH PETTY BUREAUCRACY AS WELL. GOOD RIDDANCE TO THE SURVEY, THAT'S WHAT I SAY!
AND FOR ANATOMY YOU'RE BETTER OFF WITH FREMIET AND GÉRÔME ANYWAY. AND MONSIEUR VERREAUX.
"THE TAXIDERMIST? I HAVE NOT MET..."
"I CAN PROVIDE YOU AN INTRODUCTION TOMORROW, ON THE WAY TO SEEING MY BUYER HERE. I THINK HIS TUTELAGE CAN BRING YOUR RE-CREATIONS--ALREADY SO LIFE-LIKE--TO THE NEXT LEVEL."
WELL, YES, SINCE WE DIDN'T DO SO WELL THE FIRST--
NEVER MIND THAT. A MISTAKE AND NOTHING MORE. I FORGIVE YOU.
Grenier de temps

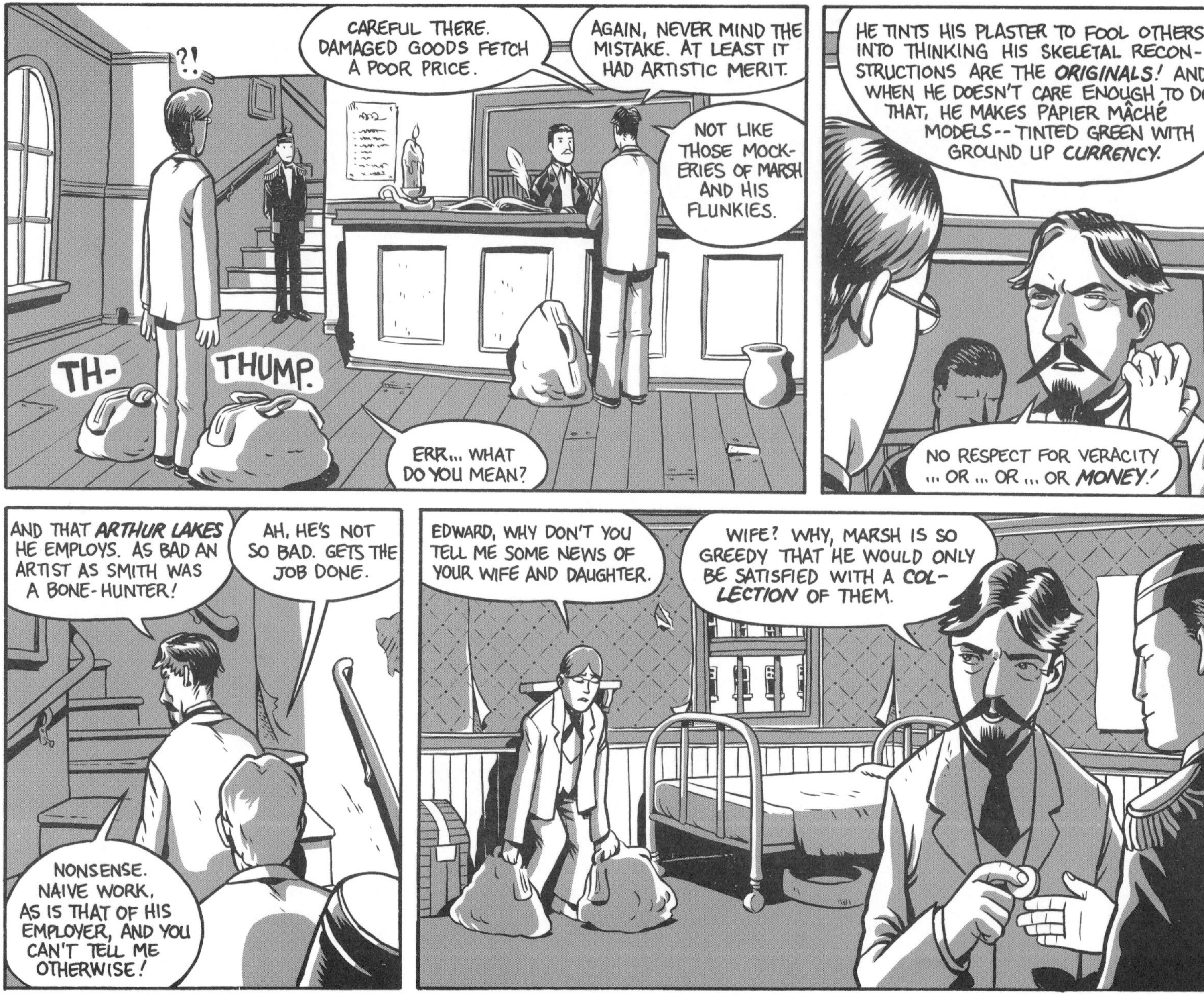
?!
TH-
THUMP.
CAREFUL THERE. DAMAGED GOODS FETCH A POOR PRICE.
AGAIN, NEVER MIND THE MISTAKE. AT LEAST IT HAD ARTISTIC MERIT.
NOT LIKE THOSE MOCKERIES OF MARSH AND HIS FLUNKIES.
ERR... WHAT DO YOU MEAN?
HE TINTS HIS PLASTER TO FOOL OTHERS INTO THINKING HIS SKELETAL RECONSTRUCTIONS ARE THE ORIGINALS! AND WHEN HE DOESN'T CARE ENOUGH TO DO THAT, HE MAKES PAPIER MÂCHÉ MODELS-- TINTED GREEN WITH GROUND UP CURRENCY.
NO RESPECT FOR VERACITY ... OR ... OR ... OR MONEY!
AND THAT ARTHUR LAKES HE EMPLOYS. AS BAD AN ARTIST AS SMITH WAS A BONE-HUNTER!
AH, HE'S NOT SO BAD. GETS THE JOB DONE.
NONSENSE. NAIVE WORK, AS IS THAT OF HIS EMPLOYER, AND YOU CAN'T TELL ME OTHERWISE!
EDWARD, WHY DON'T YOU TELL ME SOME NEWS OF YOUR WIFE AND DAUGHTER.
WIFE? WHY, MARSH IS SO GREEDY THAT HE WOULD ONLY BE SATISFIED WITH A COLLECTION OF THEM.

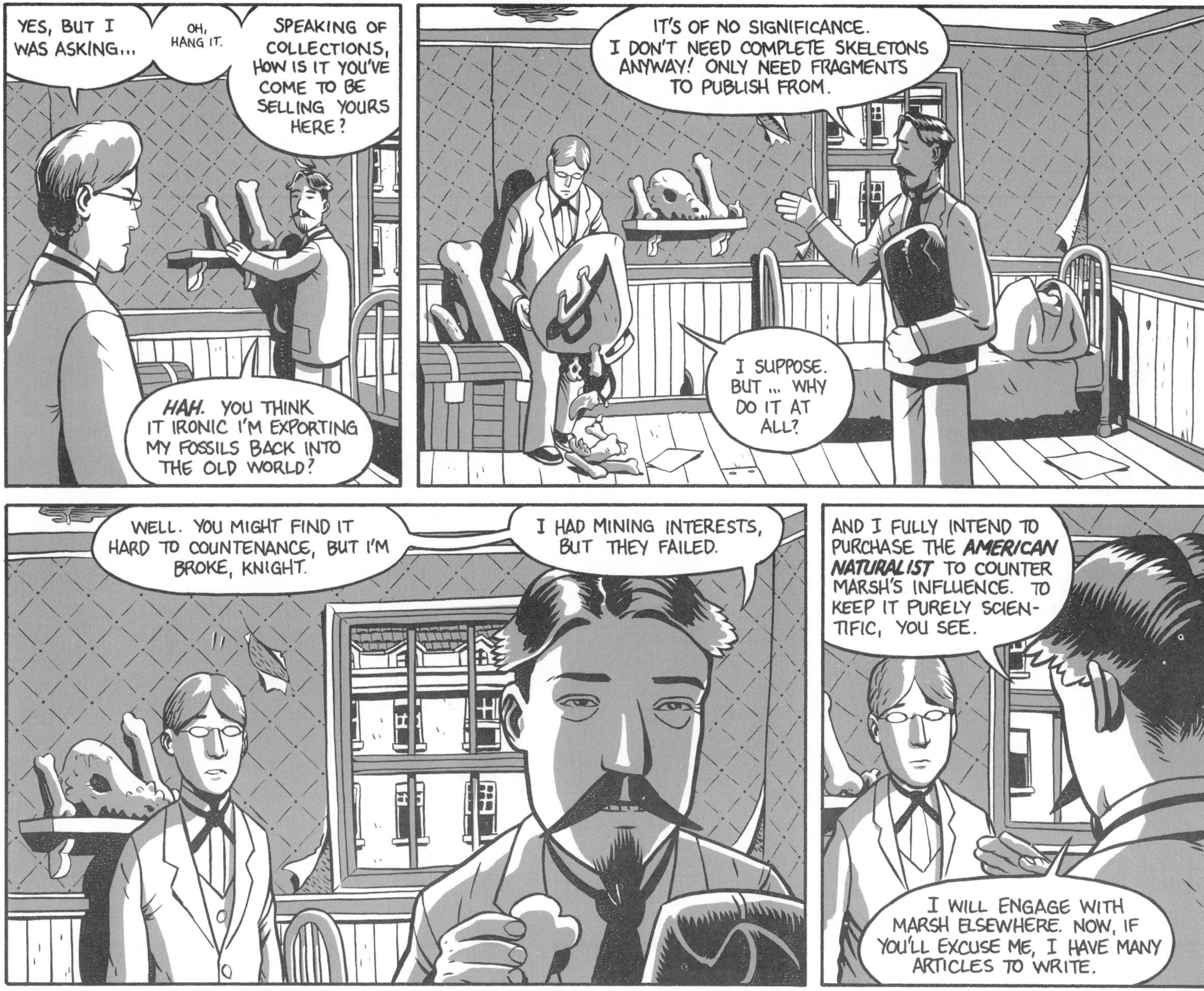

YES, BUT I WAS ASKING...
OH, HANG IT.
SPEAKING OF COLLECTIONS, HOW IS IT YOU'VE COME TO BE SELLING YOURS HERE?
HAH. YOU THINK IT IRONIC I'M EXPORTING MY FOSSILS BACK INTO THE OLD WORLD?
IT'S OF NO SIGNIFICANCE. I DON'T NEED COMPLETE SKELETONS ANYWAY! ONLY NEED FRAGMENTS TO PUBLISH FROM.
I SUPPOSE. BUT ... WHY DO IT AT ALL?
WELL. YOU MIGHT FIND IT HARD TO COUNTENANCE, BUT I'M BROKE, KNIGHT.
I HAD MINING INTERESTS, BUT THEY FAILED.
AND I FULLY INTEND TO PURCHASE THE AMERICAN NATURALIST TO COUNTER MARSH'S INFLUENCE. TO KEEP IT PURELY SCIENTIFIC, YOU SEE.
I WILL ENGAGE WITH MARSH ELSEWHERE. NOW, IF YOU'LL EXCUSE ME, I HAVE MANY ARTICLES TO WRITE.

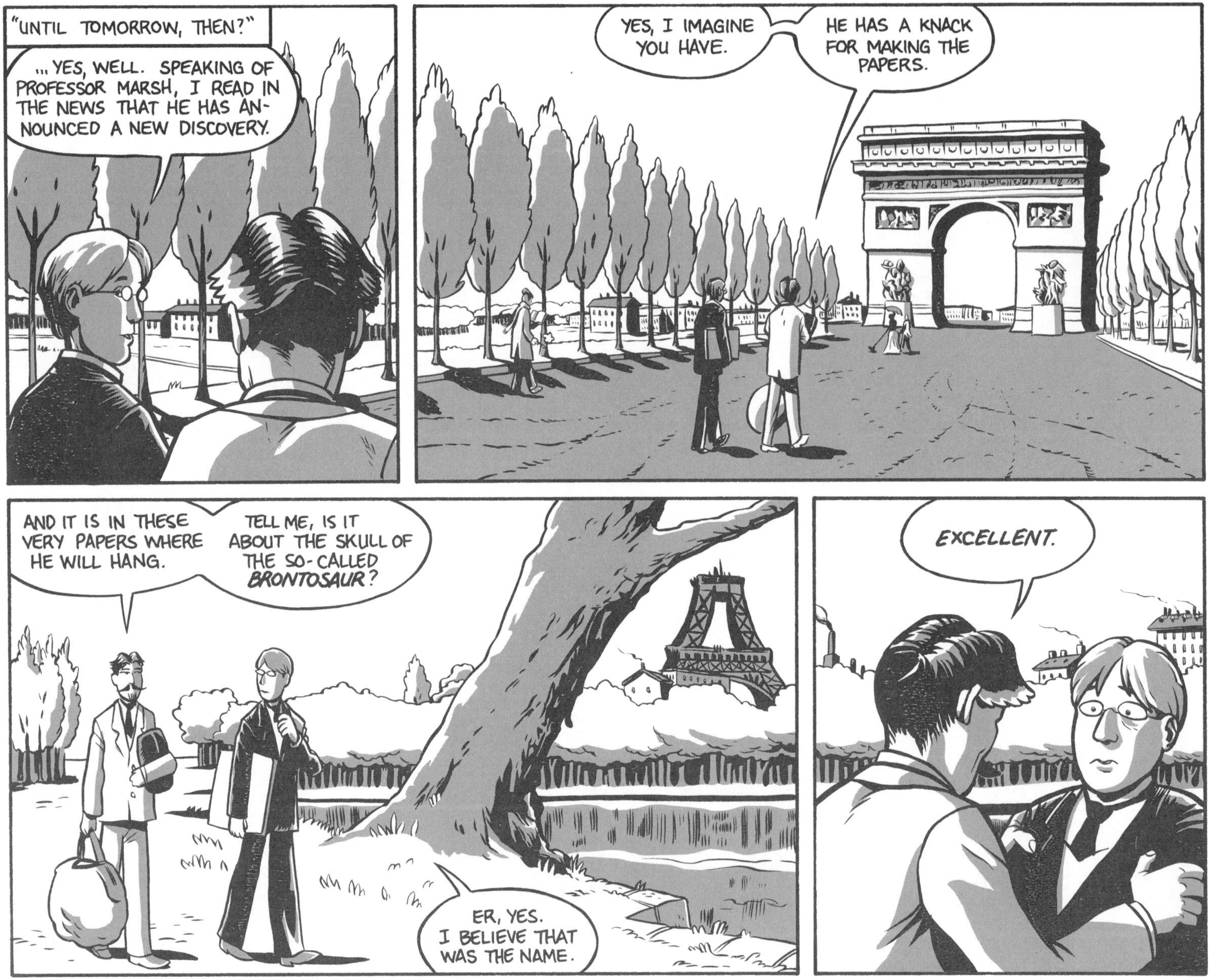
"UNTIL TOMORROW, THEN?"
... YES, WELL. SPEAKING OF PROFESSOR MARSH, I READ IN THE NEWS THAT HE HAS ANNOUNCED A NEW DISCOVERY.
YES, I IMAGINE YOU HAVE.
HE HAS A KNACK FOR MAKING THE PAPERS.
AND IT IS IN THESE VERY PAPERS WHERE HE WILL HANG.
TELL ME, IS IT ABOUT THE SKULL OF THE SO-CALLED *BRONTOSAUR*?
ER, YES. I BELIEVE THAT WAS THE NAME.
EXCELLENT.

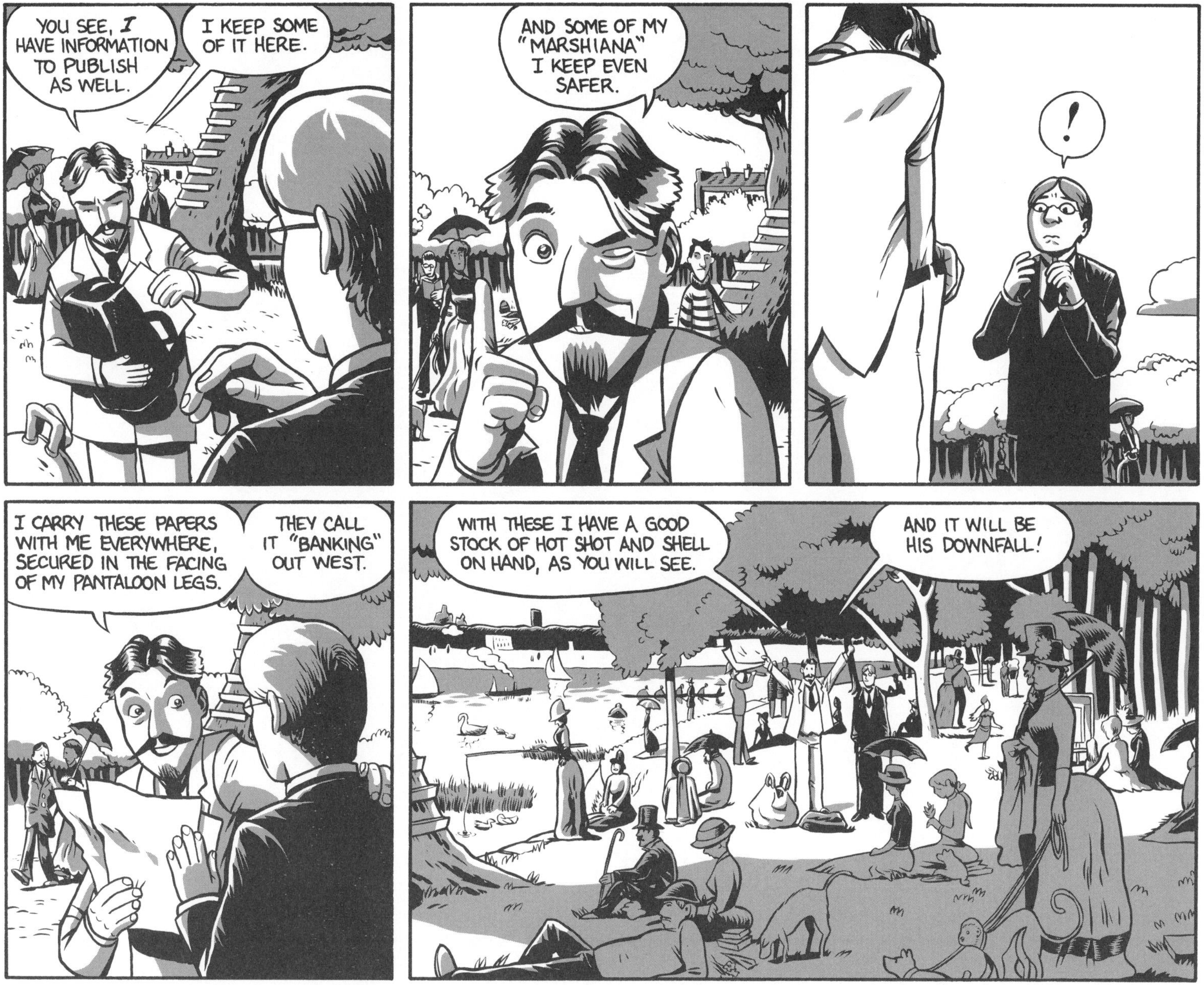
YOU SEE, *I* HAVE INFORMATION TO PUBLISH AS WELL.
I KEEP SOME OF IT HERE.
AND SOME OF MY "MARSHIANA" I KEEP EVEN SAFER.
!
I CARRY THESE PAPERS WITH ME EVERYWHERE, SECURED IN THE FACING OF MY PANTALOON LEGS.
THEY CALL IT "BANKING" OUT WEST.
WITH THESE I HAVE A GOOD STOCK OF HOT SHOT AND SHELL ON HAND, AS YOU WILL SEE.
AND IT WILL BE HIS DOWNFALL!

THUNDER LIZARDS

In which two of our protagonists make a great deal of noise, meet defeat at their own hands, &c.

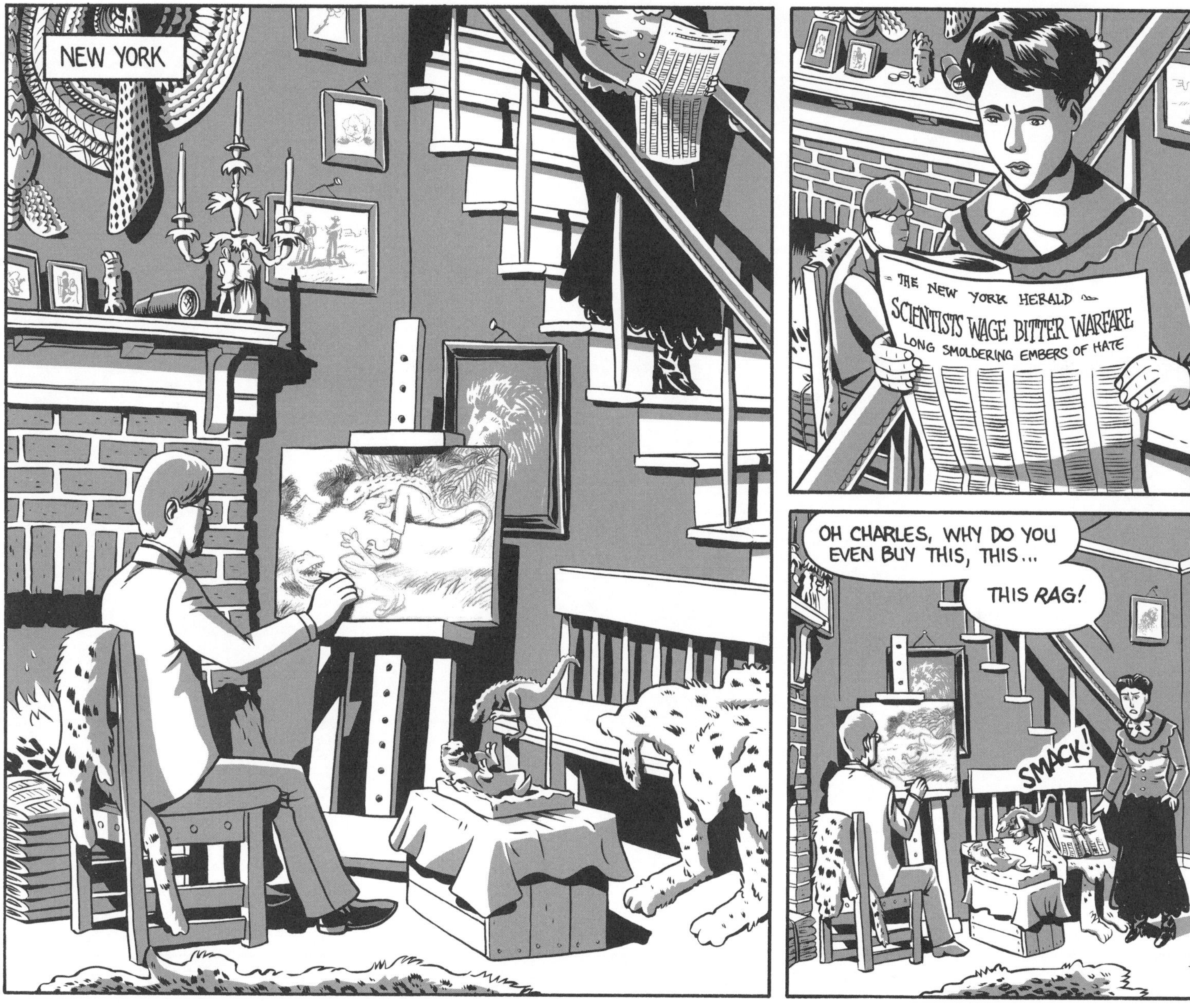
NEW YORK
THE NEW YORK HERALD
SCIENTISTS WAGE BITTER WARFARE
LONG SMOLDERING EMBERS OF HATE
OH CHARLES, WHY DO YOU EVEN BUY THIS, THIS...
THIS RAG!
SMACK!

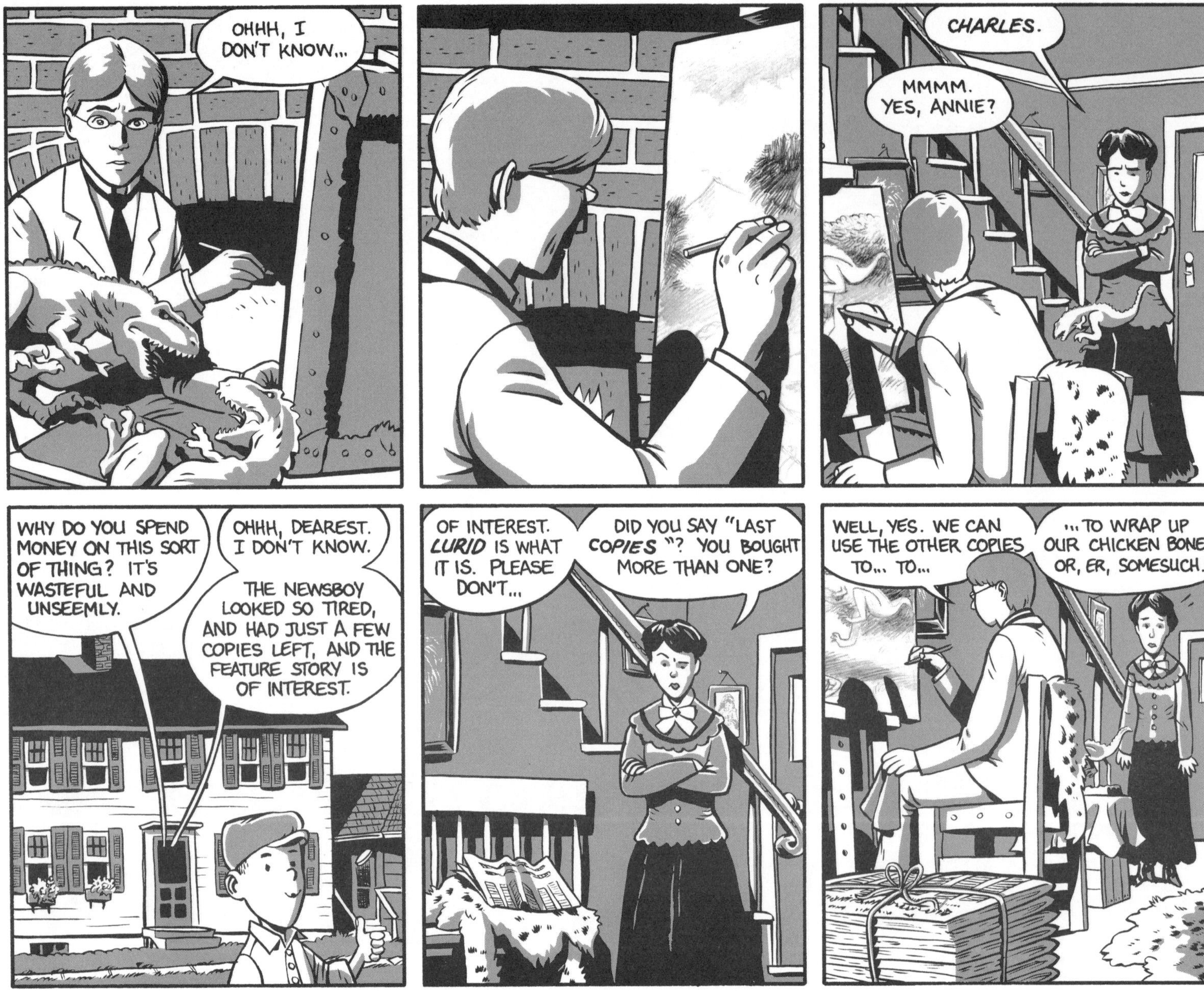
OHHH, I DON'T KNOW...
CHARLES.
MMMM. YES, ANNIE?
WHY DO YOU SPEND MONEY ON THIS SORT OF THING? IT'S WASTEFUL AND UNSEEMLY.
OHHH, DEAREST. I DON'T KNOW.
THE NEWSBOY LOOKED SO TIRED, AND HAD JUST A FEW COPIES LEFT, AND THE FEATURE STORY IS OF INTEREST.
OF INTEREST. LURID IS WHAT IT IS. PLEASE DON'T...
DID YOU SAY "LAST COPIES"? YOU BOUGHT MORE THAN ONE?
WELL, YES. WE CAN USE THE OTHER COPIES TO... TO...
...TO WRAP UP OUR CHICKEN BONES OR, ER, SOMESUCH!

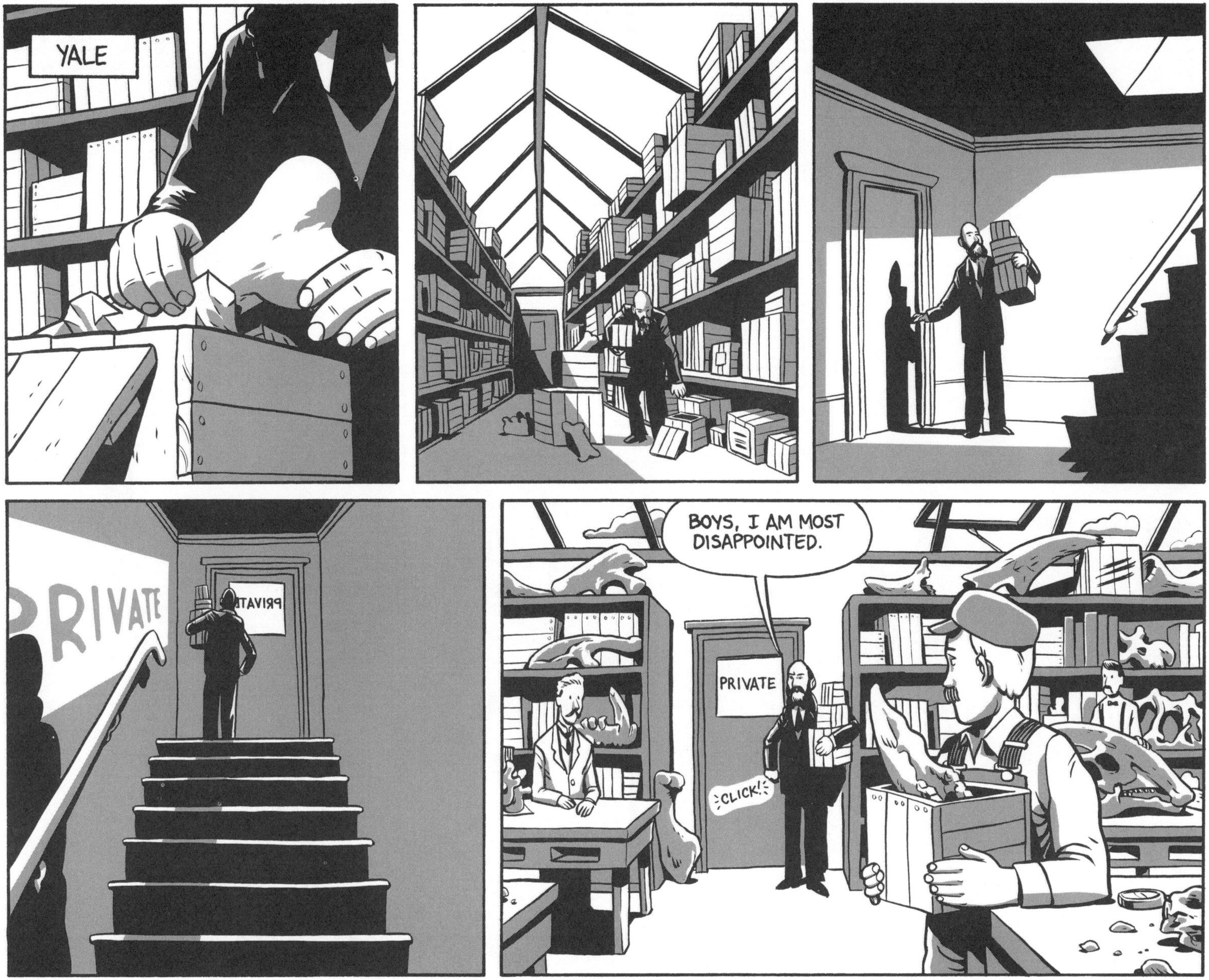
YALE
PRIVATE
BOYS, I AM MOST DISAPPOINTED.
PRIVATE
CLICK!

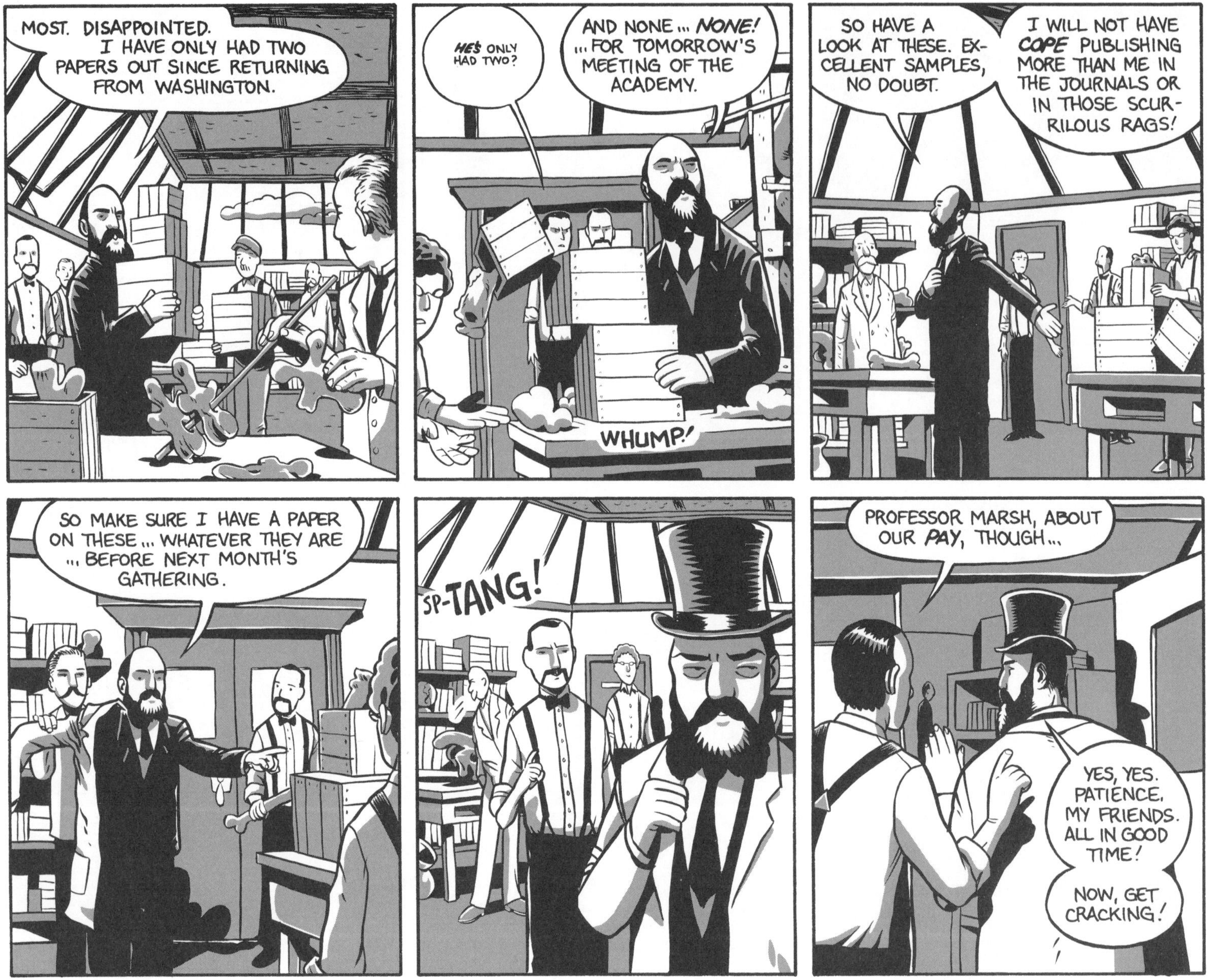

MOST. DISAPPOINTED. I HAVE ONLY HAD TWO PAPERS OUT SINCE RETURNING FROM WASHINGTON.
HE'S ONLY HAD TWO?
AND NONE ... NONE! ... FOR TOMORROW'S MEETING OF THE ACADEMY.
WHUMP!
SO HAVE A LOOK AT THESE. EXCELLENT SAMPLES, NO DOUBT.
I WILL NOT HAVE COPE PUBLISHING MORE THAN ME IN THE JOURNALS OR IN THOSE SCURRILOUS RAGS!
SO MAKE SURE I HAVE A PAPER ON THESE ... WHATEVER THEY ARE ... BEFORE NEXT MONTH'S GATHERING.
SP-TANG!
PROFESSOR MARSH, ABOUT OUR PAY, THOUGH...
YES, YES. PATIENCE, MY FRIENDS. ALL IN GOOD TIME!
NOW, GET CRACKING!

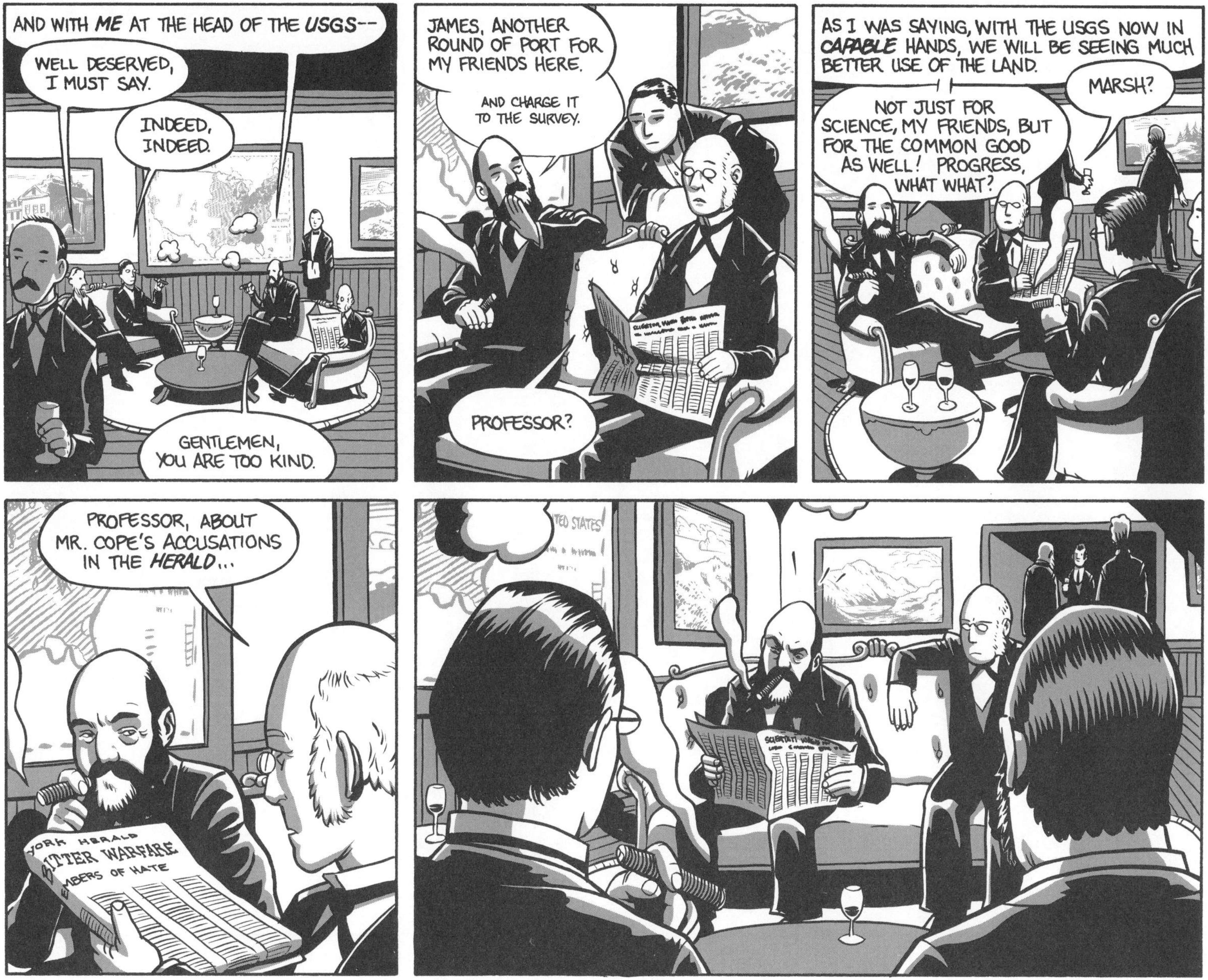
AND WITH *ME* AT THE HEAD OF THE *USGS*--
WELL DESERVED, I MUST SAY.
INDEED, INDEED.
GENTLEMEN, YOU ARE TOO KIND.
JAMES, ANOTHER ROUND OF PORT FOR MY FRIENDS HERE.
AND CHARGE IT TO THE SURVEY.
PROFESSOR?
AS I WAS SAYING, WITH THE USGS NOW IN *CAPABLE* HANDS, WE WILL BE SEEING MUCH BETTER USE OF THE LAND.
NOT JUST FOR SCIENCE, MY FRIENDS, BUT FOR THE COMMON GOOD AS WELL! PROGRESS, WHAT WHAT?
MARSH?
PROFESSOR, ABOUT MR. COPE'S ACCUSATIONS IN THE *HERALD*...
YORK HERALD
ITTER WARFARE
MBERS OF HATE

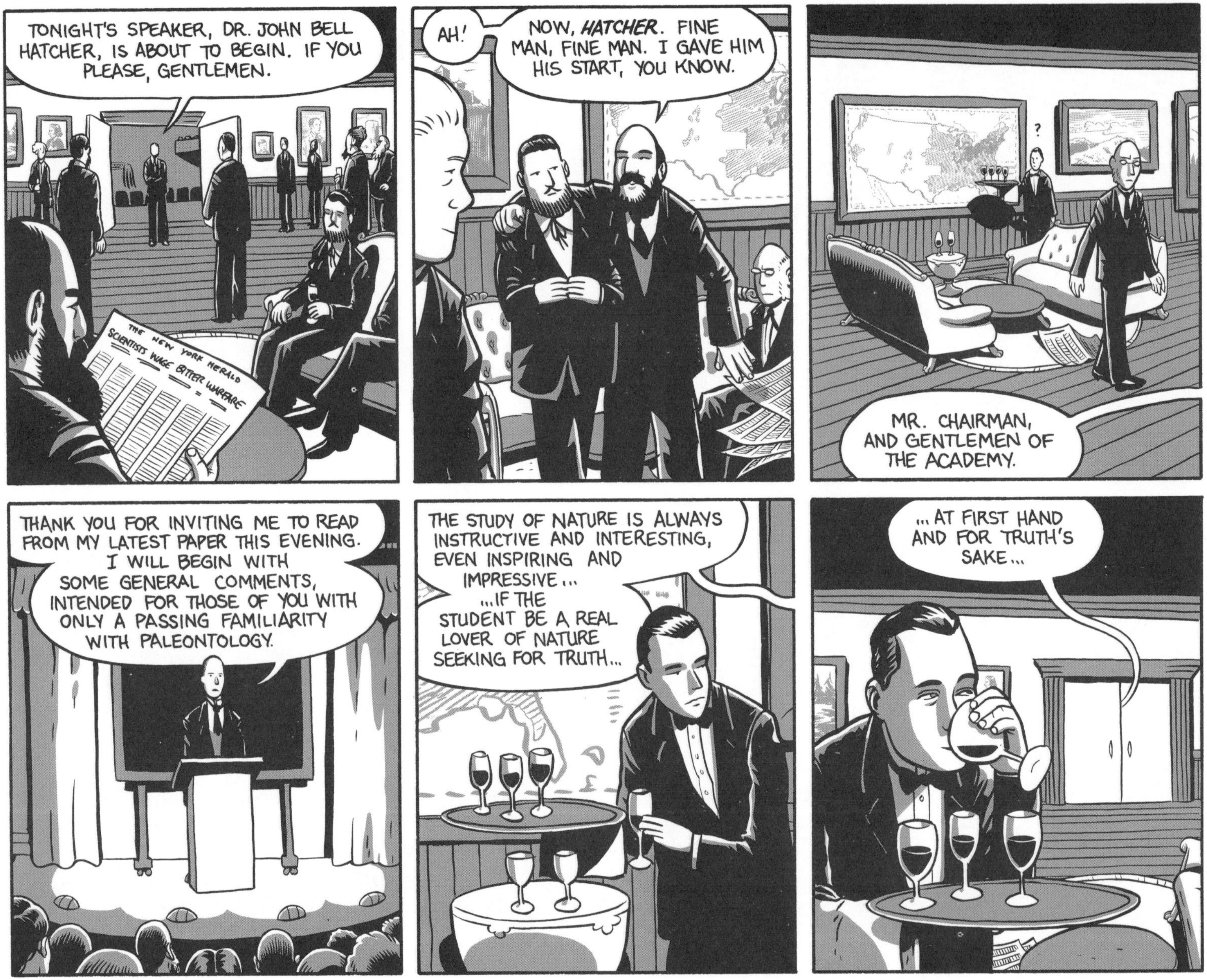
TONIGHT'S SPEAKER, DR. JOHN BELL HATCHER, IS ABOUT TO BEGIN. IF YOU PLEASE, GENTLEMEN.
THE NEW YORK HERALD
SCIENTISTS WAGE BITTER WARFARE
AH!
NOW, HATCHER. FINE MAN, FINE MAN. I GAVE HIM HIS START, YOU KNOW.
?
MR. CHAIRMAN, AND GENTLEMEN OF THE ACADEMY.
THANK YOU FOR INVITING ME TO READ FROM MY LATEST PAPER THIS EVENING. I WILL BEGIN WITH SOME GENERAL COMMENTS, INTENDED FOR THOSE OF YOU WITH ONLY A PASSING FAMILIARITY WITH PALEONTOLOGY.
THE STUDY OF NATURE IS ALWAYS INSTRUCTIVE AND INTERESTING, EVEN INSPIRING AND IMPRESSIVE...
...IF THE STUDENT BE A REAL LOVER OF NATURE SEEKING FOR TRUTH...
...AT FIRST HAND AND FOR TRUTH'S SAKE...

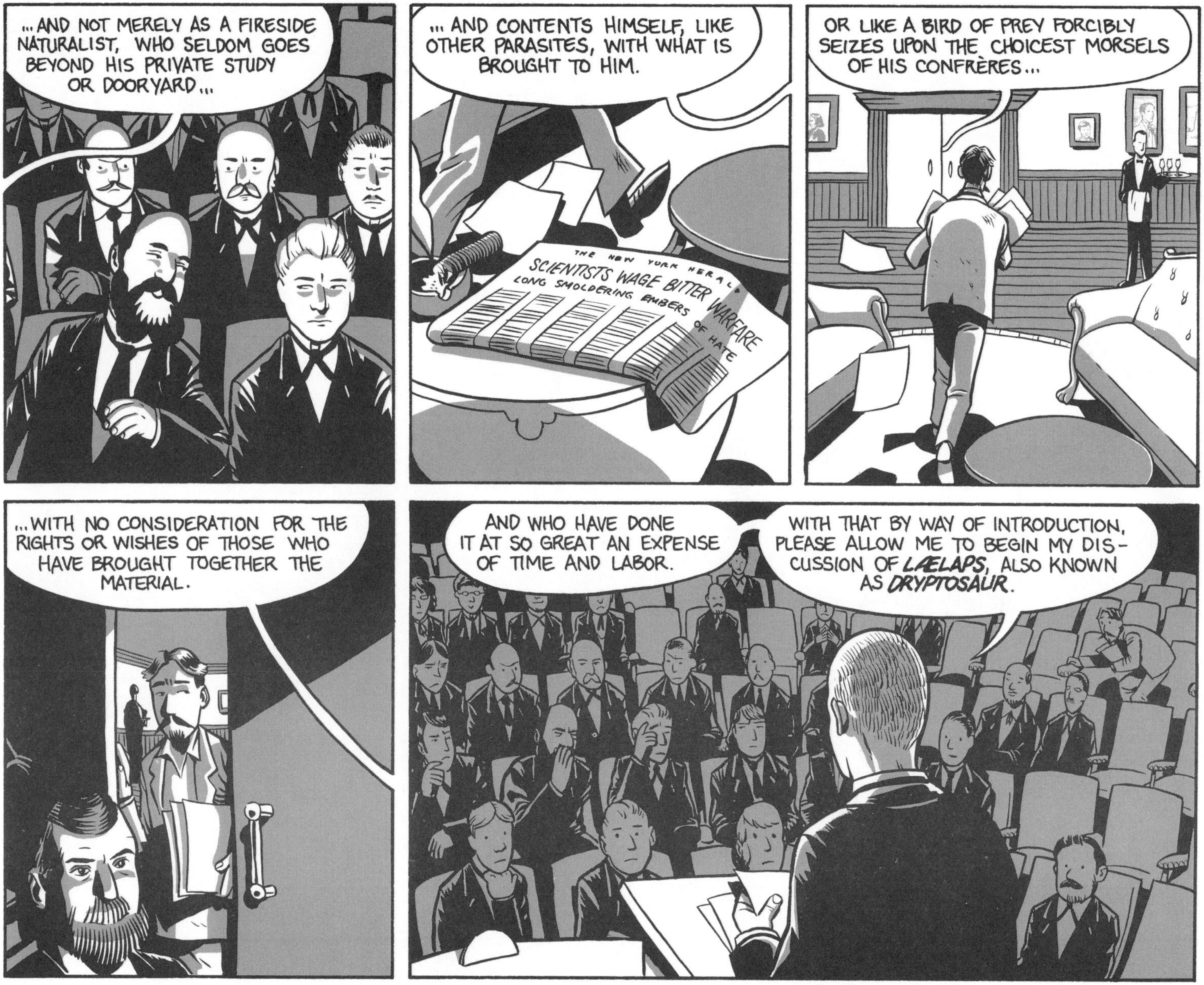
...AND NOT MERELY AS A FIRESIDE NATURALIST, WHO SELDOM GOES BEYOND HIS PRIVATE STUDY OR DOORYARD...
...AND CONTENTS HIMSELF, LIKE OTHER PARASITES, WITH WHAT IS BROUGHT TO HIM.
THE NEW YORK HERALD
SCIENTISTS WAGE BITTER WARFARE
LONG SMOLDERING EMBERS OF HATE
OR LIKE A BIRD OF PREY FORCIBLY SEIZES UPON THE CHOICEST MORSELS OF HIS CONFRÈRES...
...WITH NO CONSIDERATION FOR THE RIGHTS OR WISHES OF THOSE WHO HAVE BROUGHT TOGETHER THE MATERIAL.
AND WHO HAVE DONE IT AT SO GREAT AN EXPENSE OF TIME AND LABOR.
WITH THAT BY WAY OF INTRODUCTION, PLEASE ALLOW ME TO BEGIN MY DIS-CUSSION OF *LÆLAPS*, ALSO KNOWN AS *DRYPTOSAUR*.

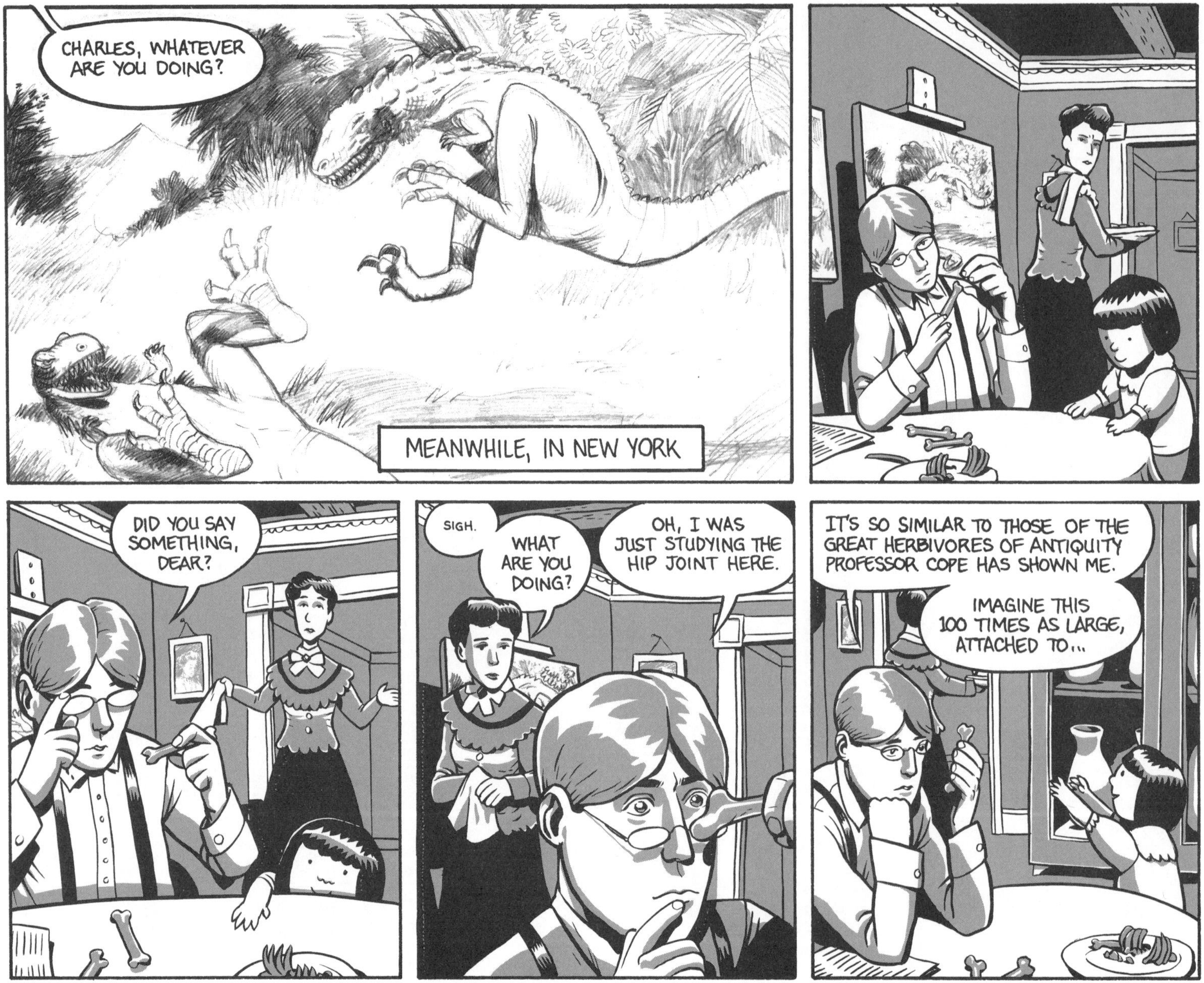
CHARLES, WHATEVER ARE YOU DOING?
MEANWHILE, IN NEW YORK
DID YOU SAY SOMETHING, DEAR?
SIGH.
WHAT ARE YOU DOING?
OH, I WAS JUST STUDYING THE HIP JOINT HERE.
IT'S SO SIMILAR TO THOSE OF THE GREAT HERBIVORES OF ANTIQUITY PROFESSOR COPE HAS SHOWN ME.
IMAGINE THIS 100 TIMES AS LARGE, ATTACHED TO...

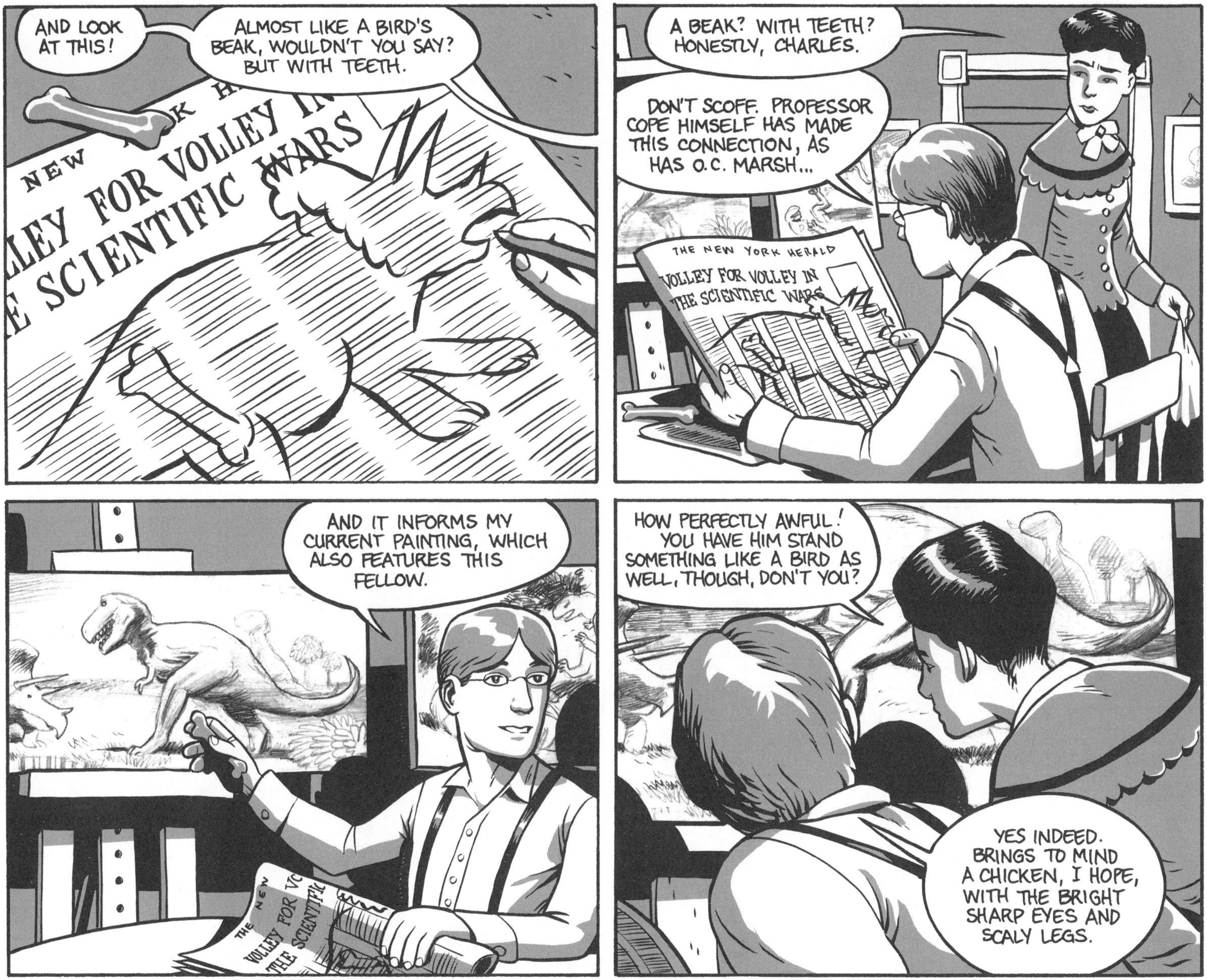
AND LOOK AT THIS!
ALMOST LIKE A BIRD'S BEAK, WOULDN'T YOU SAY? BUT WITH TEETH.
A BEAK? WITH TEETH? HONESTLY, CHARLES.
DON'T SCOFF. PROFESSOR COPE HIMSELF HAS MADE THIS CONNECTION, AS HAS O.C. MARSH...
THE NEW YORK HERALD
VOLLEY FOR VOLLEY IN THE SCIENTIFIC WARS
AND IT INFORMS MY CURRENT PAINTING, WHICH ALSO FEATURES THIS FELLOW.
HOW PERFECTLY AWFUL! YOU HAVE HIM STAND SOMETHING LIKE A BIRD AS WELL, THOUGH, DON'T YOU?
YES INDEED. BRINGS TO MIND A CHICKEN, I HOPE, WITH THE BRIGHT SHARP EYES AND SCALY LEGS.

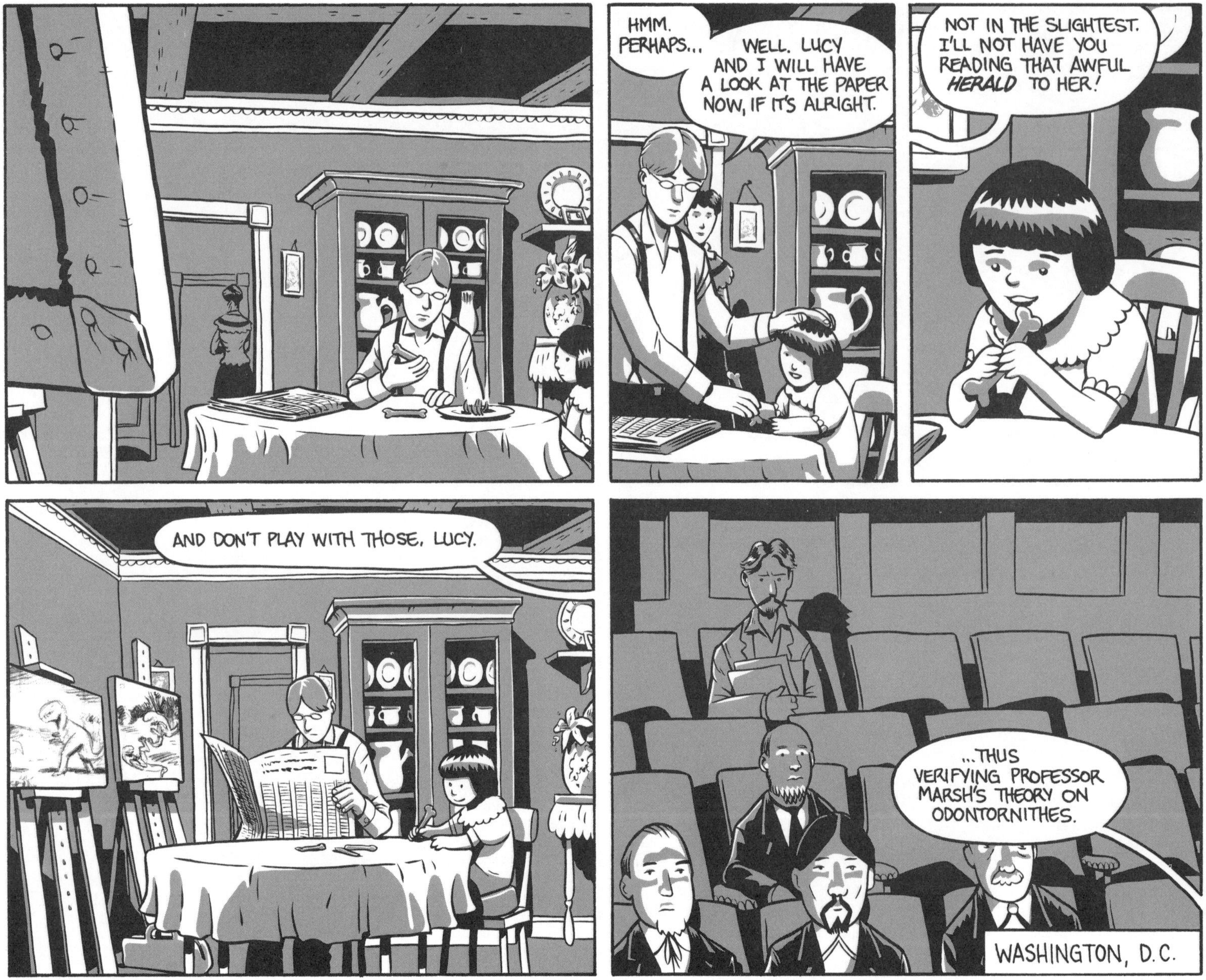
HMM. PERHAPS...
WELL. LUCY AND I WILL HAVE A LOOK AT THE PAPER NOW, IF IT'S ALRIGHT.
NOT IN THE SLIGHTEST. I'LL NOT HAVE YOU READING THAT AWFUL ***HERALD*** TO HER!
AND DON'T PLAY WITH THOSE, LUCY.
...THUS VERIFYING PROFESSOR MARSH'S THEORY ON ODONTORNITHES.
WASHINGTON, D.C.

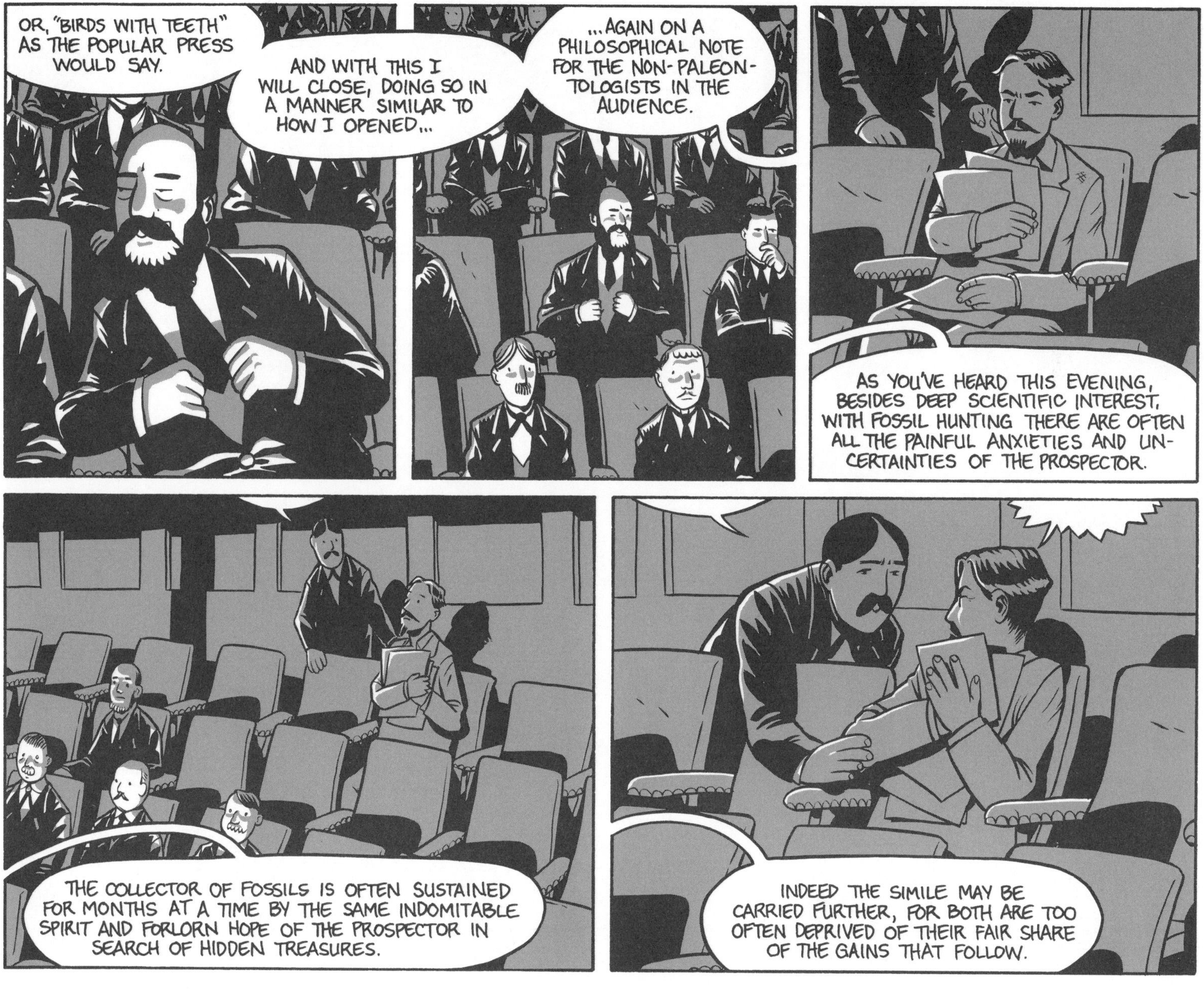

OR, "BIRDS WITH TEETH" AS THE POPULAR PRESS WOULD SAY.
AND WITH THIS I WILL CLOSE, DOING SO IN A MANNER SIMILAR TO HOW I OPENED...
...AGAIN ON A PHILOSOPHICAL NOTE FOR THE NON-PALEONTOLOGISTS IN THE AUDIENCE.
AS YOU'VE HEARD THIS EVENING, BESIDES DEEP SCIENTIFIC INTEREST, WITH FOSSIL HUNTING THERE ARE OFTEN ALL THE PAINFUL ANXIETIES AND UNCERTAINTIES OF THE PROSPECTOR.
THE COLLECTOR OF FOSSILS IS OFTEN SUSTAINED FOR MONTHS AT A TIME BY THE SAME INDOMITABLE SPIRIT AND FORLORN HOPE OF THE PROSPECTOR IN SEARCH OF HIDDEN TREASURES.
INDEED THE SIMILE MAY BE CARRIED FURTHER, FOR BOTH ARE TOO OFTEN DEPRIVED OF THEIR FAIR SHARE OF THE GAINS THAT FOLLOW.

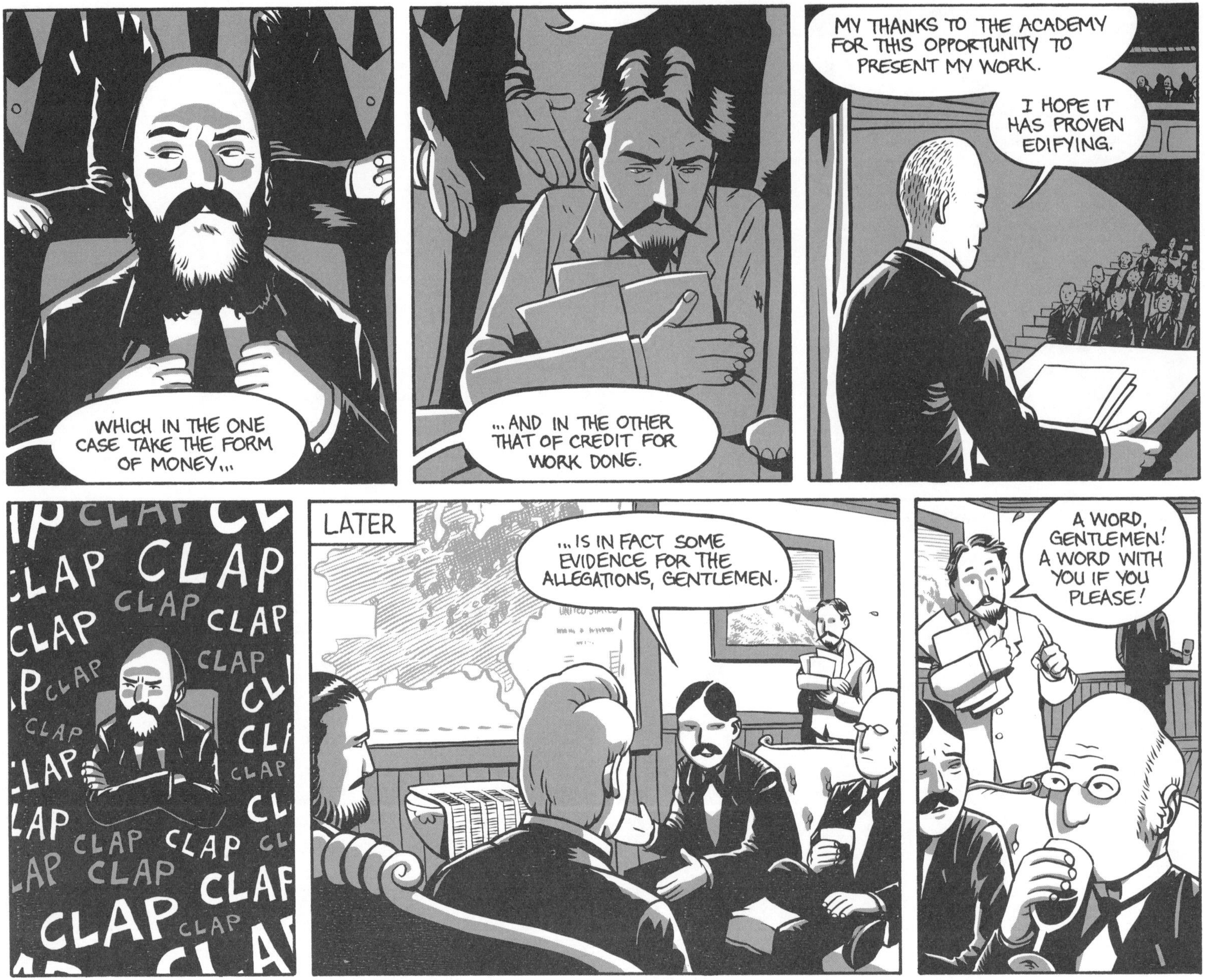
WHICH IN THE ONE CASE TAKE THE FORM OF MONEY...
...AND IN THE OTHER THAT OF CREDIT FOR WORK DONE.
MY THANKS TO THE ACADEMY FOR THIS OPPORTUNITY TO PRESENT MY WORK.
I HOPE IT HAS PROVEN EDIFYING.
CLAP CLAP CLAP CLAP CLAP CLAP CLAP CLAP CLAP CLAP CLAP CLAP CLAP CLAP CLAP CLAP CLAP
LATER
...IS IN FACT SOME EVIDENCE FOR THE ALLEGATIONS, GENTLEMEN.
A WORD, GENTLEMEN! A WORD WITH YOU IF YOU PLEASE!

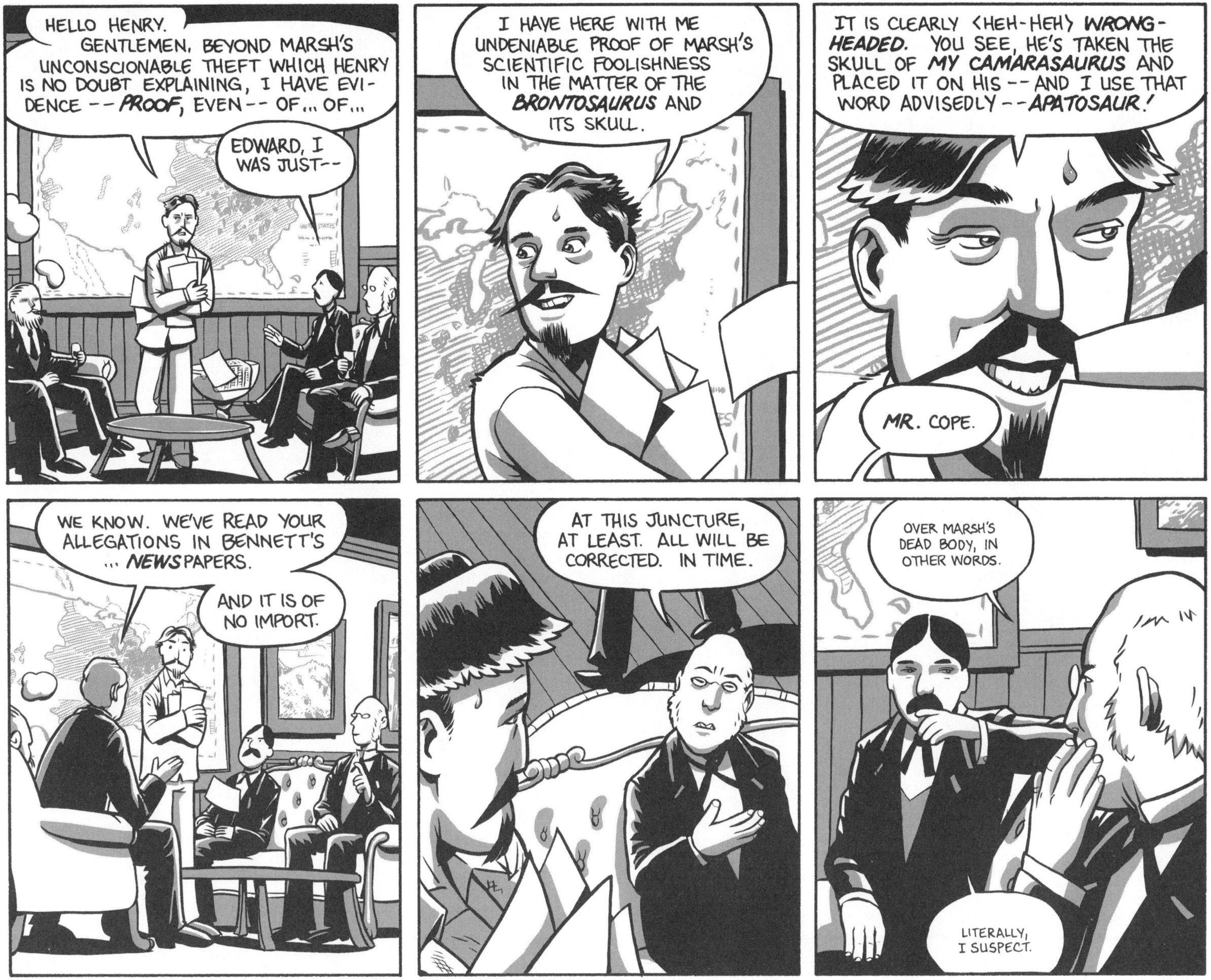
HELLO HENRY.
GENTLEMEN, BEYOND MARSH'S UNCONSCIONABLE THEFT WHICH HENRY IS NO DOUBT EXPLAINING, I HAVE EVIDENCE -- PROOF, EVEN -- OF... OF...
EDWARD, I WAS JUST--
I HAVE HERE WITH ME UNDENIABLE PROOF OF MARSH'S SCIENTIFIC FOOLISHNESS IN THE MATTER OF THE BRONTOSAURUS AND ITS SKULL.
IT IS CLEARLY <HEH-HEH> WRONG-HEADED. YOU SEE, HE'S TAKEN THE SKULL OF MY CAMARASAURUS AND PLACED IT ON HIS -- AND I USE THAT WORD ADVISEDLY -- APATOSAUR!
MR. COPE.
WE KNOW. WE'VE READ YOUR ALLEGATIONS IN BENNETT'S ... NEWSPAPERS.
AND IT IS OF NO IMPORT.
AT THIS JUNCTURE, AT LEAST. ALL WILL BE CORRECTED. IN TIME.
OVER MARSH'S DEAD BODY, IN OTHER WORDS.
LITERALLY, I SUSPECT.

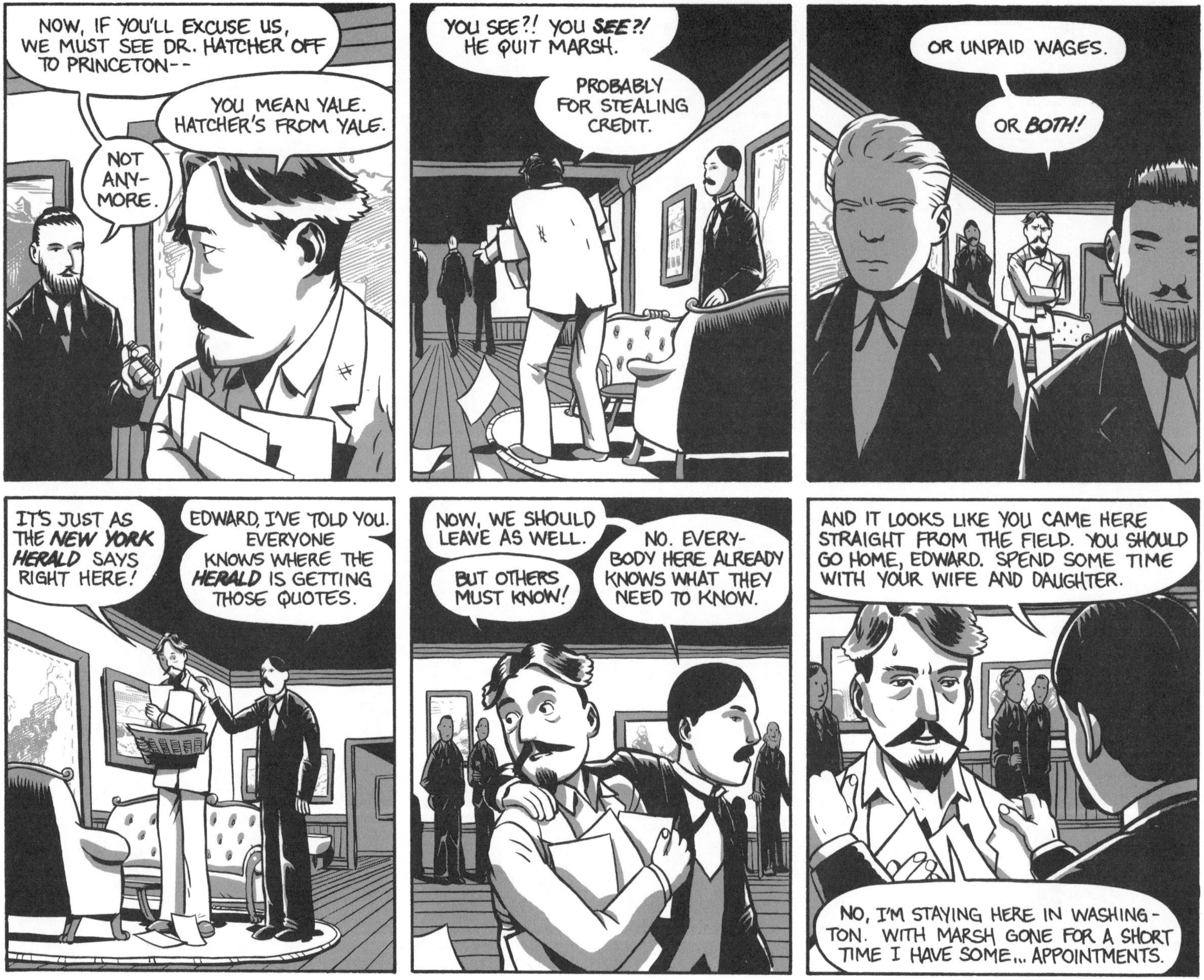
NOW, IF YOU'LL EXCUSE US, WE MUST SEE DR. HATCHER OFF TO PRINCETON--
YOU MEAN YALE. HATCHER'S FROM YALE.
NOT ANY-MORE.
YOU SEE?! YOU SEE?! HE QUIT MARSH.
PROBABLY FOR STEALING CREDIT.
OR UNPAID WAGES.
OR BOTH!
IT'S JUST AS THE NEW YORK HERALD SAYS RIGHT HERE!
EDWARD, I'VE TOLD YOU. EVERYONE KNOWS WHERE THE HERALD IS GETTING THOSE QUOTES.
NOW, WE SHOULD LEAVE AS WELL.
BUT OTHERS MUST KNOW!
NO. EVERY-BODY HERE ALREADY KNOWS WHAT THEY NEED TO KNOW.
AND IT LOOKS LIKE YOU CAME HERE STRAIGHT FROM THE FIELD. YOU SHOULD GO HOME, EDWARD. SPEND SOME TIME WITH YOUR WIFE AND DAUGHTER.
NO, I'M STAYING HERE IN WASHING-TON. WITH MARSH GONE FOR A SHORT TIME I HAVE SOME... APPOINTMENTS.

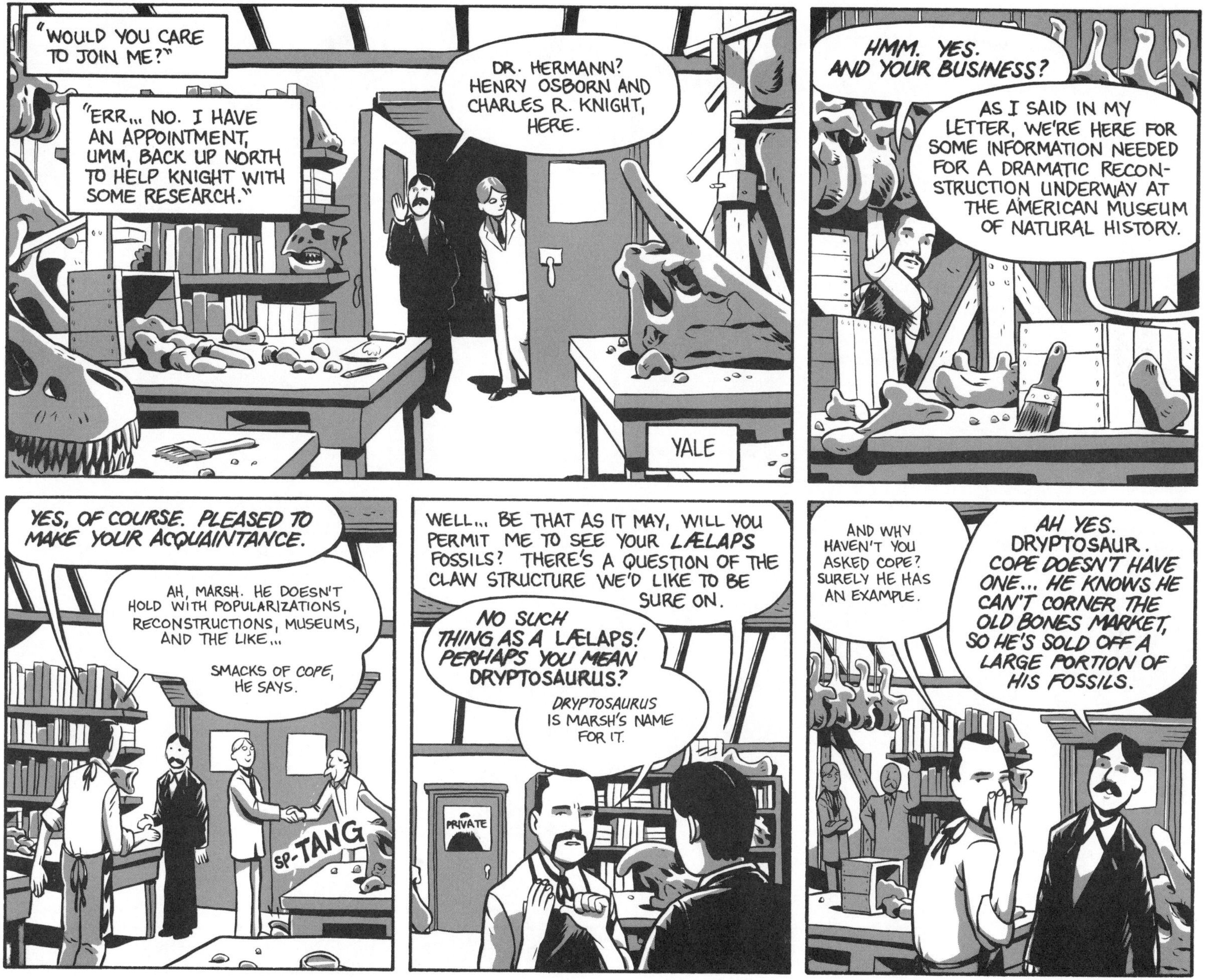
"WOULD YOU CARE TO JOIN ME?"
"ERR... NO. I HAVE AN APPOINTMENT, UMM, BACK UP NORTH TO HELP KNIGHT WITH SOME RESEARCH."
DR. HERMANN? HENRY OSBORN AND CHARLES R. KNIGHT, HERE.
YALE
HMM. YES. AND YOUR BUSINESS?
AS I SAID IN MY LETTER, WE'RE HERE FOR SOME INFORMATION NEEDED FOR A DRAMATIC RECON-STRUCTION UNDERWAY AT THE AMERICAN MUSEUM OF NATURAL HISTORY.
YES, OF COURSE. PLEASED TO MAKE YOUR ACQUAINTANCE.
AH, MARSH. HE DOESN'T HOLD WITH POPULARIZATIONS, RECONSTRUCTIONS, MUSEUMS, AND THE LIKE...
SMACKS OF COPE, HE SAYS.
SP-TANG
WELL... BE THAT AS IT MAY, WILL YOU PERMIT ME TO SEE YOUR LÆLAPS FOSSILS? THERE'S A QUESTION OF THE CLAW STRUCTURE WE'D LIKE TO BE SURE ON.
NO SUCH THING AS A LÆLAPS! PERHAPS YOU MEAN DRYPTOSAURUS?
DRYPTOSAURUS IS MARSH'S NAME FOR IT.
PRIVATE
AND WHY HAVEN'T YOU ASKED COPE? SURELY HE HAS AN EXAMPLE.
AH YES. DRYPTOSAUR. COPE DOESN'T HAVE ONE... HE KNOWS HE CAN'T CORNER THE OLD BONES MARKET, SO HE'S SOLD OFF A LARGE PORTION OF HIS FOSSILS.

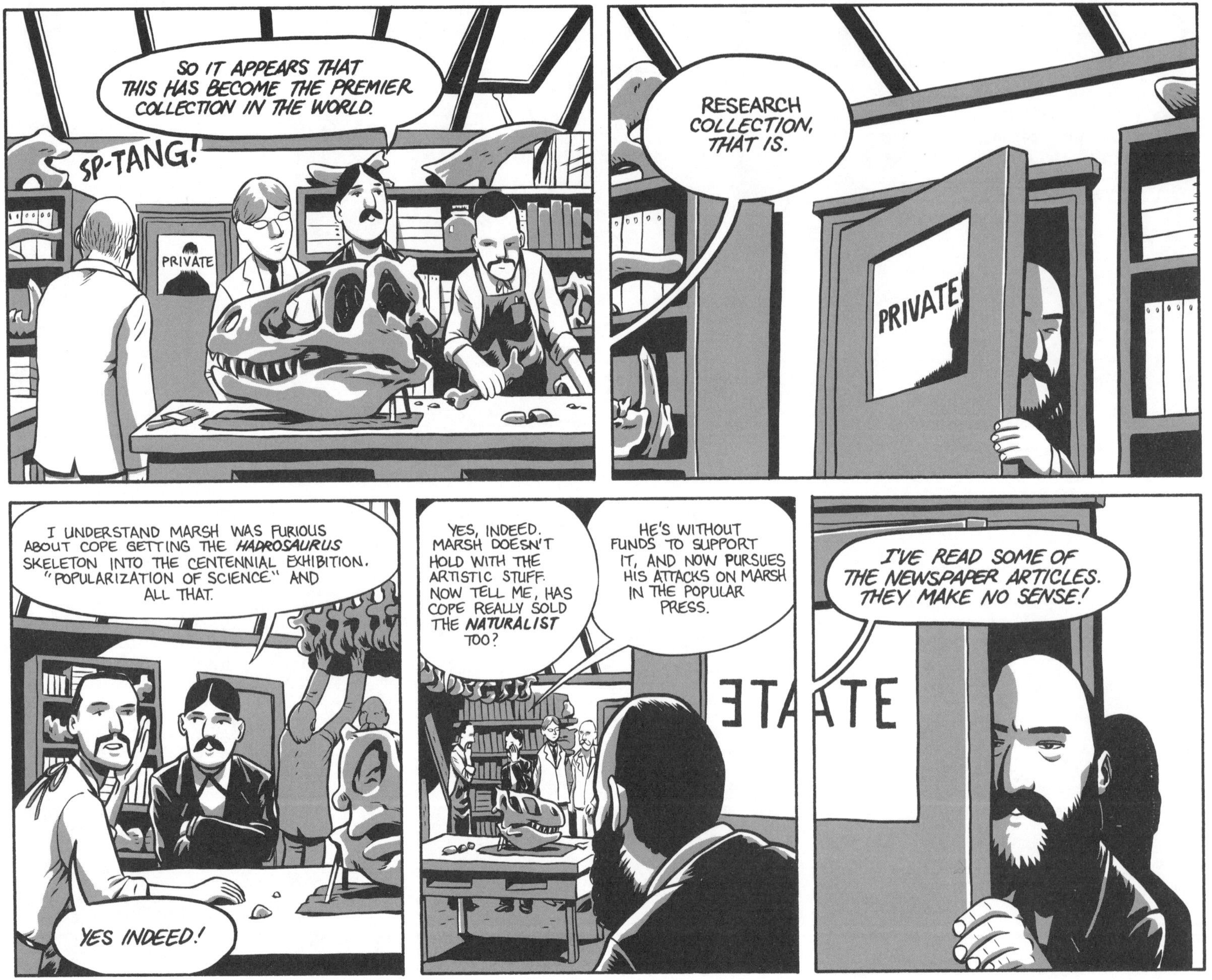
SO IT APPEARS THAT THIS HAS BECOME THE PREMIER COLLECTION IN THE WORLD.
SP-TANG!
PRIVATE
RESEARCH COLLECTION, THAT IS.
PRIVATE
I UNDERSTAND MARSH WAS FURIOUS ABOUT COPE GETTING THE HADROSAURUS SKELETON INTO THE CENTENNIAL EXHIBITION. "POPULARIZATION OF SCIENCE" AND ALL THAT.
YES INDEED!
YES, INDEED. MARSH DOESN'T HOLD WITH THE ARTISTIC STUFF. NOW TELL ME, HAS COPE REALLY SOLD THE NATURALIST TOO?
HE'S WITHOUT FUNDS TO SUPPORT IT, AND NOW PURSUES HIS ATTACKS ON MARSH IN THE POPULAR PRESS.
I'VE READ SOME OF THE NEWSPAPER ARTICLES. THEY MAKE NO SENSE!

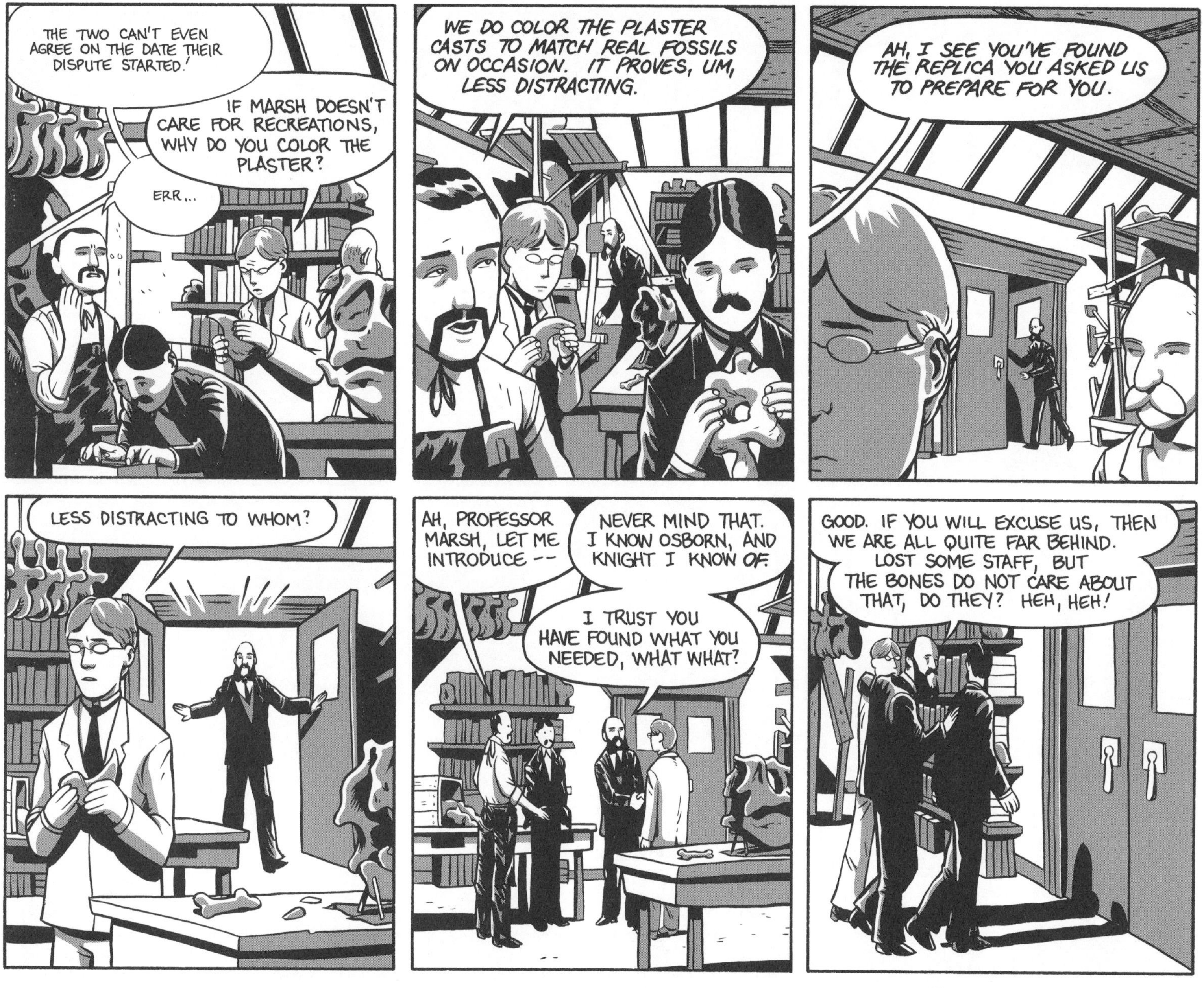
THE TWO CAN'T EVEN AGREE ON THE DATE THEIR DISPUTE STARTED!
IF MARSH DOESN'T CARE FOR RECREATIONS, WHY DO YOU COLOR THE PLASTER?
ERR...
WE DO COLOR THE PLASTER CASTS TO MATCH REAL FOSSILS ON OCCASION. IT PROVES, UM, LESS DISTRACTING.
AH, I SEE YOU'VE FOUND THE REPLICA YOU ASKED US TO PREPARE FOR YOU.
LESS DISTRACTING TO WHOM?
AH, PROFESSOR MARSH, LET ME INTRODUCE --
NEVER MIND THAT. I KNOW OSBORN, AND KNIGHT I KNOW OF.
I TRUST YOU HAVE FOUND WHAT YOU NEEDED, WHAT WHAT?
GOOD. IF YOU WILL EXCUSE US, THEN WE ARE ALL QUITE FAR BEHIND. LOST SOME STAFF, BUT THE BONES DO NOT CARE ABOUT THAT, DO THEY? HEH, HEH!

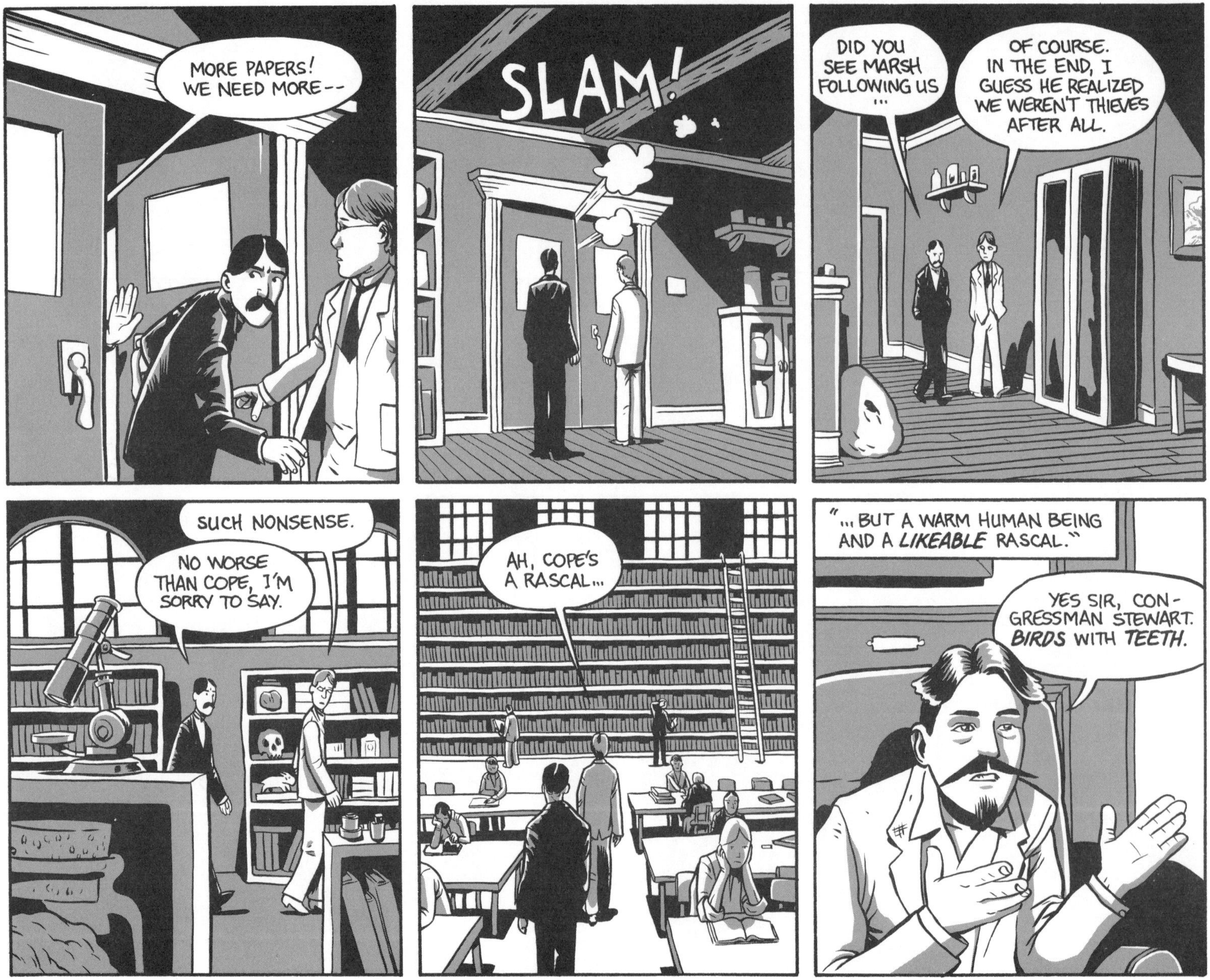
MORE PAPERS! WE NEED MORE--
SLAM!
DID YOU SEE MARSH FOLLOWING US ...
OF COURSE. IN THE END, I GUESS HE REALIZED WE WEREN'T THIEVES AFTER ALL.
SUCH NONSENSE.
NO WORSE THAN COPE, I'M SORRY TO SAY.
AH, COPE'S A RASCAL...
"... BUT A WARM HUMAN BEING AND A *LIKEABLE* RASCAL."
YES SIR, CONGRESSMAN STEWART. ***BIRDS*** WITH ***TEETH***.

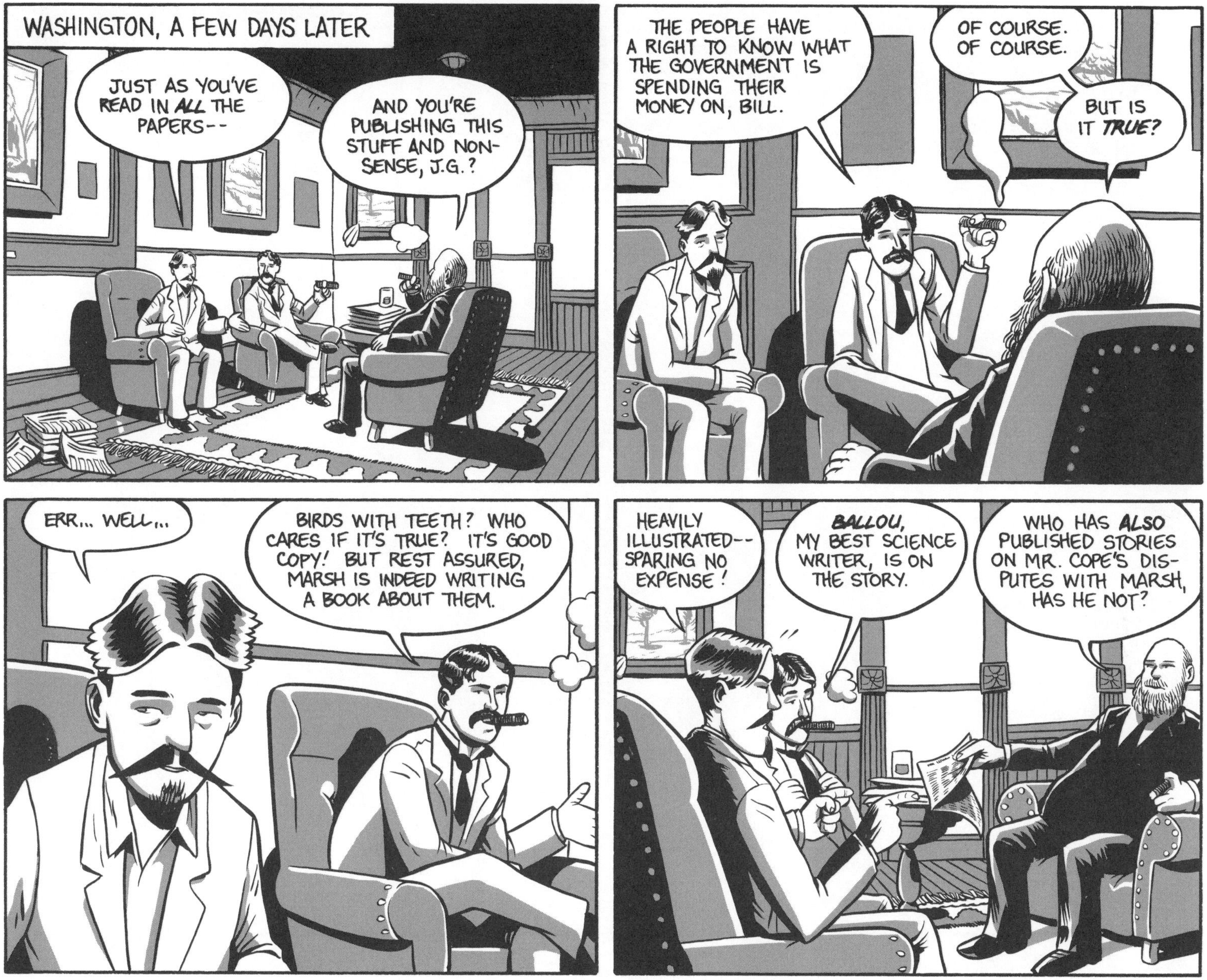
WASHINGTON, A FEW DAYS LATER
JUST AS YOU'VE READ IN ALL THE PAPERS--
AND YOU'RE PUBLISHING THIS STUFF AND NON-SENSE, J.G.?
THE PEOPLE HAVE A RIGHT TO KNOW WHAT THE GOVERNMENT IS SPENDING THEIR MONEY ON, BILL.
OF COURSE. OF COURSE.
BUT IS IT TRUE?
ERR... WELL...
BIRDS WITH TEETH? WHO CARES IF IT'S TRUE? IT'S GOOD COPY! BUT REST ASSURED, MARSH IS INDEED WRITING A BOOK ABOUT THEM.
HEAVILY ILLUSTRATED-- SPARING NO EXPENSE!
BALLOU, MY BEST SCIENCE WRITER, IS ON THE STORY.
WHO HAS ALSO PUBLISHED STORIES ON MR. COPE'S DIS-PUTES WITH MARSH, HAS HE NOT?

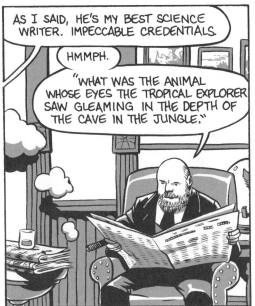

AS I SAID, HE'S MY BEST SCIENCE WRITER. IMPECCABLE CREDENTIALS.

HMMPH.

"WHAT WAS THE ANIMAL WHOSE EYES THE TROPICAL EXPLORER SAW GLEAMING IN THE DEPTH OF THE CAVE IN THE JUNGLE."

"WAS IT THE GIGANTIC *BRONTOSAURUS* OR THE FEROCIOUS *TYRANNOSAURUS?*"

IMPECCABLE CREDENTIALS. AND THAT EXPLORER STUFF SELLS PAPERS. WHY--

YES, YES, I KNOW ALL ABOUT YOUR STANLEY AND LIVINGSTON TRIUMPH.

VERY WELL. I'LL SAY THIS MUCH: IT'S ALREADY BEEN TAKEN TO COMMITTEE, MR. COPE.

NOW, IF YOU'LL EXCUSE US? OUR... NEXT APPOINTMENT IS DUE.

CERTAINLY. I'M BACK OFF ON AN EXTENDED COLLECTING EXPEDITION MYSELF IN A FEW HOURS.

CONGR

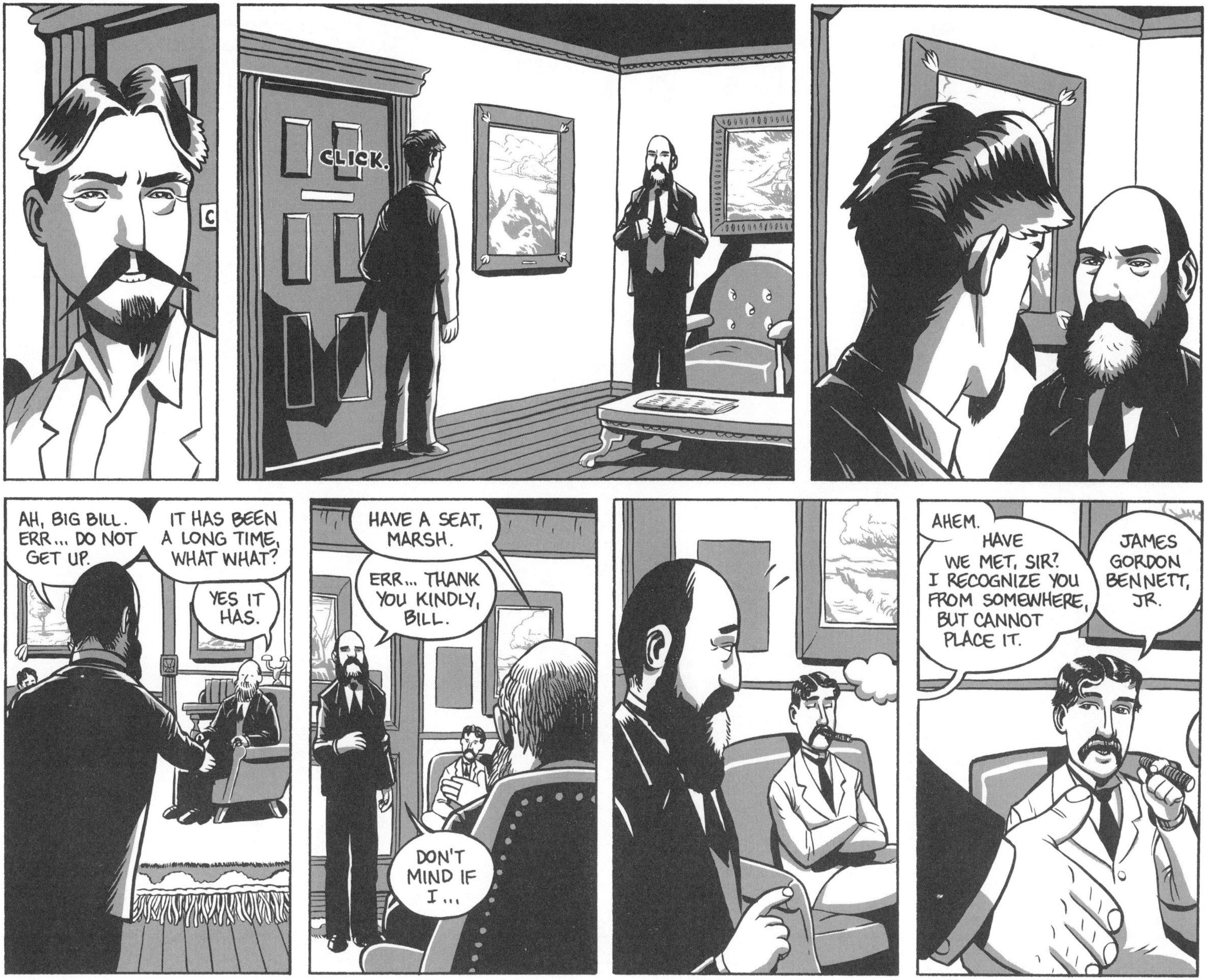
CLICK.
C
AH, BIG BILL. ERR... DO NOT GET UP.
IT HAS BEEN A LONG TIME, WHAT WHAT?
YES IT HAS.
HAVE A SEAT, MARSH.
ERR... THANK YOU KINDLY, BILL.
DON'T MIND IF I...
AHEM.
HAVE WE MET, SIR? I RECOGNIZE YOU FROM SOMEWHERE, BUT CANNOT PLACE IT.
JAMES GORDON BENNETT, JR.

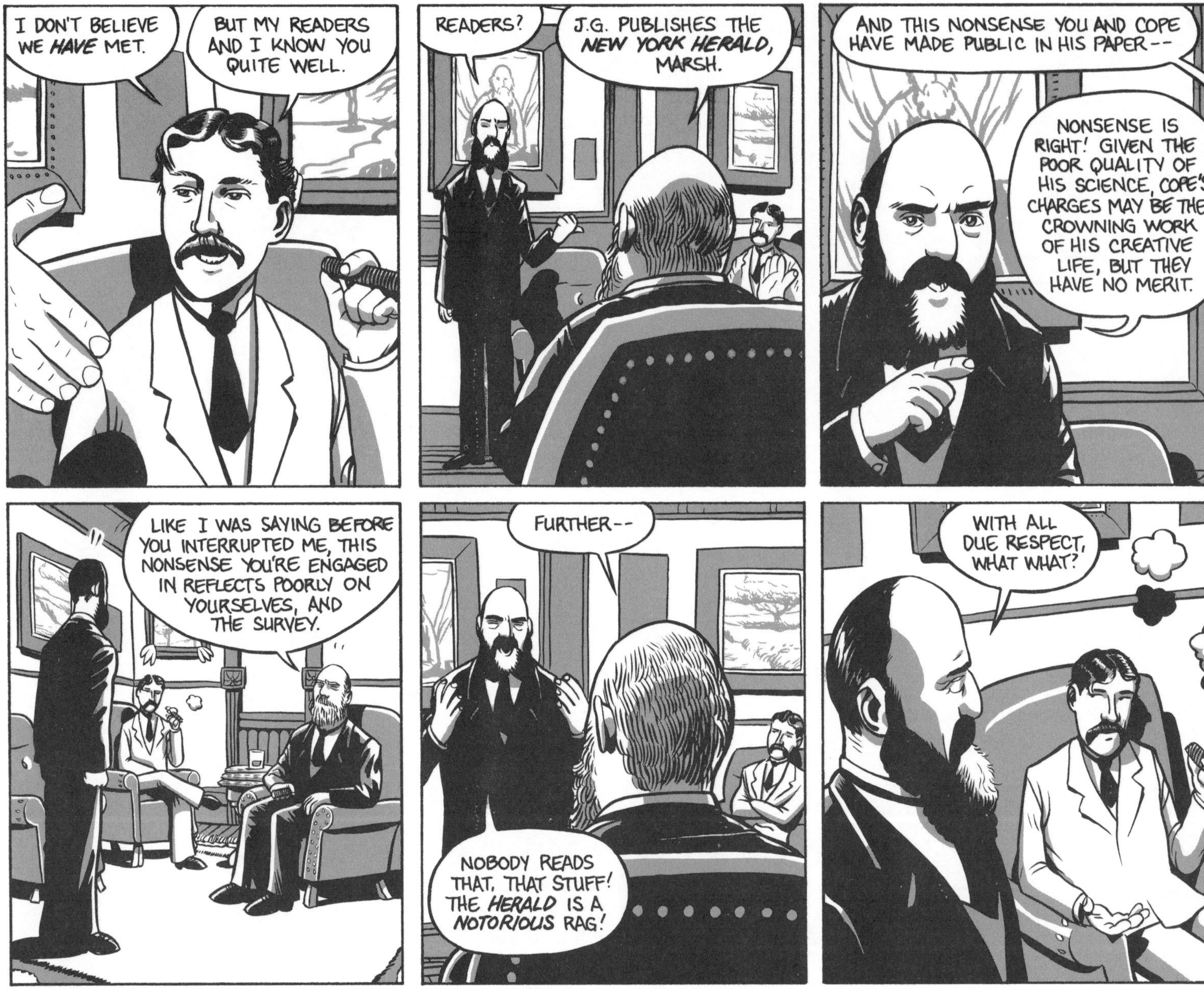

I DON'T BELIEVE WE *HAVE* MET.
BUT MY READERS AND I KNOW YOU QUITE WELL.
READERS?
J.G. PUBLISHES THE *NEW YORK HERALD*, MARSH.
AND THIS NONSENSE YOU AND COPE HAVE MADE PUBLIC IN HIS PAPER--
NONSENSE IS RIGHT! GIVEN THE POOR QUALITY OF HIS SCIENCE, COPE'S CHARGES MAY BE THE CROWNING WORK OF HIS CREATIVE LIFE, BUT THEY HAVE NO MERIT.
LIKE I WAS SAYING BEFORE YOU INTERRUPTED ME, THIS NONSENSE YOU'RE ENGAGED IN REFLECTS POORLY ON YOURSELVES, AND THE SURVEY.
FURTHER--
NOBODY READS THAT, THAT STUFF! THE *HERALD* IS A *NOTORIOUS* RAG!
WITH ALL DUE RESPECT, WHAT WHAT?

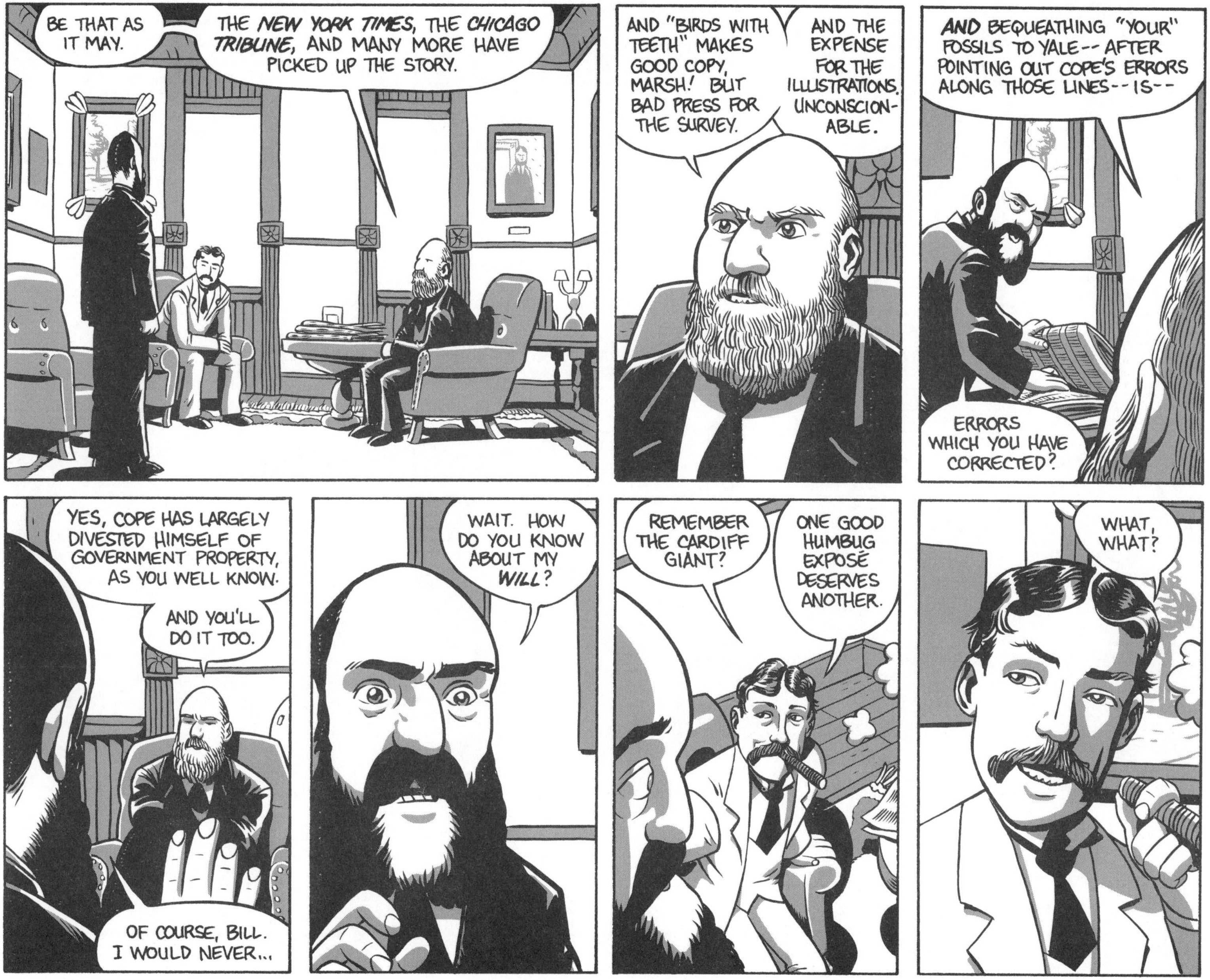

BE THAT AS IT MAY.
THE *NEW YORK TIMES*, THE *CHICAGO TRIBUNE*, AND MANY MORE HAVE PICKED UP THE STORY.
AND "BIRDS WITH TEETH" MAKES GOOD COPY, MARSH! BUT BAD PRESS FOR THE SURVEY.
AND THE EXPENSE FOR THE ILLUSTRATIONS. UNCONSCIONABLE.
AND BEQUEATHING "YOUR" FOSSILS TO YALE-- AFTER POINTING OUT COPE'S ERRORS ALONG THOSE LINES--IS--
ERRORS WHICH YOU HAVE CORRECTED?
YES, COPE HAS LARGELY DIVESTED HIMSELF OF GOVERNMENT PROPERTY, AS YOU WELL KNOW.
AND YOU'LL DO IT TOO.
OF COURSE, BILL. I WOULD NEVER...
WAIT. HOW DO YOU KNOW ABOUT MY *WILL*?
REMEMBER THE CARDIFF GIANT?
ONE GOOD HUMBUG EXPOSÉ DESERVES ANOTHER.
WHAT, WHAT?

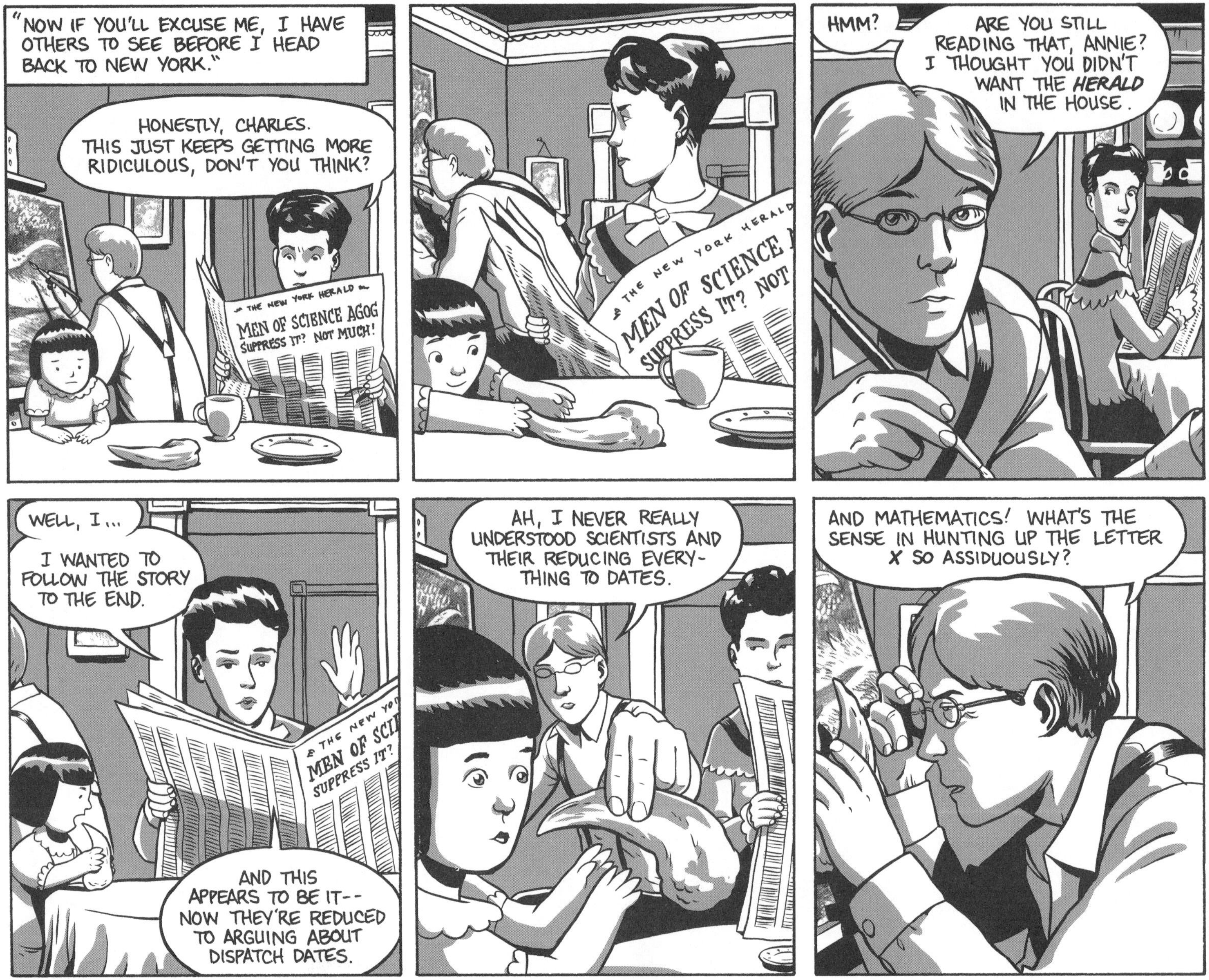
"NOW IF YOU'LL EXCUSE ME, I HAVE OTHERS TO SEE BEFORE I HEAD BACK TO NEW YORK."
HONESTLY, CHARLES. THIS JUST KEEPS GETTING MORE RIDICULOUS, DON'T YOU THINK?
THE NEW YORK HERALD
MEN OF SCIENCE AGOG
SUPPRESS IT? NOT MUCH!
THE NEW YORK HERALD
MEN OF SCIENCE
SUPPRESS IT? NOT
HMM?
ARE YOU STILL READING THAT, ANNIE? I THOUGHT YOU DIDN'T WANT THE HERALD IN THE HOUSE.
WELL, I...
I WANTED TO FOLLOW THE STORY TO THE END.
MEN OF SCI
SUPPRESS IT?
AND THIS APPEARS TO BE IT-- NOW THEY'RE REDUCED TO ARGUING ABOUT DISPATCH DATES.
AH, I NEVER REALLY UNDERSTOOD SCIENTISTS AND THEIR REDUCING EVERY-THING TO DATES.
AND MATHEMATICS! WHAT'S THE SENSE IN HUNTING UP THE LETTER X SO ASSIDUOUSLY?

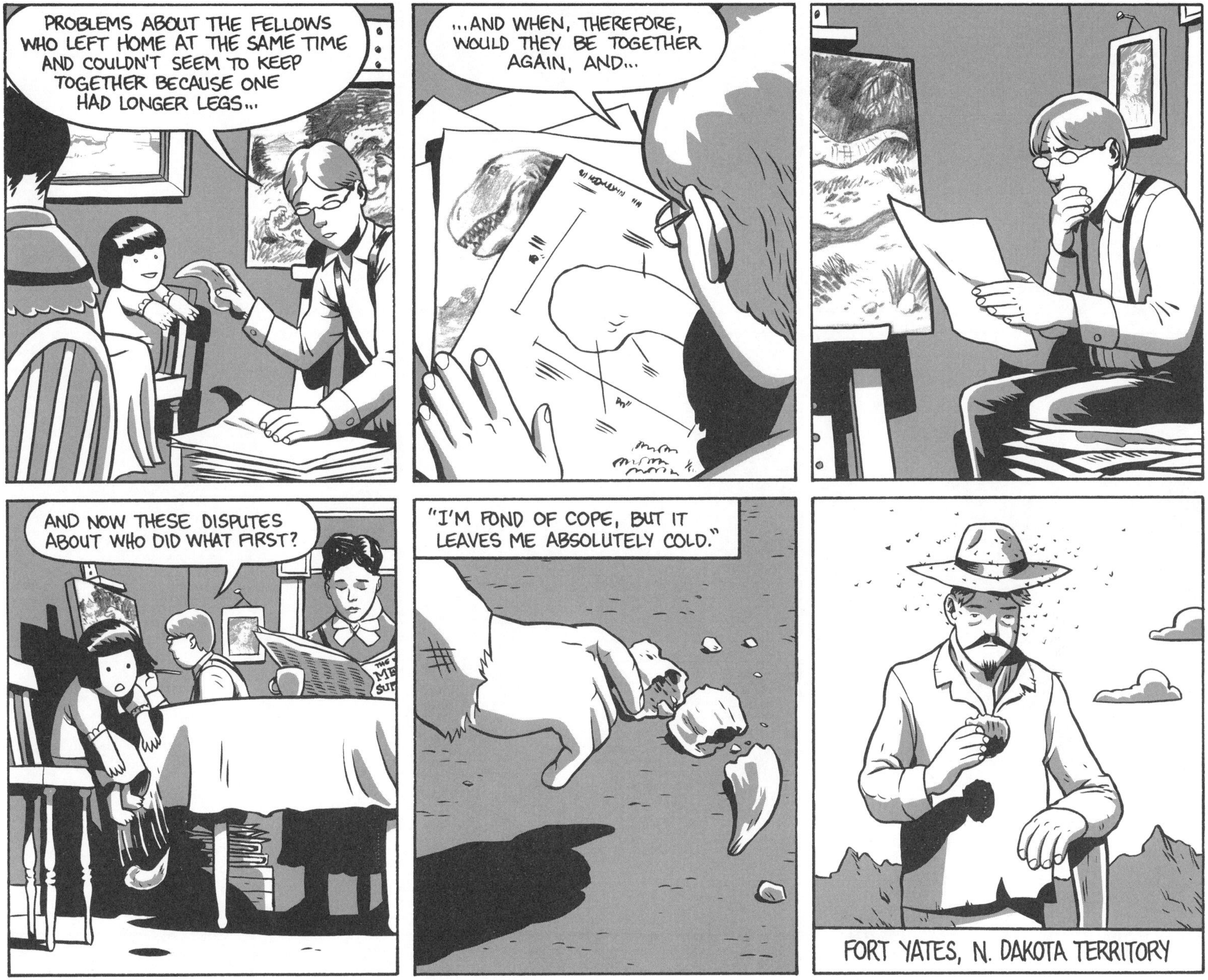
PROBLEMS ABOUT THE FELLOWS WHO LEFT HOME AT THE SAME TIME AND COULDN'T SEEM TO KEEP TOGETHER BECAUSE ONE HAD LONGER LEGS...
...AND WHEN, THEREFORE, WOULD THEY BE TOGETHER AGAIN, AND...
AND NOW THESE DISPUTES ABOUT WHO DID WHAT FIRST?
"I'M FOND OF COPE, BUT IT LEAVES ME ABSOLUTELY COLD."
FORT YATES, N. DAKOTA TERRITORY

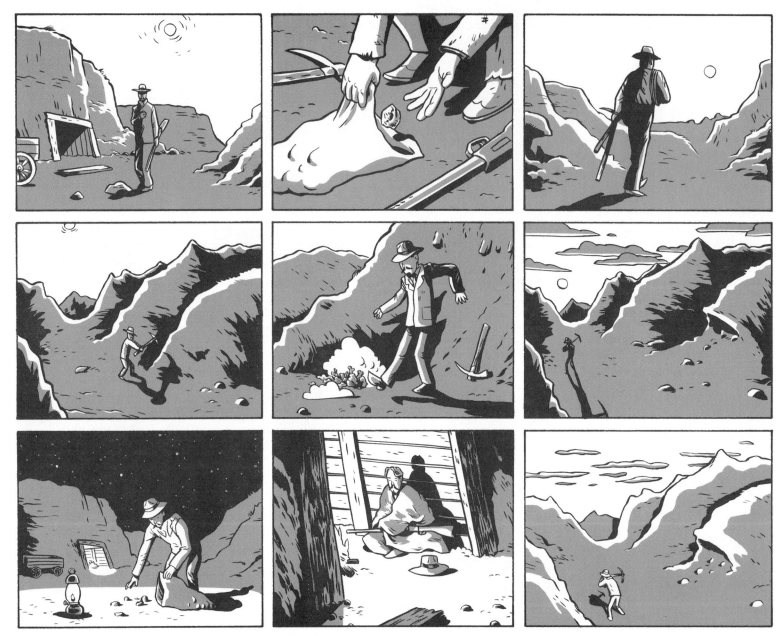

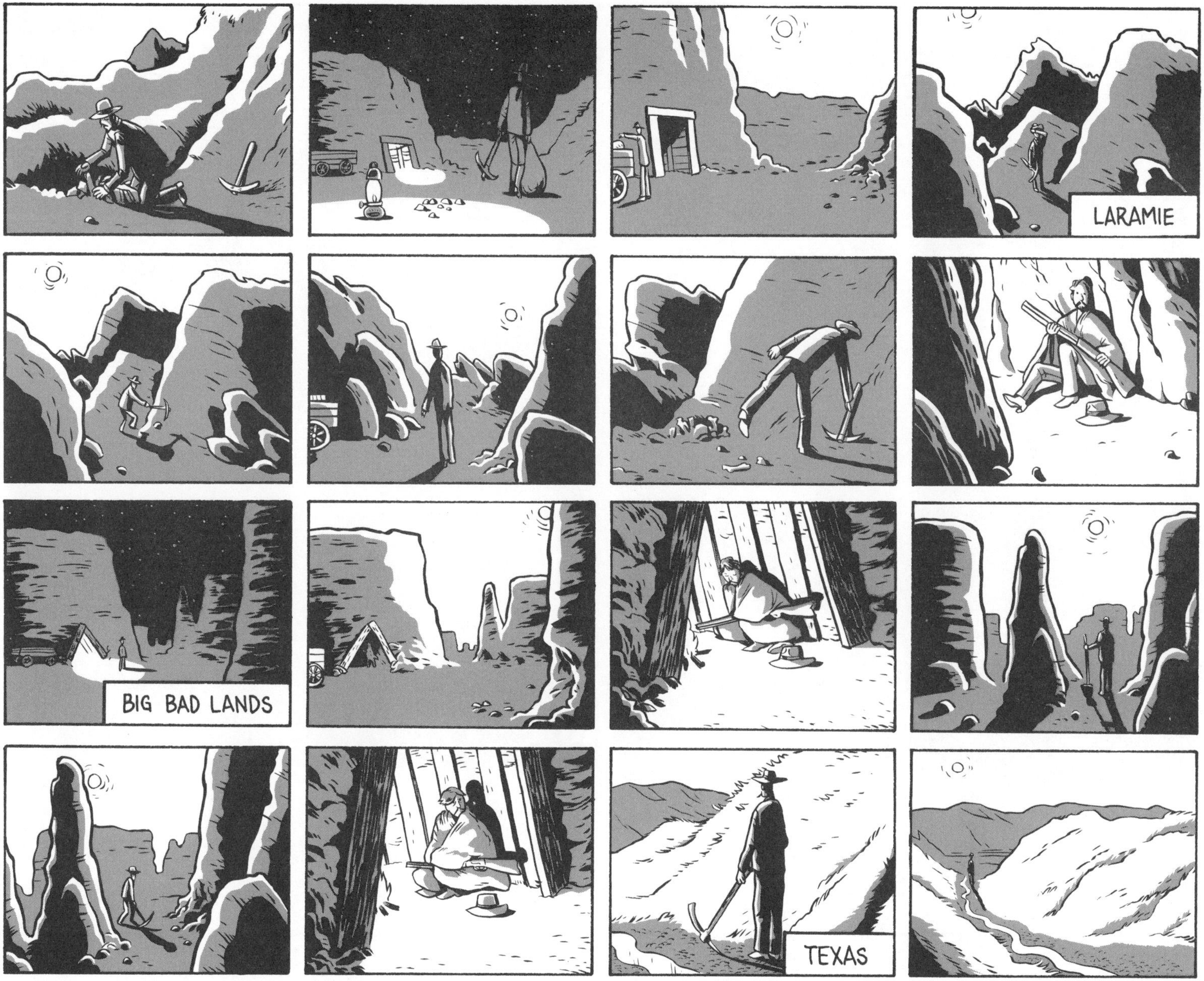
LARAMIE
BIG BAD LANDS
TEXAS

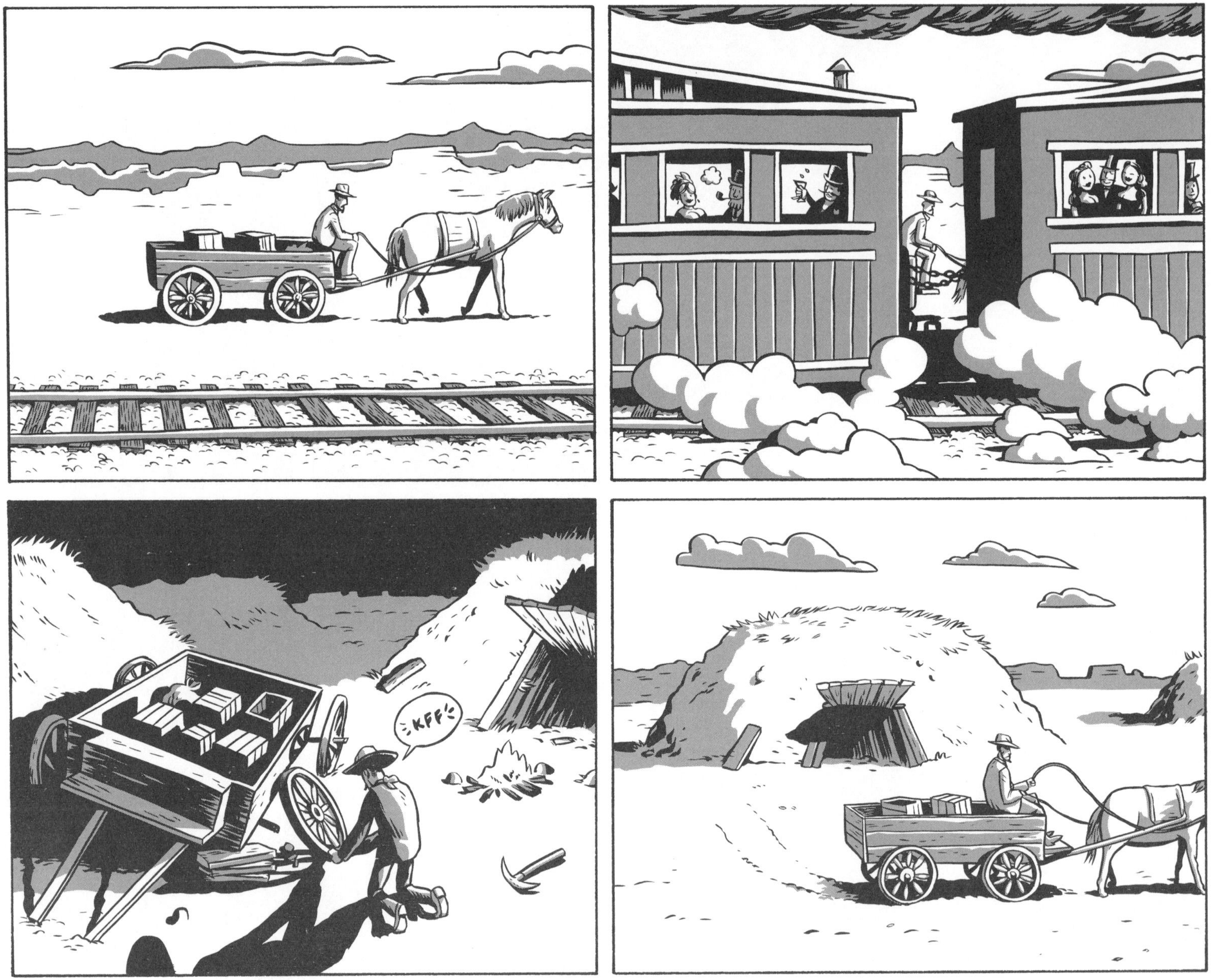
KFF

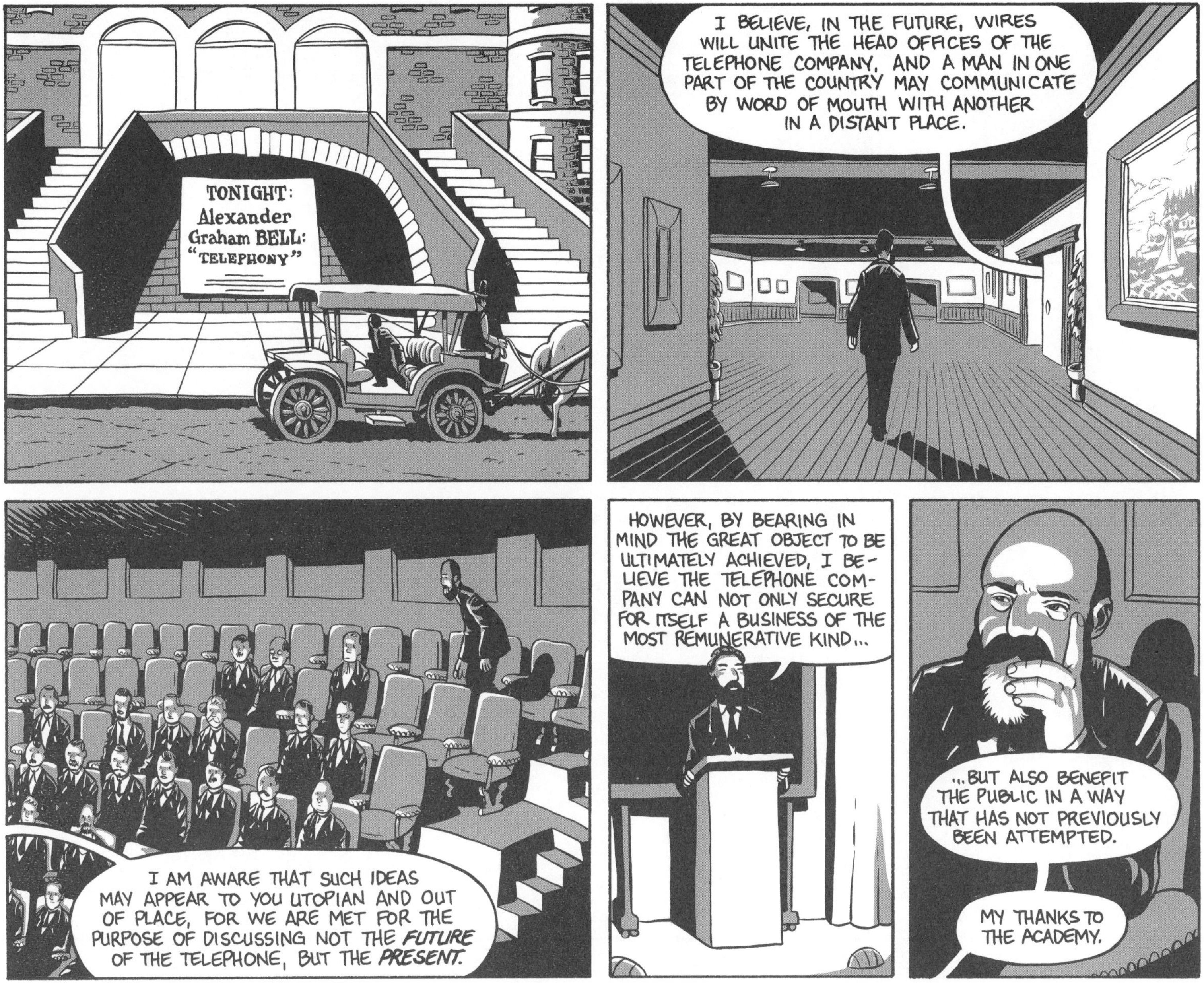
TONIGHT: Alexander Graham BELL: "TELEPHONY"
I BELIEVE, IN THE FUTURE, WIRES WILL UNITE THE HEAD OFFICES OF THE TELEPHONE COMPANY, AND A MAN IN ONE PART OF THE COUNTRY MAY COMMUNICATE BY WORD OF MOUTH WITH ANOTHER IN A DISTANT PLACE.
I AM AWARE THAT SUCH IDEAS MAY APPEAR TO YOU UTOPIAN AND OUT OF PLACE, FOR WE ARE MET FOR THE PURPOSE OF DISCUSSING NOT THE *FUTURE* OF THE TELEPHONE, BUT THE *PRESENT.*
HOWEVER, BY BEARING IN MIND THE GREAT OBJECT TO BE ULTIMATELY ACHIEVED, I BE-LIEVE THE TELEPHONE COM-PANY CAN NOT ONLY SECURE FOR ITSELF A BUSINESS OF THE MOST REMUNERATIVE KIND...
...BUT ALSO BENEFIT THE PUBLIC IN A WAY THAT HAS NOT PREVIOUSLY BEEN ATTEMPTED.
MY THANKS TO THE ACADEMY.

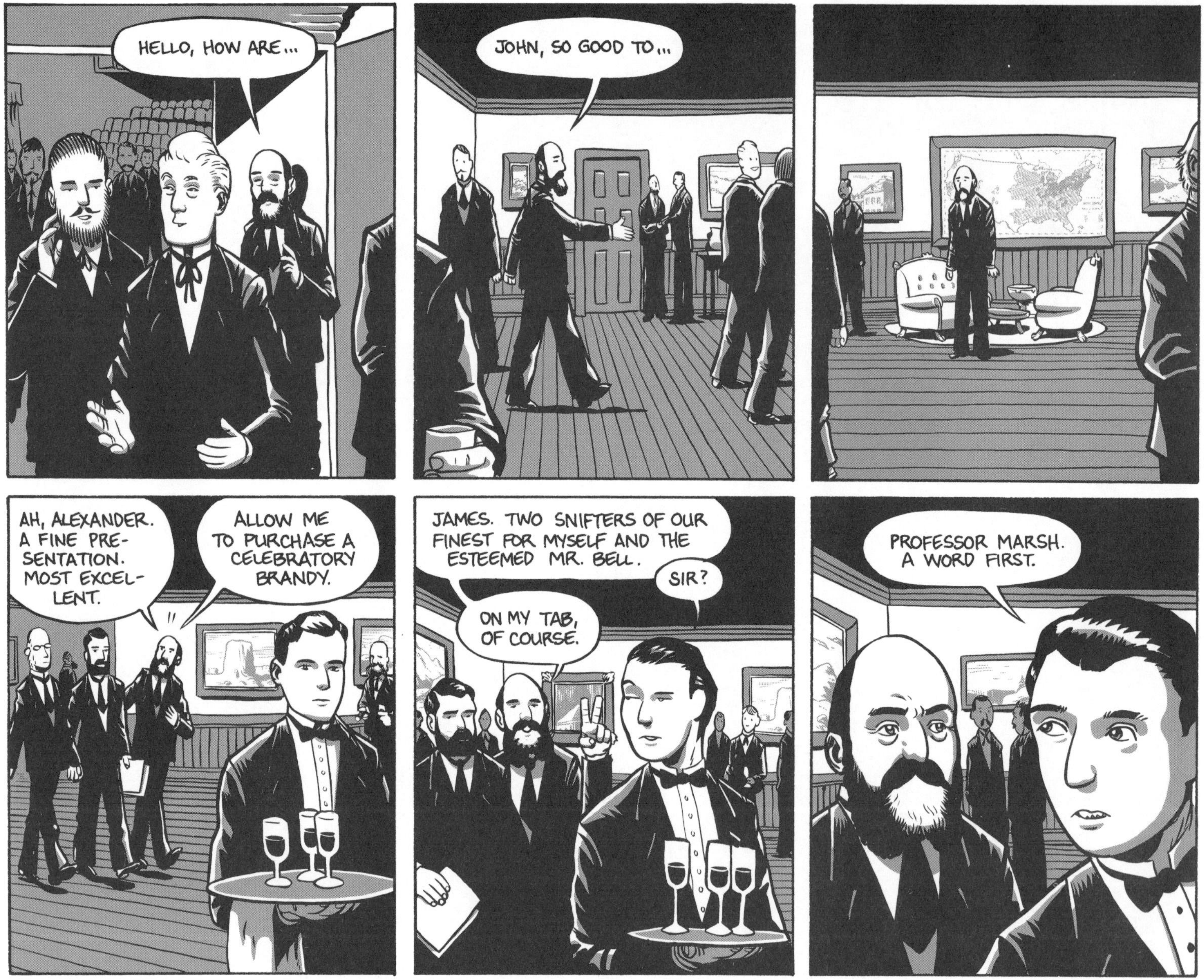
HELLO, HOW ARE...
JOHN, SO GOOD TO...
AH, ALEXANDER. A FINE PRESENTATION. MOST EXCELLENT.
ALLOW ME TO PURCHASE A CELEBRATORY BRANDY.
JAMES. TWO SNIFTERS OF OUR FINEST FOR MYSELF AND THE ESTEEMED MR. BELL.
ON MY TAB, OF COURSE.
SIR?
PROFESSOR MARSH. A WORD FIRST.

THE SURVEY IS NO LONGER SUPPORTING YOUR...

...AHH...

THERE'S NO LONGER A TAB.

OH, ER, YES OF COURSE.

UM... ALEC, YOU MUST EXCUSE ME. IT SEEMS I CANNOT TARRY AFTER ALL.

IMPORTANT DISCOVERY AT THE LAB. MUST CATCH THE NEXT TRAIN UP! THE MEN JUST CANNOT FUNCTION WITHOUT MY GUIDANCE, WHAT WHAT?

BUT I WILL SEE YOU SOON FOR OUR USUAL GET TOGETHER?

THE ASTORS AND JUSTICE HOLMES CANNOT MAKE IT, BUT I WILL HAVE A SPECIAL GUEST FROM THE WESTERN TERRITORIES, MY GOOD FRIEND, CHIEF RED CLOUD.

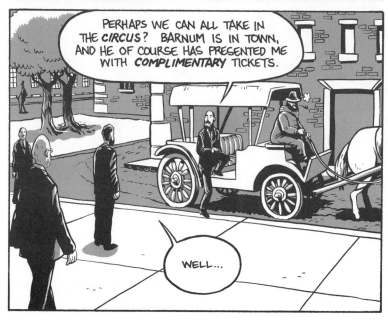

PERHAPS WE CAN ALL TAKE IN THE *CIRCUS*? BARNUM IS IN TOWN, AND HE OF COURSE HAS PRESENTED ME WITH *COMPLIMENTARY* TICKETS.

WELL...

"EXCELLENT. I WILL SEE YOU IN A FEW DAYS. NOW, I MUST BE OFF. DUTY CALLS!"

FREEZE *MY* TAB!

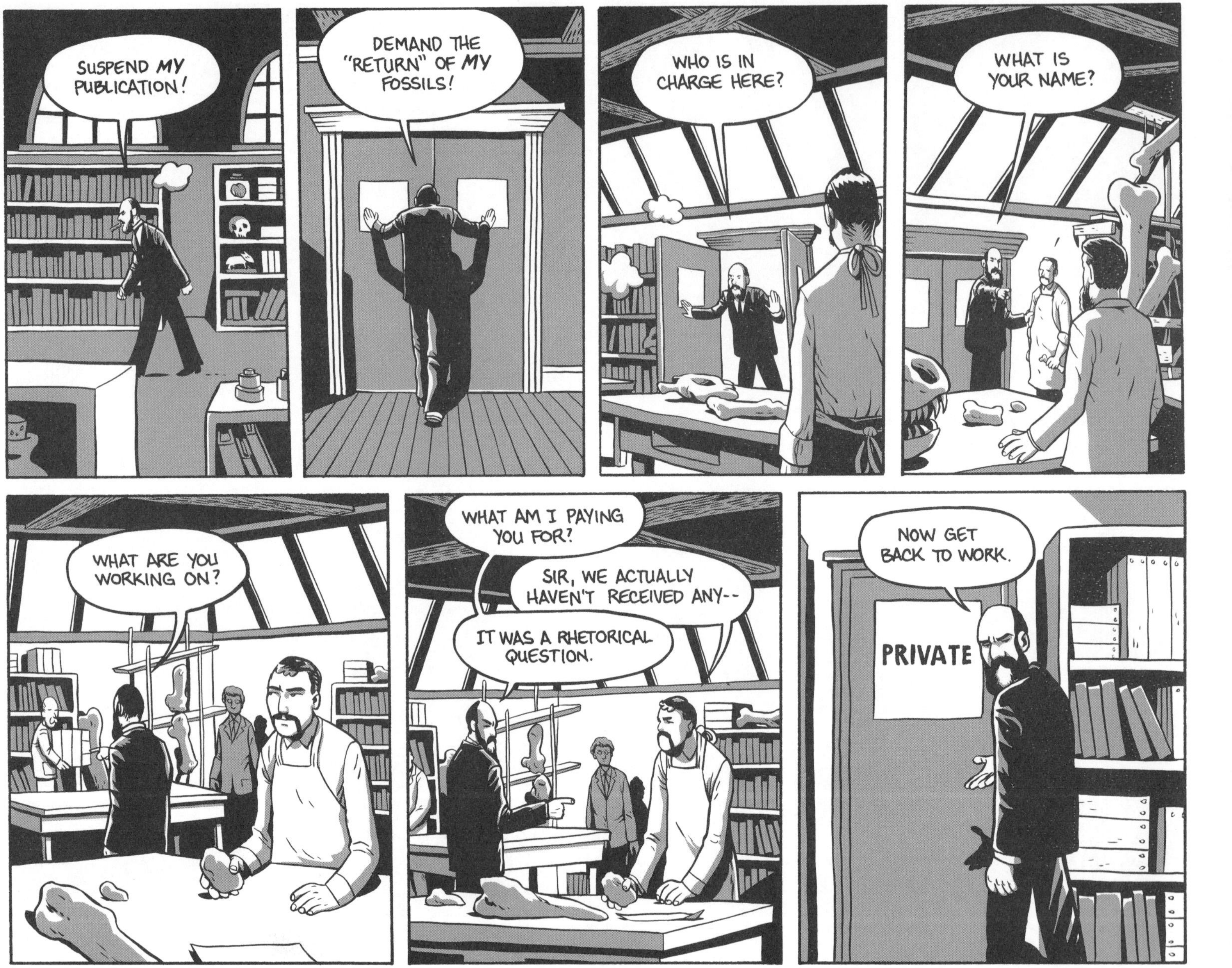
SUSPEND MY PUBLICATION!
DEMAND THE "RETURN" OF MY FOSSILS!
WHO IS IN CHARGE HERE?
WHAT IS YOUR NAME?
WHAT ARE YOU WORKING ON?
WHAT AM I PAYING YOU FOR?
SIR, WE ACTUALLY HAVEN'T RECEIVED ANY--
IT WAS A RHETORICAL QUESTION.
NOW GET BACK TO WORK.
PRIVATE

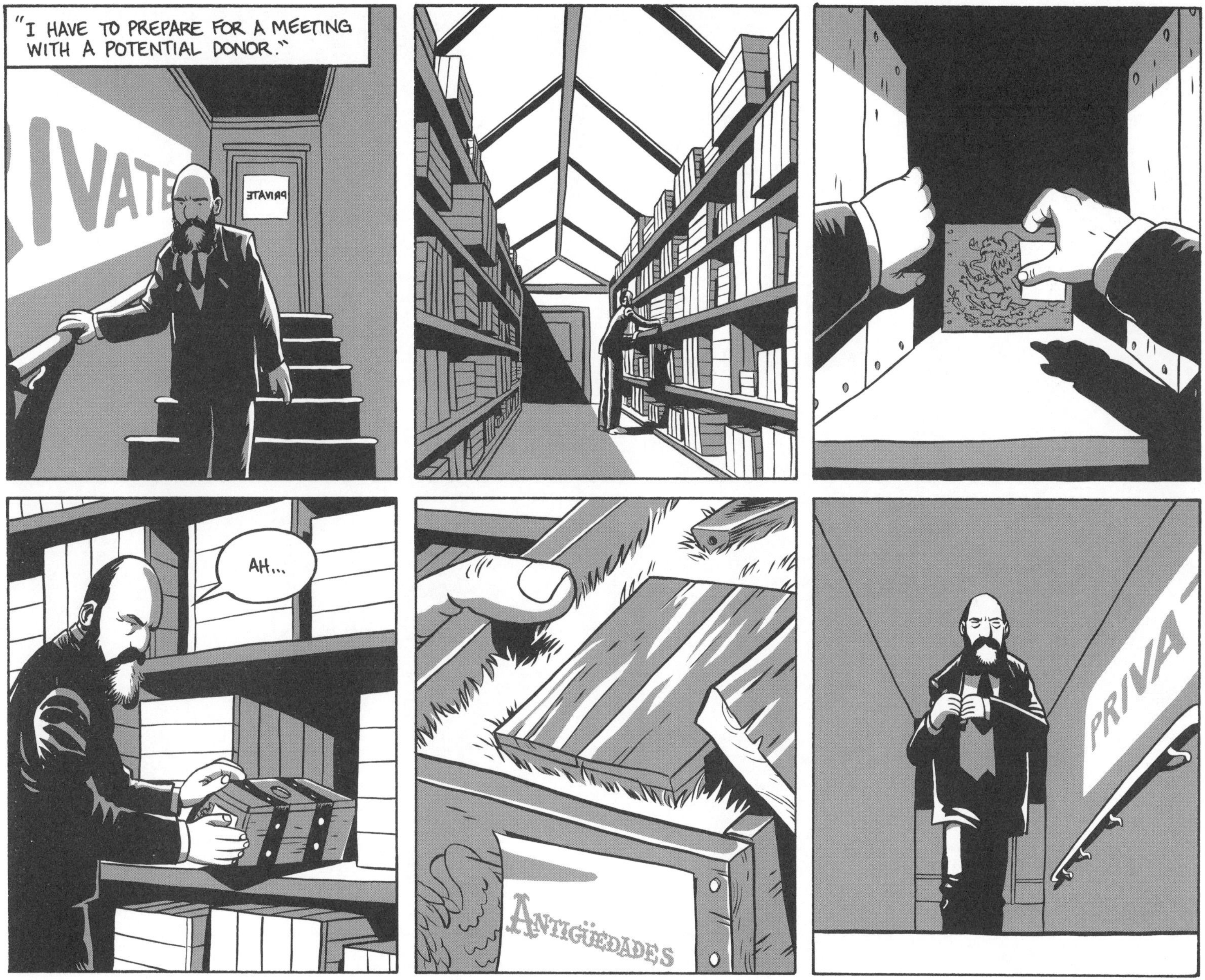
"I HAVE TO PREPARE FOR A MEETING WITH A POTENTIAL DONOR."
PRIVATE
AH...
ANTIGÜEDADES
PRIVA

2102 PINE STREET

CLUMP

CREAK

CLUMP

KFF!

PLAP.

LAST WILL AND TESTAMENT

CIGARS
TOPHAT BRAND
PASSED FLAVOUR
for the
INGUISHED GENTLEMAN

KFF!

BEST TO SAVE THIS FOR LATER, DON'T YOU THINK?

WHEN MY NEW BROADSIDE AGAINST MARSH APPEARS -- A NEW AND QUITE EXTENSIVE CATALOG OF HIS ROBBERIES!

ANXIOUS GET OUT CANNOT YET AWHILE

≀KFF!≀

YOU TWO GO ON AHEAD.

I JUST WANT TO THANK PHINEAS FOR THAT MOST AGREEABLE OF ENTERTAINMENTS.

BARNU

AH, OF COURSE. MAY WE JOIN--

I WILL BE SURE TO PASS ALONG YOUR COMPLIMENTS, ALEXANDER.

GRESS

NOW, I WILL SEE YOU AND THE CHIEF BACK AT THE WIGWAM, WHAT WHAT?

PHINEAS!

GARGANTUA
MARVEL from the HOLOCENE EPOCH
★ of the CENOZOIC AGE! ★

P.T.! A WORD, IF I MAY.

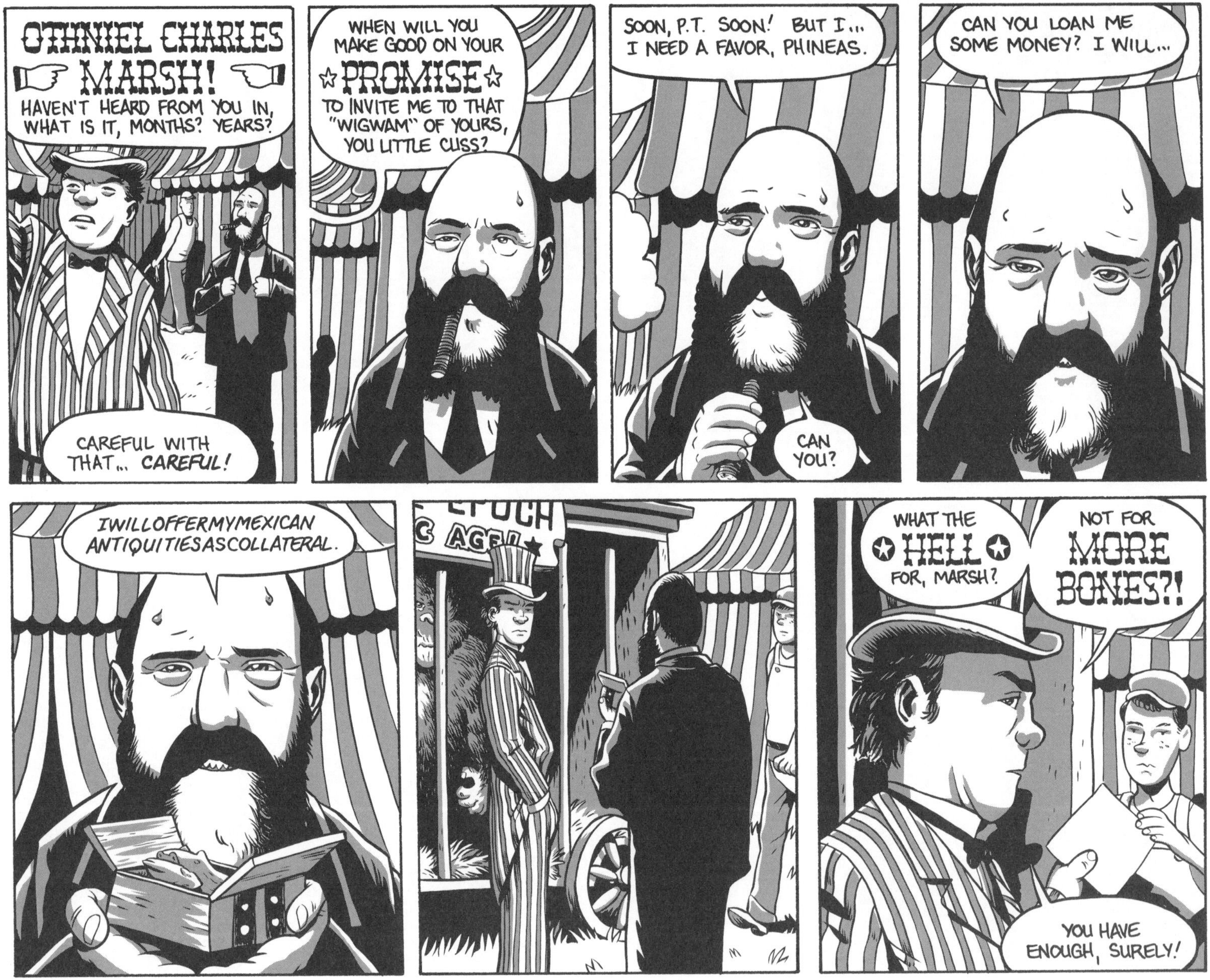
OTHNIEL CHARLES MARSH!
HAVEN'T HEARD FROM YOU IN, WHAT IS IT, MONTHS? YEARS?
CAREFUL WITH THAT... CAREFUL!
WHEN WILL YOU MAKE GOOD ON YOUR PROMISE TO INVITE ME TO THAT "WIGWAM" OF YOURS, YOU LITTLE CUSS?
SOON, P.T. SOON! BUT I... I NEED A FAVOR, PHINEAS.
CAN YOU?
CAN YOU LOAN ME SOME MONEY? I WILL...
IWILLOFFERMYMEXICAN ANTIQUITIESASCOLLATERAL.
WHAT THE HELL FOR, MARSH?
NOT FOR MORE BONES?!
YOU HAVE ENOUGH, SURELY!

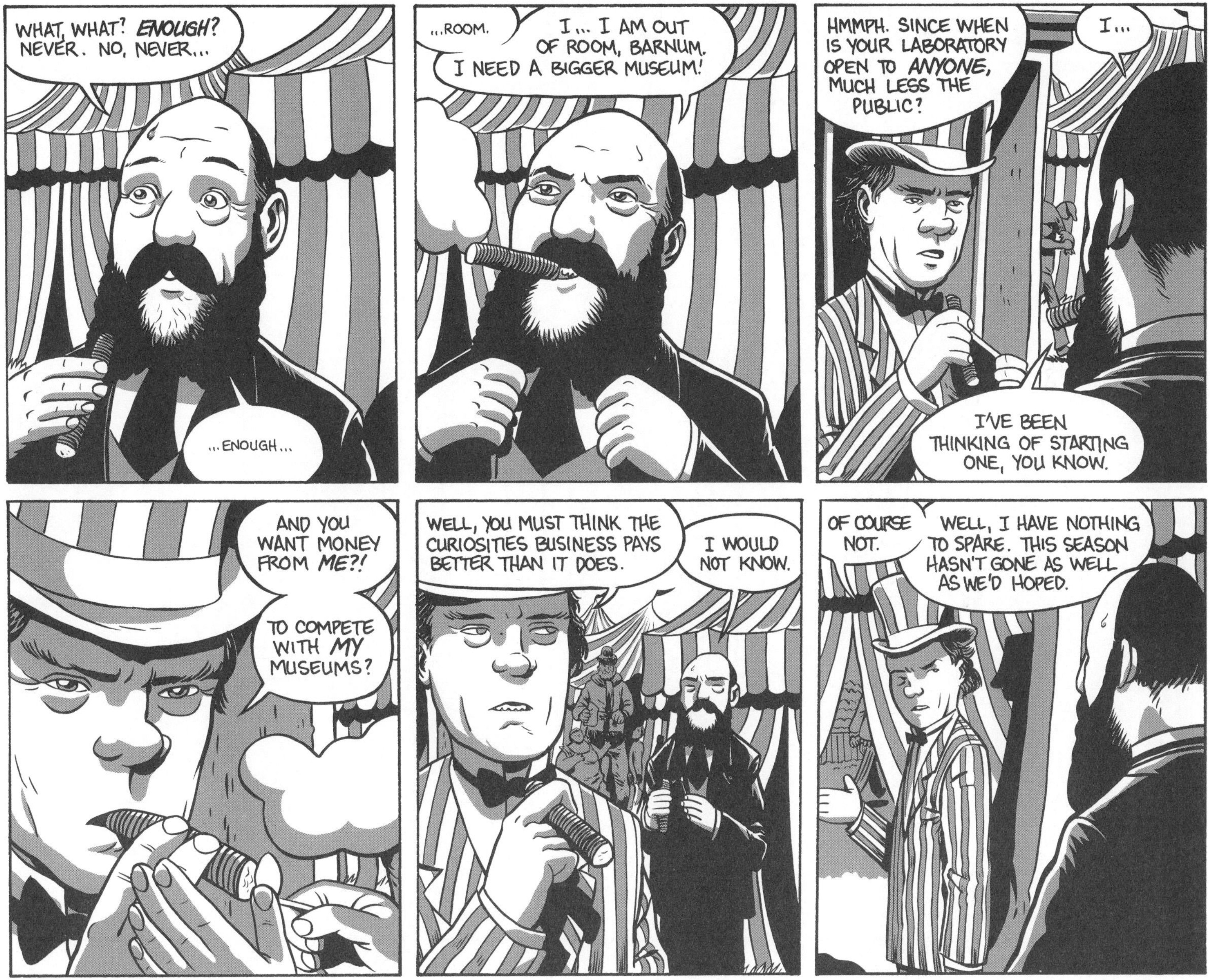
WHAT, WHAT? ENOUGH? NEVER. NO, NEVER...
...ENOUGH...
...ROOM.
I... I AM OUT OF ROOM, BARNUM. I NEED A BIGGER MUSEUM!
HMMPH. SINCE WHEN IS YOUR LABORATORY OPEN TO ANYONE, MUCH LESS THE PUBLIC?
I...
I'VE BEEN THINKING OF STARTING ONE, YOU KNOW.
AND YOU WANT MONEY FROM ME?!
TO COMPETE WITH MY MUSEUMS?
WELL, YOU MUST THINK THE CURIOSITIES BUSINESS PAYS BETTER THAN IT DOES.
I WOULD NOT KNOW.
OF COURSE NOT.
WELL, I HAVE NOTHING TO SPARE. THIS SEASON HASN'T GONE AS WELL AS WE'D HOPED.

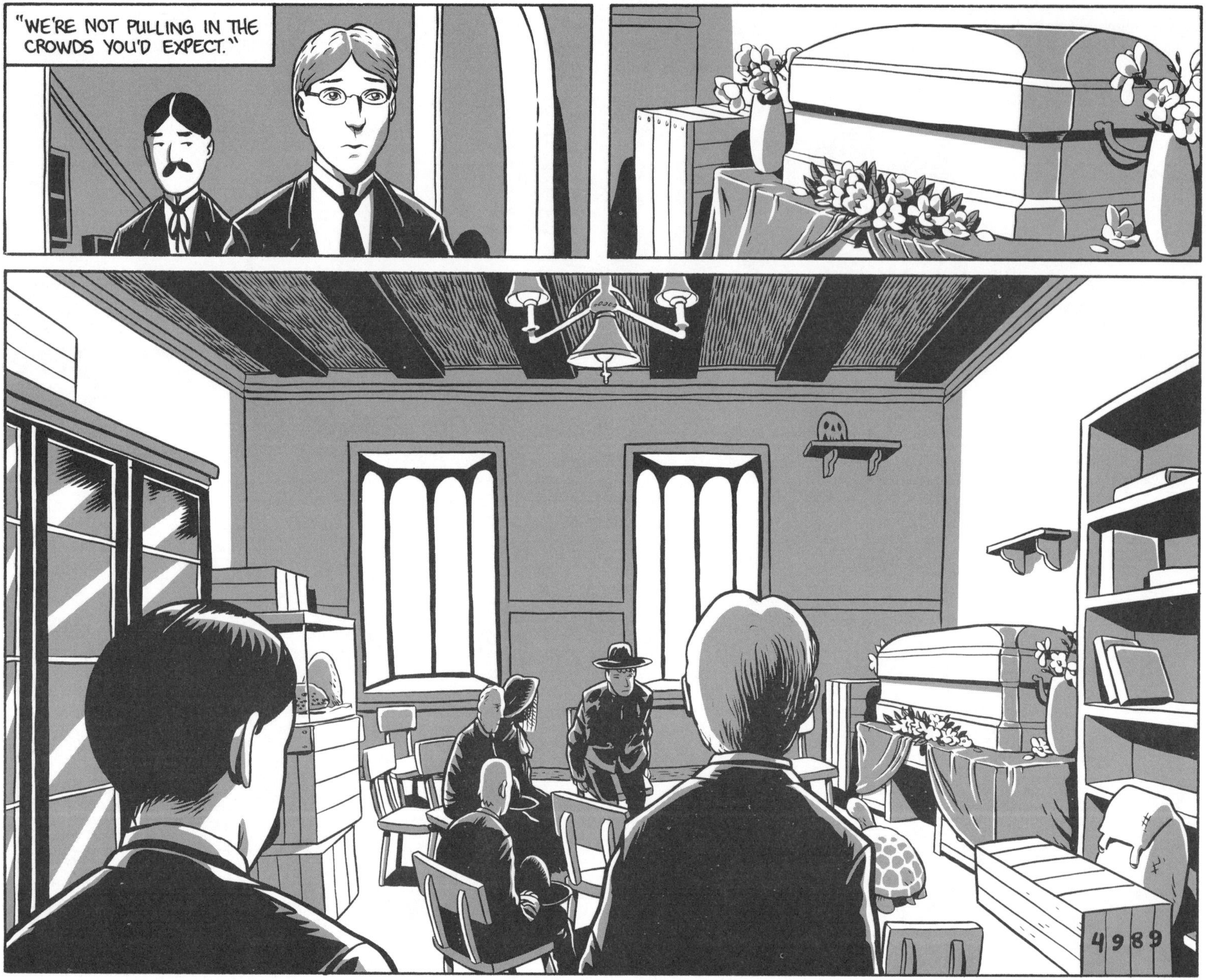
"WE'RE NOT PULLING IN THE CROWDS YOU'D EXPECT."
4989

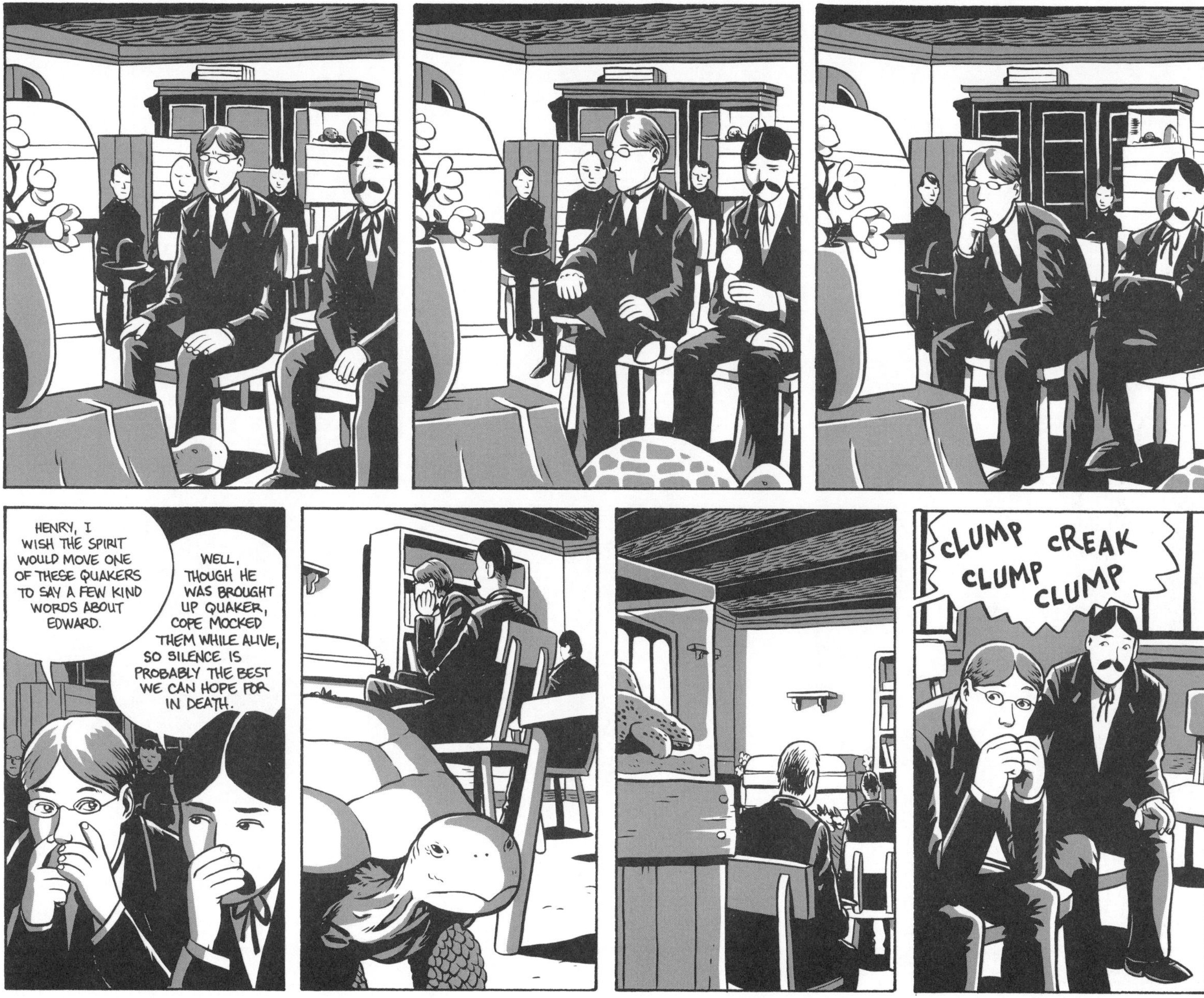
HENRY, I WISH THE SPIRIT WOULD MOVE ONE OF THESE QUAKERS TO SAY A FEW KIND WORDS ABOUT EDWARD.
WELL, THOUGH HE WAS BROUGHT UP QUAKER, COPE MOCKED THEM WHILE ALIVE, SO SILENCE IS PROBABLY THE BEST WE CAN HOPE FOR IN DEATH.
CLUMP CREAK CLUMP CLUMP

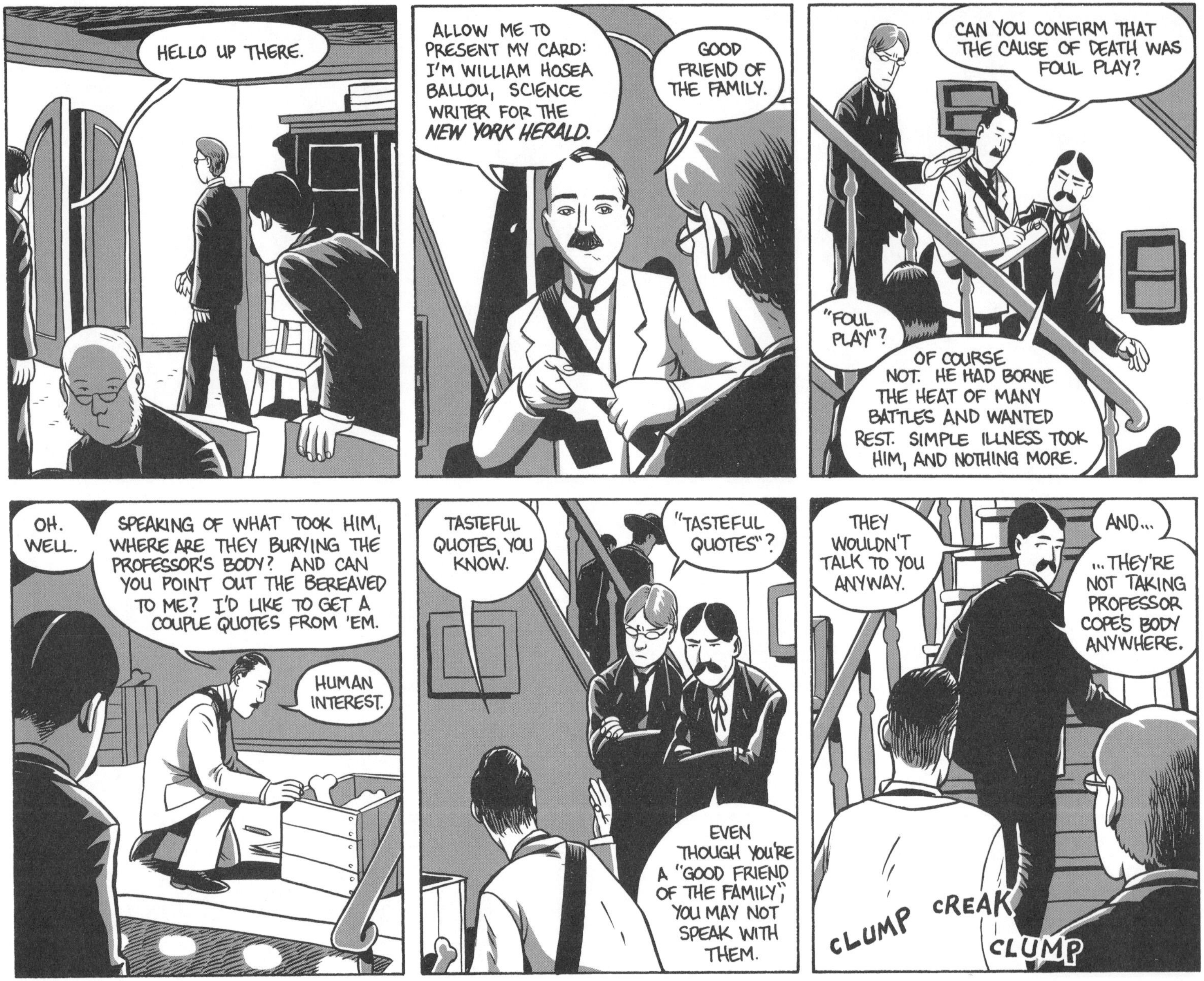
HELLO UP THERE.
ALLOW ME TO PRESENT MY CARD: I'M WILLIAM HOSEA BALLOU, SCIENCE WRITER FOR THE *NEW YORK HERALD.*
GOOD FRIEND OF THE FAMILY.
CAN YOU CONFIRM THAT THE CAUSE OF DEATH WAS FOUL PLAY?
"FOUL PLAY"?
OF COURSE NOT. HE HAD BORNE THE HEAT OF MANY BATTLES AND WANTED REST. SIMPLE ILLNESS TOOK HIM, AND NOTHING MORE.
OH. WELL.
SPEAKING OF WHAT TOOK HIM, WHERE ARE THEY BURYING THE PROFESSOR'S BODY? AND CAN YOU POINT OUT THE BEREAVED TO ME? I'D LIKE TO GET A COUPLE QUOTES FROM 'EM.
HUMAN INTEREST.
TASTEFUL QUOTES, YOU KNOW.
"TASTEFUL QUOTES"?
EVEN THOUGH YOU'RE A "GOOD FRIEND OF THE FAMILY", YOU MAY NOT SPEAK WITH THEM.
THEY WOULDN'T TALK TO YOU ANYWAY.
AND...
...THEY'RE NOT TAKING PROFESSOR COPE'S BODY ANYWHERE.
CLUMP CREAK CLUMP

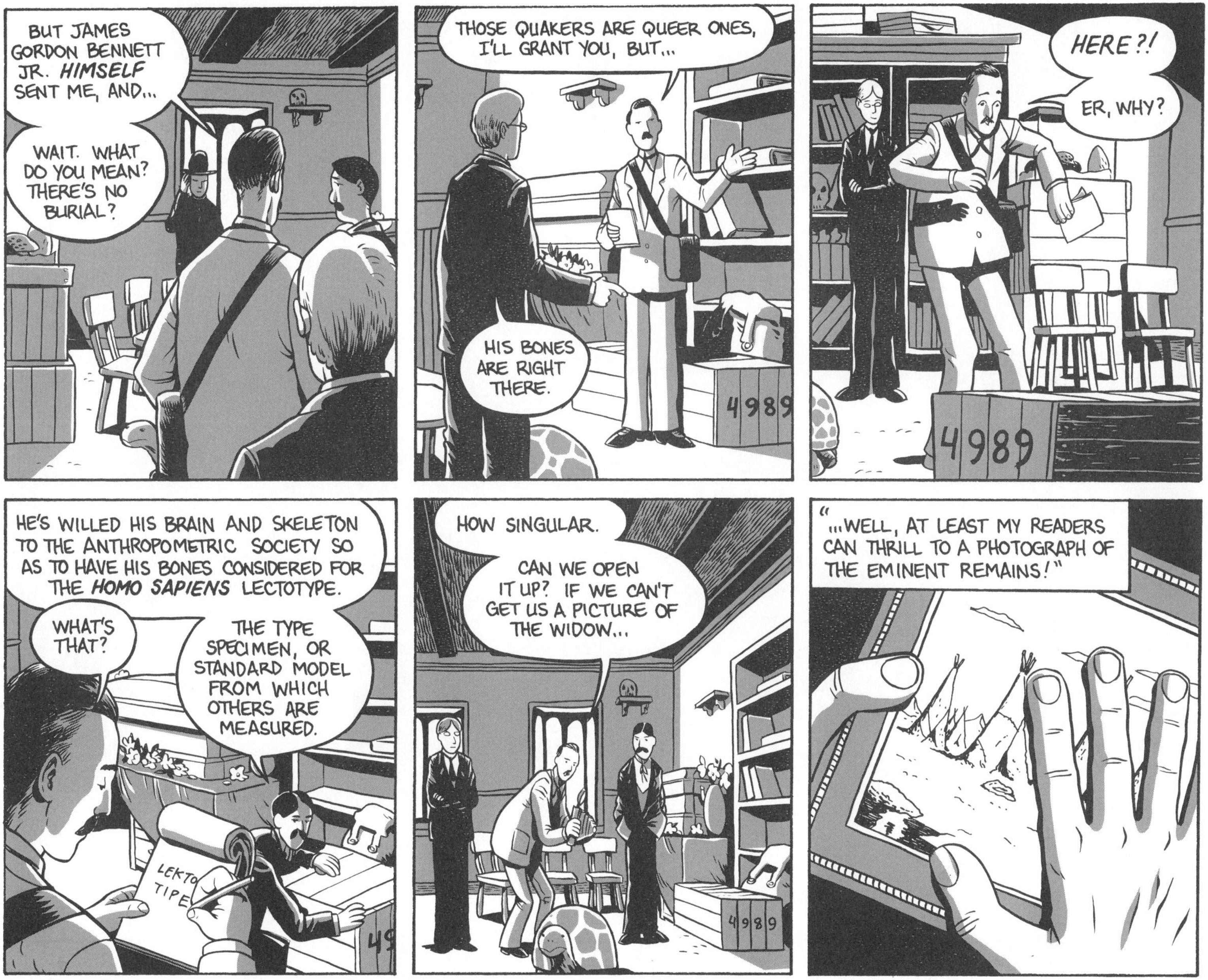
BUT JAMES GORDON BENNETT JR. *HIMSELF* SENT ME, AND...
WAIT. WHAT DO YOU MEAN? THERE'S NO BURIAL?
THOSE QUAKERS ARE QUEER ONES, I'LL GRANT YOU, BUT...
HIS BONES ARE RIGHT THERE.
4989
HERE?!
ER, WHY?
4989
HE'S WILLED HIS BRAIN AND SKELETON TO THE ANTHROPOMETRIC SOCIETY SO AS TO HAVE HIS BONES CONSIDERED FOR THE *HOMO SAPIENS* LECTOTYPE.
WHAT'S THAT?
THE TYPE SPECIMEN, OR STANDARD MODEL FROM WHICH OTHERS ARE MEASURED.
LEKTO TIPE
HOW SINGULAR.
CAN WE OPEN IT UP? IF WE CAN'T GET US A PICTURE OF THE WIDOW...
4989
"...WELL, AT LEAST MY READERS CAN THRILL TO A PHOTOGRAPH OF THE EMINENT REMAINS!"

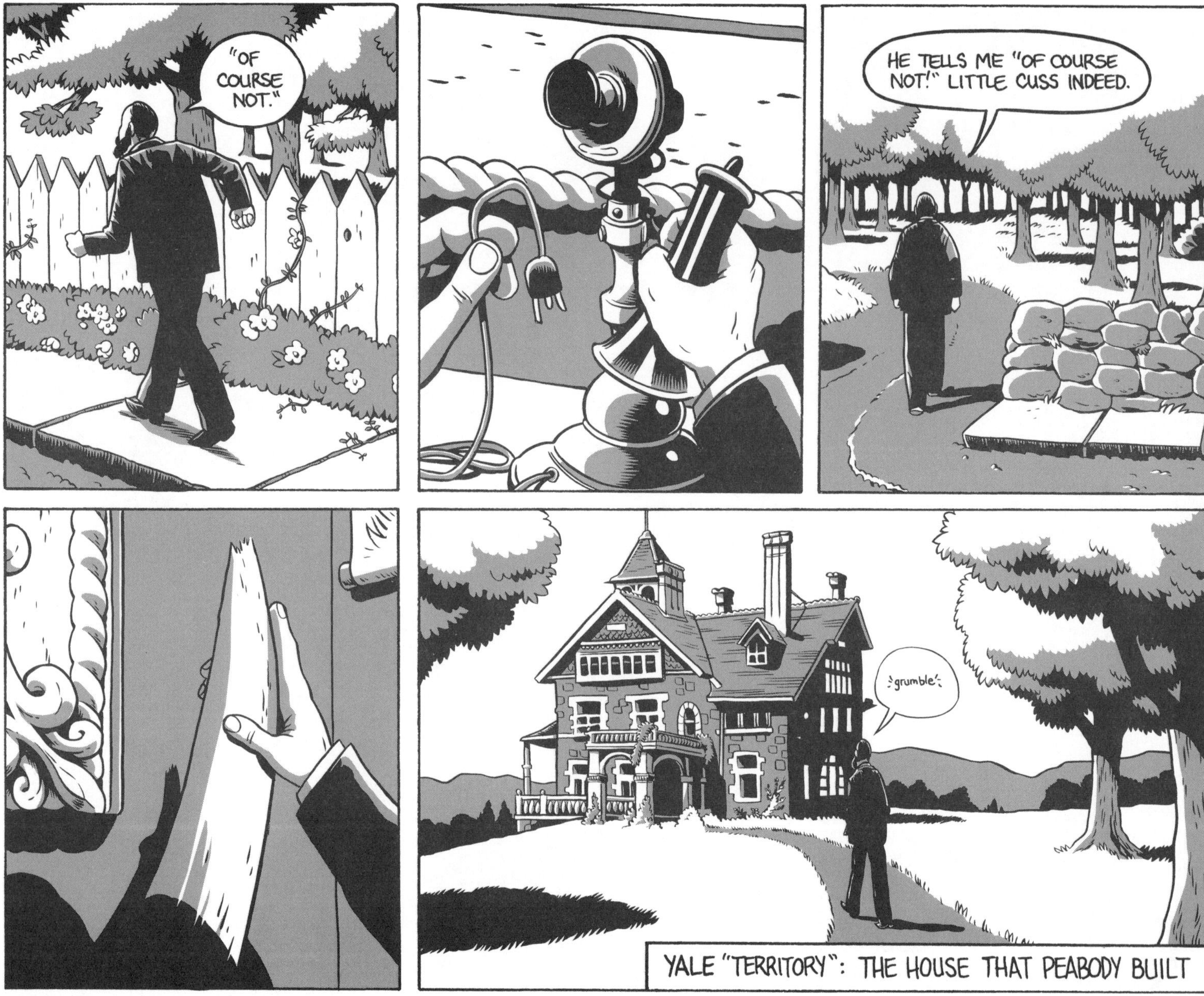

"OF COURSE NOT."
HE TELLS ME "OF COURSE NOT!" LITTLE CUSS INDEED.
grumble
YALE "TERRITORY": THE HOUSE THAT PEABODY BUILT

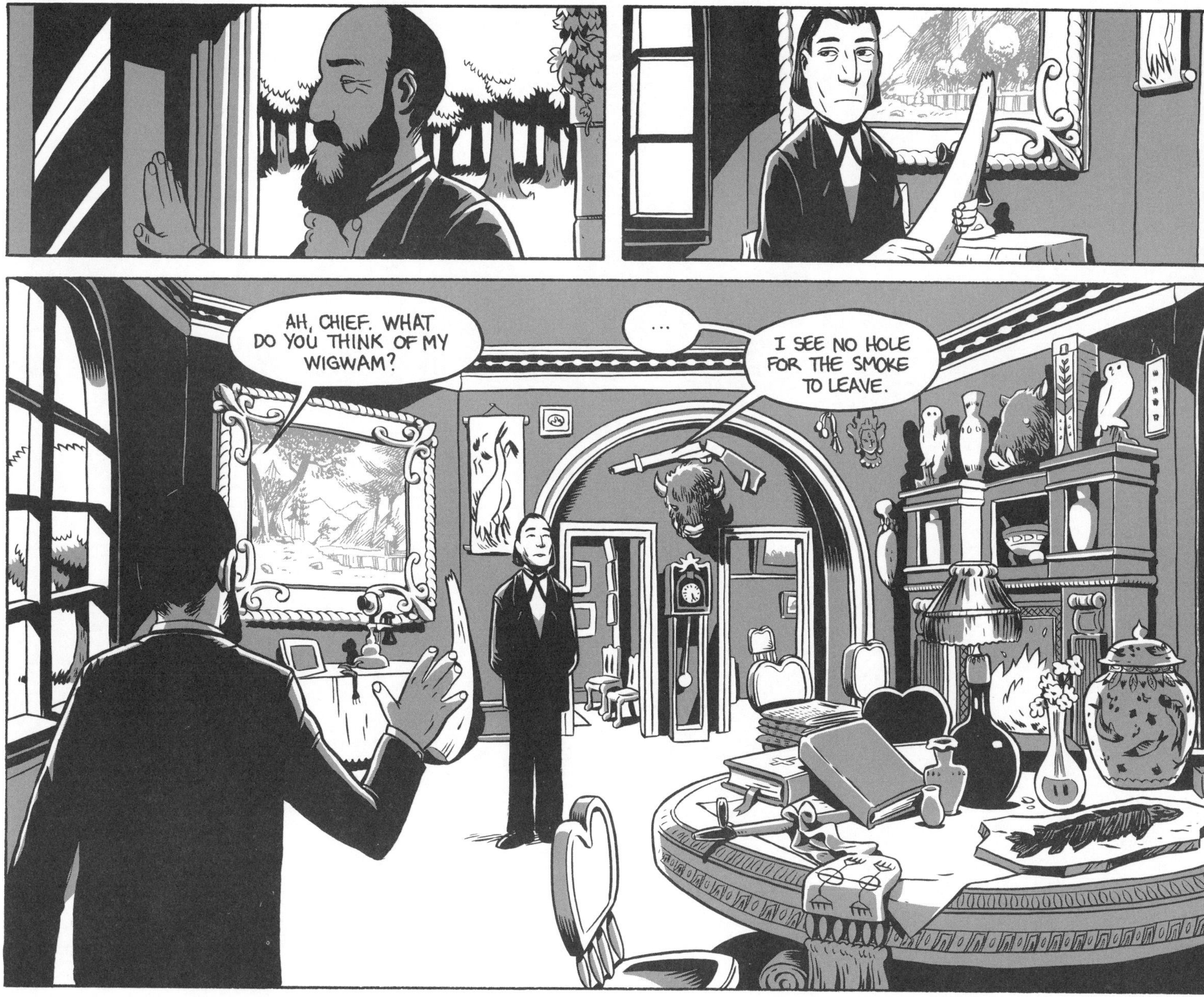
AH, CHIEF. WHAT DO YOU THINK OF MY WIGWAM?
...
I SEE NO HOLE FOR THE SMOKE TO LEAVE.

AH, CHIEF, IT GOES UP THE FLUE, RIGHT HERE.

BUT... WHERE IS MR. BELL?

HE COULD NOT STAY.

HE SAID HE WOULD CALL ON YOU BY TELEPHONE, BUT HE ASKED ABOUT THIS.

MR. BELL WONDERED WHY YOU DO NOT HAVE IT "PLUGGED IN."

THE TELEPHONE IS HERE FOR MY OWN CONVENIENCE, NOT THE CONVENIENCE OF OTHERS.

BUT NEVER MIND BELL. HOW HAVE YOU ENJOYED YOUR VISIT TO THE EAST SO FAR?

ENJOYED.

NO, THEY WOULD NOT SEE ME IN WASHINGTON.

HAH! I KNOW HOW YOU FEEL, CHIEF. BUT SURELY THERE HAVE BEEN SOME HIGHLIGHTS, WHAT WHAT?

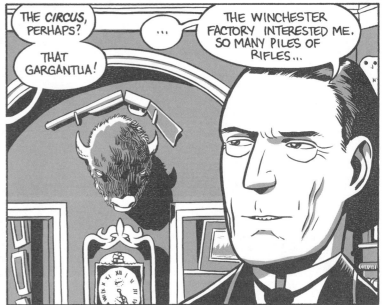

THE CIRCUS, PERHAPS? THAT GARGANTUA!

...

THE WINCHESTER FACTORY INTERESTED ME. SO MANY PILES OF RIFLES...

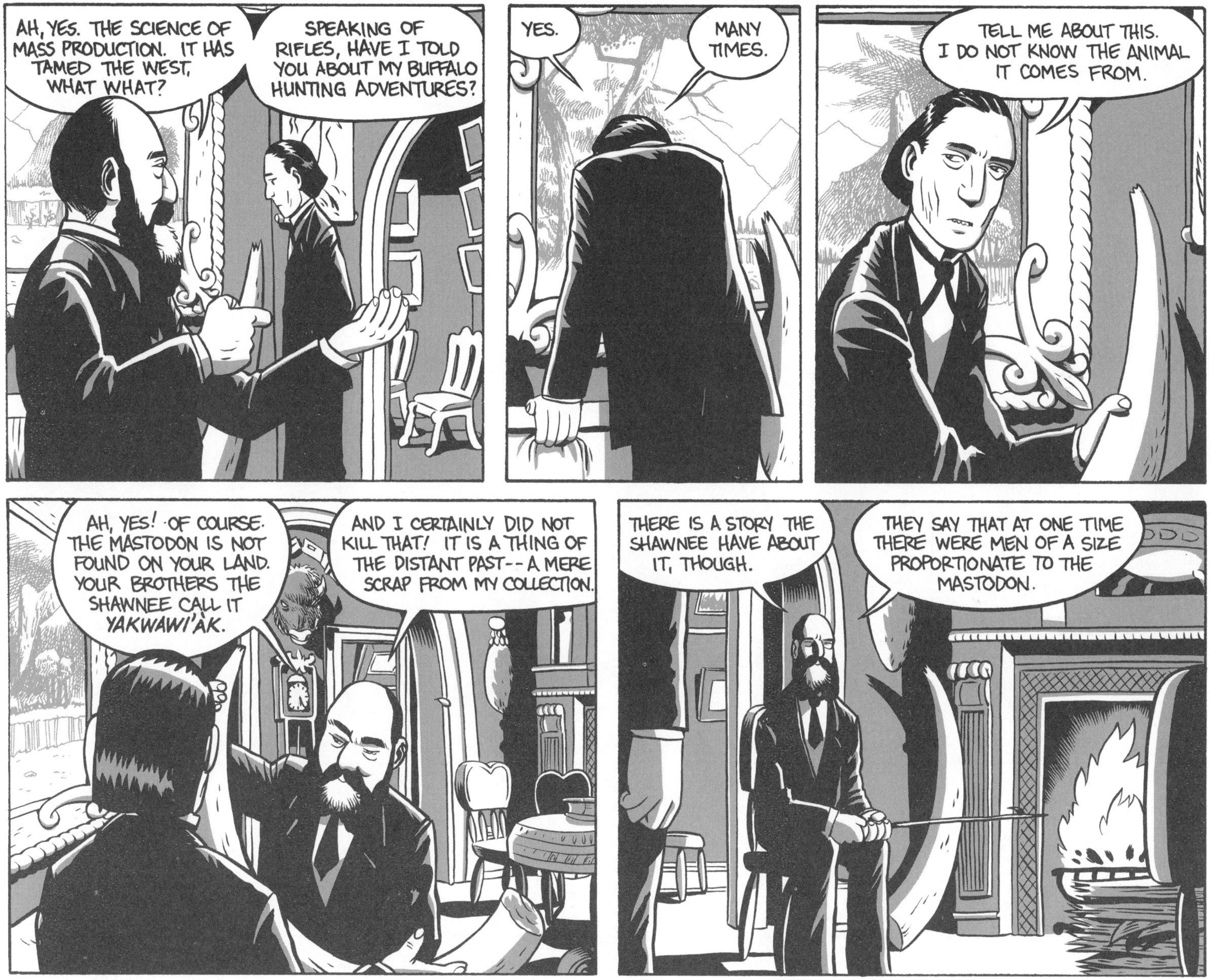
AH, YES. THE SCIENCE OF MASS PRODUCTION. IT HAS TAMED THE WEST, WHAT WHAT?
SPEAKING OF RIFLES, HAVE I TOLD YOU ABOUT MY BUFFALO HUNTING ADVENTURES?
YES.
MANY TIMES.
TELL ME ABOUT THIS. I DO NOT KNOW THE ANIMAL IT COMES FROM.
AH, YES! OF COURSE. THE MASTODON IS NOT FOUND ON YOUR LAND. YOUR BROTHERS THE SHAWNEE CALL IT *YAKWAWI'AK*.
AND I CERTAINLY DID NOT KILL THAT! IT IS A THING OF THE DISTANT PAST--A MERE SCRAP FROM MY COLLECTION.
THERE IS A STORY THE SHAWNEE HAVE ABOUT IT, THOUGH.
THEY SAY THAT AT ONE TIME THERE WERE MEN OF A SIZE PROPORTIONATE TO THE MASTODON.

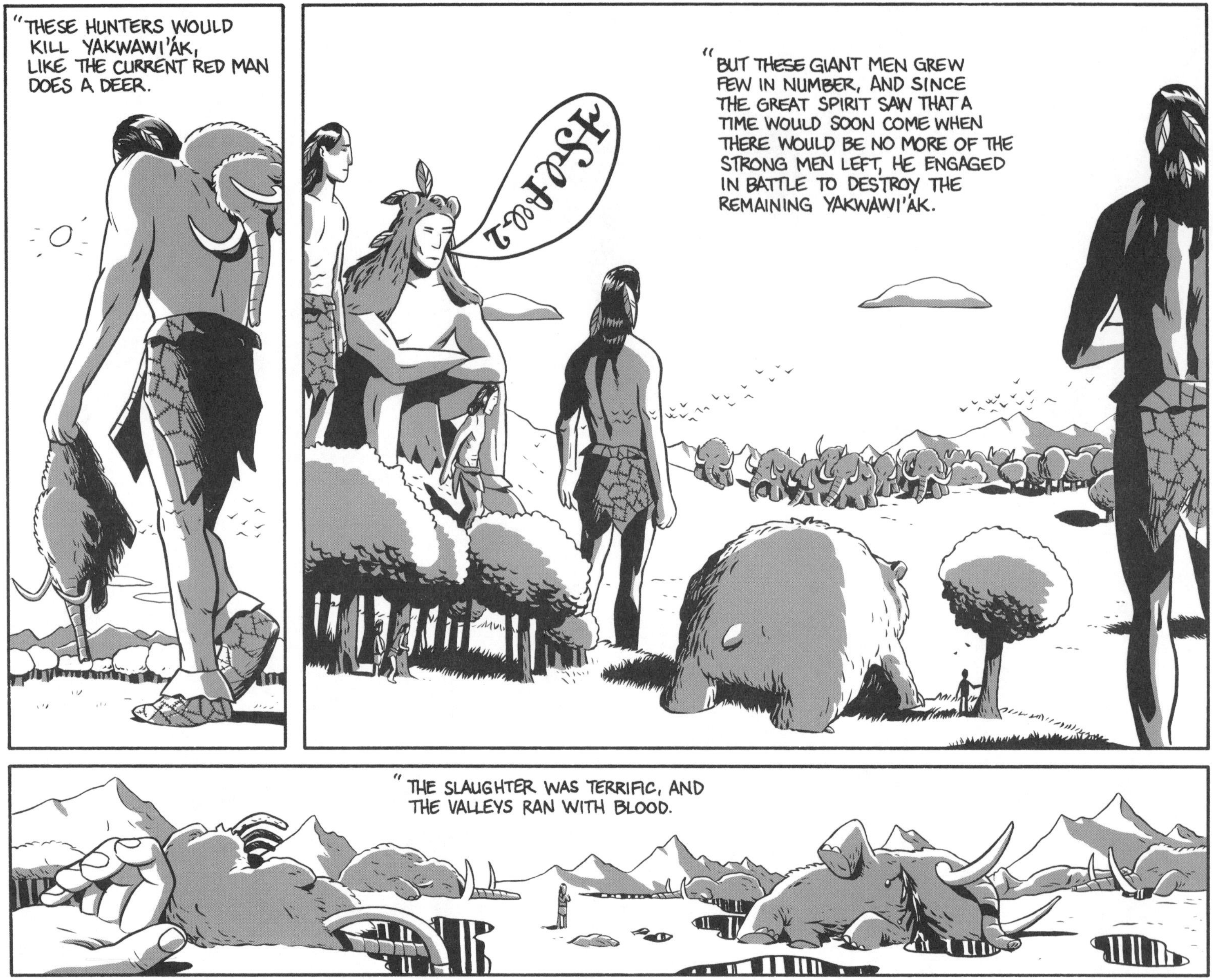
"THESE HUNTERS WOULD KILL YAKWAWI'ÁK, LIKE THE CURRENT RED MAN DOES A DEER.
"BUT THESE GIANT MEN GREW FEW IN NUMBER, AND SINCE THE GREAT SPIRIT SAW THAT A TIME WOULD SOON COME WHEN THERE WOULD BE NO MORE OF THE STRONG MEN LEFT, HE ENGAGED IN BATTLE TO DESTROY THE REMAINING YAKWAWI'ÁK.
"THE SLAUGHTER WAS TERRIFIC, AND THE VALLEYS RAN WITH BLOOD.

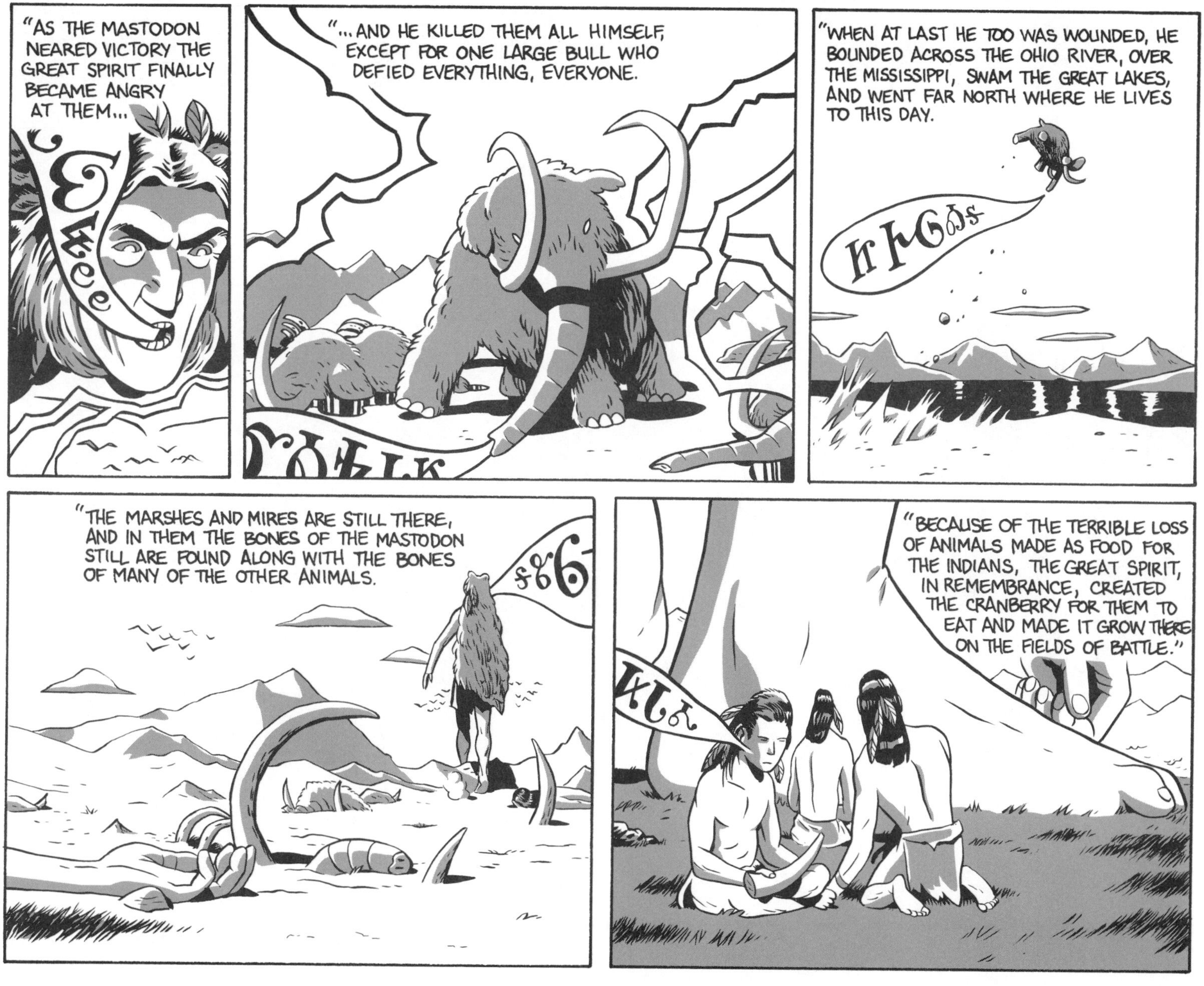
"AS THE MASTODON NEARED VICTORY THE GREAT SPIRIT FINALLY BECAME ANGRY AT THEM...
"...AND HE KILLED THEM ALL HIMSELF, EXCEPT FOR ONE LARGE BULL WHO DEFIED EVERYTHING, EVERYONE.
"WHEN AT LAST HE TOO WAS WOUNDED, HE BOUNDED ACROSS THE OHIO RIVER, OVER THE MISSISSIPPI, SWAM THE GREAT LAKES, AND WENT FAR NORTH WHERE HE LIVES TO THIS DAY.
"THE MARSHES AND MIRES ARE STILL THERE, AND IN THEM THE BONES OF THE MASTODON STILL ARE FOUND ALONG WITH THE BONES OF MANY OF THE OTHER ANIMALS.
"BECAUSE OF THE TERRIBLE LOSS OF ANIMALS MADE AS FOOD FOR THE INDIANS, THE GREAT SPIRIT, IN REMEMBRANCE, CREATED THE CRANBERRY FOR THEM TO EAT AND MADE IT GROW THERE ON THE FIELDS OF BATTLE."

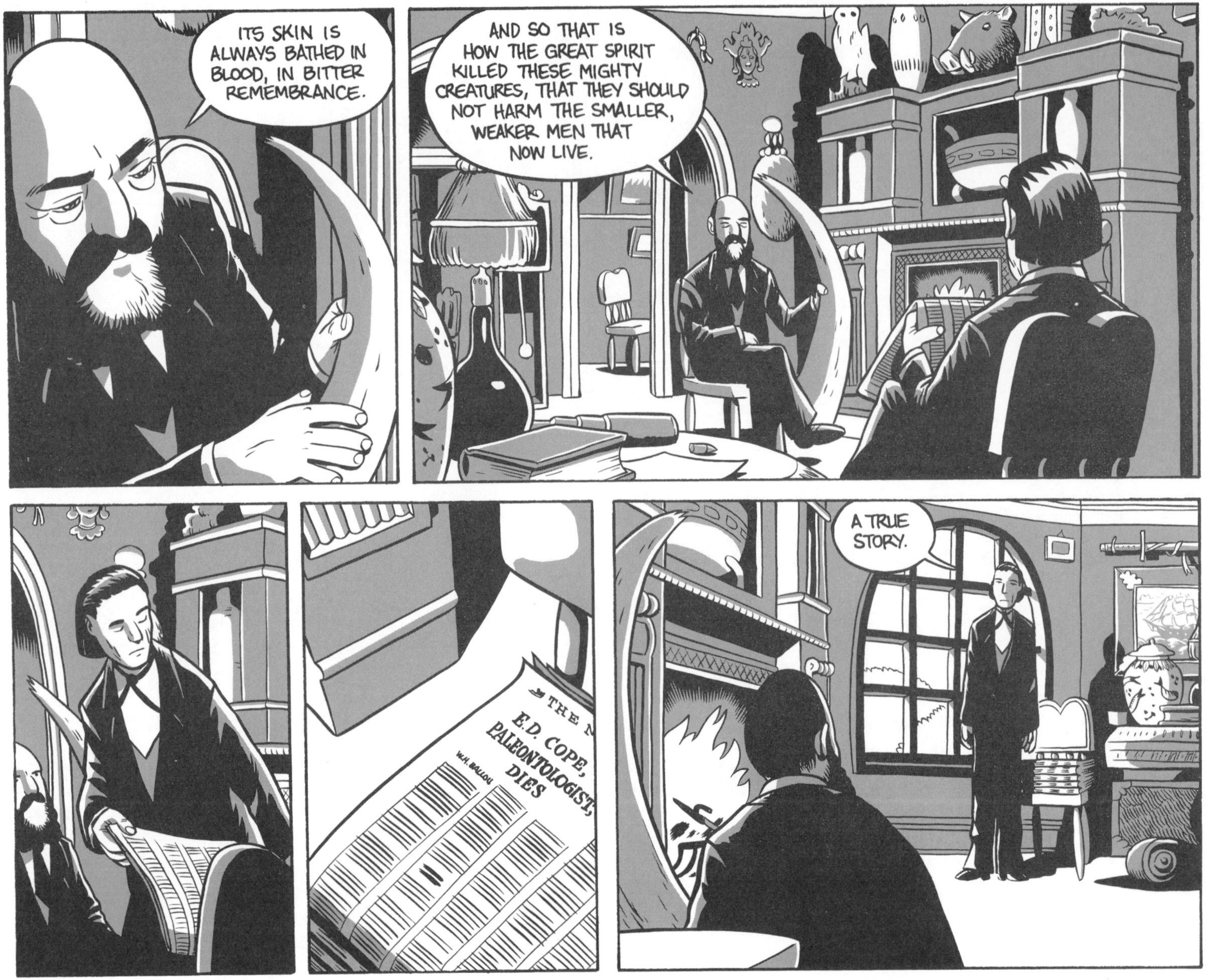
ITS SKIN IS ALWAYS BATHED IN BLOOD, IN BITTER REMEMBRANCE.
AND SO THAT IS HOW THE GREAT SPIRIT KILLED THESE MIGHTY CREATURES, THAT THEY SHOULD NOT HARM THE SMALLER, WEAKER MEN THAT NOW LIVE.
THE N
E.D. COPE, PALEONTOLOGIST, DIES
W.H. BALLOU
A TRUE STORY.

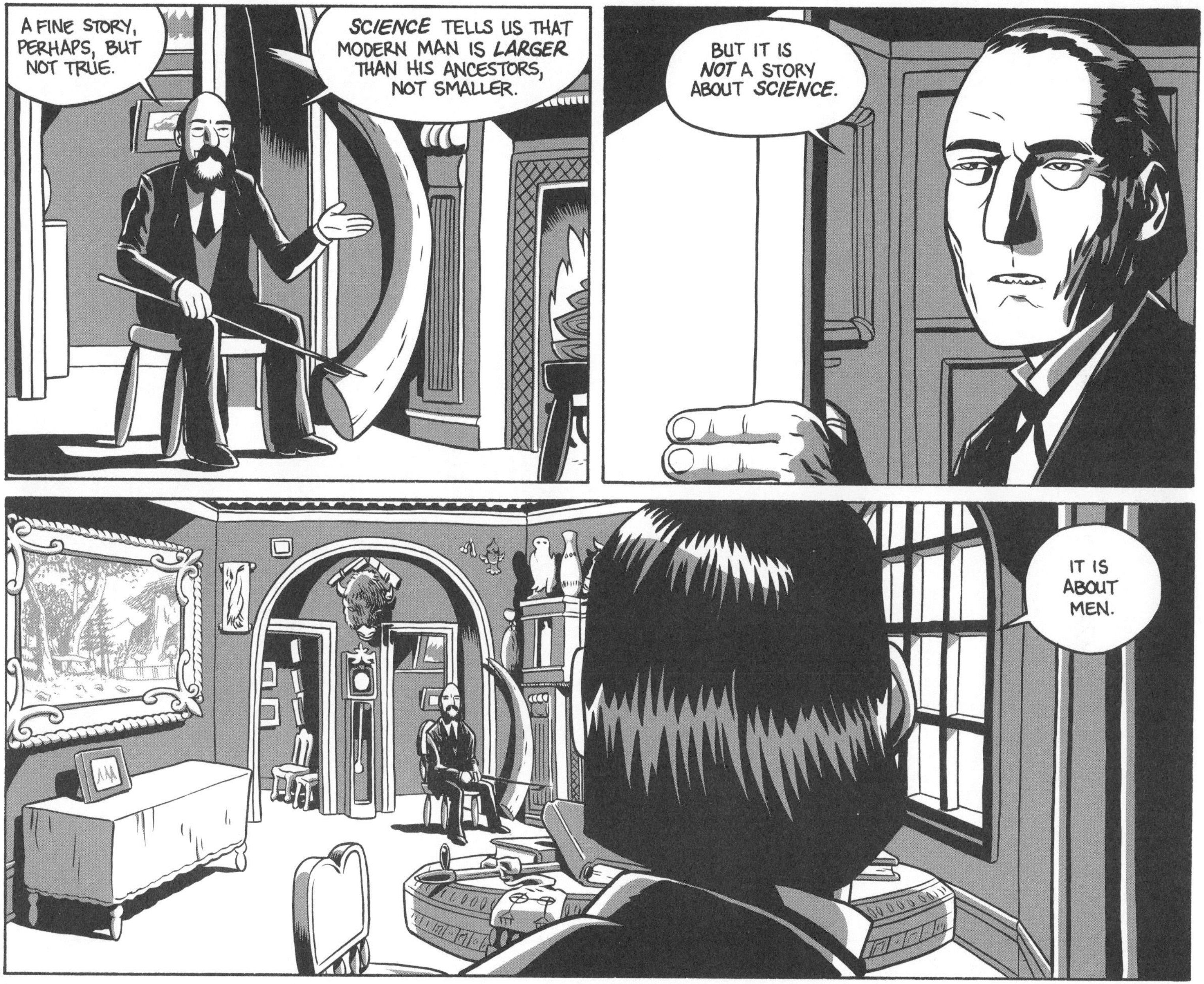
A FINE STORY, PERHAPS, BUT NOT TRUE.
SCIENCE TELLS US THAT MODERN MAN IS LARGER THAN HIS ANCESTORS, NOT SMALLER.
BUT IT IS NOT A STORY ABOUT SCIENCE.
IT IS ABOUT MEN.

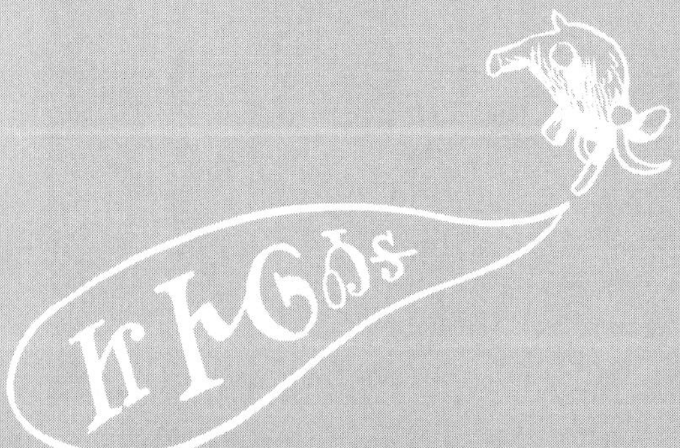

EPILOGUE

Scientia brevis est, ars longa

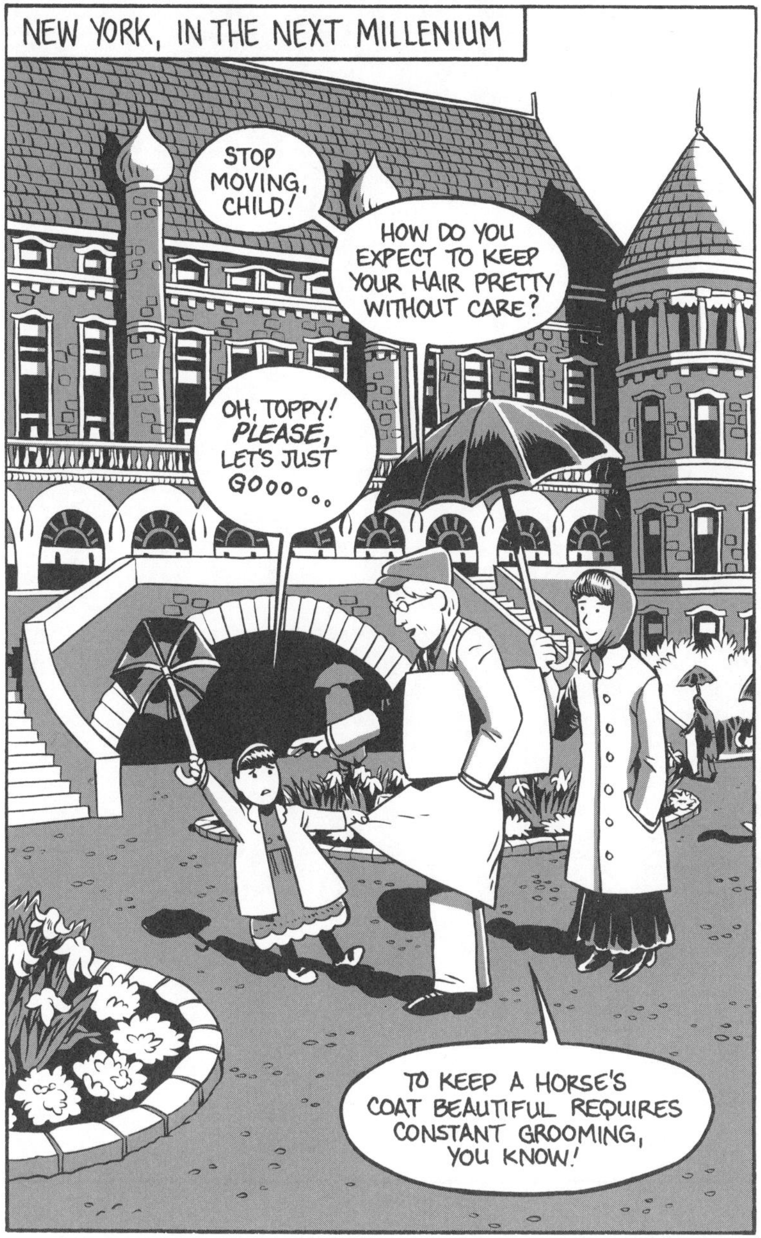
NEW YORK, IN THE NEXT MILLENIUM
STOP MOVING, CHILD!
HOW DO YOU EXPECT TO KEEP YOUR HAIR PRETTY WITHOUT CARE?
OH, TOPPY! PLEASE, LET'S JUST GOOOO...
TO KEEP A HORSE'S COAT BEAUTIFUL REQUIRES CONSTANT GROOMING, YOU KNOW!

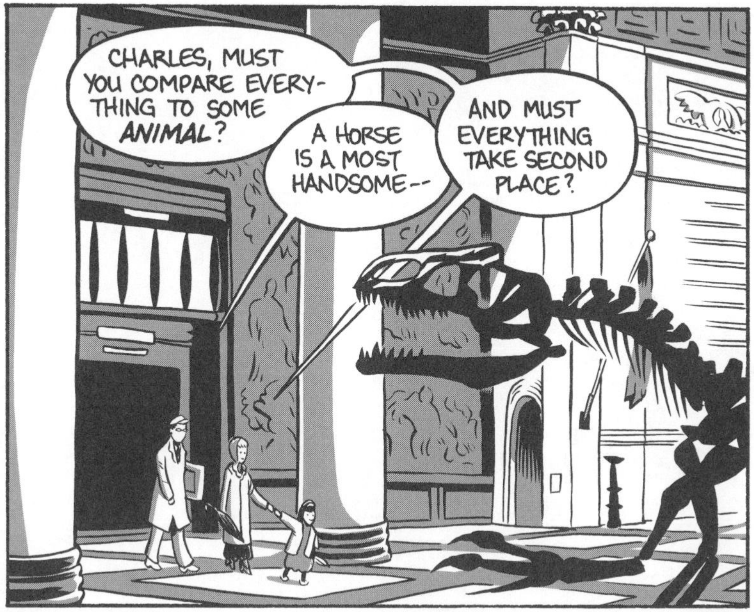
CHARLES, MUST YOU COMPARE EVERYTHING TO SOME ANIMAL?
A HORSE IS A MOST HANDSOME--
AND MUST EVERYTHING TAKE SECOND PLACE?

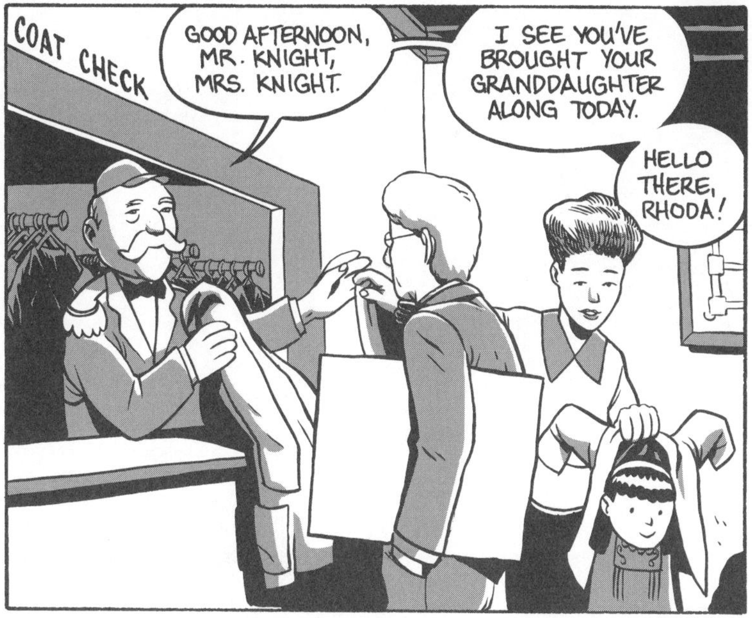
COAT CHECK
GOOD AFTERNOON, MR. KNIGHT, MRS. KNIGHT.
I SEE YOU'VE BROUGHT YOUR GRANDDAUGHTER ALONG TODAY.
HELLO THERE, RHODA!

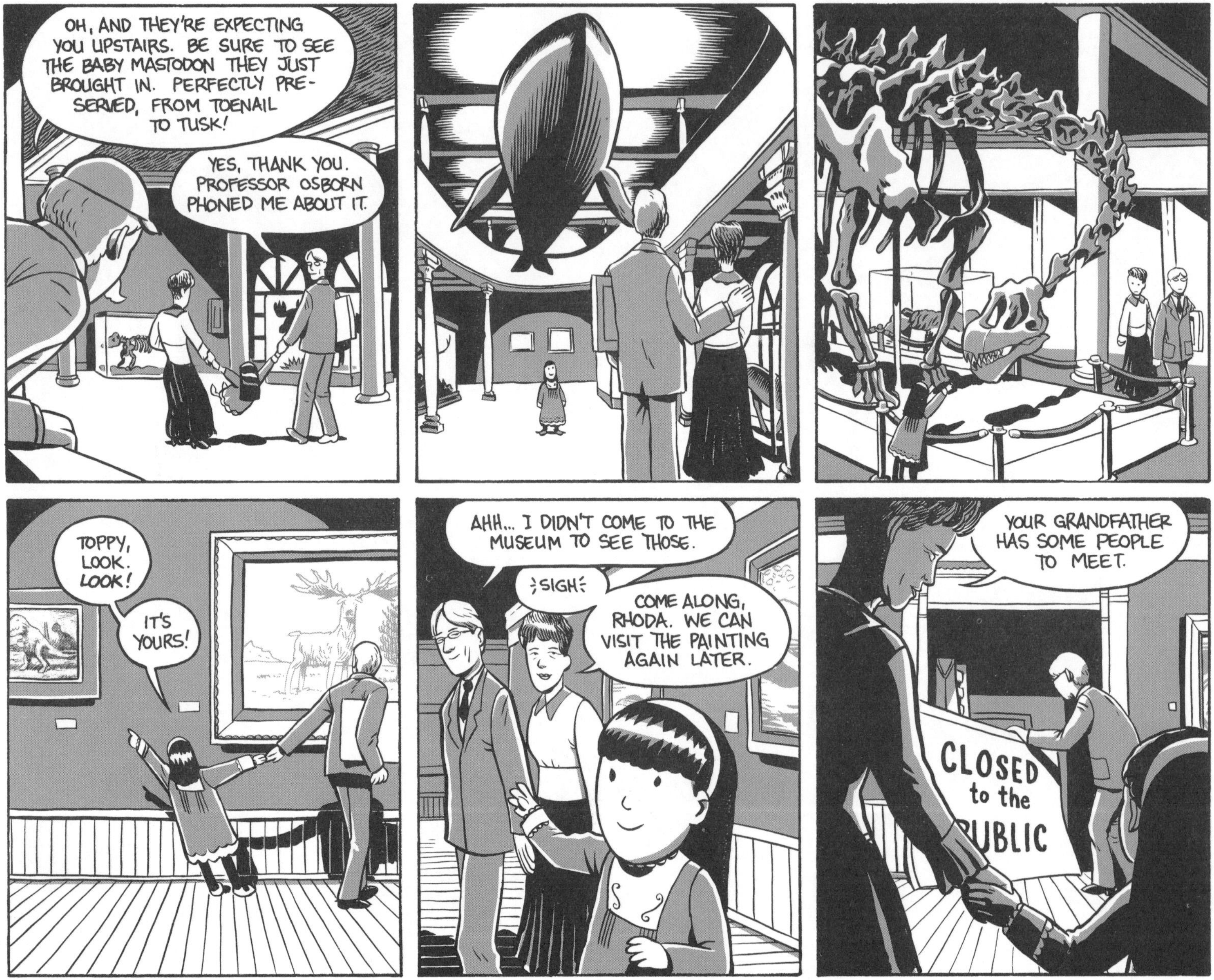
OH, AND THEY'RE EXPECTING YOU UPSTAIRS. BE SURE TO SEE THE BABY MASTODON THEY JUST BROUGHT IN. PERFECTLY PRE-SERVED, FROM TOENAIL TO TUSK!
YES, THANK YOU. PROFESSOR OSBORN PHONED ME ABOUT IT.
TOPPY, LOOK. LOOK!
IT'S YOURS!
AHH... I DIDN'T COME TO THE MUSEUM TO SEE THOSE.
SIGH
COME ALONG, RHODA. WE CAN VISIT THE PAINTING AGAIN LATER.
YOUR GRANDFATHER HAS SOME PEOPLE TO MEET.
CLOSED to the UBLIC

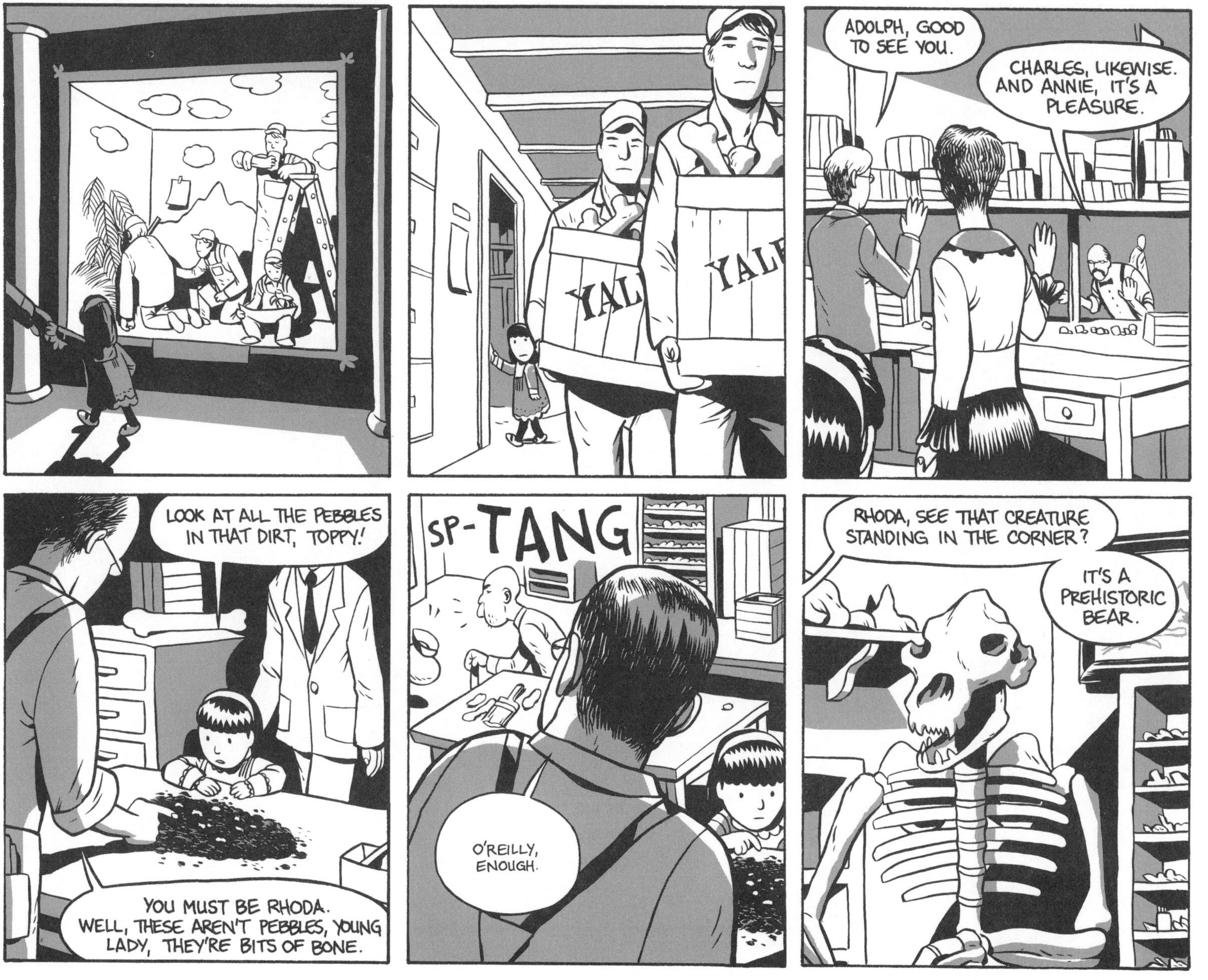

ADOLPH, GOOD TO SEE YOU.
CHARLES, LIKEWISE. AND ANNIE, IT'S A PLEASURE.
LOOK AT ALL THE PEBBLES IN THAT DIRT, TOPPY!
YOU MUST BE RHODA. WELL, THESE AREN'T PEBBLES, YOUNG LADY, THEY'RE BITS OF BONE.
SP-TANG
O'REILLY, ENOUGH.
RHODA, SEE THAT CREATURE STANDING IN THE CORNER?
IT'S A PREHISTORIC BEAR.

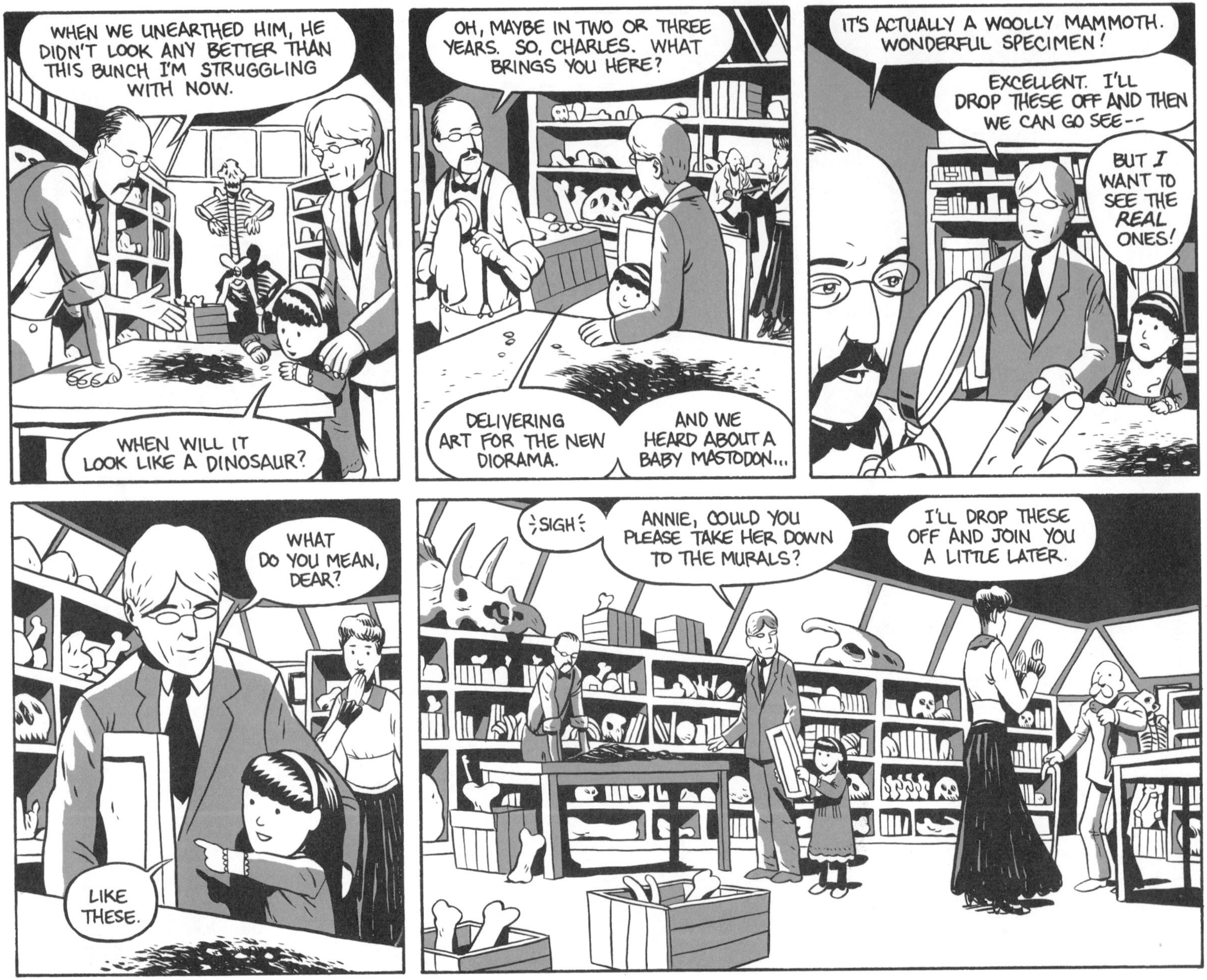
WHEN WE UNEARTHED HIM, HE DIDN'T LOOK ANY BETTER THAN THIS BUNCH I'M STRUGGLING WITH NOW.
WHEN WILL IT LOOK LIKE A DINOSAUR?
OH, MAYBE IN TWO OR THREE YEARS. SO, CHARLES. WHAT BRINGS YOU HERE?
DELIVERING ART FOR THE NEW DIORAMA.
AND WE HEARD ABOUT A BABY MASTODON...
IT'S ACTUALLY A WOOLLY MAMMOTH. WONDERFUL SPECIMEN!
EXCELLENT. I'LL DROP THESE OFF AND THEN WE CAN GO SEE--
BUT I WANT TO SEE THE REAL ONES!
WHAT DO YOU MEAN, DEAR?
LIKE THESE.
SIGH
ANNIE, COULD YOU PLEASE TAKE HER DOWN TO THE MURALS?
I'LL DROP THESE OFF AND JOIN YOU A LITTLE LATER.

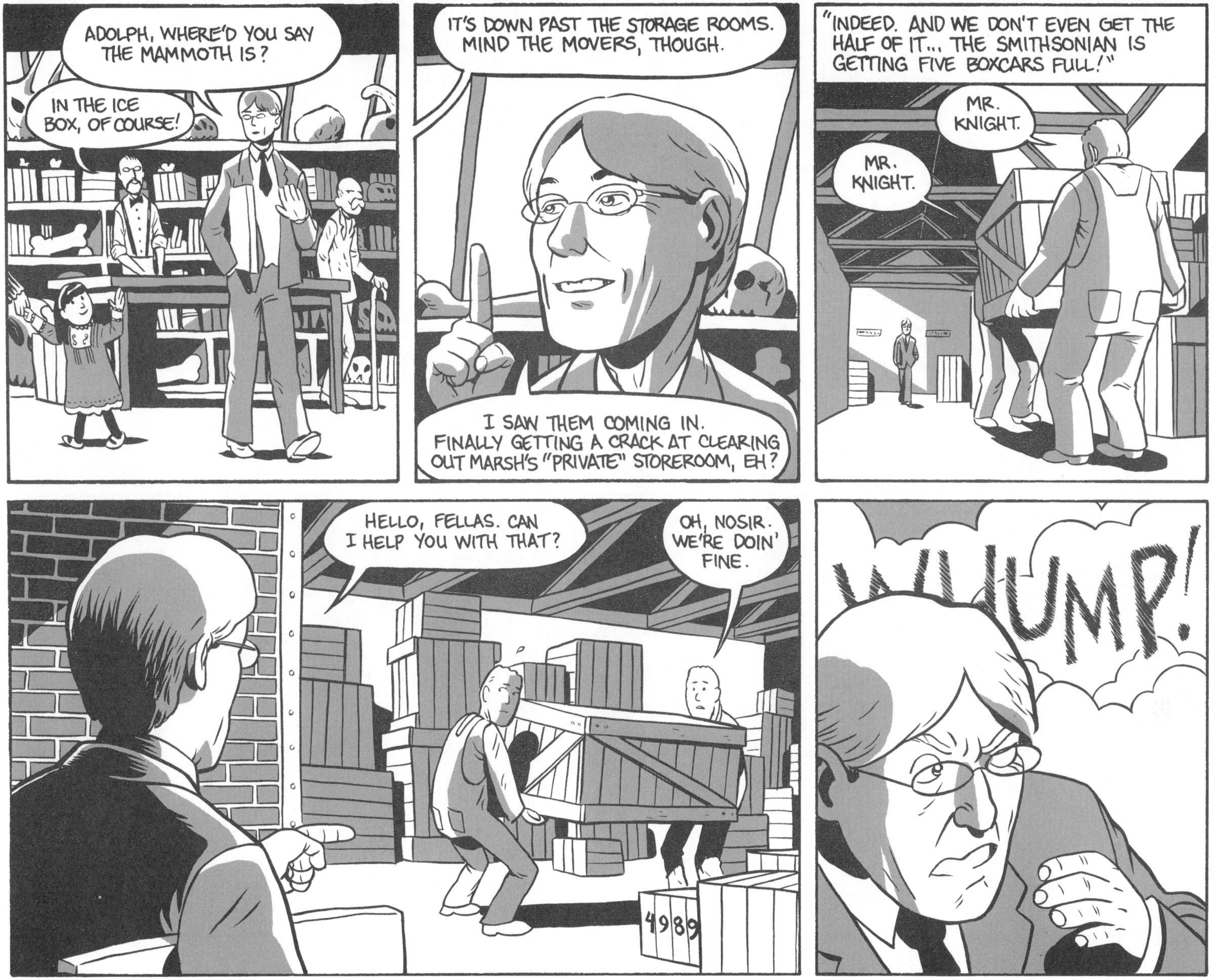
ADOLPH, WHERE'D YOU SAY THE MAMMOTH IS?
IN THE ICE BOX, OF COURSE!
IT'S DOWN PAST THE STORAGE ROOMS. MIND THE MOVERS, THOUGH.
I SAW THEM COMING IN. FINALLY GETTING A CRACK AT CLEARING OUT MARSH'S "PRIVATE" STOREROOM, EH?
"INDEED. AND WE DON'T EVEN GET THE HALF OF IT... THE SMITHSONIAN IS GETTING FIVE BOXCARS FULL!"
MR. KNIGHT.
MR. KNIGHT.
HELLO, FELLAS. CAN I HELP YOU WITH THAT?
OH, NOSIR. WE'RE DOIN' FINE.
4989
WHUMP!

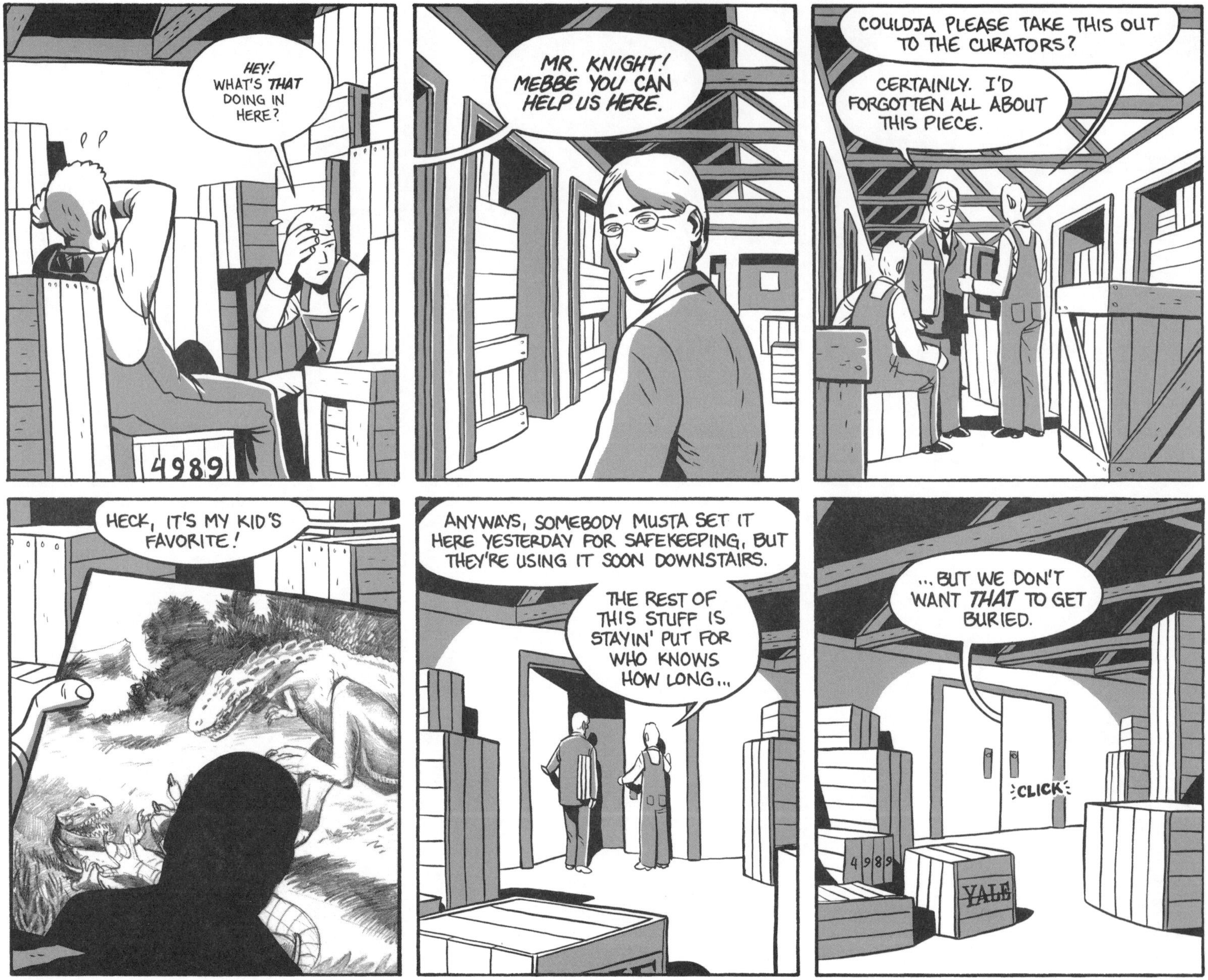
HEY! WHAT'S THAT DOING IN HERE?
4989
MR. KNIGHT! MEBBE YOU CAN HELP US HERE.
COULDJA PLEASE TAKE THIS OUT TO THE CURATORS?
CERTAINLY. I'D FORGOTTEN ALL ABOUT THIS PIECE.
HECK, IT'S MY KID'S FAVORITE!
ANYWAYS, SOMEBODY MUSTA SET IT HERE YESTERDAY FOR SAFEKEEPING, BUT THEY'RE USING IT SOON DOWNSTAIRS.
THE REST OF THIS STUFF IS STAYIN' PUT FOR WHO KNOWS HOW LONG...
...BUT WE DON'T WANT THAT TO GET BURIED.
CLICK
4989
YALE

END

FACT or FICTION?

This book is a work of historical fiction, based on real events and real people. In other words, most of what you just read is true, but read on to find out more (including illustrations which provide additional facts and quotes we liked, but that didn't fit into the story) and to learn which details we've rearranged or even made up. For instance, in the opening sequence…

FICTION: The headlines on the newspapers blowing about aren't real, nor are the news stories.

FACT: They really knew how to write titles back in the old days. The second sub-title here is adapted from Walley C. Oulton's *The Wonderful Story-teller; or Pocket Library of Agreeable Entertainment* (Boston: Joseph Bumstead, 1797).

FACT: As the headline on Marsh's newspaper says, you should check our references!

FACT: James Gordon Bennett, Jr. took naked midnight rides on his carriage… [Wallace, 5]

FICTION: …but there's no evidence that Othniel Charles Marsh ever saw him do it.

FICTION: Though saying our story takes place in the Gilded Age (ca. 1875 – 1900) is accurate, we've kept the exact dates ambiguous to allow Knight to join our story earlier than he did in reality.

FACT: Marsh exposed the Cardiff Giant as a fake. [Schuchert and LeVene, 343]

FACT: P.T. Barnum quotes his adoring public accurately, though the rube's full quote is even better: "I paid my half dollar to see the thing because my neighbor Jones told me it was a genuine petrified man, but if it's a humbug as a Yale professor says, I would pay a dollar because the fraud's such a good one." [Jaffe, 7]

FACT: Marsh and Barnum met on a train, and Barnum called Marsh a "little cuss" before knowing who he was talking to. Not that it would have mattered to him, in all likelihood! [Schuchert and LeVene, 349]

Thomas Jefferson assumed giant animals (the "Megalonyx", for example) still roamed the U.S. Interior. This is pre-Louisiana purchase, and the Eastern scientific and intellectual elite knew little about the country west of the Mississippi.

BONE SHARPS

FACT: *Elotherium/Entelodon* was Charles R. Knight's first prehistoric illustration job. [Knight, 40; Czerkas and Glut, 8]

FICTION: Though Knight knew Henry Osborn at the time, his autobiography implies that it was the reporter William Hosea Ballou (we'll meet him later) who introduced him to Edward Drinker Cope. [Knight, 72]

FICTION: Knight didn't meet or work with Cope until just weeks before Cope's death.

FICTION: Cope didn't look like this as a young man, but rather than have two paleontologists with a lot of facial hair running around for most of the story, we've given Cope's beard a trim a few decades early.

FACT: Cope's combination home/laboratory/museum/zoo was a world of wonders! [Knight, 73; Osborn, 371; Czerkas and Glut, 14; Jaffe, 305-306]

FICTION: We gave Cope some bad information about Knight here. Knight hadn't worked with Arthur Conan Doyle, but simply met him once or twice in the offices of *McClure's*. [Knight, 33]

FACT: Cope was affiliated with the United

Learned societies are largely filled with professional failures and the shifty disciples of personal expediency.

States Geological Survey, but thanks to political in-fighting did not hold his position for long. [Jaffe, 71]

FICTION: There's no evidence that Knight accompanied Cope on any of his travels.

FICTION: Cope probably never tried to impress Knight (or anyone) with his wealth by pretending he rode first class.

FACT: Cope met Marsh and showed him his dig site in New Jersey right before leaving for Fort Bridger. [Wallace, 41]

FACT: If you think a fellow who called himself "Sam Smith of the Rocky Mountains" is almost too good to be true, think again—there are even pictures of him! [Schuchert and LeVene, Plate XIII]

FACT: "OK," you might say, "Sam Smith may be real, but Gabriel O'Reilly is definitely too good to be true." Well, even though we have no photographs or daguerreotypes or even drawings to show us what he looked like, Knight knew and worked with him. [Knight, 64-67]

FICTION: Most of the description of O'Reilly, his apartment, his behavior, and his pets is accurate. However, all that chewin' tobacco-related behavior is borrowed from another acquaintance of Knight's, a certain Professor Allen.

FACT and **FICTION:** John Rowley didn't send Knight to meet O'Reilly, but Rowley was the chief taxidermist for the American Museum of Natural History, and a friend of Knight's. [Knight, 38-39]

FACT: The inland sea, also known as the American Mediterranean, was real, and Cope's description of how it must have looked and felt comes directly from his letters. [Osborn, 165-166; Lanham, 97]

FICTION: Cope did say "It was before I went there," but he said it about Fort Wallace (not Fort Bridger), and he said it to a Professor Scott, not Marsh. [Osborn, 27]

FACT: Smith spied on Cope, and (eventually) worked for Marsh. [Wallace, 81]

FACT: Marsh had his men plant fossils in Cope's path, in hopes that he'd find them and mistakenly use them. [Jaffe, 81]

FICTION: It probably wasn't Smith who planted the bogus skull, nor was this the first time Smith and Marsh met.

FACT: Buffalo Bill guided one of Marsh's Yale expeditions in the Nebraska territories. [Jaffe, 28-31]

FACT: The "deuced geology" quote is authentic, if we can trust Marsh's memory. [Schuchert and LeVene, 103-104]

FACT: Marsh met Chief Red Cloud on one of his expeditions, and promised to take up the Chief's cause in Washington when he returned. [Schuchert and LeVene, 139-146; Lanham, 148-149]

FACT: Marsh was known as "Bone Medicine Man" and "Big Bone Chief." [Schuchert and LeVene, 139]

FACT: O'Reilly only had one shirt, and Knight painted it to make it presentable before they went out to eat. [Knight, 67]

FACT: Knight painted an *Elasmosaurus*, and got the neck wrong, though not the way Cope did. [Osborn, 230]

FICTION: Marsh wasn't looking at Knight's painting when he noticed Cope's mistake. In fact, he probably would have accepted Knight's interpretation, since it at least puts the head at the right end! Further, there's no evidence of Marsh ever having met Knight.

FACT: Marsh effectively bought the rights to the New Jersey fields out from under Cope. [Shor, 30]

FACT: Marsh corrected Cope on the *Elasmosaurus* error which, as Knight said earlier, they based on a reconstruction by the well-respected and famous scientist Joseph Leidy. [Wallace, 43]

FACT: Cope saw the value of popular science exhibitions, but Marsh had contempt for making paleontology accessible to the public. [Schuchert and LeVene, 394; Jaffe, 161, 271]

Sam Smith's bones were found out in the wilderness years after he was last heard from – presumably he was murdered.

COWBOYS

FACT: John Bell Hatcher gambled to supplement his income, and as a result had to back out of at least one saloon while holding a loaded pistol in front of him. [Schuchert and LeVene, 224; Lanham, 213]

FACT and **FICTION:** The quote ending "…this place is getting too civilized." is authentic, but probably not to Smith. [Jaffe, 171-172]

FACT: Hatcher and Marsh sent each other coded telegrams. [Wallace, 145]

FACT: Trying to establish scientific precedence and assign Latin names via Morse code caused Cope a great deal of trouble. [Osborn, 178-179, 643-647; Shor, 11]

FACT: Cope cast the only vote against Marsh's election to president of the National Academy of Science, saying "I suspect that the majority will be sorry for it. Certainly they will be if they live long enough." [Schuchert and LeVene, 248; Osborn, 330]

FACT: Marsh made fun of Cope's (mis-transcribed) names, and compared them to *The Arabian Nights*. [Lanham, 122]

FICTION: It's unlikely Osborn took up Cope's cause so early in their respective careers.

FICTION: Just as Marsh intended, Cope, not Hatcher, found the planted skull. [Jaffe, 81]

FACT: Marsh's agents, and perhaps this included Smith, would rub out marks Cope had made at his dig sites in an effort to prevent him from returning to them. [Jaffe, 107]

FACT: Marsh lobbied for political power, at the expense of Cope and on behalf of Chief Red Cloud. [Lanham, 150; Jaffe, 128-129]

FACT: William Morris "Big Bill" Stewart served in Congress as a Senator from Nevada from 1864-1875 and 1887-1905.

FICTION: What Marsh said to Stewart, Congress, and President Grant is entirely made up.

FACT: The rival collectors threw rocks at each other. [Jaffe, 238; Wallace, 153]

FACT: Hatcher and other bone sharps used ants to do this detail work. [Lanham, 208-209]

FACT: Hatcher finally became disgusted enough with Marsh's behavior to quit working for him, and the "…bones here for the millions…" quote is genuine. [Schuchert and LeVene, 221]

FACT and **FICTION:** Hatcher had offered to collect for Marsh "…anywhere and at any salary." The rest of the quote is made up, though. [Simpson, 106]

FACT: Harlow and Edwards are real, and their dialogue is taken directly from a letter they wrote to Marsh… [Schuchert and LeVene, 196; Wallace, 148]

FICTION: …but they probably didn't talk, or look, like Hergé's Thompson and Thomson from *Tintin*.

FACT: Cope worked himself nearly to death in the fields, and called his resulting sickness "Bridger Fever." [Osborn, 182, Jaffe, 85]

FACT: The *American Naturalist* eventually made special rules for Cope and Marsh, charging them for each page they published in hopes of reducing their attacks on each other. In the issue after their new policy went into effect Marsh bought nine pages; Cope could only afford one. [Jaffe, 97-98]

FACT: Cope was on a stagecoach that got robbed. [Osborn, 221-222]

FICTION and **FACT:** The legend of Uncegila is real [Erdoes and Ortiz, 237-242] but Cope may not have known it, or told it to his traveling companions, or left them in the lurch as to how the story ends. We wouldn't dream of doing that to you, of course, so we now return to the story of the twin brothers, just as they are about to learn the price of power…

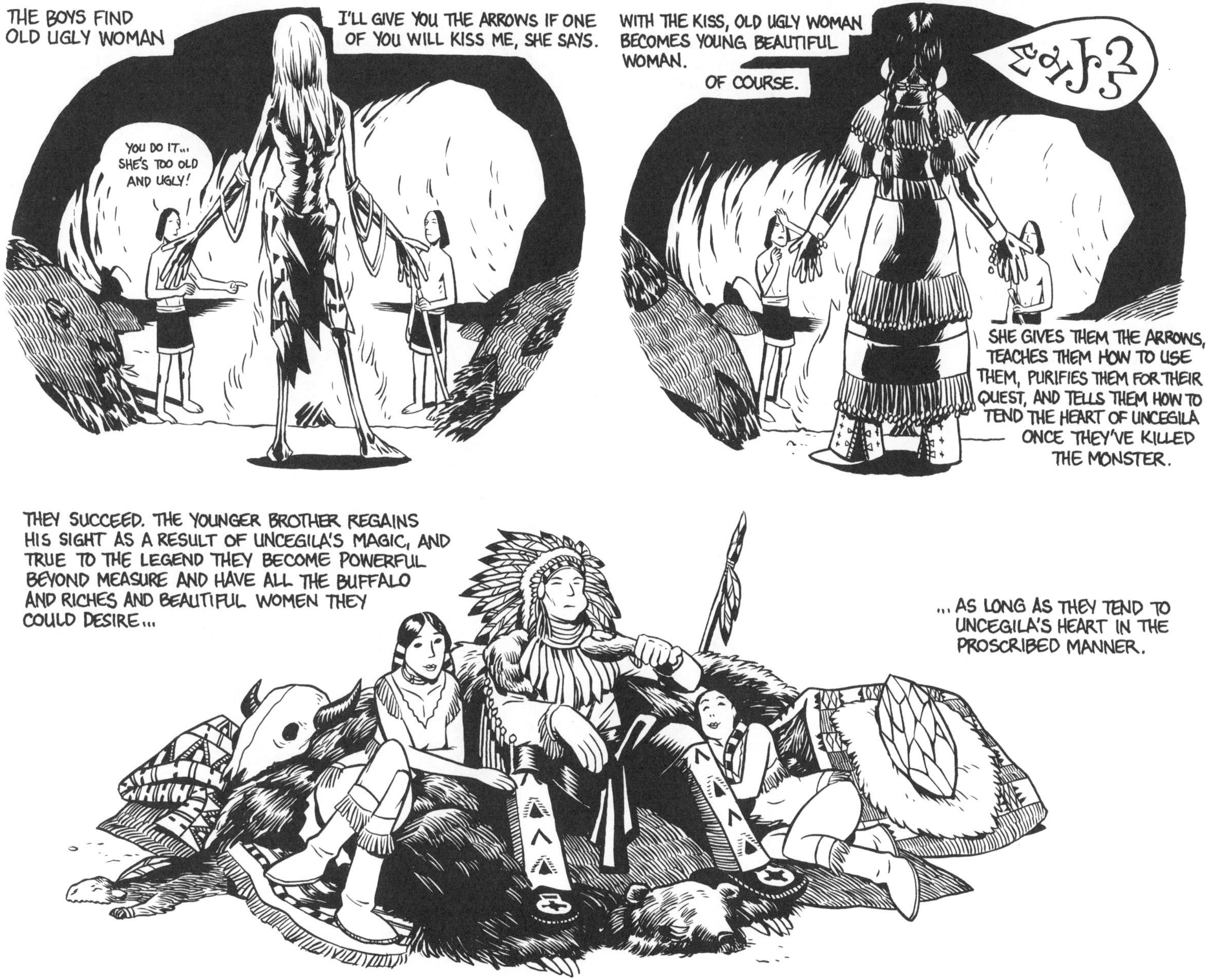
THE BOYS FIND OLD UGLY WOMAN
I'LL GIVE YOU THE ARROWS IF ONE OF YOU WILL KISS ME, SHE SAYS.
YOU DO IT... SHE'S TOO OLD AND UGLY!
WITH THE KISS, OLD UGLY WOMAN BECOMES YOUNG BEAUTIFUL WOMAN.
OF COURSE.
SHE GIVES THEM THE ARROWS, TEACHES THEM HOW TO USE THEM, PURIFIES THEM FOR THEIR QUEST, AND TELLS THEM HOW TO TEND THE HEART OF UNCEGILA ONCE THEY'VE KILLED THE MONSTER.
THEY SUCCEED. THE YOUNGER BROTHER REGAINS HIS SIGHT AS A RESULT OF UNCEGILA'S MAGIC, AND TRUE TO THE LEGEND THEY BECOME POWERFUL BEYOND MEASURE AND HAVE ALL THE BUFFALO AND RICHES AND BEAUTIFUL WOMEN THEY COULD DESIRE...
...AS LONG AS THEY TEND TO UNCEGILA'S HEART IN THE PROSCRIBED MANNER.

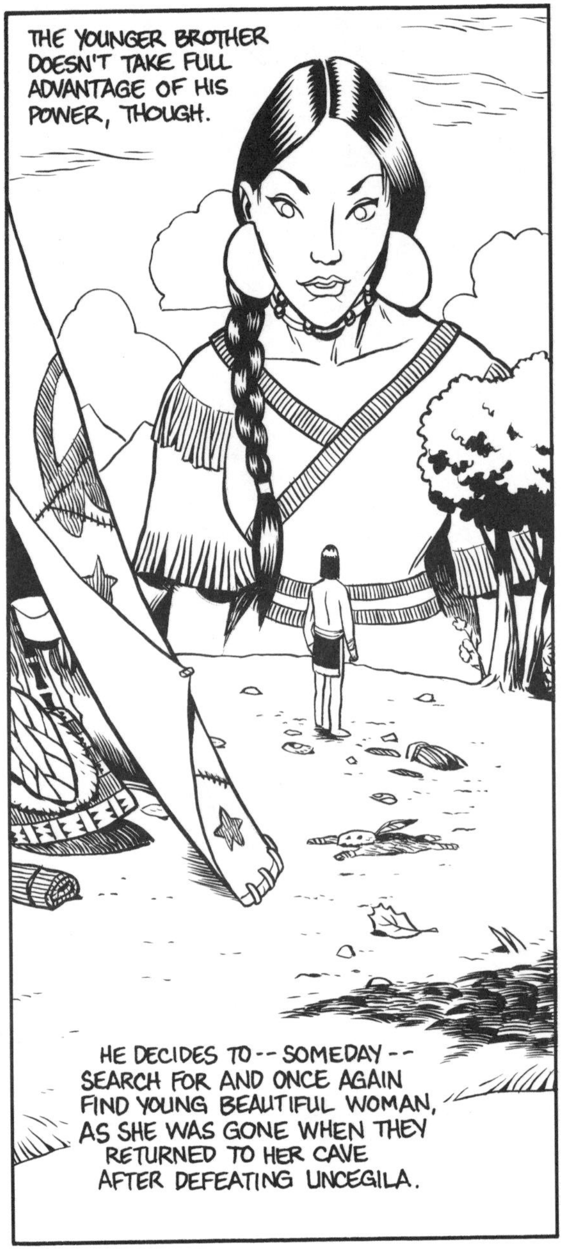
THE YOUNGER BROTHER DOESN'T TAKE FULL ADVANTAGE OF HIS POWER, THOUGH.
HE DECIDES TO -- SOMEDAY -- SEARCH FOR AND ONCE AGAIN FIND YOUNG BEAUTIFUL WOMAN, AS SHE WAS GONE WHEN THEY RETURNED TO HER CAVE AFTER DEFEATING UNCEGILA.

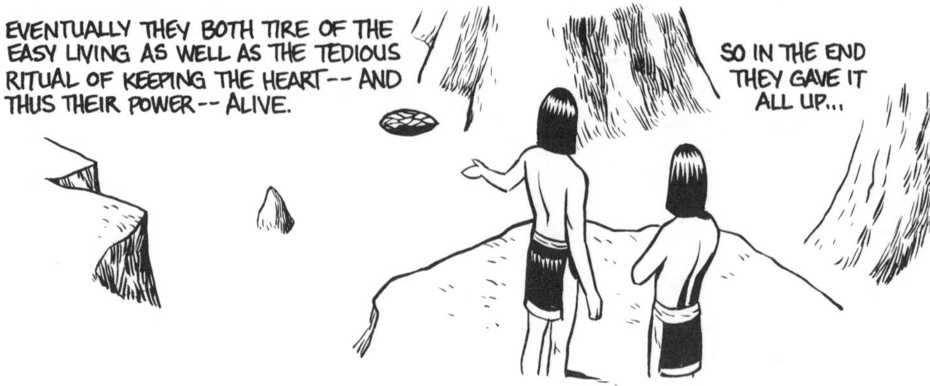
EVENTUALLY THEY BOTH TIRE OF THE EASY LIVING AS WELL AS THE TEDIOUS RITUAL OF KEEPING THE HEART -- AND THUS THEIR POWER -- ALIVE.
SO IN THE END THEY GAVE IT ALL UP...

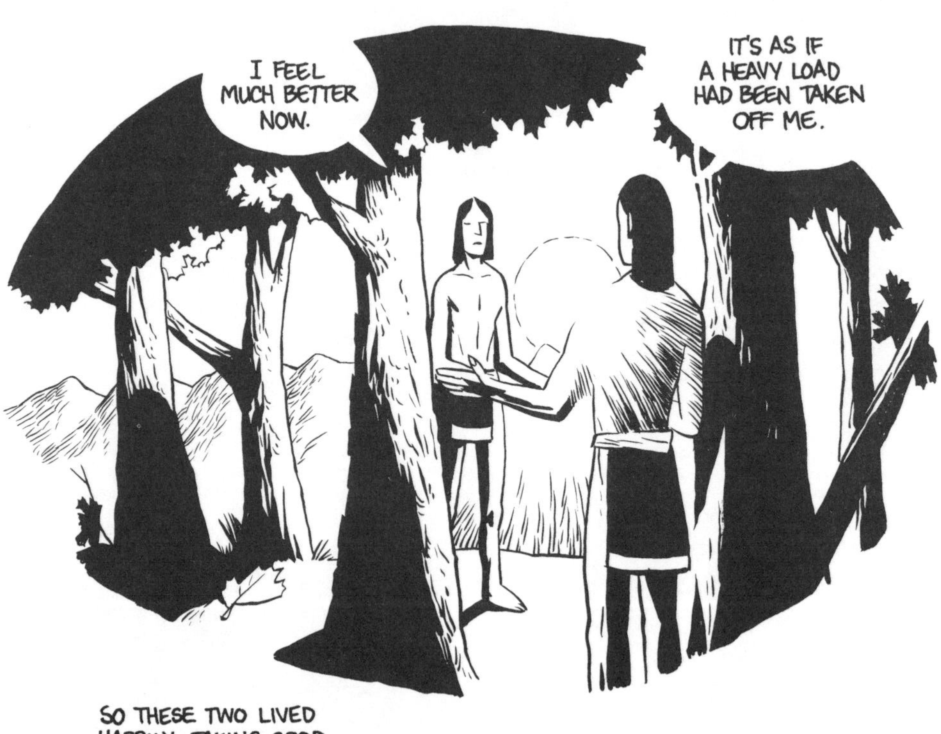
I FEEL MUCH BETTER NOW.
IT'S AS IF A HEAVY LOAD HAD BEEN TAKEN OFF ME.
SO THESE TWO LIVED HAPPILY, TAKING GOOD AND BAD AS IT CAME...
... AS MOST PEOPLE DO.

FACT: Marsh's boys sure 'nuff did rope that there '*Ceratops* skull like a steer and roll it down the hill. [Schuchert and LeVene, 214-215; Lanham, 204-205]

FACT: Marsh's efforts on behalf of the Sioux were successful, at least in terms of exposing the abuses of the Bureau of Indian Affairs. Unfortunately, treatment of Indians didn't improve substantially as a result. [Schuchert and LeVene, 162-166; Lanham, 150; Jaffe, 128-129]

FICTION: Marsh didn't get fooled by the very skull he'd had planted for Cope to find. The literary tradition of hoisting someone by his own petard was too good to pass up, though.

FICTION: Though Cope and Knight both visited Europe at roughly the same time, they didn't meet there.

FACT: The bureaucracy at French zoos irritated Knight: "There were pink tickets, blue tickets, yellow tickets, each for a different day, and for certain houses. Mondays one could work in the lion house, Tuesdays in the monkey houses, etc." On a happier note, he met and learned from the famous Fremiet and Gérôme there. [Knight, 67-70]

FACT: Marsh tinted his plaster, and used ground-up money for his papier mâché. [Osborn, 401; Schuchert and LeVene, 296-297]

FACT: The quote about Marsh not being satisfied with anything less than a collection of wives is genuine, and though probably not original to him it's reasonable to assume that Cope repeated it. With glee. [Schuchert and LeVene, 354; Shor, 28]

FICTION: Arthur Lakes was a real—and not very good—artist, but it's unlikely Cope or even Knight was aware of him.

FACT: Neither Cope or Marsh were interested in complete skeletons. If they had enough fragments to draw even a tenuous conclusion from they were happy. [Lanham, 162]

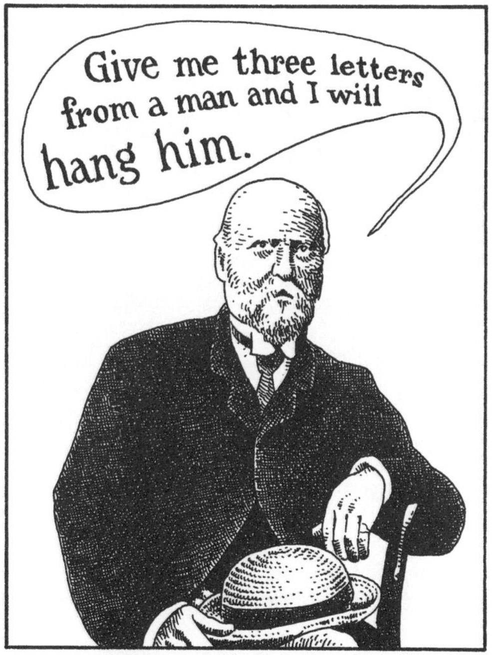
Give me three letters from a man and I will hang him.

FACT: Cope bought the *American Naturalist* and kidded himself, in public, that the only reason he did so was to keep it "purely scientific." [Shor, 9]

FICTION: Cope kept a bundle of "Marshiana" in a drawer back in Philadelphia, but probably didn't have it with him in Europe, nor would he have kept it in the "bank."

THUNDER LIZARDS

FACT: The *Herald* headlines Knight reads are authentic, and drawn from William Hosea Ballou's stories about the feud. [Shor, 65-110]

FACT: The Knights' home we show here is actually modeled after their summer residence in Long Island rather than the one in New York City. [Kalt, "The House With The Bumpy Lavender Stairs"; Knight, unpublished]

FICTION: It's unlikely Knight was working on his wonderful *Dryptosaur* painting at this precise moment, though some have speculated that it's an intentional allegory for the battle between Cope and Marsh.

FICTION: Throughout the rest of the story, when we see Knight and his wife Annie Hardcastle Knight together we often show him at his most exasperating, and her at her most exasperated. While it's true that Knight needed a partner to manage his business affairs (and keep his feet on the ground in many other ways as well), they were a devoted couple and so the brief snippets of their domestic life our story offers make Annie sound disproportionately critical of her husband.

FACT: Both Cope and Marsh ended up with more fossils than they could ever hope to handle—Marsh, because he was wealthier, acquired more than Cope. [Jaffe, 281]

FACT: As Knight mentioned back in "Bone Sharps," Professor Hermann, influenced by Marsh's disdain for mounting fossils in realistic poses, would string vertebrae along an iron rod in defiance of both logic and nature. [Knight, unpublished]

FICTION: Knight never mentioned O'Reilly working for anyone, much less Marsh. Here O'Reilly stands in for the aforementioned Professor Allen. Since he was too good to leave out of the rest of the story, he got to acquire both Allen's tobacco habit (and his snakes probably wouldn't have cared).

FACT: Marsh became the official vertebrate paleontologist of the U.S. Geological Survey in 1882. [Schuchert and LeVene, 268-269]

FACT: Hatcher's speech is adapted from a passage in his book on bone hunting in Patagonia. Given the thinly veiled anger directed at him in the quoted passage here, you'll find it surprising that he dedicated his book to Marsh! [Hatcher, 37-38, 55]

FACT: Knight was an early proponent of the dinosaur-bird connection... [Knight, quoted on the cover/dustjacket]

FACT: ...and so was Marsh... [Schuchert and LeVene, 425-444]

Osborn, that fossil completely upsets one of my favorite theories. If you were not looking I certainly would be tempted to throw it out the window.

- Cope to Osborn

FACT: …and so was Cope. [Osborn, 522-523]

FICTION: It's unlikely Cope ever took his case directly to the members of the National Academy of Sciences, and if he did, even more unlikely that he did it in this way or at this time.

FACT: Marsh got the *Brontosaurus* head wrong in just the way Cope describes. [Jaffe, 248-250, Wallace, 158-159]

FICTION: Cope probably didn't trumpet the *Apatosaurus/Brontosaurus/Camarasaurus* mistake as evidence of Marsh's incompetence, since he probably didn't recognize the mistake either. Like Marsh, he was too busy naming even more prehistoric creatures.

FICTION: If you think the implication that Marsh fooled himself by using the skull he had Smith plant for Cope to find is a little too neat, that's because you can only expect this much poetic justice from fiction.

FACT: Marsh's political power, combined with how, well, cool the *Brontosaurus* skeleton looked, meant that his reconstruction didn't get challenged or corrected for almost 100 years. [Jaffe, 250]

FACT: Knight and Osborn visited Marsh's lab, and Marsh sneaked around behind them in carpet slippers to make sure they didn't swipe anything. He had also shadowed Cope during his rival's visits. [Shor, 26-27; Osborn, 170]

FACT: Cope sold the *American Naturalist* to shore up his sagging fortunes. Besides spending all his money on more expeditions to find more bones, he had invested a lot of money in silver mines that went bust. [Jaffe, 299-300]

FACT: Knight's quote is accurate; he had a great deal of affection for Cope. [Shor, 218]

FACT: Cope lobbied Congress—though probably not Big Bill Stewart himself—unsuccessfully. [Osborn, 362-367]

FICTION: Cope almost certainly didn't have James Gordon Bennett, Jr. by his side during his lobbying.

FACT: The purple prose about the tropical explorer is pure and unadulterated William Hosea Ballou… [Shor, 60]

FACT: …or, rather, that prose is fiction, since while Bennett used Ballou as his chief science writer for the *Herald*, Ballou had no verifiable credentials to speak of. Nothing from his entry in *Who's Who*, right down to his place of birth (Oswego, fittingly enough the home of the Cardiff Giant), appears to be true. [Shor, 50-55]

FICTION: Marsh and Cope didn't meet in Washington.

FACT: Marsh said Cope's attacks on him in the *Herald* "…may thus be regarded as the crowning work of his life," intending it as a dig at Cope's scientific achievements.

FACT: Marsh's birds with teeth, while hailed by fellow scientists as a great insight—and as support for the then relatively new theories of Darwin—were mocked by Congress. Cope had also proposed the same thing in a paper about *Lælaps*, a.k.a. *Dryptosaurus* titled "Remarks on Extinct Reptiles Which Approach Birds." [Schuchert and LeVene, 231, 241, 289]

FACT: Cope had to give back the fossils he collected while with the USGS. [Osborn, 402]

FACT: Birds with teeth and printing expenses cost Marsh his position with the USGS. [Lanham, 261; Jaffe, 335-344]

FACT: Marsh willed his fossils to Yale. [Wallace, 267]

FICTION: Bennett didn't expose Marsh's will in the *Herald*.

FACT: Knight hated math, and really

didn't understand the point of finding X. [Knight, 14]

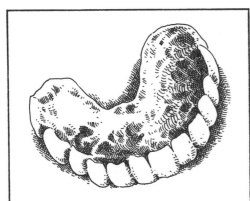

Cope impresses (and heads off an attack by) Crow Indians by repeatedly removing and replacing his false teeth.

FACT: The pick-rake-sack method, which is probably more mortifying to any paleontologists reading this than any of the other liberties we've taken with the story, was standard operating procedure back then. [Schuchert and LeVene, 171-173]

FACT: Cope would press on under almost any hardship. [Lanham, 151]

FACT: Bell's speech is authentic, though edited. [Rhodes, 45]

FICTION: Marsh probably never got shamed at the National Academy, especially by the hired help.

FACT: Marsh was almost certainly the first on his block to have a telephone, and was well known for hosting famous people like the Astors, Oliver Wendell Holmes, P.T. Barnum, and (of course) Alexander Graham Bell. [Jaffe, 268-270; Wallace, 174]

FACT: Before he died, Cope still had more things to say about Marsh, as indicated by these quotes from his letters. [Osborn, 174, 411, 468]

FACT: Marsh tried to get Barnum to donate to his so-called museum. [Jaffe, 281]

FICTION: Barnum wasn't nearly as dismissive as he appears here, saying in a letter to Marsh that he needed to be sure he could "do justice to my 2 children and 9 grandchildren," this being a "drawback to further charitable contributions from your humble servant." [Jaffe, 281]

FACT: Cope died almost broke, and was reduced to smoking half-cigars in his last days. [Wallace, 190]

FACT: The description of Cope's funeral comes from Osborn's and Knight's separate accounts, which agree on most of the details and the general pitifulness of the event. [Osborn, 587-588; Knight, 76-77]

FICTION: The service Knight and Osborn attended was in Haverford, not Philadelphia, and Ballou probably didn't crash the funeral and meet Osborn and Knight.

FACT: All Cope had left to offer science was his own skeleton. [Wallace, 288]

FACT: Marsh's "Wigwam" was an amazing room, Chief Red Cloud visited him there, and Alexander Graham Bell asked him why he didn't keep his telephone

If I make you rich, you will never do anything.
yes, uncle George.
PEABO

plugged in. [Schuchert and LeVene, 348-349; Wallace, 194]

FACT: Chief Red Cloud toured the Winchester rifle factory, and was impressed. He also toured the halls of power in Washington D.C., and wasn't impressed. [Schuchert and LeVene, 144-155, 166-168]

FACT and **FICTION:** The story Marsh tells about the Mastodon is woven from three different versions of the legend. [Adams, 57-58; Berkeley and Berkeley, 568-569; Hìtakonanu'laxk, 107-108]

EPILOGUE

FACT: Annie's comment on Knight's constant comparisons of humans with animals is real. [Kalt, "Every Afternoon A Tea Party"]

FACT: Knight, Annie, and Rhoda's visits to the American Museum of Natural History were highlights of young Rhoda's life. [Kalt, "Dinosaur's Domicile"]

FACT: Knight had free access to almost every corner of the museum, and was uninterested in revisiting his old work.

At his peak of fame (ca. 1925) Knight had more square feet of canvas and more pictures in the American Museum of Natural History than any other artist in any other museum in the world.

[Kalt, "Dinosaur's Domicile"]

FICTION: Adolph Hermann probably never met Knight at the museum, though he did eventually warm to the idea of mounting realistic displays and skeletons.

FICTION: O'Reilly would have never worked in a structured environment like this, though he probably was as unkillable as the impossible chronology we've constructed implies.

FACT: No doubt there are still boxes of fossils Cope and Marsh collected that scientists haven't gone through. [Lanham, 264]

FICTION: Though they did end up in box 4989, Cope's bones didn't end up in New York, or in a museum. [Wallace, 290]

Here are the references we encourage you to check:

Richard C. Adams, *Legends of the Delaware Indians and Picture Writing* (Syracuse, NY: Syracuse University Press, 1997), pp. 57-58.

Edmund and Dorothy S. Berkeley (ed.), *The Correspondence of John Bartam 1734-1777* (Gainesville, FL: University of Florida Press, 1992), pp. 568-569.

Sylvia M. Czerkas and Donald F. Glut, *Dinosaurs, Mammoths and Cavemen: The Art of Charles R. Knight* (NY: E.P. Dutton, 1982).

Richard Erdoes and Alfonso Ortiz, *American Indian Myths and Legends* (NY: Pantheon Books, 1984).

John Bell Hatcher, *Bone Hunters in Patagonia: Narrative of the Expedition* (originally published in 1903 as "Reports of the Princeton University Expeditions" and re-issued in 1985 by Ox Bow Press of Woodbridge, CT).

Hitakonanu'laxk (Tree Beard), *The Grandfathers Speak: Native American Folk Tales of the Lenapé People* (NY: Interlink Books, 1994), pp. 107-108.

Mark Jaffe, *The Gilded Dinosaur: The Fossil War Between E.D. Cope and O.C. Marsh and the Rise of American Science* (NY: Crown Publishers, 2000).

Rhoda Knight Kalt, "Nonnie and Toppy: An Affectionate Memoir (Childhood memories of my grandfather, the artist Charles R. Knight)," unpublished.

Charles R. Knight, *Charles R. Knight: Autobiography of an Artist* (Ann Arbor, MI: G.T. Labs, 2005).

Url Lanham, *The Bone Hunters* (NY: Columbia University Press, 1973).

Mark Norell, Lowell Dingus, and Eugene Gaffney, *Discovering Dinosaurs:*

While he was a student, Marsh's rooms had to be propped up from below because of the weight of all his books and fossils.

Evolution, Extinction, and the Lessons of Prehistory (NY: Nevraumont Publishing Company, 1995).

Henry F. Osborn, *Cope: Master Naturalist: The Life and Letters of Edward Drinker Cope with a Bibliography of His Writings Classified by Subject* (Princeton, NJ: Princeton University Press, 1931).

Douglas J. Preston, *Dinosaurs in the Attic: An Excursion Into the American Museum of Natural History* (NY: St. Martin's Press, 1986).

Frederick L. Rhodes, *Beginnings of Telephony* (NY: Harper & Brothers, 1929).

Charles Schuchert and Clara M. LeVene, *O.C. Marsh: Pioneer in Paleontology* (New Haven, CT: Yale University Press, 1940).

Elizabeth N. Shor, *The Fossil Hunters* (Hicksville, NY: Exposition Press, 1974).

George G. Simpson, *Discoverers of the New World* (New Haven, CT: Yale University Press, 1984).

William Stout, *Charles R. Knight Sketchbook, Volumes I-III* (Pasadena, CA: Terra Nova Press, 2002-2003).

David R. Wallace, *The Bonehunters' Revenge* (NY: Houghton Mifflin, 1999).

FACT: Jim thanks Kevin, Shad, Zander, and Mark for breathing life into the characters; Jeff Parker for his considerable editorial acumen; Rhoda Knight Kalt for her generosity and support, particularly in sharing her memories, photographs, and the previously unpublished memoirs of her grandfather Charles R. Knight; Adrienne Mayor for her expertise in fossil myths; my family and friends; and of course, Kat.

FACT: Big Time Attic would first and foremost like to thank Jim for unwavering enthusiasm and patience. Thanks also to our dedicated MCAD interns, Max Konrary, Jon White and Anna Bratton, as well as our friends Lonny Unitus, Bret Hummel, Tim Drabandt, Donn Ha, Jeff Parker, Michael Drivas, and Mark Schultz. Zander and Shad would like to thank their wives Julie and Anna, and Kevin would like to thank his parents.

Other books from G.T. Labs

Charles R. Knight: Autobiography of an Artist

Suspended in Language: Niels Bohr's Life, Discoveries, and the Century He Shaped

Fallout: J. Robert Oppenheimer, Leo Szilard, and the Political Science of the Atomic Bomb

Dignifying Science: Stories About Women Scientists

Two-Fisted Science

Find out more at *www.gt-labs.com*

❧ ACCEPT NO SUBSTITUTES! ❧

THIS WAY TO THE EGRESS ☞